D0898216

Alice's Adventures

ALSO AVAILABLE FROM CONTINUUM:

Will Brooker:

Batman Unmasked: Analyzing a Cultural Icon

Will Brooker:

Using the Force: Creativity, Community, and Star Wars Fans

Danny Fingeroth:

Superman on the Couch

Geoff Klock:

How to Read Superhero Comics and Why

Philip Nel:

Dr. Seuss: American Icon

Deborah O'Keefe:

Readers in Wonderland

Claire Squires:

Philip Pullman's His Dark Materials: A Reader's Guide

ALICE'S ADVENTURES

Lewis Carroll in Popular Culture

Will Brooker

continuum
NEW YORK • LONDON

2004

The Continuum International Publishing Group Inc
15 E 26 Street, New York, NY 10010

The Continuum International Publishing Group Ltd
The Tower Building, 11 York Road, London SE1 7NX

www.continuumbooks.com

Library of Congress Cataloging in Publication Data

Brooker, Will, 1970-
    Alice's adventures : Lewis Carroll and Alice in popular culture / Will Brooker.
        p. cm.
    Includes bibliographical references (p.) and index.
    ISBN 0-8264-1433-8 (hardcover : alk. paper)
    1. Carroll, Lewis, 1832-1898. Alice's adventures in Wonderland. 2.Carroll, Lewis,
1832-1898—Appreciation—English-speaking countries. 3.Popular culture—English-
speaking countries—History—20th century. 4.Carroll, Lewis, 1832-1898—
Adaptations—History and criticism. 5. Carroll,Lewis, 1832-1898. Through the
looking glass. 6. Children's stories,English—Adaptations—History and criticism.
7. Fantasy fiction,English—Adaptations—History and criticism. 8. Alice (Fictitious
character: Carroll) I. Title.
    PR4611.A73B76 2004
    823'8—dc22   2004001489

Printed in the United States of America

Contents

Acknowledgments   vii

Preface   ix

Introduction: A Mess of Souvenirs   xiii

1   The Many Lives of Lewis Carroll   1

2   The Man in White Paper   49

3   Analysing Alice   77

4   Illustrators of Alice   105

5   The Further Adventures of Alice   151

6   Adapting Alice   199

7   Dark Wonderland   229

8   Fans   265

9   Pilgrimage   307

Appendix A   349

Appendix B   357

Bibliography   369

Index

Acknowledgments

Thanks to:
    David Barker at Continuum for being the perfect editor throughout this "cultural icons" trilogy.
Fiona Graham for being the perfect research assistant.
Edward Wakeling for offering expert comments on many of the following chapters.
Alan White, Mark Richards, Roger Allen, and Harriet Tait of the Lewis Carroll Society for discussing their relationship with Alice and her author.
Darryn Reeds for the cover design.

This book is dedicated to my Nanny, Gwendoline Alice Brooker.

Preface

All references to *Alice's Adventures in Wonderland* and *Through The Looking-Glass, And What Alice Found There* in this book are to Martin Gardner's edited *The Annotated Alice: The Definitive Edition*. Charles Dodgson is referred to as Lewis Carroll throughout, for convenience; for the most part, I am discussing the man in his role as author of Alice, and it would be complicated, though more accurate, to use a different name on the occasions where I refer to his life outside children's fiction.

It has become a custom in cultural studies for the author to state his or her own position in relation to the object of study; often, and my work has been no exception, this involves a confession of partisan fandom. This book is unusual in that my attitude towards Carroll changed during the writing; at least, it is unusual in that I'm declaring this shift. I am drawing attention to this process here, at the risk of self-indulgence, because I think it illustrates a phenomenon that must be common to most research, though I have never seen it made visible. If you spend two years immersed and invested in a topic, some of that time involving a nine-to-five day of intensive writing, some of it involving a constant background ticking-over and some of it involving weeks of travel to museums, libraries, and heritage sites, you're going to develop either an intense affection for or dislike of your subject matter; perhaps sometimes both at once. Complete neutrality is, I think, difficult to maintain in a long-term relationship.

When I started writing this book, I felt relatively objective towards Lewis Carroll. My mother had introduced me to *Alice* at age seven, with *Through The Looking-Glass*; perhaps this is why the sequel remains my favourite. The inscription inside reads "William Brooker (your turn now)". Carroll, who wrote a sentimental tribute to mothers in a supplement to *Looking-Glass*,[1] would surely have approved. She bought me a copy of *The Annotated Alice* in 1979, and by the time I first visited the Alice statue in Central Park, the following year, I was certainly in love with the character and the books. But not with Carroll. Apart from *The Hunting of the Snark* and the *Selected Letters*, which I owned by the age of thirteen, I had no interest in following up more of his work, or his life, and since that point in the early to mid-1980s, my separate relationships with Carroll and Alice remained stable. I would always have a soft spot for her, but I knew little about him, and what little I did know—what I picked up from the odd newspaper story, and the hints I gathered from his letters or Gardner's annotations—didn't especially endear him to me. His apparent dislike of boys and admiration of naked girls' bodies seemed slimy even when I was a young teenager; I would remain grateful to him for *Alice*, but wasn't sure I would have liked him as a person.

The course of my research gradually nudged me away from this neutral-to-wary position. Seeing Carroll's handwritten diaries, with their crossings-out and second thoughts, cannot help but bring you closer to him; standing in front of the house where he grew up, or sitting by his grave, only a very hard-hearted researcher could resist a feeling of personal connection. On a more scholarly level, I read nine biographies and spent eighteen months as a member of the Lewis Carroll Society, which brought me into contact with people who had devoted much of their lives to celebrating the author and his work, and whose beliefs about him began to influence mine. Matthew Sweet's *Inventing the Victorians*, which seeks for traces of nineteenth-century individuals in today's geography, culture, and customs, concludes with a passionate "We should love them. We should thank them. We should love them."[2] I never grew to love Carroll—to the end, I still found too much stiffness and too much sentimentality in his writing outside *Alice*—but I developed an admiration, a respect and a loyalty for him. I developed an internal perception of the sort of man I felt he was, and this led in turn to a wish to "defend" him from misrepresentation.

This element of personal and partisan investment—my own beliefs and opinions, which lie behind more objective scholarship—will surely emerge in the chapters that follow. That I do not believe Lewis Carroll was a "paedophile" in the modern sense, and that I feel his behaviour and attitudes towards young girls should be judged within his own context rather than ours, will probably be obvious from my response to recent journalism in Chapter 2. Chapter 8, which deals with the Lewis Carroll Society, also discusses my own shift towards greater involvement in the group and affinity with their project to protect Carroll's reputation; Chapter 9 explores, in part, my personal responses to the sites that Carroll inhabited during his life. I am not the subject of this book, but the story of my gradually developing loyalty towards Lewis Carroll, or at least my idea of Lewis Carroll, is there in the background. On one level, more obviously at some points than others, my work here describes the journey towards becoming a fan.

Notes

1. Lewis Carroll, "An Easter Greeting to Every Child Who Loves *Alice*" (Easter 1876).
2. Matthew Sweet, *Inventing the Victorians* (London: Faber & Faber, 2001), p. 232.

Introduction: A Mess of Souvenirs

No thought of me shall find a place
In thy young life's hereafter—[1]

In the afternoon of the ninth of December 1891, Lewis Carroll invited Alice to his rooms at Christ Church, Oxford. This brief visit marks the last time Alice is mentioned in Carroll's diary, and it very probably represents their final meeting. Carroll was fifty-nine, Alice thirty-nine. Carroll was, of course, also Charles Lutwidge Dodgson: Alice had been, since 1880, Mrs Reginald Hargreaves.

In his short and entirely unemotional diary entry about the meeting, Carroll refers to his guest as "Mrs Hargreaves, the original 'Alice' ".[2] The inverted commas were no accident, although Carroll may not have known why he included them. In November 1888 he had been introduced to Reginald Hargreaves, and described him, with rather more passion, as "the husband of 'Alice' . . . the once-so-intimately known and loved 'Alice' . . . "[3] It had been twenty-three years since the publication of *Wonderland*, seventeen since *Looking-Glass*, and "Alice", to Carroll, was already something elusive. He couldn't call Mrs Hargreaves by her first name, even in his personal journal; but she would have been barely recognisable as little Alice Liddell, the girl he photographed in the late 1850s and early '60s.[4] The inverted commas seem to suggest a reference to the fictional heroine—the pert, ever-questioning protagonist of the two books, the pre-Raphaelite girl of Carroll's own amateur illustrations or the big-headed blonde of Tenniel's—but neither Carroll's nor Tenniel's drawings resemble Alice Liddell, and Reginald Hargreaves was clearly not married to the fictional character who was permanently stuck at seven or seven-and-a-half years old. "Alice" floated somewhere between these various

xiii

women and girls, unsettled and unsettling. She was the creature Carroll had described in the stunningly bleak poem that ends *Looking-Glass*:

> Echoes fade and memories die:
> Autumn frosts have slain July.
>
> Still she haunts me, phantomwise,
> Alice moving under skies
> Never seen by waking eyes.[5]

Just as "Lewis Carroll" had become a myth in his own lifetime, then—a closely-guarded front for Dodgson, a mask of kindly innocence that shielded Dodgson's internal conflicts—so Alice Liddell carried "Alice" with her like a ghostly child-companion, even when she visited the man who made her name famous.

As Karoline Leach points out, Lewis Carroll has survived Dodgson by more than a century, very much alive and gathering new meanings independently of his creator.[6] "Alice" trailed Mrs Hargreaves into the 1930s, when she was invited to New York to receive an honorary degree from Columbia University and recall her memories of Carroll/Dodgson for the benefit of the American media. Morton Cohen reprints a news photograph of the game old lady arriving in New York: the caption announces " 'Alice' here for Fete", with the more proper "Mrs R. L. Hargreaves" in a smaller font beneath.[7] On her return to England, declining further appointments, she confessed to her son Caryl—the name, she stressed, was "from a novel"[8]—that she was "tired of being Alice in Wonderland. Does it sound ungrateful? It *is*—only I do get tired!"[9] Mrs Hargreaves was experiencing life tied to a cultural icon. They float more freely after the death of the flesh-and-blood human who inspired or created them; in November 1934, with the passing of Mrs Hargreaves, "Alice" was released like a helium balloon, to roam and to be caught by others.

This is not, for the most part, a book about Charles Lutwidge Dodgson and Alice Pleasance Hargreaves, or even a book about Lewis Carroll and Alice Liddell. It is, more accurately, a book about "Lewis Carroll" and "Alice", and the bundles of meaning attached to those names; the way those names function for us in the early twenty-first century, just over a hundred years since Carroll's death and approximately one hundred and fifty since Alice Liddell's birth.[10] It is based on the idea that Carroll and Alice currently circulate as cultural myths, cultural icons—often far removed from the historical figures of Alice Liddell and Charles Dodgson—and it investigates the contemporary role and meanings of these cultural icons through an analysis of texts about them.

I use "texts" in a broad sense; during the course of this book I analyse hotels, fields, films, computer graphics, paintings, and theme park rides, as well as books and articles. By "contemporary", what I actually mean in practice is 1990 to 2003. This may seem a small sample, but I found more than enough uses of Alice and Carroll across various media from 1990 onwards to fill a book; to stretch the net wider would have meant a shallower investigation, although I refer to earlier examples to provide context and history. For the same reason, this study is primarily concerned with Anglo-American popular culture. An attempt to trace Alice and Carroll's journeys in France, Japan, Greece, Denmark, or any of the other many countries that have their own translated versions of *Wonderland* and *Looking-Glass*[11] would be fascinating but again, falls beyond the bounds of this project.

My approach here does have an agenda. It is not just an open trawl, with no aim but to present the more interesting catches of the chosen period. Rather, it looks at the contemporary traces of two specific discourses around Carroll and "Alice"—the books and the Liddell girl—one that evolved during Carroll's lifetime, and the other with its origins in the 1930s. Both of these ways of seeing Carroll and Alice are still extant. In the first discourse, Carroll is a sainted innocent, his books are joyous nonsense and Alice is his muse. In the other, Carroll is a paedophile, his books are dark allegories, and Alice is his obsession.

When Dodgson died in 1898, he was buried at a quiet ceremony in Guildford as he had wished, while his possessions were auctioned, burned, or carelessly stored by his family. So much for the man and his belongings; his reputation fared better. Carroll was mourned around the world, and his name, already saintly, was further deified. Gertrude Thomson, his artist friend, reported the passing of "the sweetest soul / That ever looked with human eye". Letters written to his family paint him as "a sort of missionary to all in need", as "the kindest and gentlest of friends", full of "pure innocent fun" and "countless acts of kindness".[12] The first biography of Carroll, published by his nephew Stuart Collingwood in 1898, is described by Karoline Leach as a "portrait of an already famous image, the benign and beloved St Lewis."

> It was affirmed, in line with popular expectation, that he lived the life of near perfection, always calm, godly, uncomplaining and charitable; "no outward circumstance could upset the tranquillity of his mind" because he "resembled the Stoic philosophers"; he avoided all coarseness and impropriety, "always rose at the same early hour" and was "very abstemious always" . . . Collingwood's "Carroll" made almost no concessions to common humanity. He was a saint and he was eccentric.[13]

In 1933, A. M. E. Goldschmidt published "*Alice in Wonderland* Psycho-Analysed". This essay, first delivered at Oxford University and considered by some to be a parody of Freudian interpretation,[14] discovers in the fall down the rabbit hole "perhaps the best-known symbol of coitus", followed by "the common symbolism of lock and key representing coitus." Having transformed the first pages of Alice's adventures into a coded message saturated with sex, Goldschmidt tells us what this reveals about the author's unconscious concerns:

> The interest is centered on the little door, which symbolizes a female child; the curtain before it represents the child's clothes. The colourful language suggests the presence, in the subconscious, of an abnormal emotion of considerable strength. [. . .] It is difficult to hold that [Carroll's] interest in children was inspired by a love of childhood in general, and in any case based on a mental rather than a physical attraction, in view of two facts: that he detested little boys, for whom, writes a biographer "he had an aversion amounting to terror," and that his friendships almost invariably ended with the close of childhood.[15]

No matter that Carroll's letters and diaries put the lie to both assertions: the ball was rolling now, gathering myth. Five years later, Paul Schilder took up Goldschmidt's Freudian approach to Carroll at greater length, and with no hint of parody. Rather than an innocent fairy-tale by a storyteller caught in childhood, Schilder sees "preponderant oral sadistic trends of cannibalistic character."[16] "This is a world", he pronounces, "of cruelty, destruction and annihilation."[17] The text is viewed in black light and seen as grotesque: next it's the turn of Carroll himself.

> What was his relation to his sex organ anyhow? [. . .] There may have been in Carroll the wish for feminine passivity and a protest against it . . . the little girl is his love object, substituting for the mother and substituting for the sister . . . we are reasonably sure that the little girls substitute for incestuous love objects. [. . .] The promiscuity in Carroll's relationship to children is interesting. He seemingly tried to get in contact with a very great number of children and to "seduce" them in this way.[18]

Whether Goldschmidt's original had been tongue-in-cheek or not, the damage was done: this vision of Carroll as repressed pervert and his books as a coded expression of abnormal desires was repeated across a range of psychoanalytic studies in the 1930s, '40s and '50s, and formed the basis for an understanding of Carroll that persists to the present day. As Leach describes it:

> The influence of Goldschmidt's article can be found in almost everything that has been said about Carroll and his work for the past sixty years. If it was a joke, it was one of the best.[19]

Yet surprisingly, this reading did not obliterate the idealised view of Carroll and his work that Collingwood had put forward in 1898. It developed in parallel, sometimes keeping its distance from the notion of Carroll as reserved, kindly, and sexless, and sometimes meshing with this interpretation, resulting in a portrait of the author as repressed yet conflicted, harbouring forbidden desires but keeping them properly buttoned-up.

Both "Carroll" and "Alice", already myths within their originators' lifetimes, are shadowed now by sinister twins, warped looking-glass reflections. *Wonderland* still sells in bright new editions to young children while it inspires horror-genre PC games for teenagers. Carroll's relationship with Alice is retold as carefree friendship in picture books and museum displays, while journalists make sly references to the author's supposedly deviant sexuality as if it were a joke everybody knows. The *Alice* books are still adapted to film and television as Christmas family specials, while novelists describe Alice Liddell teasing Carroll as he photographs her in the nude. Astonishingly, these twin interpretations—"good" Carroll and "bad" Carroll, "good" Alice and "bad" Alice—exist side by side. While we are supposedly all familiar with the rumour that Carroll was a paedophile, we continue to buy his books for our children.

My primary aim is not to seek the "truth" about Charles Lutwidge Dodgson and the girl who became Mrs Reginald Hargreaves. However many biographies we read, Dodgson still evades categorisation, seemingly impossible to pin down. As Virginia Woolf put it in 1939, "we ought to be able to grasp him whole and entire. But we fail—once more we fail. We think we have caught Lewis Carroll; we look again and see an Oxford clergyman. We think we have caught the Reverend C. L. Dodgson—we look again and see a fairy elf. The book breaks in two in our hands."[20] The last century of scholarship has not, in my view, made us any more certain of knowing for sure who Dodgson was, what he meant to Alice, and what Alice meant to him. So this book is not really about Dodgson and Alice and what they meant to each other. It is about "Carroll" and "Alice" and what they mean to us.

Notes

1. Lewis Carroll, prefatory poem, *Through the Looking-Glass* (London: Penguin, 2001), p. 139.
2. Lewis Carroll, diary entry (9 December 1891), quoted in Morton N. Cohen, *Lewis Carroll: A Biography* (London: Macmillan, 1995), p. 510.
3. Lewis Carroll, diary entry (1 November 1888), quoted in Cohen, ibid., p. 508.
4. His portrait of her in 1870 shows a sullen young woman, tragically distant from the playfully coy subject of his photographs a decade before. See Roger Taylor and Edward Wakeling, *Lewis Carroll, Photographer* (Princeton: Princeton University Press, 2002), pp. 62, 63, 65, 79.
5. Lewis Carroll, "A Boat, Beneath A Sunny Sky", *Through the Looking-Glass and What Alice Found There*, reprinted in Martin Gardner, ed. *The Annotated Alice: The Definitive Edition* (London: Penguin Books, 2001), p. 287.
6. Karoline Leach, *In the Shadow of the Dreamchild: A New Understanding of Lewis Carroll* (London: Peter Owen, 1999), p. 9.
7. Cohen, *Bibliography*, p. 520.
8. See Cohen, ibid., p. 523; Michael Bakewell, *Lewis Carroll: A Biography* (London: Mandarin, 1996), p. 262.
9. Cohen, ibid., p. 521.
10. Of course, my "now" is already out of date. I began researching the book in autumn 2001 and wrote it during the summers of 2002 and 2003.
11. See Jo Elwyn Jones and J. Francis Gladstone, *The Alice Companion: A Guide to Lewis Carroll's Alice Books* (London: Macmillan, 1998), pp. 266–70.
12. Quoted in Donald Thomas, *Lewis Carroll: A Portrait With Background* (London: John Murray, 1996), pp. 353–54.
13. Leach, *Dreamchild,* p. 21.
14. See Thomas, *Portrait*, p. 364.
15. A. M. E. Goldschmidt, "*Alice in Wonderland* Psycho-Analysed," in Robert Phillips, ed., *Aspects of Alice: Lewis Carroll's Dreamchild as Seen Through the Critics' Looking-Glasses* (New York: Vintage Books, 1971), pp. 280–281.
16. Paul Schilder, "Psychoanalytic Remarks on Alice in Wonderland and Lewis Carroll," in Phillips, ibid., p. 286.
17. Ibid., p. 289.
18. Ibid., p. 291.
19. Leach, *Dreamchild*, p. 36.
20. Virginia Woolf, "Lewis Carroll," in Phillips, ed., *Aspects of Alice*, p. 47.

In the house where Alice lives,
Alice is
It's a mess of souvenirs
There to remind you, telling the time

The Psychedelic Furs, *Alice's House*

Through a two-way looking-glass
You see your Alice
You know she has no sins, for all your jealousy
In a sense she still smiles very sweetly

Elvis Costello, *Beyond Belief*

I think it was about "malice".

Lewis Carroll[1]

---

[1]Lewis Carroll, letter to Agnes Argles (28 November 1867), reprinted in Morton N. Cohen, *The Selected Letters of Lewis Carroll* (London: Macmillan, 1982), p. 38.

THE MANY LIVES OF LEWIS CARROLL

Think of me in the year 1924.

–Lewis Carroll[1]

With little primary evidence to go on, biographies of Lewis Carroll from the mid-twentieth century tended to simply refer to previous biographies for their basic material and pad the rest with speculation. Karoline Leach provides a convincing account of the way secondary text built upon secondary text, repeating half-truths until they seemed wholly common sense, and I draw partly on her survey here.

In the 1930s, Florence Becker Lennon, denied access to Dodgson family papers or to Alice Hargreaves, tried to build a sensible hypothesis from existing material. Examining Stuart Collingwood's 1898 tribute to his uncle through the lens of recent psychoanalytical theories, she arranged the material into a new story of Carroll's emotional development. There was no mention in Collingwood of any adult romance; there were seventy-two pages about "child-friends". The conclusion seemed inevitable. "People have wondered what he did with his love-life," Lennon announced. "Now it can be told. He loved little girls, but, like Peter Pan, he had no intention of marrying them."[2]

This reading was a form of hybrid, the Freudian approach cross-bred with the "Saint Lewis" theory; it resulted in the potent image of Lewis Carroll as emotionally restrained, "innocent" in his lack of actual sexual activity, but obsessed with female children.

Though much of Carroll's insomnia was due to theological conflicts, some of it arose from the complete negation of his sexual needs. He had an odd, and of course frustrated, love for little girls—in part identifying with them, in part substituting "child-friends" for more difficult and responsible adult relationships.[3]

No one contends that Carroll ever attained the stage of adult love. It seems likely that he once made an effort to grow up and marry, but perhaps he was psychologically doomed to fail.[4]

Her main justification for the notion that Carroll may have suffered a romantic heartbreak is a passage in Collingwood's biography. This brief, almost offhand paragraph, which conceals with one hand what it almost reveals with the other, is so important to the biographies of the mid-twentieth century that it is worth quoting in its entirety. Collingwood is himself constructing a wistful, guarded theory around Carroll's posthumous *Three Sunsets*, a collection of "adult" poetry about betrayal and loss.

One cannot read this little volume without feeling that the shadow of some disappointment lay over Lewis Carroll's life. Such I believe to have been the case, and it was this that gave him his wonderful sympathy with all who suffered. But those who loved him would not wish to lift the veil from these dead sanctities, nor would any purpose be served by so doing.[5]

Based on this apparently authoritative suggestion of a frustrated love affair, and on the theory that Carroll's "emotional tone dried and stiffened between the writing of the two *Alices*,"[6] Lennon took the further step of suggesting that Carroll could have been in love with Alice Liddell, and may even have "proposed honourable marriage to her."[7] It was an original proposal at the time, a tentative idea—"we do not know for certain that he ever contemplated matrimony, or that if he did, his queen was Alice"— but it would soon become an integral feature of the Carroll-Alice myth.

Lennon's *Lewis Carroll* appeared in 1945. Seven years later, in 1952, Alexander Taylor published *The White Knight*. According to Karoline Leach, this biography had begun life as a scholarly account of mathematical and theological analogies in the *Alice* books—many of the pages are crammed with pedantic attempts to "prove" that, for instance, the Red and White Queens represent "Reason and Dogma" and that Alice stands for "the True Church".[8] This dry and implausible thesis had been jazzed up with theories of Carroll's personal life in order to secure a publisher.[9] Taylor worked up a notion, borrowed from Lennon, that the author had been infatuated with Alice; accordingly, he read Stuart Collingwood's passing reference to "the shadow of some disappointment" over Carroll's life as a coded reference to this lost love.[10] "[Carroll] determined that the secret should die with him, except that he told Collingwood, who respected his confidence and left it out of his biography."[11]

"There is no doubt in my mind," Taylor states plainly in his Preface, "that Dodgson was in some sense in love with his heroine or that the breakdown in their relationship which occurred as Alice grew up was the real disappointment of his life."[12] In extraordinary language, he then asserts that Alice haunted Carroll for life: "The facts speak louder than any opinion that she and she alone was his lost love, the withered rose in his filing-cabinet, the little ghost that was to come crying in the night to the windows of his bachelor rooms in Tom Quad."[13]

The idea was tacked-on, speculative, without recourse to new evidence, but it was presented with confidence and, more importantly, it seemed to fit. It worked with the "virginal don" theory and the repressed paedophile theory; it allowed Carroll to retain the Victorian chastity that was part of his nostalgic charm, yet incorporated the psychoanalytic complexity that the twentieth century demanded. Lennon's guess had become Taylor's bold statement: Alice was Carroll's lost love, his unattainable infatuation.

The persuasiveness of this image of a repressed obsessive is suggested by the fact that a further biography by Derek Hudson, appearing in 1954 and attempting to return Carroll to his original status as an almost totally sexless innocent, failed to catch the public imagination. Hudson strongly disapproved of Taylor's theory that the "shadow of some disappointment" was a reference to Alice Liddell, or indeed that it was anything but a passing, offhand speculation. As evidence, he quotes a letter written in 1932 from Collingwood to Carroll's niece, F. Menella Dodgson, in which Collingwood seems to dissemble and bluff his way out of his earlier suggestion:

> Nothing that I have read in L.C.'s diaries or letters suggested—to the best of my memory—that he had ever had any affaires de coeur.
>
> I *think* that Aunt Fanny once told me that it was the family's opinion that Uncle Charles had had a disappointment in love, and that they thought . . . that the lady in question was Ellen Terry.
>
> I don't think I ever had the *complete* diary . . . the "shadow" I hinted at had no other basis than what I had heard from Aunt Fanny. When Ellen Terry was just growing up . . . she was lovely beyond description . . . and it is highly probable that he fell in love with her; he may even have proposed to her. Whereas, in regard to the Liddells it was *Alice* who was undoubtedly his pet; and it was his intense love for her

(though she was only a child) which pulled the trigger and released his genius. Indeed it seems quite likely that Alice's marriage to Hargreaves may have seemed to him the greatest tragedy in his life.[14]

Although Hudson quotes this letter as if it constituted an absolute authority—"these doubts can now be set at rest"[15]—Collingwood's memory is, as Hudson himself subsequently admits, clearly unreliable, for he should have known full well that he did possess the complete set of diaries in 1898. Leach suggests that this letter is "massively disingenuous", written as an "apology to posterity" and in the knowledge that it would be made public. She shrewdly notes that Collingwood's letter makes several about-turns—he initially states that he knows nothing about any love affair, then suddenly remembers that Carroll probably fell in love with Ellen Terry, and a moment later adds that he also felt so passionately for Alice that her marriage cast a shadow over his life.[16]

Overall, Hudson's biography is more valuable than Taylor's, as it introduces a significant amount of original primary material—hitherto unpublished letters and documents—in place of Taylor's attempts to map everything in the *Alice* books to Oxford politics and theological debate. However, the decision to spend half a chapter investigating Carroll's possible romance with Ellen Terry, on the basis of Collingwood's dubious evidence, seems a waste of energy. This theory is only really pertinent in as much as it helps Hudson to tie down and muffle the rumours about Carroll and Alice. To Hudson, the author's love for the Liddell girl merely

> . . . crystallised and consecrated his love for children. As she passed out of childhood, it became clear that neither her family background nor her own interests offered any reliable foundation for adult love. Just at that time he met Ellen Terry—at seventeen half woman and half-child—whose radiant character and genius stirred all his artistic sensibilities. Here perhaps came his one clear romantic call—it was not one that he could attempt to answer. As the years went by, the news of Alice's marriage may yet have brought him a pang, as Collingwood suggests, for he was not without jealousy.[17]

Hudson and Taylor's clashing interpretations of the Alice-Carroll relationship led them to a public conflict in the pages of *The Spectator*. In a letter to F. Menella Dodgson of 1953, Hudson discussed the controversy: Taylor was responding furiously to Hudson's negative review of *The White Knight*, and Hudson was aware that he might have to issue a counter-statement.

> Mr Taylor has written to *The Spectator* a long and rather angry letter of reply. I don't know whether or not the editor will want to publish it

4

and I have told him I must leave that entirely to him, of course—but
if he does, I shall probably have to write a short reply. I wonder whether
I might say, what I think I remember your telling me, that S. D.
Collingwood himself assured you he had no *particular reason* for C.L.D.'s
unhappiness in his mind when he wrote the famous passage about the
"shadow of disappointment"? . . . for really I think Mr Taylor ought to
be pulled up. As you will see from what I have quoted, he has read all
sorts of deep meaning into the passage which is completely misleading,
I feel sure.[18]

Despite the keen support of the Dodgson family for Hudson's interpretation, it was Taylor who had the last word, and his entirely speculative
theory about Carroll's shadowy, secret love for Alice took root. "The
twentieth century had more empathy with the repression theories and
surreptitious dirt-dishing of Taylor's hypothesis, and this is what stuck,"
Leach decides. "Through invention and fantasy and the sheer determination
to believe, posterity had acquired the Carroll it wanted."[19]

Carroll's diaries, edited by Roger Lancelyn Green, were published in
1953; the original volumes were presented to the British Museum in 1969.
Neither Hudson's reissued biography of 1976 nor Anne Clark's new *Lewis
Carroll* of 1979 took account of this new and potentially sensational material.
Hudson, despite a new preface, reiterated his view of the "gentle pre-
Freudian", while Clark, according to Leach, "conveyed a life untouched
by normal human shadows and therefore all but featureless, uncontaminated
even by the one unambiguous shred of humanity he had ever been ac-
corded—his nascent deviancy."[20]

Meanwhile, Carroll's nine diary volumes sat in storage until 1982,
when Morton Cohen declared he had discovered six razored pages and
pointed the finger at Dodgson's niece F. Menella.[21] Subsequent researchers
into Carroll's life chose not to challenge his announcement and analysis—
which Leach describes as incorrect in its detail, though accurate in its
basic discovery of sabotage and deliberate censorship. Writing in the late
1990s, Leach came to the weary conclusion that "biography has continued
to tell the familiar story."[22] Carroll was at once deviant and controlled,
devoted to the company of little girls yet rigidly holding himself back
from any improper contact.

Which is where we come in. This chapter examines eight sources:
biographies by Christina Bjork and Inga-Karin Eriksson (1994), Morton
N. Cohen (1995), Michael Bakewell (1996), Donald Thomas (1996),
Stephanie Lovett Stoffel (1997), and Karoline Leach (1999), along with
Jones and Gladstone's *Alice Companion* (1998) and Edward Wakeling's

commentary to the fourth volume of Lewis Carroll's *Diaries* (1997). Rather than attempting to take on a comparison of these texts as a whole, I am choosing to focus on the way they depict key moments in Carroll's life or discuss key debates around it. So we drop in on Carroll at specific points in these multiple, parallel stories, and examine the different retellings to see what picture they give, what myth they perpetuate. The points I am concentrating on are as follows: the "golden afternoon" of July 4, 1862, when Carroll first told *Alice's Adventures* to the Liddell children; the social split with the Liddell family; the pleas for divine forgiveness in Carroll's diary; and the nude photographs he took of young girls.

The Golden Afternoon

" 'Alice' is Carroll's twin in mythology," writes Leach.

> With our modern love of literalism we have interpreted his "Alice" as the real-life Alice he knew when he wrote the story. We confuse their separate identities . . . the consensus in modern biography is that Alice Liddell is the "dreamchild" and, beyond that, the key to Dodgson's inner mind, his muse, the love of his life, the cipher by which we read his soul.[23]

While accounts of the now-famous boat trip during which *Alice* was originally told to Alice are only indirectly related to the modern reading of Carroll as "deviant", it is worth examining the ways in which 1990s biography and commentary treat this moment of origin, in order to see how it has been steeped in idealised nostalgia. Although there is evidence to suggest that the day seemed unremarkable at the time, even to the author, this collaboration between Alice as muse and Carroll as genius at the birth of *Wonderland* has been built up from subsequent reminiscences into a sacred myth that few biographers, even now, bother to challenge. It also serves as a key plank in the story of Carroll's supposedly doomed love for Alice Liddell. As Leach scornfully relates the received wisdom about their relationship:

> Dodgson "fell in love" with Alice Liddell soon after he met her. It was his unprecedented adoration of her, his passionate desire to please her, that made him create the story of "Alice" just for her. After he told the story in the boat on that dreamy afternoon of 4 July 1862 his devotion inspired him to sit up all night writing the whole tale down for her. Thus, in a spirit of distorted sacrifice, was a work of genius born.[24]

As such, while the origin story is usually presented as a clear case of Carroll's innocent skill at weaving fairy-tales and knowing the childish mind—the saintly Peter Pan image—it leads into the episode about his alleged proposal of marriage to Alice Liddell, and what contemporary discourse now considers his "paedophilia".

There are seven key pieces of evidence that give us a sense of what happened during the boat trip of July 4, 1862, when Carroll and his friend Robinson Duckworth took Lorina, Alice, and Edith Liddell up the Isis for tea on the riverbank at Godstow.

The first is Carroll's diary entry, now reprinted in full as part of Edward Wakeling's mammoth project to edit and publish all of Carroll's nine surviving journals. It is surprisingly plain in nature.

> Duckworth and I made an expedition *up* the river to Godstow with the three Liddells: we had tea on the bank there, and did not reach Ch.Ch. again till quarter past eight, when we took them on to my rooms to see my collection of micro-photographs, and restored them to the Deanery just before nine.[25]

The best part of a year later, Carroll added "a note on the blank page opposite"[26]: "On which occasion I told them the fairy-tale of 'Alice's Adventures Under Ground', which I undertook to write out for Alice . . . " Not an especially sparkling record of the day. At the time, it seems that the boat trip failed to stand out as exceptional for Carroll, who declined to mark the day with his traditional blessing, a metaphorical "white stone".

The next piece of evidence is also by Carroll's hand, although this recollection takes a very different tone: it is the prefatory poem to *Wonderland*, "All in the Golden Afternoon." The matter-of-fact diary entry has been transformed into a romanticised flight of fancy where even the Liddell girls are renamed in Latin as Prima, Secunda, and Tertia, and Carroll's dreamy pen-portrait is punctuated by exclamations like "Ah, cruel Three!"

> And ever, as the story drained
> The wells of fancy dry,
> And faintly strove that weary one
> To put the subject by,
> "The rest next time"—"It *is* next time!"
> The happy voices cry.[27]

Just as Carroll's journal entries were generally fairly dry, so his "serious" poetry, as opposed to parody or nonsense, tended to what we might now see as a rather grandiose style within rigid rhyme schemes: as such, this poem is entirely characteristic.

In his essay " 'Alice' on the Stage" of 1887, Carroll returned to the scene with a description that owes far more to the verses than to his original memories.

> Full many a year has slipped away, since that "golden afternoon" that gave thee birth, but I can call it up almost as clearly as if it were yesterday—the cloudless blue above, the watery mirror below, the boat drifting idly on its way, the tinkle of the drops that fell from the oars as they waved so sleepily to and fro, and (the one bright gleam of life in all the slumberous scene) the three eager faces, hungry for news of fairy-land, and who would not be said "nay" to . . . [28]

The fourth and fifth accounts were supplied by Robinson Duckworth and Alice Hargreaves to Stuart Collingwood, for his 1898 biography. Alice mistakenly remembers that this trip was "down the river" rather than up, and contradicts Carroll's poem—but not his vague journal entry—by recalling that he began the story not in the boat, but on the bank, "under a new-made hayrick".[29] Otherwise, her story sticks very closely to the versions we have already heard.

> Here from all three came the old petition of "Tell us a story," and so began the ever-delightful tale. Sometimes to tease us—and perhaps being really tired—Mr Dodgson would stop suddenly and say, "And that's all till next time." "Ah, but it is next time," would be the exclamation from all three . . . [30]

This merry account of her exchange with Carroll is almost identical to the poem stanza quoted above, to the extent that we might suspect Mrs Hargreaves of giving Collingwood's readers what they wanted to hear; that is, a confirmation that the poem was based on "fact". Alternatively, she may actually have begun to rely on the fiction in place of her own memories, just as Carroll seems to have referred to his poetic reconstruction of the afternoon rather than to his own diary.

Duckworth supports Carroll's recollection that the story was told during the boat trip itself, rather than on the bank.

> I rowed *stroke* and he rowed *bow* . . . when the three Miss Liddells were our passengers, and the story was actually composed and spoken *over my shoulder* for the benefit of Alice Liddell, who was acting as 'cox' for our gig. I remember turning round and saying, "Dodgson, is this an

extempore romance of yours?" And he replied 'Yes, I'm inventing as we go along."[31]

Mrs Hargreaves's final offering was made to the public of the 1930s who demanded more recollections of "Alice". It is perhaps arguable how much an eighty-year-old would accurately recall of a boat trip seven decades ago, and so we can hardly be surprised that she adds little to the previous reports. However, she still seems to imply that, contrary to Carroll and Duckworth's memories, the story unfurled as they sat by the haycocks—a more plausible suggestion, given that *Wonderland* (like *Under Ground*) begins on a riverbank, not on a river.

> Nearly all of *Alice's Adventures Under Ground* was told on that blazing summer afternoon with the heat haze shimmering over the meadows where the party landed to shelter for a while in the shadow cast by the haycocks near Godstow . . . I have such a distinct recollection of the expedition . . . [32]

Lastly, and with sad irony, we must nod to a more prosaic source: the meteorological report from July 4, 1862, that records the day as "cool and rather wet" with rain after 2 PM, 10/10 cloud cover and maximum shade temperature of 67.9 degrees Fahrenheit.[33] Somehow Carroll and Alice have apparently, on two occasions each—deliberately or otherwise— got the weather wrong, and it is their idealised memory of a blazing sun and cloudless blue that passed into myth.[34]

Christina Bjork and Inga-Karin Eriksson's *The Story of Alice in Her Oxford Wonderland* is a book for young readers; not "a learned essay, because so many already exist"[35], but a lively, well-researched portrait of Dodgson from Alice's point of view, with rich illustrations based on sketches of modern Oxford. Carroll is referred to very properly—appropriately, as this is Alice's story—as "Mr Dodgson", and the pictures of cheeky brunette Alice Liddell far outnumber those of prim, petticoated Alice from Ten- niel's drawings.

The importance of the boat trip as the pivotal moment in the story of Alice and Dodgson, Carroll, and *Alice*, is stressed by placing it out of sequence, at the start of the book. Its chronological place comes on page 48, but as "everyone who has heard it knows that this story is something *special*,"[36] the golden afternoon is shifted back to the beginning of the narrative. The page title, "Once Upon A Time", immediately provides a fairytale framework, and Eriksson fills in two-thirds of the page with the picture of a summer idyll: three giggling girls in white crammed at the end of the boat, matched by kindly Dodgson and Duckworth in white suits and boaters.

The illustration, with its gorgeous details of oars gently stirring water, the pale city in the distance, and even an Edenic gathering of horses on the far bank, could have been snatched from Carroll's own sugar-coated memories of the day. That he barely mentioned the expedition in his diary of the time, that he only connected this trip to the first telling of *Wonderland* in a later note, and that the weather that afternoon was less than perfect, have been omitted. The legend is prettier than the truth, so we print the legend; and Eriksson illustrates it.

Bjork's account of the boat trip is clearly drawn from Carroll's prefatory poem and 1887 article, combined with the 1898 recollections of Robinson Duckworth and Alice Hargreaves's two reports from 1898 and 1932. The "All till next time"/ "It is next time" dialogue is reproduced as authentic—we are assured that "the text and illustrations in this book are based on the real facts"[37]—and the exchange that originated in Carroll's poem becomes, more or less, biographical reportage.

> Sometimes Mr Dodgson pretended to be asleep, to give himself time to work out the next bit.
> "That is all till next time," he said, in the middle of the story.
> "Oh yes," said Alice, "and now it is already next time."
> And so the story went on after all. When they had found a good picnic place in the shade of a big haystack, Mr Duckworth asked:
> "Dodgson, is this an extempore romance of yours?"
> "Yes," said Mr Dodgson. "I'm inventing as we go along."[38]

Note that Bjork's retelling favours Alice's version—placing the group under the haystack—and in doing so, contradicts Carroll's description of the girls asking for a story in the boat. More crucially, it deliberately misappropriates the evidence from Duckworth's account. In the latter, as cited above, Duckworth's question about an "extempore romance" was called back over his shoulder while "I rowed *stroke* and he rowed *bow*" and Alice acted as cox: here, the exchange has been shifted to the bank.

Just as Eriksson's illustration allows for artistic license, so Bjork's prose adapts the evidence from the poem and the three reminiscences— hardly reliable in themselves—for her own convenience. Alice's account fails to tally precisely with the prefatory poem, Carroll's recollection, or Duckworth's report; but there is no place at the start of a children's book for competing versions or debates over accuracy, so Bjork, naturally enough, has to make sense from conflict and iron out inconsistency.

It is hardly surprising that Bjork and Eriksson's charming, simplified story softens the corners and blurs the lens. However, it is striking that this trend towards pretty myth is also so obvious in "adult" biographies of the last decade. The heat haze of the "golden afternoon" dominates almost all contemporary accounts of *Alice*'s origins, with recollections from decades after the event preferred to the mood struck by Carroll's diary of the time. It seems trivial to complain that these biographies play down the official report of weather conditions over Oxford on July 4, but I think their treatment of this small point, this objectionable rain on the parade, demonstrates their need to confirm the myth at the price of ignoring, undermining, or playing down any elements that threaten to contradict it.

Michael Bakewell's 1996 biography, for instance, favours the romanti-cised versions over the two documents that would seem more reliable—the Meteorological Office report and Carroll's diary—to the extent that he questions the scientific record of the weather.

> *All in the golden afternoon*
> *Full leisurely we glide . . .*
> begins the poem which prefaces *Alice's Adventures in Wonderland*. Alice Hargreaves remembered 4th July, 1862, as "a blazing summer afternoon." [. . .] it is most unlikely that Dodgson would have set out on the river in rainy weather . . . even accounting for their sentimentalising that memorable day after the event, the weather could scarcely have been as bad as the report suggests, or the tale would never have got told at all. Dodgson remembered: "the cloudless blue above, the watery mirror below, the boat drifting idly on its way, the tinkle of drops as they fell from the oars, as they waved so sleepily to and fro . . . " Even Duck-worth, who had no need to sentimentalise the event, referred to it as a "beautiful summer afternoon." And so, on what we must accept was an idyllic summer day . . . "[39]

There is some logic in Bakewell's protest that Carroll would not have begun an expedition if the weather had been poor. On the other hand, he had spent an enjoyable afternoon with the same group on the seventeenth of June, despite torrential rain—the drenched walk from Nuneham to Sandford inspired the "Pool of Tears" episode.[40] Bakewell's argument—that "we must accept" the notion of a blazing hot day because Carroll tells us it was in a clearly idealised piece of writing—seems quite peculiar. The fact that Alice Hargreaves and Robinson Duckworth corroborated this 1887 account when Collingwood probed their memories twenty-six years after the event is hardly conclusive evidence—Carroll had just passed away, and they were unlikely to contradict his myth even if they remembered the afternoon as pleasantly cool. The fact is that we "must accept" this version only because it suits us far better to have the origin of a great children's book set on an exceptional, unforgettable day, with every detail of sky and water just so, rather than believe that while the story was unique, the day itself may have been fairly ordinary.

Bakewell's need to keep the idyll intact leads him to rely on Carroll's poem as a key source. Filling in details from his own informed guesswork— "finding a suitable boat would not have been an easy matter"—he incorporates snatches from the prefatory verses as if they were objective reporting. "Alice [did] her best to steer them on their course: *While little hands make vain pretence / Our wanderings to guide . . .* "[41] The "All till next time" / "It is next time" routine is brought in again, and while Bakewell notes the clash between Carroll's and Alice's memories as to whether the story was begun in boat or on bank, he declines seriously to question the accuracy of either recollection.

Morton Cohen's three pages on the afternoon, in his massive *Lewis Carroll* of 1995, are essentially given over to lengthy quotations from the key existing sources. He begins with Carroll's underwhelming diary entry, then moves through the later, romanticised revision of 1887 to Alice's recollections of 1898 and 1932, winding up with Duckworth's account. There is no questioning of these texts' authority, or mention of their inconsistency with each other. While Cohen makes surprisingly few personal interjections during these pages—content for the most part to link the quotations and let them speak, unchallenged, for themselves—he notes that the trip was "destined to make literary history" and calls it an "exceptional adventure".[42] The former is impossible to deny, but the latter description only applies if we take Alice's perspective—or rather, Alice's adult perspective with decades of hindsight.

Given that he starts this section with Carroll's uninspiring diary entry, for Cohen to claim that the afternoon was either exceptional or adventurous is, like Bakewell's account, a falling back upon myth and a deliberate ignoring of anything that contradicts it. He knows full well that Carroll and the Liddells had made many other river trips—he notes only two pages beforehand that "the rowing parties became routine"[43]—and that the rain-soaked trip of the previous month was technically far more adventurous than the journey to Godstow and the picnic on the bank. The day itself is celebrated because of the book that resulted, and the glory of *Alice* reflected back until its origin is also bathed in light.

As a sidenote, we should observe that although Wakeling, Cohen, and Bakewell all quote the same passage from the diary, these quotations differ from each other with regard to the time of the group's return to Oxford. Cohen reports "we . . . did not reach Christ Church again till $^1/_2$ past 8," while Wakeling reproduces it as "did not reach Ch. Ch. again till quarter past eight." Bakewell has them arriving at "a quarter-to-eight", forty-five minutes before Cohen and half an hour before Wakeling.[44] In fact, the original manuscript of the diary reveals that Wakeling is correct, allowing for his transcription of fractions: Carroll wrote "till $^1/_4$ past 8."[45] The point may seem trivial and minor errors are entirely understandable, but these inconsistencies do encourage scepticism about biographical references to the "facts" of primary documents.

Both Donald Thomas—in his 1996 portrait of Carroll against the "background" of Victorian social context—and Stephanie Lovett Stoffel, in her slim but glossily illustrated guide to Carroll's "life and times" (1997), make a wry distinction between the afternoon itself and the way it evolved in the participants' memories. "The weather on Friday 4 July 1862 was not particularly good," Thomas says flatly.

> Yet the memories of those who went in the little boat to Godstow were of blazing sun and perfect summer. Perhaps, in the six hours of absence from Christ Church, the weather cleared sufficiently to give that impression. Or perhaps they sailed into another dimension of eternal summer, commemorated by Dodgson in his concluding verses to the famous story.
>
> A boat, beneath a sunny sky
> Lingering onward dreamily
> In an evening of July—[46]

Similarly, Stoffel notes that the "dreamy afternoon . . . is described in the official weather records as cool and rainy, but those involved remembered it as a blazingly sunny day, with a heat haze shimmering over the meadow at Godstow."

> In reality or in the glow of memory it truly was the golden afternoon that Dodgson conjures up in the introductory poem to *Alice in Wonderland*. The warmth of the sun, the gentle rocking of the boat, the murmur of the river, the rapt listeners together stimulated that great mind to an unparalleled flood of mingled logic and whimsy.[47]

In both accounts we find the same approach—whatever the truth, whether the travellers dreamed it or not, on one level the afternoon was just as Carroll described it in his poem. It is strange, though, that the lines Thomas cites as "the concluding verses to the famous story" are from the spectral, doom-laden poem that closes *Looking-Glass*, rather than *Wonderland*'s preface.

Just as Stoffel takes a romantic view of the story's creation, presenting it as the singular rush from Carroll's "great mind," when added, like elements of a chemistry set, to the perfect setting and the prodding of his muse, so Thomas comments that "seldom had literary inspiration of such genius been so public."[48] The suggestion is that the entire story emerged during that afternoon, "composed and polished"[49] as Thomas puts it, in a flow of consummate brilliance.

Finally, two sources take a comparatively sceptical approach to the romance that now surrounds *Alice*'s origins. Although Jo Elwyn Jones and J. Francis Gladstone's glossary *The Alice Companion* locates the story of 4 July under "Golden Afternoon", they are more critical of received wisdom than most writers on *Alice*, and unpack various conflicting points of view. The authors' pragmatic angle is perhaps best illustrated by another entry that touches on the realities of river trips with young girls, and suggests that Alice and her sisters would "inevitably . . . have to pee"[50]—a detail I have certainly not seen elsewhere in Carrollian scholarship.

Jones and Gladstone are the first in this group of 1990s commentators to use the word "myth".

> Myth has it that the first *Alice* story was told to Alice, her two sisters and Robinson Duckworth on a single river expedition on 4 July 1862.
>
> All in the golden afternoon
> Full leisurely we glide;[51]

Again the poem is brought in, but this time not as talisman of authenticity but as a contrast to Carroll's practical, commonsensical diary entries, which describe the creation of *Alice* as "interminable". The authors' contention is not focused on whether the day itself was commonplace or exceptional, but on whether the story was composed on that specific occasion. "Twenty-five years later," they remark, "there was a change. [Carroll] began to establish the myth that *Under Ground* was the spontaneous creation of a single afternoon . . . since then, an assumption about the 'golden afternoon' has influenced many Carroll studies."[52]

Jones and Gladstone's argument is that the complexity, the in-jokes, the real-world satire, and the sheer longevity of the first *Alice* story combine to suggest that it was gradually and carefully built up over time, rather than invented over a few hours.

It would have taken a genius indeed to come up with *Under Ground* on a single "golden afternoon". Not everyone, however, wishes to face this.[53]

As we have seen, biographers like Thomas and Stoffel deal with the problem very simply by accepting that Carroll was a "genius indeed"; that both he and the telling of the story were exceptional. But the truth is that Carroll never actually makes this claim in the passage referred to by Jones and Gladstone. If he suggests at all that the *Adventures* were completed by the evening of July 4, it is only in the prefatory poem:

Its quaint events were hammered out—
And now the tale is done,
And home we steer, a merry crew,
Beneath the setting sun.[54]

Contrary to their complaint, his romanticised 1887 account does not present the story as the finished product of one afternoon. It was, he says, the "golden afternoon" that "gave [the story] birth", but he goes on, even in this lyrical recollection, to describe how he refined and developed the basic tale: "In writing it out, I added many fresh ideas, which seem to grow of themselves upon the original stock; and many more added themselves when, years afterwards, I wrote it all over again for publication . . ."[55]

The only real distinction Carroll makes between his stories of July 4 and those of other occasions is that Alice demanded this one be written down; indeed, the other tales that "lived and died, like summer midges", are given equal status by the author, "each in its own golden afternoon."[56] It was not Carroll but Alice who claimed, seventy years after the event, that "nearly all of *Alice's Adventures Under Ground* was told on that blazing summer afternoon"[57]—and by this time, we can hardly blame her for misremembering, or for choosing to confirm the notion of Carroll as creative genius.

The myth of a single flood of invention is there in Stoffel and Thomas, certainly—and Cohen also buys into the idea, with his gushy "out it poured, the story of Alice down the rabbit hole"[58]—but even during his high-flown, "full many a year" fancy, Carroll gives a humbler and more plausible account of the story's evolution. To accuse Carroll of trumpeting his own creative abilities is misguided; he remade the afternoon as idyllically golden, but the secondary myth, that the story was virtually finished by evening, seems to have been dreamed up by others, long after his death.

Karoline Leach is the most radical commentator of this group; indeed, her entire project is to present "a new understanding of Lewis Carroll". Overturning the notion that Carroll was fixated on little girls—and that Alice was his lost love—Leach constructs in its place a theory that he was involved in an affair with Mrs Lorina Liddell, Alice's mother. Inevitably, she has no truck with the idea of Alice as muse, and the idealisation of the "golden afternoon" is viewed scornfully for its role in the broader myth of Alice Liddell. "With our modern love of literalism we have interpreted his 'Alice' as the real-life Alice he knew when he wrote the story. We confuse their separate identities . . . "[59]

Leach mentions July 4, 1862, only in passing, as part of the received narrative that she locates at the heart of traditional Carrollian criticism: "After he told the story in the boat on that dreamy afternoon . . . his devotion inspired him to sit up all night writing the whole tale down for her."[60] She offers a refreshingly revisionist approach to the Carroll life story, identifying key points in the conventional biographies and suggesting that they fail to measure up against primary evidence. "Dodgson's extant and aggravatingly elliptic diaries give no indication that he had any special attachment to Alice over and above his affection for the entire family. She appears mostly as one of the undifferentiated 'Liddells' . . . "[61] Leach's theory here, like so many about Carroll, is open to dispute: in the diary, we see that Alice is mentioned by name on the day in question—"on which occasion I told them the fairy-tale . . . which I undertook to write out for Alice"[62]—and it is hard to believe that the real Alice, at this very early stage, was not closely connected in Carroll's mind with the protagonist of *Alice's Adventures Under Ground*.

Be that as it may, it is hard to discount Leach's argument that recent biographers perpetuate the romantic, Alice-as-muse theory. Stoffel depicts their meeting as a portentous crossing of destinies—"one of these girls, Alice Liddell, was about to inspire him to become an author of rare destiny"[63]—and we have seen a similar line about "literary inspiration of such genius" in Thomas. Leach's scepticism works as a useful antidote, encouraging a more challenging, critical approach to the available evidence even if we choose not to go along fully with her project of demolishing the existing story and building a new one.

The meeting and creating is only the first part of the myth as Leach retells it: the second half involves loss and longing.

> Alice the child was the love of his life and the passion of his tragically deviant soul, and for a brief while she gave him happiness. But then, goes the story, things got out of hand. He became too obvious in his

affection, may have even proposed marriage to the eleven-year-old girl. This is said to have precipitated a crisis in his relationship with her family, dated in the summer of 1863. A particular page, cut from his diary by a later hand, is assumed to have told the story of this confrontation. Her shocked parents are said to have banned him from her presence . . . [64]

Less than a year after the golden afternoon, dark clouds begin to gather around the twin myths of Carroll and Alice.

The Censored Diary

On June 25, 1863, Carroll took a boat trip to Nuneham with Lorina, Alice, and Edith in the company of their father, mother, paternal grandfather, little sister Rhoda, and Lord Newry, an undergraduate protégé of the Liddell family. It was a "pleasant expedition with a *very* pleasant conclusion"[65], as Carroll had escorted the three girls home alone. On the twenty-seventh he wrote to Mrs Liddell "either to send the children to be photographed"— and here there is a gap in the journal until June 30. The incongruous "either" has been crossed out in an attempt to make a false sentence from the remaining words.[66]

There is no further mention of the Liddells in the diary for more than five months. On December 5 (not the second, as Cohen has it[67]) Carroll meets them at a Christ Church theatrical: "but I held aloof from them, as I have done all this term."[68] His encounters with the family after this point are infrequent. In 1864, Mrs Liddell told Carroll that he would no longer be allowed to take her daughters on the river. The relationship with Alice is generally accepted to have faded and cooled to formality after this point, flattening into the letters to "Dear Mrs Hargreaves" that Carroll wrote in the 1880s and '90s.

The missing pages in Carroll's diary, according to Cohen, Leach, Wakeling, Stoffel, Bakewell, and Bjork, were deliberately censored. "This omission is unique," writes Cohen.

> He accounted for those days, but the page on which he wrote was later cut out. In fact, by her own admission many years later, Charles's niece Menella Dodgson owned to having cut some pages from the diary, and this page was evidently one of them. It contained information that offended her sensibilities, and she took a razor to it. That the page recorded a crisis in Charles's relations with the deanery is certain.[69]

Bakewell explains that "'Either' has been crossed out and a harmless sentence has been cobbled together (probably by Dodgson himself) . . . the next page has been torn out."[70] The implication is clearly of self-censorship: a theory shared by none of the other contemporary biographers. Bjork, despite her young readership, doesn't shrink from addressing the issue, and blames another hand for the editing. "A page has been torn out of his diary just after that delightful boat trip. The words have been slightly altered on the next page so the gap would not be noticed—but the writing is not Mr Dodgson's."[71] Stoffel agrees—"the very next page has been cut out with a razor . . . the deletion of three days from the diary was made not by Dodgson but by his niece, after his death"[72]—and Wakeling confirms.

> The next page has been removed from the journal, and the perpetrator is almost certainly not Dodgson. The handwriting which has crossed out the word "either" is not his, and neither is the pen the same style used by Dodgson. Clearly, Dodgson offered Mrs. Liddell an alternative which is now missing, together with the rest of the entry for Saturday 27 June . . . in that time, something written by Dodgson was deemed to be too sensitive by a descendant, and while the family had the journal, the page was removed.[73]

Leach airily tells her readers that the original diaries "can now be viewed by anyone who cares to look . . . there for anyone to see are the scissored and razored stumps . . . "[74] In fact, the diaries are kept at the highest level of restricted access, guarded by multiple gatekeepers: I had to present the Manuscripts department of the British Library with a book contract and a letter of support from my department chair before they would even consider letting me view the books. But they are there, and they clearly show the short, jagged cuts of small scissors, rather than a rip. The "either" is crossed through in thick, dark pen very different from Carroll's own writing, but very similar to the other erasure in the same volume—the attempt to scribble over an unflattering reference to Alice on April 21.

Bakewell's opinion that the removal of "either" was Carroll's own doing—like the assumption he shares with Bjork that the page was "torn" out, as opposed to cut or razored—is surely due to carelessness and a lack of familiarity with the original manuscript. Leach's detailed account of the edits accurately describes this page as "chopped out untidily by one of his descendants with what seem to have been nail scissors"[75]; by comparison, "torn" sounds like a guess at the more likely way of removing pages, rather than an observation of the document. While we can excuse mistakes in Bjork's simplified history (translated from the Swedish in any case), the careless imprecision in Bakewell's account might lead us to doubt his contentious suggestion of self-censorship.

Thomas makes no mention of any censorship of Carroll's diaries, treating Mrs Liddell's refusal in 1864 to let her daughters accompany him on further river trips as the key factor in his "parting with Alice Liddell."[76] Jones and Gladstone advise that notions of censorship need to be "cautiously interpreted"[77], offering no detail of this specific editing. But if we accept the plausible theory that the page in question included sensitive details of Carroll's reasons for breaking company with the Liddells—at least temporarily, and with lasting effects—and that it was censored not by Carroll's hand, but by one or more of his descendants, then we have to ask what secrets were being withheld, and why. As Stoffel observes, "in censoring the diary the Dodgson family unwittingly focused the unquench-able curiosity of posterity on the very issue they had wished to obscure."[78] What was being hidden? The most obvious answer, according to these commentators, is that the missing page told of Carroll's marriage proposal to Alice; but they add that the obvious answer is not always the most accurate.

"The explanation most frequently brought forward," says Bakewell, "is that Dodgson asked for Alice's hand in marriage . . . the evi-dence . . . however, is decidedly slim."[79] He concludes "it is more than likely . . . that the whole story of his proposal is no more than a myth".[80] As evidence of a more likely reason for the split, Bakewell offers a letter written from Lorina to Alice in 1930, following Lorina's interview with Florence Becker Lennon.

> I suppose you don't remember when Mr Dodgson ceased coming to the Deanery? How old were you? I said his manner became too affectionate to you as you grew older and that mother spoke to him about it, and that offended him so he ceased coming to see us again, as one had to give some reason for all intercourse ceasing . . . [81]

This letter "goes some way to accounting for what happened," Bakewell argues. "Something must have trigged an alarm bell in Mrs Liddell's mind."[82] The explanation is that the break was caused by a more general concern, nothing specific; Bakewell ignores, or does not notice, the fact that Lorina seems to be telling her sister that she invented a reason for Lennon's benefit.

Stoffel is equally sceptical. "The obvious conclusion is that Dodgson has asked the dean if he might court Alice, then 11 years old, when she came of age . . . [but] there are many other possible explanations for such an estrangement." Again, the reasons offered are vague: "The Liddells may have asked him to keep company less often with the girls as they grew up. A suggestion of ungentlemanly behavior would have been a great insult to him."[83] Jones and Gladstone are also careful:

> Why Mrs Liddell put a stop to Carroll's friendship with Alice, Lorina and Edith may remain a secret. The reasons for speculating that Carroll proposed to Alice are strong, but they are entirely circumstantial.[84]

Thomas and Wakeling choose not to entertain the possibility of a proposal.

We have seen that Jones and Gladstone generally take a sceptical approach to the stories circulating around Carroll. However, Bakewell and Stoffel were content for the most part to let the "golden afternoon" glow in memory as Carroll described it in his poem, and tended to an idealised view of *Alice*'s creation: we might wonder that they tend to downplay the plausibility of the marriage proposal. The most obvious explanation is that they suspect such a declaration, to an eleven-year-old, would seem a bridge too far for contemporary readers, and that to give the idea any serious credence would alienate us from Carroll. Despite all the evidence that it would have been acceptable within the cultural context of 1863,[85] the inevitable "paedophile" sexuality suggested by a marriage proposal to a child risks despoiling the contemporary image of Carroll as odd but fundamentally harmless.

We can find endearing the idea that the author was fond of little girls, as long as he kept his hands to himself; we can deal with his photographs, his letters with a thousand kisses, his love gifts of nonsense literature, but for him to want an eleven-year-old in his bed is too much for a society with such a hatred for the "paedophile"[86] and the idea needs to be handled carefully. On the one hand, Carroll must be kept separate from our bogeyman figure of the child abuser; on the other, his celibate adoration of children is a key feature of his contemporary image.

Stoffel, while presenting the likelihood of a marriage proposal as only one of many possibilities, says in the same breath, "it is plausible to think that Dodgson may have been in love with Alice."[87] A distinction is apparently being made between unrequited infatuation and the less palatable idea of Carroll wooing a child-bride; the latter is barely acceptable, the former seems crucial to the current myth of Carroll. He must be charmingly eccentric, but not weirdly abnormal; it is a strange balance.

In this respect, Bakewell's to-and-fro response to the issue also seems telling. He has already stated plainly that Carroll's photographs of the

Liddell girls "tell us, if nothing else, that he is in love with Alice."[88] This "love", held at the respectable distance between camera and subject, has nothing to trouble the contemporary reader; indeed, it confirms the idea of a man endearingly enamoured with childhood. However, the idea that Carroll wanted a physical union is tossed from hand to hand instead of being grasped firmly; Bakewell theorises, "if Dodgson really contemplated marriage with Alice," it was because he envisaged sliding "gradually into matrimony through a long engagement" and therefore conquering "his fear of a real sexual relationship".[89]

Immediately after this psychoanalytical justification comes the blunt closure I quoted above: more than likely, the whole story is "no more than a myth." The marriage proposal is made more acceptable through this explanation that Carroll was using Alice to bridge the gap between the childhood he idealised and the adult sexuality that terrified him, but anyway, we are assured that it probably didn't happen; the prospect must be entertained for the sake of completeness, and rationalised through psychoanalytic guesswork, but this thread, a loose live wire, is quickly run to ground and made safe.

Carroll, through this lens, remains a naïve innocent rather than a risk to society; his requisite oddness is retained but controlled. Of course, the reluctance of these commentators to accept the proposal theory may simply reflect a lack of evidence; but Cohen, the only one of this group who believes the theory plausible, makes a good show of finding proof for it. Even in his support of this notion, though, Cohen is careful to define his conception of Carroll's love for Alice so as not to disturb our contemporary sensibilities.

> The fact that Alice is Charles' "ideal child friend", that she sparked his creative energy, that he devoted so much of his time to her and fashioned his two remarkable fantasies with her as heroine is proof enough of a deep attachment, certain affection, even a kind of love. That he might desire a holy union with her is understandable.[90]

Cohen leads us to the idea gradually, moving from the more acceptable position that Alice was Carroll's muse, the girl at the heart of his most important creative work, to a suggestion that his feelings coalesced into the wish for a sacred intimacy. That the theory is so tentatively expressed shows, I think, how sensitive this area is for modern readers. Carroll's feelings for Alice are described with almost comical hesitancy—"a deep attachment, certain affection, a kind of love"—and the marriage proposal is stressed as leading to "holy union", not the honeymoon suite.

Cohen offers several clues to this "certain affection" between the man and the girl. Firstly, he suggests that there were rumours of Carroll's proposal at the time—"Oxford gossip has it so."[91] According to Margaret Woods, daughter of the Master of University College, "when the Alice of his tale had grown into a lovely girl, he asked, in old-world fashion, her father's permission to pay his addresses to her."[92] Despite quoting this opinion, Cohen describes it twice offhandedly as "gossip", and Bakewell dismisses it in a similar vein as "little more than a report of Oxford gossip", offering plausible reasons for its unreliability.[93] However, Cohen has another scrap from a man he considers a more trustworthy source: Lord Salisbury. "Now, Lord Salisbury was an archenemy of gossip," Cohen assures us, and so his report, "they say that Dodgson has half gone out of his mind in consequence of having been refused by the real Alice (Liddell). It looks like it,"[94] is regarded as having more weight.

Next, there is an entry in Carroll's diary from October 1866. At this time, Carroll's brother Wilfred had, by coincidence, fallen in love with the fourteen-year-old Alice Jane Donkin. Dining with his uncle, Skeffington Lutwidge, Carroll raised the problem of this relationship: "we had a good deal of conversation about Wilfred, and about A. L. It is a very anxious subject."[95] This line is enough for Cohen to state—in contrast to his more tentative suggestions immediately above about the possibility of "a kind of love"—that "the two brothers . . . were attached to two teenage youngsters named Alice."[96]

The letter from Lorina to Alice, written in 1930, is also marshalled to this cause, though Cohen admits that Lorina seems to be withholding information in her apologetic report that "I said his manner became too affectionate . . . one had to find some reason for all intercourse ceasing." Finally, there is some hint of the past in a letter from Carroll to Mrs Liddell, from 1891, asking whether Rhoda and Violet, the youngest daughters, could visit him. "I am close on 60 years now, and all romantic sentiment has quite died out of my life: so I have become quite hardened to having lady-visitors of *any* age!"[97] Cohen suggests that if there had never been any romantic sentiment involved in his break with the Liddells, Carroll need not have brought it up here.

The puzzle pieces arrange to form some kind of picture; but overall we can't help feeling that there are gaps, that we are being asked to fill in a fair amount from imagination, and that some of the pieces could have been turned another way. Bakewell, for instance, also quotes the "A. L.—a very anxious subject" document, but slants it to back up his own interpretation of the relationship, that Alice was probably Carroll's beloved, lamented child-friend rather than a prospective fiancée. "Dodgson must have been haunted by the spectre of what he had lost."[98] Thomas, in turn, draws an altogether different conclusion, stating flatly, "there is nothing apart from initials" to suggest that Alice was even referred to. "Wishful thinkers might conclude that the conversation also dwelt on Alice Liddell as a child bride . . . [the initials] might as easily refer to someone like Arthur Lewis."[99]

In this detail, Thomas is closest to Karoline Leach, who touches on many of the same documents as Cohen, but only to destroy their credibility. Lord Salisbury's opinion in the private letter of 1878 is a "slightly jokey aside"; a "fragile piece of evidence"[100], backdated fifteen years so it can apply to Carroll's supposed proposal of 1863, and existing in conjunction with a bunch of other rumours that Carroll courted Alice's mother, sisters and the governess Miss Prickett. The diary reference to A. L.? "The most obvious explanation is a slip of the pen . . . Dodgson, in a momentary slip, wrote 'A. L.' in mistake for 'A. D.' "[101] or Alice Donkin. This suggestion may seem unlikely, given that Carroll was notoriously controlled and consistent in his diary-keeping;[102] for good measure, Leach provides another two alternatives: that A. L. referred to "Aunt Lucy" or to "some man lost in history to whom Wilfred owed money."[103] The letter from Lorina to Alice, written in 1930, is analysed as a case of denial and alibi.

> She told the "Alice story" because she "had to give some reason" for all intercourse ceasing and did not want to bring the awkward reality out into the light of day. In the grip of the myth Lennon let her get away with it and did not notice the sleight of hand.[104]

> The elderly Ina's letters to her sister . . . make it evident that she used Lennon's own Alice story as some form of camouflage for whatever had really been going on between Dodgson and her family at the time, presumably because it was too private or too potentially harmful to be revealed.[105]

Leach's real coup, though, relates to the cut page that, in its scandalous absence, seems to keep fuelling the possibility that something happened between Carroll and Alice. She claims to have found a small piece of paper at the Dodgson Family Collection, Guildford, in 1996. Supposedly written in Violet Dodgson's hand, it describes the contents of "cut pages in diary". One of these pages is "*the* page, the one for 27–29 June 1863, that all the fuss is about, the one described as 'crucial' by Cohen, the one assumed to have contained the story of Dodgson's marriage proposal and his banishment from the Deanery."[106] It reads as follows, according to Leach:

> Vol. 8 Page 92. L. C. learns from Mrs Liddell that he is supposed to
> be using the children as a means of paying court to the governess—He
> is also supposed [unreadable] to be courting Ina.[107]

With this ammunition, Leach seeks to destroy the myth of Carroll-Alice,
the two figures who walk hand-in-hand through over a century of popular consciousness.

> Currently, Alice Liddell—and Dodgson's supposed passion for her—is
> used as a cipher for interpreting almost every aspect of his work, as
> well as his emotional and creative life. She is, after all, the ultimate
> demonstration of his strangeness. But it is apparent that the evidential
> justification of this is—has always been—almost non-existent. [. . .]
> There is no evidence that he was in love with her, no evidence that
> her family worried about his attachment to her, no evidence that they
> banned him from her presence. [. . .] There is no evidence, either
> prima-facie or secondary, cryptic or elliptic, to suggest he proposed to
> the eleven-year-old girl or even considered doing so.

Having demolished one house of cards and cleared the foundation,
Leach sets out to build another. "He is supposed to be courting Ina" would
have been a good enough reason on its own for Carroll to hold back from
the Liddells socially, either on their instruction or from his own discretion.
There is no reason to suppose the rumour true, any more than we should
imagine that Carroll was really courting Mary Prickett. Leach, however,
sets up the framework of an alternate myth through various, and arguably
thin, examples of Carroll's apparent affection towards Lorina—he refers
to her as "tall", notes the number of times she has joined them on the
river, and remained friends with her until his death.[108] However, the real
project of Leach's book is to persuade the reader—Alice now being out
of the picture—that Carroll enjoyed a lengthy and secret romance with
Mrs Lorina Liddell, the girls' mother.

Persuasive in places, Leach's grand argument is inevitably just as
speculative as Cohen's theory that Alice was Carroll's lifelong love. It
relies on the intelligent arrangement of scant evidence and on the reader's
willingness to accept the author's joining of dots. The "cut pages" document
is not really convincing as the basis of a romance between Carroll and
Mrs Liddell—it would seem peculiar for Carroll to refer to her as "Ina"
on just one isolated page, when his diary has her as "Mrs Liddell" throughout, and strange for Violet Dodgson, if she was the author, to use both
the formal title and shortened Christian name in the same personal note.
Indeed, on the reverse of the "cut pages" document the same hand has

noted down birth and marriage dates of the Liddell girls, including the line "Lorina (Ina) married Mr Skene Feb 1874."[109] The nickname is unambiguously linked to Alice's sister here, so why should the note writer turn over the page and use the same name to refer to Alice's mother?

As with the examples above, it may seem trivial to point out minor lapses in attention to detail, but as Leach's research is so dependent on a close re-reading of primary texts, it is surprising to find that she misquotes a key passage in Carroll's diary. On April 21, 1863, Leach says, Carroll described Alice as being "in an unusually imperious and ungentle mood, not at all improved by being an invalid."[110] The line has been disguised by heavy scribble in black pen, but it is clear that it reads "by no means improved by being an invalid";[111] the strokes of "by" are entirely legible. Obviously, this makes no difference to the meaning, but once more I think it encourages a degree of caution about the accuracy of these secondary texts.

More seriously, Leach's flourish of producing a scrap that had never been "published or even seen before"[112] is misleading to the point of being fraudulent. Her reports of the discovery consistently imply a startling personal find, as though this little document had fallen out of a book onto her lap. The following is from her original 1996 article in the *Times Literary Supplement*:

> While researching a screenplay for a forthcoming film, quite by chance I came across a small piece of paper, tucked away among a mass of Dodgson family records in the archive at Guildford. About five inches by three, torn rather inaccurately from what seems to have been an account book, at first glance it hardly looked sensational or revelatory. And yet written on this tatty scrap was, apparently, an answer to one of the most haunting of literary mysteries . . . this scruffy little bit of scribble-pad that has lain in the public record unnoticed for seventeen years contains the only surviving account of what actually occurred during those few vital days in late June.[113]

Visitors to the Surrey History Centre in Woking, where the Dodgson Family Collection is now held, may be surprised to find the listing "Cut pages in diary 3 Feb 1932" as item DFC.F/17/1 in a bound catalogue. The fact that this entry is typewritten rather than laser-printed alone suggests its age; the "cut pages" document appears to have been identified and described[114] not long after the last papers in the Dodgson family's Carrolliana were donated to the Guildford Muniment Rooms in 1981.[115] It is surprising that nobody thought to publicise or comment on this readily available item before Leach used it as her calling card in 1996, but for her to claim that it was "never . . . even seen before" and that she is the "discoverer"[116] of the document is absurd.

Wakeling's annotated edition of the diaries includes a note on Leach's discovery, though it could hardly be more icily detached: he pointedly refuses to admit that it was she who uncovered the crucial scrap of paper, and credits her only with her article about the find in the *Times Literary Supplement*. There is no comment on the plausibility of a romance between Carroll and Lorina Liddell, and by adding a cross-reference to earlier rumours that Carroll was courting Miss Prickett, Wakeling implies that these suppositions are equally meaningless.[117] On this earlier occasion, in 1857, Carroll "learned to my great surprise that my notice of . . . [the children] is construed by some men into attentions to the governess," and resolved not to take "any public notice of the children in future unless an occasion should arise when such an interpretation is impossible."[118] That his "holding aloof" from the Liddells during 1863 was simply an echo of this dignified caution may be the least exciting, but the most common-sense explanation for the apparent split.

The Guilty Prayers

"A noticeable feature of this journal," Wakeling notes in the introduction to the 1862–1864 diaries, "is the use Dodgson makes of these pages for recording prayers and supplications to help him lead a better life."

As Wakeling's approach to the diaries is on the reserved side, with a mannered, formal tone and barely any comment of his own or venture at interpretation—beyond his reconstruction of Carroll's four missing diaries from available evidence—it is worth quoting his remarks here at length, as they constitute a rare personal interjection.

> Although prayers occurred in earlier volumes, the frequency and earnestness began to take on greater proportions in this journal. There has been much speculation about the reasons and purposes of the prayers. Reading them in the context of his unfolding life, there is no clear and obvious reason which can account for them. They do show that he experienced great self-doubt and guilt. Some prayers indicate that slothfulness and lack of attention to his duties as mathematical lecturer were causes of regret. However, there are some prayers which are more personal and poignant. In transcribing them I have felt a deep sense of Dodgson's inability to come to terms with the troubles in his mind,

and a feeling that he was unable to control these feelings which caused him such anguish and concern, whatever the cause may have been. Perhaps he was troubled by dreams, or maybe his personal standards of diligence and duty were hard to maintain.[119]

That Wakeling comments at all on this in the introduction is un-usual—he makes no such comment here on the cut diary pages, for instance, or indeed on any other aspect of the diaries' content rather than their form and convention. The personal aspect of this paragraph is also noteworthy, as Wakeling is otherwise so perfectly detached and proper in his annotations; here he implies that the lengthy, dedicated process of transcription encouraged a form of bond between author and editor and enabled a deeper, emotional understanding of the text.

Overall he seems to play down the importance of the prayers—he stresses "context" here and again in a later sentence, where he advises "any interpretation, in my view, should carefully consider the prayers as a whole, and the sporadic nature in which they occur."[120] Wakeling makes no direct guess as to what the prayers might signify, and urges caution in drawing conclusions from what he sees, in terms of the overall picture, as infrequent religious appeals.[121] It seems unlikely that he would feel inclined to mention the prayers at all, though, and offer his view on their interpretation—however guarded his suggestions are—were it not for the fact that these passages of the diary had been used by some recent biogra-phers to support various theories of Carroll's emotional and sexual life.

Stoffell, Thomas, and Bjork make no mention of the prayers: Jones and Gladstone mention them only briefly, and ignore any shift in the prayers' tone or frequency, implying that they increased only around each New Year.[122] These commentators effectively chose to excise this puzzling and sometimes unsettling aspect of the writer, just as Roger Lancelyn Green did when he edited Carroll's diaries in the 1950s. As such, they are even more reticent than Stuart Collingwood, who noted that the prayers were characterised by "modest depreciations of himself and his work", and occasionally more "earnest" pleas "that God would forgive him the past, and help him to perform His holy will in the future."[123] Colling-wood murmurs that these latter entries are "too sacred and private to be reproduced here", and sees only the best motives behind them:

And all the time that he was thus speaking of himself as a sinner, and a man who was utterly falling short of his aim, he was living a life full of good deeds and innumerable charities, a life of incessant labour and unremitting fulfilment of duty. So, I suppose, it is always with those who have a really high ideal: the harder they try to approach it the more it seems to recede from them . . . [124]

So, Collingwood, the only one of Carroll's biographers to have access to all his diaries, once again draws the veil back a tad before closing it securely over the "dead sanctities". However, Bakewell, Leach, and Cohen all construct quite extensive theories of Carroll's internal struggle from these moments of private appeal, and all these theories are at least slightly different.

Bakewell, like Wakeling—and indeed, Collingwood, despite his avoidance of any detail—draws our attention to a "change in tone" between the prayers Carroll recorded in his 1856 diary and those in the volumes of 1862.[125] In the earlier example, "the tone is calm and measured, even complacent." After 1858, however, there is a four-year gap in the record, comprising two missing volumes,[126] and "when the diary resumes, the prayers occur every few weeks, sometimes every few days . . . their tone is now immediate and urgent."[127] Bakewell quotes lines from earlier in 1862—"Oh God help me to live a better and more earnest life"—then a passage from July 24, 1862, when Carroll was invited to preach:

till I can rule myself better, preaching is but a solemn mockery—"thou that teachest another, teachest thou not thyself? God grant this may be the last such entry I may have to make! that so I may not, when I have preached to others, be "myself a castaway".[128]

"This is not a formal, dutiful response," Bakewell suggests, calling these prayers "anguished and hysterical"; "he really is asking for God's help."[129] In 1863, Bakewell points out, Carroll's pleas continue, as he begs with God to "help thou the weak flesh . . . help me put away my old sins and lead a new life."[130] As with the cut diary pages, these passages pose a mystery to biographers. "What kind of personal crisis is being chronicled? The most obvious explanation," says Bakewell, is Carroll's "failure to overcome the Victorian demon of masturbation."

As supporting evidence, he points us to Carroll's book of mathematical puzzles, *Pillow Problems*, which was written—according to the preface—to distract the reader from "unholy thoughts, which torture, with their hateful presence, the fancy that would fain be pure."[131] Collingwood, almost a century before, had presented this preface as a further example of Carroll's devotion to "a higher purpose", and quoted the above passage as "a momentary glimpse" into his uncle's "refined and beautiful character".[132] That recent biographers read the same words as clear evidence of an inner torment constitutes a remarkable interpretive shift. With the generosity of a mid-1990s perspective, Bakewell concludes that for Carroll to have occasionally fantasised about sex "would not be very surprising . . . it would, in fact, make him more human."[133] This may indeed be what Wakeling is implying with his reference to being "troubled by dreams", or to Carroll being unable to maintain "personal standards".[134]

However, as with the idea that Carroll proposed to Alice Liddell, Bakewell seems to immediately feel the need to qualify any notion of Carroll as a sexual being—even if masturbation is far less peculiar to late twentieth century mores than wanting to marry an eleven-year-old. "With a personality as complex as Dodgson's, nothing is ever simple."[135] Bakewell goes on to propose that reservations about not giving enough time to God rather than worldly frivolities, "as much as auto-erotic malingering, may well be the sins he is recording."

Of course, it is sensible to entertain alternative explanations for lines in a private diary whose meaning can never be confidently understood, but it seems strange that Bakewell is able to read the passages as referring to both intense guilt at masturbation and the feeling that more time should be devoted to holy pursuits rather than the theatre. There is a persuasive impression that Bakewell is once again seeking the difficult balance between a modern portrayal of Carroll as a "human" figure with active sexual desires—the figure Karoline Leach and Morton Cohen are both invested in depicting, though in quite distinct ways—and retaining the more traditional, enduring, and endearing image of a buttoned-up innocent. Leach, as we have already seen, is eager to throw out the old fuddy-duddy in favour of a virile but tormented figure; Cohen's analysis leads him to a position that is in many ways similar, though he proposes a different love-object and stops well short of saying that Carroll actually had a physical affair.

Bakewell's position is far more ambivalent, and though he shuttles from one to the other, he tends to return to the comfort of the familiar myth. His fall-back option, that the prayers could signify no more than pangs of conscience about a lack of religious devotion, is barely less cosy than the explanation Roger Lancelyn Green offered in 1953: the "sins" were

> entirely those of wasted time, wasted opportunities for doing good . . . and self-condemnation of personal failings . . . the worst of which seems to have been his tendency to sleep, or at least idle away, some hours after the early (and rather heavy) College dinner.[136]

Bakewell's unwillingness to allow Lewis Carroll a mature, even a teenage sexuality is confirmed by his subsequent discussion of Carroll's "serious poem" of 1862, "Stolen Waters". By bringing up this uncharacteristic text—the story of a temptress who becomes an old hag after a symbolic coupling—Bakewell raises the idea of Carroll entertaining intense, adult sexual fantasies, but immediately drops it again in favour of the reassuring, familiar image of the childlike man who loved children without actually desiring them. By focusing on the concluding verses, where the speaker finds solace in the vision of "an angel-child",[137] Bakewell finds a way back to Carroll as emotionally retarded innocent.

> It is unlikely that Dodgson actually fell for the wiles of a witchy lady . . . he is telling himself that if he were to engage in a real-life physical love affair, the gates of the garden of childhood would be closed to him for ever. The delights he found in the company of children were more important to him than the uncertainties of sexual reality.[138]

These are incredibly bold conclusions about a man's deep personal beliefs to draw from a single poem. Of course, the reading is valid—we can't say it is "wrong"—but it seems to serve Bakewell's need to keep touching base with a safe image of Carroll every time he proposes a more radical possibility. That the poem does not mean what Bakewell wants it to mean in any absolute sense is amply demonstrated below, if demonstration is needed, by Leach's very different use of the same text.

Leach reckons that Cohen and Bakewell draw identical conclusions from the evidence of Carroll's prayers—Cohen phrasing more delicately what Bakewell chooses to express in "earthy" language.[139] "Victorian demon of masturbation" may not seem particularly explicit, but Cohen's "the nights brought troubled thoughts for which he saw himself a miscreant"[140] is indeed euphemistic to the point of ambiguity. However, Cohen's theory of the troubled thoughts themselves is more developed and direct than Bakewell's; rather than merely ascribing Carroll's pillow problems to a natural but repressed sex drive, Cohen links them to Carroll's passion for children, more specifically the Liddells, and more narrowly yet, to Alice.

Like Bakewell, Cohen treats the prayers as another unanswered puzzle, a series of clues and gaps akin to the cut diary pages and their surrounding entries. Such impassioned pleas cannot merely stem from "ordinary failings like idleness or indolence".[141]

> What, then, lies behind and beneath those guilty appeals, these protests against past sins? Why should he characterize himself as vile and worthless, weak and selfish; why is he caught in the chains of sin; why does he confess to a rebellious will; what makes him yearn for a new life?

What does he mean when he writes of mental troubles, sceptical or unholy thoughts "which torture the fancy that would fain be pure," blasphemous thoughts "which dart unbidden into the most reverent souls"? What temptations besiege him, to which, by his own admission, he succumbs?[142]

"We have no proven answers," Cohen admits, but again he is prepared to build a theory. Like Bakewell, he cites "Stolen Waters" as an expression of Carroll's probable sexual fantasies, while stressing "it is probably not the report of anything he has experienced; at most, his Circe is the lithe creature of his dreams."[143] The poem was written, Cohen points out, "when his attention to the deanery children was focused most intensely . . . when he had reason to hope that the affection the children bore him would ripen even further." A skillful and persuasive writer himself, Cohen is surely aware of the echoes between his own language and the sexual metaphors of fruit and juice in Carroll's poem; while Bakewell sees Carroll finding inner salvation and peace by turning to his child-friends and sacrificing any hope of adult love, Cohen strongly implies that the child-friends were, in fact, the source of all the trouble.

> For the most part he convinced himself . . . that his intentions were innocent and honorable, and on the conscious level, they certainly were. For this stern self-disciplinarian never permitted himself to cross into the forbidden territory where he sent his knight of "Stolen Waters" . . . as tight-lipped as he was, however, the images that surface in his letters, diaries and works reveal his sexual nature.[144]

All the examples Cohen goes on to provide are directed at children—a letter, dripping with innuendo, to Gertrude Chataway, a mock-lovers' tiff with Agnes and Evie Hull.

> Charles's sexual promptings are evident. Because they could not be ritually fulfilled, he repeatedly felt frustrated, and saw himself as an inconsolable sinner. He became inhibited, irritable when his child friends did not respond to his advances . . . But the sexual force did not retreat; it was there and victimized him with nocturnal incursions.[145]

Cohen envisions Carroll not as a naïve innocent but as a man of conflicted passions—"a master at regulating his life"[146]—whose repressed but raging sexual desires emerged in his imaginative writing and in his dreams. Carroll has, in this account, an attachment for Alice that troubles him and that he may not truly understand himself. While these feelings are not restricted to her alone, she is one of the most important love-objects in his life and, as discussed above, Cohen believes he may well have seen marriage to her as the logical expression of his emotional and sexual feelings.

The period of most frequent and abject prayer is therefore linked in Cohen's analysis to Carroll's engagements with the Liddell family; even when there seems no obvious connection, Cohen lists meetings with the children alongside private appeals to God.

> On the seventh, in London, Charles meets the Liddells . . . on the tenth, back in Oxford, he enters another plea for help . . . on the sixteenth he . . . sees "Mrs Liddell and the children." On the twenty-second he writes "God help me to lead a new and better life."

Two days later, Carroll files the resolution quoted above by Bakewell, that he must not preach until he can rule himself better, for fear that "I may not, when I have preached to others, be myself a castaway."

> On August 8 the Liddells leave Oxford . . . Charles too leaves Oxford, and while he and the Liddells are apart, his lamentations and prayers disappear. He returns to Oxford on October 11, and six days later, on the seventeenth, while out walking, falls in "with Mrs Liddell and the children." That very day, the appeals to heaven resume.[147]

The fact that Carroll enters a prayer in his diary up to a week after seeing the Liddell family may not seem conclusive proof that the meetings prompted the guilty suffering, but it is clear that Cohen wants to suggest as much. "During this time of exultant companionship with the Liddells [the self-rebukes] are there, and in unprecedented numbers."[148]

The meetings and the prayers do not end at the same time—"when he is not in touch with them, we find thirteen recantations and prayers"[149]— and though Carroll's visits to the Deanery cease in 1867, "the last time any of the Liddells enter the diary until over three years later", the self-recriminations continue. As Cohen never explicitly states that the Liddells are the only source of Carroll's anguish, merely indicating "correlations" and making strong hints, it is difficult to know how he reconciles the apparent discrepancy here: we can observe that the prayers do become far less frequent after 1867, according to his tally (from twelve a year to nine to eight in 1869, compared to twenty-four in 1863),[150] and that the continued torment may be put down to what Cohen calls the "wrench" and "constant ache" following from the break with, in his own treacly words, the "idyllic trio . . . the Liddells, the three darlings."[151]

Ultimately, Cohen argues, the lack of contact does lead to a winding down in Carroll's spiritual conflicts. "His self-rebukes, his protests about his sinful life . . . decline as the thread that connects his life to the deanery unwinds: as the mentions of the Liddell children vanish, his complaints and resolves subside."[152] Again, Cohen claims nothing more than "coincidence", but makes the strongest case he can without stating an unequivocal link. "The conjunction of these two currents, flowing side by side, must signify something."[153]

It will come as no surprise that to Leach, they signify something different; and we can guess by now what she makes of the coincidence between prayers and encounters with the Liddells. The source of the guilt is not Alice or even her sisters, but her mother.

As is so often the case with these recent biographies, Leach uses the same limited information available to researchers one hundred years after Carroll's death; she merely arranges the key points into a different pattern and, as if sketching a constellation from a collection of stars, draws a new picture around them. It is "unlikely, if not impossible" that masturbation or dreams are the soul cause of Carroll's anguish; firstly, because he would have discovered this aspect of himself through noctural emission before his mid-twenties, and secondly, because the torment this discovery prompted would not, logically, last four years and then cease.[154]

Leach notes, as did Bakewell, Wakeling, and Cohen, that the prayers enter a new phase of intensity around 1862; "the change that has been wrought in four short years is immediately obvious . . . [the diary voice is] more clipped, more tight-lipped . . . interspersed, for the first time, with elliptic painful references to his own sin."[155] Like Bakewell and Cohen, Leach quotes the "castaway" prayer, a reference to a verse of Corinthians; she also notes additional biblical allusions in the appeals, "most frequently of all, Psalm 51, David's hymn of repentance after his adultery with Bathsheba."[156] We can see where Leach is going with this. The reading of Carroll's pleas as guilt at masturbation or sexual dreams—radical as it is in comparison to alternative theories of worries about indolence—confirms the "mythic images of his chastity, his isolation and his rejection of adult sexuality."

> It is in fact a reaffirmation of his quasi-religious symbolism; the myth of his unassailable "otherness". His sexual guilt has to be commensurate with his virginity. Masturbation and nocturnal emissions are the only sexual "sins" reconcilable with Carroll's monkish iconism.[157]

The references to the sin of David therefore allude, in Leach's interpretation, to Carroll's sexual congress with another person. "Stolen Waters" reveals not an experiment with the thrills and terrors of a never-tasted adult love, not an attempt to channel his troubling attachment to the Liddell children into a fantasy of danger and desire, but "a man helpless in the grip of intoxicating adult passion."[158] Bakewell and Cohen were certain that the temptress was an imaginary figure: Leach believes that "life and poetry overlap" in the poem and that the woman is a barely disguised Mrs Lorina Liddell.

Like Cohen, Leach maintains "we can never be entirely sure" of the precise cause or connection, "because we do not have the lost record."[159] Like Cohen, she is more than happy to speculate, though, and like him, she constructs her theory through the convergence of Dodgson's writing— "Stolen Waters", the prayers—and the dates when he encountered the Liddells. "This is a synchronicity of life and art that certainly seems to be beyond coincidence, and for the next few years poetry and private prayers continue to echo each other . . . "[160] Her conclusion is quite different from Cohen's, but the method, even the wording of the argument, is remarkably similar.

> The period of enforced absence [from the Liddells] was, we know, a troubled time for Dodgson. He was guilty and he was restless. He spent his summer periodically asking for strength to "leave my old life behind" and "amend." And as the time approached for his return to Oxford this anxiety intensified . . . he returned on the evening of 14 October. Two days later his diary contains the single observation "met the Liddells", without further comment, and three days after that he asks God once again to help him "amend my life, for Christ's sake."[161]

On the fifth of December, as we have seen above, Carroll met the Liddells but "held aloof". "Two days later," Leach notes, "he filled an entire entry with this warning to himself: 'Exactly a month ago I find a prayer for grace to lead to a better life. I now repeat that prayer . . . ' "[162]

Leach locates the end of the truly despairing appeals to Heaven in the summer of 1866, when a moment of epiphany—for a reason she admits she can't identify—signals the beginning of a climb "out of the pit and back into the light."[163] Carroll's rare visit to the Deanery in May 1867, and his "long chat" there with Mrs Liddell, is seen as symptomatic of this new internal peace; paralleled by and perhaps the result of his renewed, albeit courteously reserved, acquaintance with the Liddell family. "This would be rather an odd conclusion to a situation in which Dodgson is putative child-molester," Leach wryly observes, puncturing the notion that Carroll was banished for inappropriate attentions to Alice, "but it is a very natural, very human resolution to a love affair finally gone cold enough to talk over."[164] At this point, she sums up her case:

> I think the facts presented here suggest that biography must make the massive adjustment necessary to include the possibility, if not the probability, that Lorina Liddell, the Dean's wife, was central to Lewis Carroll's life and work in a unique and extraordinary way. She was the root of his otherwise rootless love poetry; the source of his transforming guilt; his deepest experience of passion and of desire . . . [165]

Three distinct pictures of Carroll emerge from these case studies around the mysterious prayers. We have Bakewell's blurry double-exposure of a fundamentally innocent figure who may have harboured sexual urges but barely understood them; Cohen's man of intense but unusual passions, rigidly controlled and internally fired-up; and Leach's portrait of the author as shockingly "normal" in his desires but hiding them behind a myth of celibate child-loving. Already—and especially if we factor in the work of Thomas, Stoffel, Bjork, Wakeling, Jones, and Glad-stone—we can see that a troop of men with quite diverse personalities cluster around the name "Carroll" in the 1990s; the photographs on the cover invariably show the familiar gentle figure, but the main protagonist is never quite the same person from one book to the next.

The next chapter examines the extent to which these various shades of Carroll—based for the most part on primary research and careful assessment—affect the dominant popular, as opposed to scholarly, view of the man; the image of Carroll as constructed by journalism. What emerges from this more mainstream discourse, as we might expect, is a comparative lack of interest in subtle distinctions of interpretation, or a weighing-up of alternative options without definite conclusion. There is a preference for clear hooks to hang the story on, rather than an availability of several possible readings; for a black-and-white line drawing of Carroll rather than a shot of him moving, defying focus. As such, the final case study in this section is perhaps the most important in terms of our broader conception of Carroll around the turn of the twentieth century. It concerns something irrefutably documented and, to our contemporary culture, potentially shocking: the fact that he photographed little girls in the nude.

The Nude Portraits

Most of Carroll's nude photographs were destroyed, at his instruction, when he died. Until comparatively recently, the idea that he took pictures of naked little children was based only on written evidence, and the precise nature of the images could only be imagined. Four of the six surviving nudes we have today were discovered in the Rosenbach collection in the 1970s, and published by Morton Cohen in 1978—approximately a century after they were taken—as *Lewis Carroll, Photographer of Children: Four Nude Studies*. The other two are, contrary to expectations, of young boys: one, identified by Edward Wakeling from an auction catalogue, has never been published, and the other is not widely known.[166] These biographers only mention the four portraits of girls—of Evelyn and Beatrice Hatch, and of Annie and Frances Henderson—and so those are the only images in question here.

All four of these portraits are professionally coloured, with a fantasy setting painted in behind the models. Beatrice Hatch sits on a rock with white cliffs behind her; Evelyn Hatch poses on a riverbank and, in another picture, stretches out on grass; Annie and Frances Henderson stand in the surf, shipwrecked as their boat sinks in the distance. Whether or not the images are shocking depends, of course, on personal notions of acceptability. Only the picture of Evelyn Hatch lying in a watercolour field shows "full frontal" nudity, with chest and genital area exposed; in the white cliffs and the riverbank pictures, she and her sister have their legs crossed and knees drawn up, and the colourist of the shipwreck portrait has apparently added a rough skirt and a covering of leaves to the naked bodies of the Henderson girls. Viewed objectively, they could be described as whimsical, coy, even trite, and the painted settings in particular have a garishly amateur quality.

That overtones of suspect sexuality have been read into them is surely due less to the pictures themselves than to the fact that they confirmed an existing myth about Lewis Carroll. Even in his lifetime, Carroll was renowned as a lover of children: through the psychoanalytic readings of the 1930s and 1940s, this relationship acquired connotations of sinister sexual deviancy that no biography was able to completely contain or repress. The theory that Carroll's attachments were dubious or distasteful had required only visual proof, the nude portraits slotted neatly into the case against him, exhibits A to D. "It is here," writes Leach, "that we find our most familiar images of Carroll."

> The fact of these small nude bodies, the fact that this grown man chose not simply to associate with girl-children but to admire and photograph their nakedness is seen, both in biography and popular culture, to have only one interpretation. His photography is the centrepiece of the delicate indictment of Dodgson as a man who "desired the companionship of female children" in an extreme and disquieting way.[167]

Leach's response to this accusation is quite simple. If Carroll was a pervert, she argues, then so was the rest of his surrounding culture, from J. Ashby-Sterry's poems about little girls' "snow white pantalettes" through Dante Gabriel Rossetti's tribute to a nine year-old's "virginal bosom" to the drawings of naked nymphs that adorned Christmas cards.[168] To view Carroll's portraits as evidence of paedophilia, she persuasively suggests, is to completely misunderstand a culture where "paedophilia", had the word even existed, would have been taken to mean a laudable, innocent love of childhood purity. "We inevitably speculate about repression and sublimated desires, but this is more about incomprehension than insight." We look at the Victorian age "across a great chasm of cultural incomprehension."[169]

Of course, Leach's key and most contentious argument is that Carroll had perfectly conventional sexual desires for adult women. Why, then, did he apparently only photograph young girls? In fact, he did not—Wakeling and Taylor's *Lewis Carroll: Photographer* suggests that only half of Carroll's extant photographs are of male or female children, and that his subjects fell into a range of categories from landscapes to skeletons—but Leach is addressing the myth rather than the reality here, and her answer is that young girls were simply easier to get hold of than adult models. "He was, perhaps, before anything else, a man who adored and relished every aspect of femaleness, who responded sensually and emotionally to female company . . . "[170] He certainly tried to find young women, rather than little girls, who would pose for him, but met with comparative failure due to his snobbishness about using professional models and the reluctance of parents to allow their older daughters to undress for his camera.

Within this reading, Carroll's professed adoration of female children is, at least in part, a clever front. To truly love the form and company of a child was viewed by his society as a "badge of intellectual and moral distinction", a seeking after purity, a "synonym for moral integrity."[171] The notion of Saint Lewis the child-lover—which twentieth-century biography has tended to see as deviant or at least unusual—was, Leach argues, an image Carroll helped to build around himself for safety and camouflage.

Do other biographies of the 1990s respond as Leach suggests to the nude portraits? Stoffel's few pages on the matter actually echo many of Leach's arguments. We are reminded of the very different context within which Carroll took his portraits—the Wordsworthian ideal of the child "freshly arrived from the presence of God, uncontaminated and asexual",[172] the photographs by Julia Margaret Cameron, the nude cherub as stock figure on Victorian greetings cards. Indeed, Stoffel's explanation is very similar to Leach's in its acknowledgement of contemporary suspicions and its response to them by stressing the cultural divide between our perspective and Carroll's own.

> His delight in the company of children, especially little girls, has inevitably led to much speculation that his interest in them was not entirely innocent. His photographs of them included some nudes, and though this was by no means an uncommon genre at that time, it is viewed today with some suspicion. The assumption is made that a bachelor's interest in little girls must be sexual, and that a photographer of little girls must be a voyeur . . . but to view him so is to judge him by the standards of our time, while taking no account of the culture in which he lived.[173]

However, Stoffel declines to take the further and more radical step of suggesting that this love of children was a convenient mask for a love of all female company. Her defence of Carroll is more traditional: there was no sexual interest in girls not because his sexual interests lay in women, but because he was "ill at ease with the sexual side of human life . . . he had many deep friendships with adult women, but seems to have had no real romances or sexual liaisons with them."[174]

While utterly denying the notion that Carroll could have been an active paedophile in the way we currently understand the word—"such behaviour [would] be contrary to everything we know about Dodgson—and indeed profoundly shocking to him"[175]—she entertains the possibility that his pleasures in female children may not have been entirely pure. "We can never be sure if there was a sublimated sexuality with the intellectual and spiritual pleasures he derived from his friendships . . . "[176]

Stoffel's brief justification for the nude portraits is the least complex of those under discussion here. The pictures are unremarkable within their context; we cannot be wholly sure of a man's personal sexuality in every detail; we have no evidence whatsoever of any sexual advances towards girls, or of any sexual motive behind the photography. Carroll, in these pages, is a strange man, an unusual man, but an utterly harmless man. There is barely a note of "deviance" in Stoffel's analysis—the accusation is mentioned only to be explained away, or for the sake of including all remote possibilities. There is no "paedophilia", not because Carroll was involved with adults but because he held himself apart from physical sexuality as a whole. Other commentaries from the 1990s entertain a similar image when dealing with the case of the nude portraits, but they add suspicions of a more worrying, potentially sinister "otherness" that seems to escape around the edges of the biographer's best assurances.

Of this selection, Bakewell's account comes closest to what Leach expects from contemporary criticism. Once again, Bakewell walks a wavering line between the twin myths of deviant and innocent, and—apparently inadvertently—constructs a strangely ungraspable, ambiguous figure. Although he stresses that Carroll's photography was entirely platonic—any suggestion of a sexual element to the photographs "would have outraged him"—he suggests at the end of the same paragraph that "the act of photography was beginning to come perilously close to a kind of substitute for the sexual act."[177] Between these two poles, which Bakewell seems to supply as Carroll's conscious and unconscious motivation, we find the familiar image of the emotionally retarded author, the harmless freak. There is no evidence given for this theory, but it is proposed with absolute confidence; perhaps because it has circulated for so long.

> His relationships ended with kissing and cuddling—nothing even remotely approaching the sexual act was required of him. Children for Dodgson were a defence against the impossible reality of sexuality. Sex would have destroyed his sacred vision of the innocence of children which was so central to him that it was virtually a religious belief.[178]

Despite this assurance that there was nothing even slightly suspect in Carroll's photography, Bakewell seemingly cannot help but shadow his account with hints of impropriety. True, there were whispers of disapproval around the nude portraits even at the time Carroll took them—he was apparently very much aware that harmful gossip had begun to circulate by the late 1870s[179]—but there is an odd sense that while Bakewell plainly states his belief in Carroll's innocence, he also wants to give his narrative an edge of suspense. As such, he has it both ways; Carroll is charming, harmless and naïve, but with an edge of threatening, titillating otherness about him.

At the end of one chapter, then, we have the cliff-hanger: "Dodgson's obsession with taking pictures of little girls scantily dressed or 'in Eve's original dress' was threatening to become dangerous."[180] Ten pages on, Bakewell brings us back to the "dangerous obsession . . . he seems to have been compelled by a desperate and irresistible desire to photograph his little girl-friends without their clothes on." This interest in his friend's daughters is "hazardous" and would make him "a subject of gossip and scandal."[181] Again, the latter is undeniable, but Bakewell's language suggests the scandal was entirely justified.

We are led through Carroll's correspondence with the Mayhews, who turned down a request to allow their daughters to be photographed unchaperoned and prompted a formal but clearly incensed response from Carroll at the implication that he could not be trusted. The story is told with Mrs Mayhew's perspective as the normative standard: Carroll's suggestions about the girls are "alarming . . . she was understandably unnerved."[182]

Later, he found success with the Henderson family, who willingly let Annie and Frances pose nude; even when the mother has no objections, however, Bakewell describes Carroll's need to "skate on thin ice". "There was a kind of reckless abandon in what he was doing and courting danger always gave him a certain excitement. He simply could not see that he was putting himself at risk."[183] Even these two sentences wrestle with contradiction as Bakewell at once claims Carroll as a naïve innocent and a seeker after unconventional thrills.

Like Bakewell, Donald Thomas makes a case for Carroll as rigidly pure in his feelings for young girls, although he reminds the reader that Carroll would have been entirely aware of contemporary pornography, that he took a direct interest in the problems of prostitution and also owned several volumes of scientific sexual enquiry along the lines of *The Physical Life of Women*.[184] While Bakewell's version implies darker urges lurking unrecognised beneath Carroll's wholehearted belief in his own purity, Thomas suggests that Carroll was well aware of sin even in himself, and was engaged in a constant struggle to fight it down. Occupying himself with children, or thoughts of children, according to Thomas, provided him with a valuable focus to protect himself against spiritual pollution.

> He was vigilant for purity. He dreaded evil against children, as he repeatedly insisted. [. . .] The control of sexual feeling, preferably its suppression, was important enough to be a main reason for compiling his book of mathematical problems for bedtime, *Pillow Problems*, in 1893. [. . .] When he was fortunate enough to "centre in a focus" the nakedness of Lily Gray, or Ethel Hatch and Beatrice Hatch, or Annie and Frances Henderson, or Ella Monier-Williams, he saw only the purity of "fairies". Those who saw evil in such images by the 1880s misunderstood. Children offered him a refuge because even in these circumstances he was safe from having sexual demands made upon him or from feeling that he need entertain such thoughts himself. They were, as he put it, a "tonic" to his mind.[185]

Thomas, like Bakewell, uses the contrasting examples of the Mayhew and Henderson families as key illustrations; and again, despite the claims that there was nothing remotely sexual about the portraits, the biographer is unable to remain fully neutral. Carroll had a "wild hope . . . it was not enough for him . . . his appeals grew more imploring and importunate . . . then came the explosion which any rational being might have foreseen . . . a dispassionate observer might wonder how long Dodgson's activities could continue without gossip or scandal."[186]

Once more, we see the implication that Carroll was somehow possessed, driven, that his needs and requests went beyond Victorian standards of propriety however their attitudes towards nude children differed from our own. Thomas observes that the nudity itself was not the problem—it was the manner in which Carroll described his models that unnerved mothers like Mrs Mayhew; "his importunate correspondence and appallingly coy euphemisms."[187]

Carroll saw only fairy purity in his portraits, Thomas reassures us. Anyone who sees them otherwise is mistaken. Carroll was, in this account, not innocent but determined to surround himself with innocence in the form of children—and yet, we have this contradictory message that other people of his society and his period found something odd and uneasy in his need for young girls to photograph. Thomas's version of Carroll is safely buttoned-up, but there is a dark, troublesome urge somewhere inside him. Like Bakewell, Thomas effectively retains both the "pure" and the "deviant" conception of the author, although he more explicitly suggests that they were part of the same man, the celibate bachelor repressing his own sinful curiosity and perhaps only making it stronger in the process.

Cohen's version of the events surrounding the nude portraits also has a strange double voice to it: the plain statements of the biographer's theory about Carroll's emotional life, and then an echo that says something slightly different. Cohen's vision of Carroll, as already discussed, is that he was a "highly charged, fully grown male, with strong, mature emotional responses."[188] He was not emotionally stunted; "he did not suffer from arrested development." He was not a childlike innocent but "a person with a passionate orchestra playing within his breast."[189] As Cohen wryly points out,

> His responses were not those of a schoolboy. Schoolboys do not spend their energies or their time cultivating the friendship of young females or pursuing their companionships; they are more interested in sweets, sports and their fellow schoolboys.[190]

However, Cohen does propose that Carroll's passions followed an unusual path, that his "emotional targets clearly differed from most men's . . . that his inner springs differed from most men's, that his heart beat to a different drum."[191] At the book's conclusion, he develops this notion into the more explicit "his sexual energies sought unconventional outlets."[192] By all this he means that Carroll found his deepest satisfaction—on many levels—in the company of young children, primarily girls.

> For Charles, his child friends were more than a source of pleasure—they were his mainstay, as essential as the air he breathed. They provided the impetus for his actions, regulated and punctuated his daily rounds, defined the purpose of his labors, fired his energies, and sparked his imagination.[193]

While he was aware of the gossip circulating around him and his photographic activities in the late 1870s, Carroll was not afraid of this "current of whispers" because he knew himself to be clear of conscience: "he knew that he had not compromised his standards of moral rectitude."[194] Cohen's account differs from Thomas's version here; Thomas sees the society of children as Carroll's attempt to defend himself against sin, not as his overwhelming source of emotional pleasure and quasi-romantic attachment. However, the two biographers agree that he controlled himself rigorously. "He sought to live a respectable life and succeeded," says Cohen.

> His stern rules of thought and behavior ensured rectitude even with his child friends. He convinced himself that his interest in these dyads was purely social, aesthetic, and spiritual, and if we see a hidden sexual force as well, we know, too, that he effectively suppressed it.[195]

Overall, though, there is little explicit mention of a sexual undercurrent, as opposed to a more general passion, in Cohen's defining statements of Carroll's emotional framework; once more, this element comes across not so much in what the biographer says outright, but in the tone and language he uses to tell the story. Photography was, says Cohen, a passport for Carroll into the acquaintance of "beautiful, pure, unaffected, natural female children"[196]—implying a means to an end, rather than a pleasurable and challenging art form in itself.

The slight hints of cynicism continue as we are taken through the encounters with the Mayhews, the Hendersons, the other families with photogenic daughters. From his overall position on Carroll, Cohen does not seem to intend any suggestion of dubious motives, but it is hard not to pick up an air of the predatory when he tells us that Carroll had "access to many homes and the children they sheltered."[197] Again, Cohen echoes the metaphors of Carroll's most sexual poem with his explanation that "if the season was right and the acquaintanceship ripe enough, the next adventure was to photograph the young sitters"; and there is either an irony or an acknowledgement of alluring sensuality in his description of a child-model as "one young charmer."[198]

"How did he manage it?" Cohen asks, implying a process of stealth and persuasion; a sense of surprising achievement that needs explanation, rather than something quite unremarkable within the Victorian social context. "His letters and diaries trace the way he approached parents, first to get their permission to photograph the children and then, if all went well, to photograph them unclothed."[199] "In a sense he worked his way slowly toward the nude child model."[200] Although the term was apparently a common enough description of photography, with its messy chemicals and potential to stain the hands, Cohen must be aware of a sinister double-meaning, for modern readers at least, in his phrase, "Charles practiced the black art."[201]

Cohen is more outspoken than most biographers about the possibility that Carroll's relationship with children involved unrealised sexual aspects as well as emotional and spiritual pleasures. He proposes openly that Carroll had drives of the same intensity as any "normal" adult, but that he found them directed towards an unusual focus. Though he makes no claims for Carroll's naïve innocence, he does stress that these desires were entirely, rigidly held in check; however, there are undertones to his writing that suggest a scheming obsession rather than a successful repression. Just as Carroll, according to many of these contemporary accounts, fought down aspects of his own persona, so many of these contemporary accounts also seem to contain a second voice, emerging unbidden, that suggests alternative, more troubling possibilities in contradiction to the official authorial line.

One man, many parallel lives published a hundred years after his death. These reports of Carroll's life invariably build their stories from the same blocks—the same diary entries, the same letters, the same events—and only rarely bring in original or surprising primary documents. Most of them will confirm what the reader already knew, or suspected, about Lewis Carroll; as such, they fill out detail and shading on a pre-existing picture. Only one or two of them could be said to offer any radical theories about Carroll's internal or external life.

Taken as a group, they present an unwieldy bundle of ideas about who Carroll might have been: variations, contradictions, different tellings of the same story. Collectively, their images of Carroll overlap and clash. Laying one over another like a series of transparencies, we build up a picture with some strong features—where the biographies agree—but with faint shadows and blurred edges, and with phantom limbs where a biographer goes out on his or her own to stake a new claim. Carroll becomes a solid man moving through fog; there is a real person somewhere there, but he seems impossible to catch. And perhaps this shifty elusiveness is the nearest we can hope to get to a very private individual who died a century ago—nearer to the historical truth than a clear, over-confident portrait of someone who never really existed.

Comparatively few people will reach this point, where a few certainties—or strong probabilities—about Carroll can finally be glimpsed through a whirl of conflicting rumour and speculation. Only an enthusiastic Carrollian or a researcher on a mission would bother to read several biographies on the same man from the same decade. Yet popular culture thinks it knows who Lewis Carroll is. The broader talk outside Carrollian scholarship thinks it knows who Lewis Carroll is. Journalism thinks it knows, and it assumes its readers agree. The next chapter is about this wider discourse, and how, if at all, it is shaped by the recent interpretations discussed above.

Notes

1. To Ethel Hatch, quoted in Morton N. Cohen, ed., *Lewis Carroll: Interviews and Recollections* (London: Macmillan, 1989), p. 114. Also quoted in Leach, *Dreamchild*, p. 179, as "Remember me in 1924".
2. Florence Becker Lennon, *Lewis Carroll* (London: William Clowes & Son, 1947), p. 190.
3. Ibid., pp. 186–87.
4. Ibid., p. 191.
5. Stuart Collingwood, *The Life and Letters of Lewis Carroll* (London: T. Fisher Unwin, 1899), p. 354.
6. Lennon, *Lewis Carroll*, p. 192.
7. Ibid.
8. Alexander Taylor, *The White Knight* (Edinburgh: Oliver & Boyd Ltd, 1952), p. 108.
9. Leach, *Dreamchild*, p. 42.
10. Taylor, *White Knight*, p. 32.
11. Ibid., p. 198.
12. Ibid., p. v.
13. Ibid., p. 32.
14. Stuart Collingwood, quoted in Derek Hudson, *Lewis Carroll* (London: Constable, 1954), p. 191.
15. Hudson, ibid.
16. Leach, *Dreamchild*, p. 167.
17. Hudson, *Lewis Carroll*, p. 207.
18. DFC.F/2/4/39–45, Derek Hudson to F. Menella Dodgson (26 February 1953), document in Surrey History Centre, Woking.
19. Leach, *Dreamchild*, p. 43.
20. Ibid., p. 55.
21. Morton N. Cohen, "Who Censored Lewis Carroll?" *The Times* (23 January 1982), quoted in Leach, ibid., p. 56.
22. Ibid., p. 57.

23. Ibid., p. 161.
24. Ibid., p. 162.
25. Edward Wakeling, ed., *Lewis Carroll's Diaries*, vol. 4 (Bedfordshire: Lewis Carroll Society, 1997), pp. 94–95.
26. Cohen, *Interviews*, p. 89.
27. Lewis Carroll, "All in the Golden Afternoon," *Alice in Wonderland*, p. 8.
28. Lewis Carroll, " 'Alice' On the Stage," *Theatre* (April 1887), quoted in Cohen, p. 90.
29. Alice Hargreaves quoted by Stuart Collingwood, *Life and Letters* (1898); see Cohen, p. 90.
30. Ibid.
31. Robinson Duckworth quoted by Collingwood; see Cohen, *Biography*, p. 91.
32. Alice Hargreaves, "The Lewis Carroll That Alice Recalls," *New York Times* (1 May 1932), cited in Cohen, ibid.
33. Helmut Gernsheim, *Lewis Carroll: Photographer* (New York: Dover, 1969), quoted in Gardner, *Annotated Alice*, p. 9.
34. Edward Wakeling points out that this weather report "appears to have been made in a different part of Oxford, and is likely to be very general. Locally, at Binsey and Godstow, the weather may have been different (better)." Wakeling, personal correspondence (23 July 2002).
35. Christina Bjork and Inga-Karin Erikssonn, *The Story of Alice in Her Oxford Wonderland* (London: R&S Books, 1994), p. 8.
36. Ibid., p. 48.
37. Ibid., flyleaf blurb.
38. Ibid., p. 13.
39. Bakewell, *Biography*, pp. 114–115.
40. See Wakeling, *Diaries*, pp. 81–82.
41. Bakewell, *Biography*, p. 115.
42. Cohen, *Biography*, pp. 89–90.
43. Ibid., p. 88.
44. Ibid., p. 117.
45. Lewis Carroll, diary entry (4 July 1862), original manuscript in British Library, London.
46. Thomas, *Portrait*, p. 145.
47. Stephanie Lovett Stoffel, *Lewis Carroll in Wonderland: The Life and Times of Alice and Her Creator* (New York: Abrams, 1997), p. 65.
48. Thomas, *Portrait*, p. 146.
49. Ibid.
50. Jones and Gladstone, *Alice Companion*, p. 215.
51. Ibid., p. 107.
52. Ibid.
53. Ibid., p. 108.
54. Carroll, "All in the Golden Afternoon," *Alice in Wonderland.*
55. Carroll (1887), quoted in Cohen, *Biography*, p. 90.
56. Ibid.
57. Alice Hargreaves (1932), quoted in Cohen, *Biography*, p. 91.
58. Cohen, ibid, p. 123.
59. Leach, *Dreamchild*, p. 161.
60. Ibid., p. 162.
61. Ibid., p. 163.
62. Wakeling, *Diaries*, p. 95.
63. Stoffel, *Life and Times*, p. 65.
64. Leach, *Dreamchild*, p. 163.
65. Wakeling, *Diaries*, p. 213.
66. Ibid., p. 214.
67. Cohen, *Biography*, p. 100.

68. Wakeling, *Diaries*, p. 264.
69. Cohen, *Biography*, p. 100.
70. Bakewell, *Biography*, p. 127.
71. Bjork and Erikkson, *Alice in Oxford*, p. 72. In fact the writing is altered on the preceding page, not the "next page".
72. Stoffel, *Life and Times*, pp. 81–82.
73. Wakeling, *Diaries*, p. 214, footnote.
74. Leach, *Dreamchild*, p. 52.
75. Ibid., p. 169.
76. Thomas, *Portrait*, p. 148.
77. Jones and Gladstone, *Alice Companion*, p. 62.
78. Stoffel, *Life and Times*, p. 82.
79. Bakewell, *Biography*, pp. 129–130.
80. Ibid., p. 129.
81. Lorina Skene to Alice Hargreaves (1930), cited in Bakewell, *Biography*, p. 129.
82. Bakewell, ibid.
83. Stoffel, *Life and Times*, p. 82.
84. Jones and Gladstone, *Alice Companion*, p. 164.
85. See Bakewell, *Biography,* p. 127; Cohen, *Biography*, p. 102.
86. See James R. Kincaid, *Child-Loving: The Erotic Child and Victorian Literature* (London: Routledge, 1992).
87. Stoffel, *Life and Times,* p. 82.
88. Bakewell, *Biography*, p. 104.
89. Ibid., p. 129.
90. Cohen, *Biography*, p. 101.
91. Ibid., p. 100.
92. Margaret Woods, "Oxford in the "Seventies," *Fortnightly Review* 150 (1941), quoted in Cohen, ibid.
93. Bakewell, *Biography*, p. 128.
94. Lord Salisbury to Lady John Manners (1878), quoted in Cohen, *Biography*, p. 101.
95. Lewis Carroll, diary entry (7 October 1865), quoted in Cohen, ibid.
96. Cohen, ibid.
97. Lewis Carroll to Mrs Lorina Liddell (19 November 1891), quoted in Cohen, ibid.
98. Bakewell, *Biography*, p. 149.
99. Thomas, *Portrait*, p. 271.
100. Leach, *Dreamchild*, p. 164.
101. Ibid, p. 165.
102. On the other hand, Edward Wakeling suggests that Carroll "often made errors and slips of the pen. He wasn't as consistently accurate as people make out." Wakeling, personal correspondence (23 July 2002).
103. Leach, *Dreamchild*, p. 165.
104. Ibid., p. 178.
105. Ibid., p. 181.
106. Ibid., pp. 170–71.
107. Ibid., p. 171. The "unreadable" words are decipherable as "by some".
108. Ibid., p. 180.
109. DFC.F/17/1, "Cut Pages in Diary" (3 February 1932), document in Surrey History Centre, Woking.
110. Ibid., p. 173.
111. Lewis Carroll, diary entry (21 April 1863), original manuscript in British Library, London.
112. Leach, *Dreamchild*, p. 170.
113. Karoline Leach, "Ina in Wonderland," *Times Literary Supplement* (3 May 1996), p. 15.
114. Edward Wakeling identifies the archivist as Shirley Corke: Wakeling, personal correspondence (23 July 2002). He dates the catalogue to 1989.

115. Catalogue introduction, Dodgson Family Collection, Surrey History Centre, Woking.
116. Karoline Leach, letter to *The Carrollian* 9 (Spring 2002): 55.
117. See Wakeling, *Diaries*, pp. 214–215.
118. Lewis Carroll, diary entry (17 May 1857), quoted in Cohen, *Biography*, p. 68.
119. Wakeling, *Diaries*, p. 7.
120. Ibid.
121. He did make it clear in correspondence with me that he believed the prayers were probably concerned either with Carroll's dreams or guilt at his own laziness. Edward Wakeling, personal correspondence (22 June 2002).
122. Jones and Gladstone, *Alice Companion*, p. 206.
123. Collingwood, *Life and Letters*, p. 65.
124. Ibid.
125. Bakewell, *Biography*, p. 110.
126. See Leach, *Dreamchild*, pp. 48–49, for comment on what may have happened to these lost diaries.
127. Bakewell, *Biography*, p. 110.
128. Wakeling, *Diaries*, pp. 107–108.
129. Bakewell, *Biography*.
130. Ibid.
131. Lewis Carroll, preface to *Pillow Problems* (1893), quoted in Bakewell, ibid.
132. Collingwood, *Life and Letters*, pp. 321–22.
133. Bakewell, *Biography*.
134. Wakeling, *Diaries*. As noted in the footnote above, he stated his view more plainly in personal correspondence.
135. Bakewell, *Biography*, p. 110.
136. Green, quoted in Leach, *Dreamchild*, p. 149.
137. Lewis Carroll, "Stolen Waters" (1862), reprinted in Leach, ibid., pp. 273–76.
138. Bakewell, *Biography*, p. 112.
139. Leach, *Dreamchild*, p. 149.
140. Cohen, *Biography*, p. xxi.
141. Ibid.
142. Ibid., p. 219.
143. Ibid., p. 224.
144. Ibid., p. 228.
145. Ibid., p. 230.
146. Ibid., p. xxi.
147. Ibid., p. 210.
148. Ibid., p. 207.
149. Ibid., p. 210.
150. Ibid., p. 204.
151. Ibid., p. 213.
152. Ibid., p. 219.
153. Ibid.
154. Leach, *Dreamchild*, p. 150.
155. Ibid., p. 140.
156. Ibid., p. 142.
157. Ibid., pp. 149–150.
158. Ibid., p. 157.
159. Ibid., p. 195.
160. Ibid.
161. Ibid., pp. 206–7.
162. Ibid.
163. Ibid., p. 213.

164. Ibid.
165. Ibid., pp. 213–3.
166. Edward Wakeling, personal correspondence (23 July 2002).
167. Leach, *Dreamchild*, pp. 61–62.
168. Ibid., pp. 64–65.
169. Ibid., p. 66.
170. Ibid., p. 77.
171. Ibid., p. 64.
172. Stoffel, *Life and Times*, p. 46.
173. Ibid., p. 40.
174. Ibid., pp. 46–47.
175. Ibid., p. 47.
176. Ibid., p. 47.
177. Bakewell, *Biography*, p. 245.
178. Ibid.
179. See for instance Cohen, *Biography*, pp. 171, 183, 189.
180. Bakewell, *Biography*, p. 220.
181. Ibid., p. 231.
182. Ibid.
183. Ibid., p. 234.
184. See Thomas, *Portrait*, p. 265, pp. 277–80, p. 272.
185. Ibid., pp. 266–67.
186. Ibid., p. 263.
187. Ibid.
188. Cohen, *Biography*, p. 192.
189. Ibid., p. 530.
190. Ibid., p. 192.
191. Ibid., p. 190.
192. Ibid., p. 530.
193. Ibid., p. 181.
194. Ibid., p. 171.
195. Ibid., p. 531.
196. Ibid., p. 152.
197. Ibid., p. 161.
198. Ibid., p. 162.
199. Ibid., p. 168.
200. Ibid., p. 165.
201. Ibid., p. 173.

2

THE MAN IN WHITE PAPER

> *Any*body who is spoken about at all, is *sure* to be spoken against
> by *somebody*.
>
> —Lewis Carroll[1]

Imagine a Victorian Internet, a web of Babbage engines linked across the Britain of 1899. You punch out "Alice in Wonderland" and "Lewis Carroll" on two cards, feed them in, pull a lever. What comes back from a trawl of the contemporary media? The almost uniformly enthusiastic reviews of the *Alice* books, perhaps, which applaud them as delightfully innocent frippery:

> Our young friends may rest assured that the exquisite illustrations only do justice to the exquisitely wild, fantastic, impossible, yet most natural history of "Alice in Wonderland."[2]

> A children's feast of triumph and nonsense; it is nonsense with bonbons and flags . . . never inhuman, never inelegant, never tedious.[3]

> It would be difficult to over-estimate the value of the store of hearty and healthy fun laid up for whole generations of young people by Mr. Lewis Carroll . . . [4]

The search might turn up eulogies to Carroll, equally generous and refined, like this verse in *Punch*—

> Farewell! But near our hearts we have you yet,
> Holding our heritage with loving hand,

> Who may not follow where your feet are set
> Upon the ways of Wonderland.[5]

—or this misty-eyed farewell in Collingwood's biography.

> A marble cross, under the shadow of a pine, marks the spot, and beneath his own name they have engraved the name of "Lewis Carroll", that the children who pass by may remember their friend, who is now—himself a child in all that makes childhood most attractive—in that "Wonderland" which outstrips our dreams and hopes.[6]

Those critics with reservations—mainly based on Carroll's later work such as the titanic and turgid *Sylvie and Bruno* (1889)—expressed them elegantly and gently.

> Lewis Carroll had really been lost to us for some time: the magic wand was broken, and it is certain that he would never again reach the level of his best work.[7]

> We shall miss him for a long time to come . . . not for his books, for his story-telling days were past, but for himself.[8]

Only one anonymous obituary described Carroll in anything but glowing terms: "a humorist oppressed with a sense of gravity . . . the stiff but courteous don, all chastened eyes and repellent silence."[9]

Overall, a quick search through the Victorian media for traces of Carroll's name and *Alice*'s adventures would, it seems, give a sense of almost unanimous praise for the books' frivolous, essentially meaningless fun and for the many personal qualities of their creator. Wonderland is a gay realm in the most innocent sense, and even rises to heaven with Carroll in Collingwood's eulogy. Carroll at his most sinister, in the unflattering obituary quoted above, displays no greater sins than being awkwardly quiet and forbiddingly dull.

Needless to say, offering the same keywords up to an Internet search in 2002 yields quite different results. Perhaps most surprisingly, some have no direct connection to the author or his work, but nevertheless trade on the associations that both "Carroll" and "Alice" gained in the twentieth century.

Lucy's Little Wonderland[10] is the home page of transvestite "Lucy Robinson", who first indulged his love of female clothes as a thirteen-year-old. "At the end of the first term, each class did a short play: We did the

Mad Hatter's tea party from *Alice in Wonderland*, and guess who played Alice in a pretty blue dress with a white apron and stockings?" This moment of origin aside, there is nothing to link Lucy's portfolio of glamour shots with Carroll's books apart from their common interest in transformation. Alice, after all, stretches, shrinks, shuts up like a telescope; changing sex would almost be a logical next step for her.

The same parallel presumably informs *Alcie's Web Page*, home of "the prettiest blonde bitch transvestite"; whatever the spelling, the fact that Alcie's site features a graphic of a manga-style Alice in blue dress and white apron makes its cultural debt clear.[11] *Alice's Wonderland* has even less relevance to the 1865 story, but again, this is the home page of a "fun-loving bisexual transvestite"[12]: the author's *femme* name and site title are presumably born from a perceived affinity with Carroll's shape-shifting heroine. Three cross-dressing Alice sites do not, perhaps, make a trend, but they suggest an interesting adoption of the character that clearly goes beyond pure coincidence.

More unnervingly, an amateur piece of erotic fiction on *Lady Moonwise*'s site, "Daddy's Little Girl", draws on the myths of a paedophile Lewis Carroll[13] to dress up its fantasy of sex between father and daughter:

> The note said "Daddy's little girl . . . " She opened the box and took out the things inside. Then she quickly undressed. First she took a bubble bath. As she dried off she studied her twenty-eight year old body in the mirror. Then she got dressed.
>
> She walks in dressed as Alice in Wonderland. Her long hair held back by a pink ribbon. Looking at her you smile . . . but something is not quite right. Her shoes are high heels. She smiles a Cheshire cat smile . . . then turns so you can see the zipper on the dress . . . you unzip it slowly pulling the dress off her shoulders. She is left standing in a black lace teddy, black lace undies and the white silk stockings . . . she dances for you, a slow erotic . . . little girl . . . [14]

This use of Carroll will be tawdry and disturbing to many readers, more so to dedicated Carrollians who, as we shall see in Chapter 8, have an interest in protecting his reputation. It is not, to my mind, an inspiring appropriation of the *Alice* texts; I had to doctor the punctuation just to make the above quotation readable. However, the association of Carroll and Alice with sexualised images of children is not isolated to Lady Moonwise. Dragging their names across the net also pulls in references to the "Wonderland Club",[15] an international child pornography ring whose reference to Carroll's creation can, again, hardly be unintentional. The charm that Victorian reviewers, for the most part, saw in *Alice*, has been tainted by twentieth-century perceptions of Carroll's child-friends and nude portraiture, and become a twisted myth, a name and image for abusers to use as their mascot and motto.

It would not be remotely practical to use the results of a general, global Internet search as the basis of this discussion: there would simply be too much material to sort and analyse. Instead, I am restricting my data to newspaper and popular magazine articles from 1992–2002, the results of a search on the LexisNexis electronic network of British journalism using various combinations of "Lewis Carroll", "Alice", and "Wonderland". Almost all of the articles were British in origin, but a handful of American texts were also returned.

In total, the search yielded seventy-seven articles. Five were about child pornography, paedophilia, or child abuse, referring to Carroll or Alice in connection with the club's name and motifs. Seven were concerned with the discovery or auction of documents—letters, papers, photographs and personal effects—related to Lewis Carroll or Alice Liddell. One was about the 125th anniversary of *Alice in Wonderland*'s publication, another commemorated the July 4 river trip, and two marked the centenary of Carroll's death. Three were features or reviews on the American McGee PC game *Alice*, and will be saved for discussion in Chapter 8. Two were "heritage" articles about Carroll's connection with Oxford and Ripon in Cheshire. One mentioned Carroll in relation to J. M. Barrie, one in terms of Victorian culture, and two in the context of nude child photography, whether from the nineteenth or twentieth centuries.

The remaining articles were all about Alice-related books or plays. Two reviews of Katie Roiphe's novel *Still She Haunts Me*, which will be discussed in Chapter 5, and an essay by the author. Seven features on the Royal Shakespeare Company's production of *Alice in Wonderland*, which ran during autumn 2001 and spring 2002. One interview with Christopher Hampton about his play *Alice's Adventures Underground* of 1994. A surprising twenty-one reviews of Helen Oxenbury's new illustrations for *Alice*— discussed at length in Chapter 4—and two of Lisbeth Zwerger's. Two further articles that mentioned both versions are included, for convenience, in the Oxenbury tally.

Finally, the search returned reviews of biographies and commentaries, many of which we encountered in the previous chapter—four of Cohen, one of Jones and Gladstone, two of Thomas, one of Bakewell; three reviews of Martin Gardner's definitive *Annotated Alice*, one of Edward Wakeling and Roger Taylor's *Lewis Carroll: Photographer*, and seven articles either by Karoline Leach or about *In The Shadow of the Dreamchild*.

It seems, then, that—where not prompted by the appearance of a new critical work or creative adaptation—British journalism of the 1990s links Lewis Carroll with heritage and history, with the occasional notable sale of private documents, with nude photography or child pornography. These four categories neatly fit the twin contemporary readings I suggested in the Introduction. Carroll is safely buried in nostalgia, emerging in museum pieces or alternatively dragged into the company of criminals and abusers, his own photography tarnished by association with the exploitative obscene images of the last decade. The rest of this chapter examines more closely the way Carroll is constructed by the press of the 1990s, then asks how Alice herself emerges from these reports.

Paedophilia and Promiscuity

On Valentine's Day 2001, seven British men were sentenced for their involvement in the "Wonderland Club", an online, international network whose joining fee was ten thousand new pornographic photographs of children. The precise reasons behind the name are presumably known only to the members; the *Western Daily Press* in Bristol made the connection to "Lewis Carroll's fantasy novel", and noted that one of the society's chat room "bots"—programs that act as artificial intelligences to keep out unwanted guests—was called Alice, "a further link to Carroll's 1865 dreamworld fantasy."[16] Detective Chief Inspector Alex Wood offered his own reading: "I can only assume the names Wonderland and Alice were an indication of youthful, pre-teen pleasure. But I don't know what interpretation the club put on it."[17]

Unrelated to the Wonderland society—but trading on similar associations—the magazine *Alice Club* is mentioned in a 1999 *Guardian* article on Japanese child pornography. Although its specialty is "nude pictures of young teenagers" rather than children, the reporter makes it clear that the magazine "derives its title from the work of Lewis Carroll".[18] As with the transvestite uses of Alice and Wonderland, we have to guess that these publishers, like the paedophile ring, sense an affinity with Lewis Carroll on the basis of his association with and photographs of young girls.

We might baulk at the connection between Carroll's coy portraits of Beatrice Hatch and a Japanese porn magazine—even more so at any link with images of six-month-old children being raped or abused—but we cannot ignore the fact that some people clearly believe the two have something in common. Note, though, that the Detective Chief Inspector quoted above constructs "Alice" as a sign of innocence and childish pleasure, implying that the concept itself is abused by its appropriation as an in-joke for sex offenders.

Mary Kenny's *Express* article on the justifications used by "man-boy" organisations confirms that "paedophile propagandists . . . like to claim Lewis Carroll (the author of *Alice in Wonderland*) . . . among their number."[19] Matthew Sweet underlines the link in his review of Wakeling and Taylor's *Lewis Carroll: Photographer*, though he blames Cohen's "now standard" biography for lending the idea scholarly weight. Cohen, "probably the world's most prominent Carroll authority", tells us that his subject's "sexual energies sought unconventional outlets."

> Small wonder that popular accounts of Carroll's life—Dennis Potter's *Dreamchild* (1985), Katie Roiphe's novel *Still She Haunts Me* (2001)—have engaged with this idea so enthusiastically. Paedophiles themselves have made the most energetic use of these ideas: Dodgson's case is cited endlessly in their apologist literature, and his name and works have provided sobriquets for organisations involved in distributing child pornography: the *Wonderland Club*, the *Lewis Carroll Collectors Guild*.[20]

However, Sweet reminds the reader that recent studies have "sought to prize Dodgson away from such company"; Wakeling and Taylor's book insists there is "not a shred of evidence" for the paedophile claim, and Leach has provided "campaigning work" to save Carroll's name.[21] This critical championing of Leach as a form of defence lawyer is quite common in reviews of her book, as we'll see below.

Finally, Jim Harding reviews "the most vile and perverted novel I have ever read", a novel that will be discussed in Chapter 5 below.

> It is called *The End of Alice* and it describes in gloating and pornographic detail the physical and sexual abuse of a young girl, Alice, by an unrepentant paedophile. Alice—the cynical reference to Lewis Carroll's creation is quite deliberate—is a child whose sorry end, after a long period of sexual abuse, is to be mutilated and killed.[22]

Harding suggests that the use of Alice's name is a nasty piece of emotional manipulation—presumably because of the juxtaposition of a word that signifies childish fantasy with the reality of graphic abuse, and the attempt at shock value by placing *Alice*'s perceived innocence next to horrific exploitation. As with the Detective Chief Inspector's suggestion, Harding's comparison actually returns Wonderland to the level of purity and wholesomeness that it occupied in Collingwood's 1898 eulogy, and there is a sense of resentment from all these writers about the attempt to defile Victorian icons. Carrollians who mourn the association of their hero and his creation with modern sex abuse can at least be assured that any direct link between the two tends, in this sample at least, to be rejected.

Indeed, outright claims that Lewis Carroll was a paedophile are very rare in this particular case study. Of my seventy-seven articles, only two ventured so far, and these were both by writers with a degree of celebrity status, who may see "daring provocation" as part of their remit. One was by Waldemar Januszczak, the art critic and sometime TV presenter; the other was by novelist and game show regular Will Self.

"What's Tate Britain for?" asks Januszczak at the start of his piece on a new exhibition at the London art gallery. "Even those of you who are the same tender age as the naked girls photographed by the disgusting Lewis Carroll should be able to answer that one." Following this startling sideswipe, Januszczak doesn't mention Carroll again until the final paragraph, when he discusses "Exposed", the gallery's opening show.

> Exposed plods through assorted excuses for painting naked girls, employed by various subspecies of the Victorian lecher . . . most of this is merely sad. Occasionally, it slips into something much worse, as when the paedophile longings of Lewis Carroll are made absolutely clear in his images of the tiny Evelyn Hatch reclining naked. Should this show have set out to prove that the British are frequently sick on the subject of sex, it would have had a point. But since it has been mounted to entice visitors, it is just as disquieting as its own worst moments.[23]

In fairness to Januszczak, his response is based on a very understandable disgust at the exploitation of women and children. However, he clearly makes no attempt to identify with or even recognise the very different set of attitudes that produced the artwork—a shift of perspective that Stoffel and Leach easily managed—and allows his own contemporary attitudes towards the abuse of children to shape his judgement. "Paedophile longings" are read into Carroll's portrait because, presumably, it resembles the type of image that would today be circulated secretly as child pornography. However, as Januszczak is unwilling to explain his judgment beyond the fact that Carroll is disgusting and that his paedophilia is obvious, it is difficult to investigate this reading in any more depth.

Will Self proposes a slightly more complex argument about why Carroll was "indisputably a paedophile—just not an active one." Any commentary on Carroll, he proposes—he mounts this hobby-horse while reviewing Martin Gardner's *Annotated Alice: The Definitive Edition*—must "acknowledge one vital fact about his sexuality" or become "an exercise in wilful distortion."[24] There is no room for manoeuvre in this argument—he's a paedophile, and if you don't agree, you're wrong.

What, then, is Self's proof? We will recognise the various exhibits in his evidence from the previous chapter's brief tour through biography:

> Carroll's obsession with pre-pubescent girls, his photographing and sketching of them in the nude, his delight in kissing them, his revulsion from boys at a similar age, his apparent revulsion from adult sexuality in all forms.[25]

We will also recognise many of these exhibits as misleading, meaningless, or false. That Carroll enjoyed kissing little girls carries no significance on its own, and only speaks of "paedophilia" if our minds are already made up that the man is a pervert. His "revulsion from boys" is contradicted by his close friendship with Hallam and Lionel Tennyson, "the most beautiful boys of their age I ever saw"[26], and with Alice's brother Harry Liddell.[27] His "revulsion from adult sexuality" is harder to maintain when we consider the adult nudes that Leach reveals in his private collection.[28] Self's case, in short, is not solid.

However, after agreeing with Nabokov (or "Vladimir", as Self calls him) that Carroll enjoyed a "wretched perversion . . . in dim rooms", Self winds up with a conclusion similar to Cohen's view of Carroll, albeit more direct.

> What, in my view, makes the *Alice* books so enduringly central to the English literary canon is precisely their quality of heightened repression: the struggle by a tormented paedophile to keep the manifest object of his desire straitjacketed in a fallacious—yet socially condoned—dreamlike realm of sexual ignorance.[29]

He never calls his subject "a dirty old man" as Self does, but the idea of an unusual passion that was controlled and channelled into creative writing is central to Cohen's argument. In the end, Self's viewpoint is no more radical than that of many recent biographers—he even calls upon *Pillow Problems* as witness to Carroll's displacement of "unholy thoughts" into writing—but by pinning the loaded word "paedophile" to Lewis Carroll, he deliberately brings a late twentieth-century moral panic to bear on a Victorian writer. The basic theory that Carroll struggled with urges that shamed him is not remarkable; to bluntly call those urges "paedophilia" or "perversion" rather than the possibility of "a hidden sexual force . . . that he effectively suppressed"[30] is to put Carroll on trial in 2000 and convict him by modern standards.

By contrast, the only articles in this sample that explicitly deny and argue against accusations of Carroll's paedophilia are—as Matthew Sweet's article suggested—the reviews of Karoline Leach's *In The Shadow of the Dreamchild*. The right-wing newspaper *The Mail on Sunday*, for instance, embraces Leach for her efforts to clear Carroll's name.

> Pervert, paedophile, pornographer: it seems unbelievable that such words should adhere so easily to the reputation of the writer of that most innocent of fantasies, *Alice in Wonderland*. And yet, after a century of revisionist dirt-digging, they do. Since Lewis Carroll's death 100 years ago, regiments of researchers and biographers have deconstructed his work, examined the ephemera he left behind and seen in their looking glasses a dark vision: an anguished loner who got his excitement from photographing little girls naked and who misused his talent for storytelling to pursue his friend's daughters. So heavily does Carroll's current reputation hang over his work that some schools and parents, particularly in America, now question whether the *Alice* stories are even fit for children.[31]

Carroll's image, the *Mail*'s William Langley rejoices to report, "may be salvaged" by Leach's book. Langley's stance is traditionalist and conservative, but in some ways it, like the arguments of Self and Januszczak above, is shaped by late twentieth-century codes of sexual behaviour. As such, his attempt to protect Carroll's reputation—although he explicitly rubbishes the biographical "revisionism" of the past century—is entirely different from the way Stuart Collingwood preserved his subject's integrity.

While Carroll's society would have seen adultery and dalliance with unmarried women as scandalous, Langley grasps this possibility as proof of Carroll's "robustly normal" erotic urges, far preferable to what he calls the "newer, darker vision"[32] of paedophilia. Social sins have traded places in the last one hundred years: the child-love that served as a badge of respectability in the mid to late 1800s is now Carroll's curse, providing his detractors with evidence to twist into an "unnatural obsession with little girls",[33] while any hint of his womanising is now his route to salvation. We might note that Carroll's "robustly normal" desires are subtly contrasted with those of the "notoriously boring and reputedly homosexual" Dean Henry Liddell; passionate affairs are apparently more laudable than repressed gayness and dullness on the *Mail*'s scale of manly virtues.

Langley tends to sensationalise and exaggerate a view of the Alice-Carroll relationship that recent biography only implies. "The modern view," he claims, "is that he was fixated with her; that he schemed endlessly to visit her and tricked her parents into allowing him to photograph her in erotic poses."[34] I argued in the previous chapter that Bakewell, Thomas, and Cohen almost inadvertently give a vague sense of the predatory, but nothing so blatant as this. We see here, I think, journalism's drive to make stories bigger, starker, less accurate but more dramatic, and we can see it again in a second review of Leach's book.

Graeme Woolaston depicts the Carroll of current imagination as "nursing a forlorn, and originally paedophile, love for Alice Liddell." Summing up Leach's 294 pages in 374 words, he relates that Carroll

> . . . was first portrayed as a bachelor academic whose innocence was expressed in happy associations with girl children. Then, of course, the world was changed by Dr Freud and he became a potentially dangerous pervert. [. . .] There is no doubt that Carroll was strongly heterosexual and was fascinated by females of many ages.[35]

That "of course" is priceless as an example of the blithe transformation of vague assumptions into common sense, stuff everyone knows: Woolaston's "no doubt" is of the same order. Similarly, Geoffrey Heptonstall's warm reception of the book in *Contemporary Review* simply replaces outdated "facts" about Carroll with new ones, making certainties from Leach's comparative subtlety. After sceptically breaking down the myths around Carroll, Heptonstall boldly sets out "truths" that have little more substance.

> Everyone knows about Lewis Carroll, yet almost everything . . . is an invention. [. . .] The truth is that Carroll was a philanderer of scandalous notoriety. His interest in children, including Alice, was by his own account perfunctory. In the guise of telling fairy-tales he could write absurd satiric fantasies which are part of general consciousness. The imagery of Carroll is everywhere. So too is the reputation which long since turned sour . . . commentators have made inventions of their own, ignoring the realities to be found in Dodgson's private papers. [. . .] By such legerdemain speculation is given authority without reference to other interpretations: "What I tell you three times is tree."[36]

The mangling of Carroll's "what I tell you three times is true", from *Hunting of the Snark*, is presumably a typo, but it aptly illustrates Heptonstall's blatant repetition of the very crimes he denounces. In his review, speculation does indeed become authority—the piece claims to reveal "the real Lewis Carroll"—and the arguments that Leach herself only presents

58

as plausible alternatives are firmed up into "the whole truth with an intelligent advocate."[37]

On one level, these reviews will be welcomed by Carrollians who deplore the "paedophile" label. The journalists discussed here display a common zeal to rescue Carroll as if he were falsely imprisoned or libelled. Heptonstall observes that "the hostility has been extraordinary"; Leach's "defence . . . is more than chivalrous; it is just."[38] Langley describes the "paedophile" rumour as a "grotesque betrayal" of a man who made such a contribution to our literature; "only a modern world obsessed with finding imaginary victims and villains could fail to thank him."[39] Like the articles discussed below that try to reopen the intrigue of Alice's relationship with Carroll, these writers make the defence of Carroll into an urgent mission, treating his case as newsworthy and current. In practice, however, they are just as careless with their evidence as the writers who scorn Carroll as a dirty old man; it is surely just as absurd to announce that he was "obviously" a womaniser as it is to brand him a child-abuser.

When theories pass from the measured argument of more scholarly discourse to the bold statements of popular discussion, we find crudely drawn caricatures forming in the public consciousness. Most readers will come to associate these cartoonish but powerful images, rather than the cautiously indecisive portraits we gain from recent biographies, with the name Lewis Carroll. There is no room for subtlety or tentative suggestions in this kind of writing, and whether we agree with these authors' supremely confident conclusions or not, we should be aware that their articles will do more than any scholarly work to shape most people's understanding of Carroll, and convince them of what "we", as a culture, "know" about him.

The claims for Carroll as either paedophile or promiscuous lover fall at either extreme of these newspaper reports. The majority of opinions found in this sample are equally bold and stark, but they hover between the stereotypes, resulting not in carefully modulated suggestion but in shifting positions and contradictory assertions. As the next section shows, newspapers need little excuse to call up and reassess the contemporary image of Lewis Carroll; a newly discovered letter or a recent anniversary is reason enough to rehearse the old stories.

Heritage and Intrigue

Several original documents related to Carroll came to light or up for sale during the first years of the twenty-first century. One of these, an unpublished letter auctioned in November 2001, prompted a broader discussion of Carroll's relationship with children: the document was said by a

Sotheby's spokesman to represent "the most explicit expression of his sense of the loss of innocence entailed in what elsewhere he called 'the transition' ".[40] In a brief summary of the changing discourses around his sexuality, the *Scotsman*'s David Robinson ran through various theories familiar from the biographies in Chapter 1:

> For such a chaste Victorian clergyman, tenderness towards children was only part of a Christ-like renunciation of the pleasures of the adult world. After his death, a radically different interpretation soon arose. This, after all, was a minister who proposed marriage to an 11 year-old girl; whose photographs of pre-pubescent girls even his defenders admit verge on paedophilia. To the modern mind, Charles Dodgson—the man who was Lewis Carroll—looks like a pervert. [. . .]
>
> After so much paedophile sex abuse in our own age, it is difficult for us to accept the reasons anybody gives for wanting to take pictures of naked children. All we really know about Dodgson's sexuality is that if he was indeed a paedophile it was in thought rather than deed. Whether he was too emotionally immature or controlled, he never acted on those particular impulses.

This breakneck race through conflicting interpretations is a clear case of journalism grabbing for easy hooks and clear, unambiguous stories; when this approach is applied to someone as elusive as Lewis Carroll, the result is a choppy argument, both confidently unequivocal and internally contradictory. There is no room here for carefully built theories, and so the cautious wavering we find in Bakewell and Thomas becomes, as we saw in the articles above, what we "know" about Carroll.

Instead of speculation backed up by diary entries and letters, we have statements like "Dodgson did indeed believe that their beauty had an almost divine purity." Instead of potential explanations held up against other alternative possibilities, we have "a minister who proposed marriage to an 11 year-old girl." The assertions fail to either add up into a focussed snapshot or to offer the ambiguity we would find in a book-length portrait: instead of shades of grey, Robinson gives us stark lines pointing in different directions. The article concludes, almost as if realising that the fragmented "facts" fail to slot together, "for all that, Carroll's sexuality remains an enigma."

Fiachra Gibbons's report from the same month, about an export ban on Carroll's original photographs of the Liddell girls, transforms speculation into fact in a similar manner. The opening paragraph neatly conveys the twin contemporary discourses around Carroll and Alice, as embodied by his images of children. "They are either some of the sweetest images of

childhood innocence, or they are the first photographs of little girls seen
through the looking-glass of suppressed paedophile desire."[41] The rest of
the article, though, performs much the same routine as Will Self did in
his character assassination: Gibbons unapologetically imposes a twenty-
first-century perspective on examples of a Victorian aesthetic, and presents
his own opinion unblushingly as the simple truth.

> Dodgson's relationship with Alice Liddell . . . has always raised uncom-
> fortable questions. A pioneer and an early master of portrait photography,
> Dodgson shot Alice—the first of his many child-friends—in several
> ambiguous poses, conferring upon her a kind of adult knowingness.
> [. . .] The 13 glass negatives and prints, which attracted a temporary
> export ban from the arts minister, Lady Blackstone, yesterday, show
> Alice and her siblings in a variety of romanticised settings. She is seen
> lying on a couch in one: in another her sister Ina holds a doll; a further
> photograph is entitled, in a rather unsettling way, "Open Your Mouth
> and Shut Your Eyes."

Because Gibbons sees a worrying overtone of "knowingness" in the
portraits—presumably due in part to his (imperfect) knowledge of the
Carroll-Alice relationship, and informed by our modern sensitivity to any
hint of paedophilia—every aspect of them is held up as potentially sinister.
That Alice lies on a couch and Ina holds a doll is clearly devoid of any
inherent significance, but the details are mentioned as if they were clues
to a crime; in turn, "Open Your Mouth and Shut Your Eyes" is invested
with vaguely sexual connotations and its subject—the three girls eating
cherries—deliberately ignored.

With a marked shift, however, the end of Gibbons's article constructs
the photographs—and by extension Carroll, Alice Liddell, and "Alice"—as
nostalgic treasures with a vital place in British heritage. Lady Blackstone,
who opposed their sale, is given the final word with her view that the
Alice books

> are known and loved throughout the world . . . they are regarded as
> classics of English literature enjoyed by children and adults alike. More
> and more people who have read them know of the connection between
> their author and Alice Liddell . . . I very much hope [the photographs]
> can stay in this country.[42]

After heaping doubt on Carroll's motivation and inviting a view of the
portraits as unhealthily sexualised, Gibbons allows the piece to end with
a quite different reading of the man and his work: again, what emerges

is our culture's see-sawing ambivalence towards these Victorian texts. As in David Robinson's report, confident but contradictory interpretations clash throughout the article, and Gibbons ultimately has to resolve that Carroll and Alice had a "to modern sensibilities, inexplicable friendship."[43]

We find the same odd pattern—uncertainty half-concealed by bluff—in coverage of the sale of Alice Liddell's personal collection of letters and photographs. The documents, according to *The Scotsman*'s Karen McVeigh, reflect the alleged "obsession" between Carroll and "the seven-year-old girl who became his muse" and are "expected to shed light on the relationship between the two."[44] The curator of Sotheby's auction house confirms that the collection is crucial "in terms of what it shows between Carroll and Alice."[45]

We are led to expect some kind of revelation about the mysterious bond that "has fascinated people for decades"; the documents, we are told, have "never been seen outside of Liddell's family." Again, the author presents the Carroll-Alice relationship as an enduring, intriguing mystery. However, the letter cited within this article, "written in 1891 to the then 39 year-old married Alice, which shows the author yearning for the little girl she once was", is reproduced in Cohen's *Letters* of 1979.

My dear Mrs Hargreaves,
I should be so glad if you could, quite conveniently to yourself, look in for tea any day. You would probably prefer to bring a companion; but I would leave the choice to you, only remarking that if your husband is here he would be ~~most~~ very welcome (I crossed out most because it's ambiguous; most words are, I fear.) I met him in our Common Room not long ago. It was hard to realise that he was the husband of one I can scarcely picture to myself, even now, as more than 7 years old! Always sincerely yours,
C. L. Dodgson[46]

McVeigh's explanation of what this formal, even mundane document "shows" is, contrary to her assertion, open to dispute—Leach, for example, suggests that the same letter implies a lack of any lasting passion for Alice.[47]

Robert McCrum's report on the same story in the *Observer* repeats this approach. Alice and Carroll had a "strange and, to modern eyes, scarcely explicable relationship"; the collection gives us "a tantalising glimpse into the intense, strange and relatively brief relationship between the shy, stammering Oxford mathematician . . . and the fascinating, seven year-old daughter."[48] The scraps of evidence are confidently interpreted to fit in with the reporter's idea of a weird fascination and a lifelong love.

"There is Dodgson's heartrending request to Mrs Liddell for the grown-up Alice Hargreaves's address . . . most movingly of all, there is Dodgson's letter directly to Mrs Hargreaves . . . inviting her to tea." This, again, is the polite note quoted above; to see it as heartrending requires us to believe that Carroll cherished a repressed passion throughout his life, expressing it only in clipped tones.

> And then there are the photographs: Alice as a Beggar Maid, Alice by a potted fern, Alice with her sisters (titled: "Open Your Mouth and Shut Your Eyes"); Alice dressed as a gypsy, playing a ukulele . . . and so on. Who knows what other poses have been lost to posterity?[49]

By listing the photographs of Alice so breathlessly together, McCrum wants to give the impression of what he calls "Dodgson's obsession with Alice Liddell [which] runs through every part of this archive like an unanswered question."[50] In the context of Carroll's photographic career—even in terms of the 407 pictures collected in Edward Wakeling and Roger Taylor's recent volume[51]—these few portraits of Alice do not suggest a fixation with the girl. Only if we are drawn into McCrum's vision—and the casual reader would surely have no reason to question it—do we see "Alice playing a ukulele" as symptomatic of an unhealthy infatuation. Note that "Open Your Mouth" is again subtly drawn to our attention as if it had some double meaning, and the question about potentially lost photographs also seems to insinuate that the other poses may have been more sexually explicit.

McCrum, in common with his fellow journalists in this sample, wants the Carroll-Alice story to be "at once passionate yet innocent; idealised, romanticised and yet ultimately mysterious." Carroll, though "a writer of genius and . . . one of the greatest photographers of his age" also raises "our contemporary anxieties about child welfare."[52] When his name is associated with actual child abuse, as we have seen, the part of us that cherishes his literary and cultural importance, his nostalgic value, and connotations of Victorian "innocence", is quick to protect him: yet at the same time, the consensus emerging from these newspaper reports suggests that some part of Carroll's appeal to journalism lies in his slightly uncanny, abnormal aspects.

The popular media like an ongoing mystery, with new clues to uncover; hundred-year-old secrets and a hint of kinky sexuality give the story a keener edge. These writers like the quaint, heritage associations of Carroll; they like him to belong to yesterday, with its sepia associations of a lost, golden age. But to keep him newsworthy, to keep the story current, they have to examine his relationship with Alice from our own very different perspective and revive it with knowing hints of paedophilia—not enough to bring Carroll down from his platform in the literary canon, not enough to make him a criminal like the perverts in the Wonderland Club, but enough to give the man a shadow and keep the intrigue alive.

This attempt to have Carroll both ways, as both a national treasure and a vaguely suspect enigma, is not confined to these specific reports on papers up for auction. Indeed, the tendency to identify strange desires within Carroll but to stress that, in true "Victorian" fashion, he kept them buttoned inside, is not confined to popular journalism. We have seen variants on this reading in Bakewell, Thomas, and Cohen, and these biographies have, no doubt, informed the way McCrum, McVeigh, Gibbons, and Robinson approach Lewis Carroll. In journalism, however, the conflicts and subtleties that a biographer has room to explore over hundreds of pages are boiled down to basics and, as noted above, reduced to bold but often inconsistent statements reflecting Carroll's two-faced status as a contemporary icon. Any new discovery or sale of private papers is less a story about the auction than an opportunity to recycle familiar stories that ultimately say more about our ambiguous attitudes towards Carroll— genius but obsessed with children, a beloved part of our literary history but a troubling enigma—than they do about the man himself.

For a further example of this unsettled approach towards Carroll and his work, we can turn to one final source in the "heritage" category. Here the occasion and excuse is not a new cache of documents but the centenary, in 1998, of Carroll's death. The feature appeared in *History Today* magazine, and we might expect it to value established facts over comfortable myths; but to a large extent, it repeats the ideas that we saw in the reports above.

The article opens with the legendary moment of origin, and the same heavily loaded sense of literary destiny that we encountered in some biographical retellings: compare Cohen's dramatic "It had to happen" at the start of his chapter on the *Alice* books.[53]

> When Charles Lutwidge Dodgson climbed into the small boat moored on the river at Oxford in July, 1862 . . . he could little have known that the outcome of an innocent boat trip would be *Alice's Adventures in Wonderland* (1865), one of the best-loved children's stories ever written—and one of the darkest and fiercest controversies ever surrounding an author and his motivations.[54]

Already the author, Ian Fitzgerald, has introduced both the adored, "innocent" Carroll of heritage and the "dark", shadowy figure who still threatens to scandalise us. The next paragraph develops this notion of a double life.

At the time of his meeting with the Liddells, Dodgson had been a quietly
dull mathematics tutor at the college, the very model of an upright—and
uptight—Victorian gentleman. Ten years later, when Alice was published
under Dodgson's pseudonym, Lewis Carroll, his world had been turned
upside down: true, he had become the author of a timeless children's
classic, but he had also been forced to end his friendship with the Liddell
girls, being branded a morally suspect "friend" to Alice and her sisters.
By the time [Wonderland] was published Dodgson had severed all links
with the Liddells. Although they had allowed him much access to their
children, it seems the Liddell parents had always had their reservations
about the attention he paid their children and in 1863 something happened that caused an irreparable breach.[55]

There is more than a spoonful of fantasy in this "history". In 1865,
Carroll did not know, of course, that he was the author of a "timeless
children's classic"; this is a retrospective assessment. The image of Carroll
as tediously stuffy and conventional—with the implication that the Liddell
girls prompted him to both a rush of creativity and unhealthy fascina-
tions—is not especially justified: in 1855 he had recently published light-
hearted fiction and poetry in local newspapers[56] and just prior to meeting
with the Liddell children had, according to Cohen, enjoyed "a busy, sociable
vacation in the north and four days swanning about London."[57] However,
the construction of Carroll as a dry and prematurely middle-aged don is
necessary for the contrast with his other two contemporary roles, the
creator of enduring fantasy and the suspected pervert.

As we saw in Chapter 1, there is no proof that Carroll was "branded
a morally suspect 'friend' " to the girls—the sly inverted commas around
"friend" are presumably meant to suggest a sexual element—we only know
that there was a social split, a holding aloof, and then a gradual, partial,
more formal resumption of the acquaintance. The breach was not wholly
"irreparable", there was not a severing of all links, and there is no suggestion
that the Liddell parents had always harboured reservations about Carroll.
As Leach points out, if they had suspected him of being a sexual threat
to any of their children in any way, they would hardly have invited him
back to the Deanery in December 1866 and May 1867.[58]

Fitzgerald, like the biographers discussed in the previous chapter,
sees the rift with the Liddell family as a puzzle to solve. "Something
happened . . . that 'something' may never be known."

The common explanation is that the indulgence of the Liddells towards
their daughter's friend ended when the thirty-one year old Dodgson
asked for the hand in marriage of the eleven year-old Alice. One of

Dodgson's most recent biographers argues that this is too presumptuous, and forwards the more innocent explanation that Mrs Liddell, worried by Dodgson's intimacy with Alice, confronted him and that Dodgson, who saw his friendship as totally innocent, took mortal offence and broke off all contact with Alice and her sisters.[59]

Note that the theory of a marriage proposal has now become a "common explanation", despite having no evidence behind it apart from Oxford gossip, an ambiguous diary entry about "A. L.", and a ripped-out page that demanded to be filled in with guesswork. Florence Becker Lennon's speculation in 1945 that Carroll may have "proposed honourable marriage" has snowballed, gaining status over the decades to the point where a popular history treats it as the most likely truth.

In fact, as the previous chapter suggested, more than one of Carroll's "recent biographers" either reject or propose less sensational alternatives to the marriage theory. Fitzgerald fails to identify the author he has in mind but it could be Stoffel, who explains, "the Liddells may have asked him to keep company less often with the girls as they grew up. A suggestion of ungentlemanly behaviour would have been a great insult to him."[60]

Overall, the impression given by the latest biographies was that a proposal of marriage seemed unlikely, with only Cohen giving the idea much credence. It is telling, then, that the quasi-scholarly discourse of *History Today* prefers a far older, less rigorously researched version of the story. Fitzgerald is suspicious of the "recent" argument, which he describes as making Carroll into "a kind of holy innocent, an infant trapped in an adult's body whose true nature only reveals itself with other children." This is a strange response to the suggestion that there may have been less dramatic reasons for the social rift: it equates the Stoffel school of explanation—sensibly moderate, offering various possibilities—with the Stuart Collingwood conservatism that paints Carroll as an angelic celibate.

"The truth," Fitzgerald proposes, "probably lies somewhere in the shady area between the innocent and the sinister."

In later life he became notorious for his penchant for photo studies of partially-clothed and naked young girls. In fact, he eventually gave up photography when a whispering campaign against him in Oxford became too loud to ignore. Clearly, Dodgson's obsession with prepubescent girls cannot be discounted in any discussion of his work. At one extreme, psychologists have detected elements of 'cruelty, destruction and annihilation' and 'oral sadistic trends of a cannibalistic nature' in his work, others see it as a delightful and invigorating piece of nonsense.

At face value, this is precisely the dynamic I tried to pinpoint in my Introduction the dual image of Carroll as an innocent with an alter ego, of almost absolute goodness and sinister darkness, of naïve Victorian readings versus cynical Freudian interpretation. Yet as I argued of Bakewell and Thomas, the language makes its own insinuations, nudging us towards suspicion of Carroll's motives. While Fitzgerald claims he sees Carroll somewhere between innocence and perversion, the phrase "penchant for . . . partially-clothed and naked girls" is loaded with ideas of sexual fetish, and the idea that Carroll had an "obsession" with these girls is stated as a plain fact that "cannot be discounted." This is not a neutral portrait—"obsession" is enough to taint the reader's impression of Carroll—and Fitzgerald reveals his own beliefs more plainly in the closing sentence: "Whatever the truth, it is the case that most parents today would be happy for their children to listen to the story of *Alice's Adventures in Wonderland*—but they probably would not want Dodgson to be the man to read it to them."[61]

It is a wry ending, and it neatly conveys our contemporary ambivalence towards Carroll. He retains his nostalgic status as author of a much-beloved story, and yet modern journalism cannot resist hinting at his suspect sexual tastes: the contemporary intrigue and ongoing mystery must be balanced with Carroll's role in the "past" of English heritage. Fitzgerald ultimately handles these mixed feelings by separating author from text, Carroll from *Alice*—the book remains innocent and uncontaminated, but we are far from sure about the man who wrote it.

Alice's Lost Innocence

The articles so far have given some idea of the way journalism of the last decade regards Lewis Carroll and his relationship with Alice Liddell. What about the *Alice* books? Fitzgerald treasures them as an enduring treat for children, and as we have seen, many of the writers in the "heritage" section above still separate *Alice* from any of the more dubious rumours around Carroll. To Fitzgerald, *Wonderland* is "one of the best-loved children's stories ever written"[62]; to Langley, it is "that most innocent of fantasies"[63], while McVeigh calls it "one of English literature's best-loved stories."[64] Yet such uncritical perceptions of the *Alice* books as innocent and adored are actually in the minority; most discussions of Carroll's work in these recent articles look for more complex and often for "darker" meanings.

Robert McCrum's review of Gardner's definitive *Annotated Alice* conflates the real girl with the fictional character.

> He rowed Alice (and her sisters) on long boat rides up the Thames . . .
> adopting another persona—Lewis Carroll—he took her into the place
> he called 'Wonderland' and subjected her to all kinds of disagreeable
> imaginary friends, from the child-beating mother (the Duchess) to the
> psychotic chaperone (the Queen of Hearts).[65]

This over-simplistic assumption that Alice Liddell is precisely the same person as the *Wonderland* protagonist is unusual, but McCrum's perception of the books as a child's view of a brutal adult world is fairly typical of this sample. Adrian Mitchell, who adapted the two *Alice* stories for the Royal Shakespeare Company's Christmas 2001 production, proposes that once down the rabbit-hole, Alice is "a child among grown-ups and it's not a pretty picture."

> There are a lot of bad-tempered people, like the Queen of Hearts,
> shouting at her, the Mad Hatter is hectoring and the Caterpillar sneers
> at her. It's bewildering and frightening but then, for far too much of
> the time, it is frightening to be a child. Alice is put-upon but she deals
> with it. She dances into each encounter, is friendly with the White
> Queen and with the White Knight who is Carroll himself.[66]

This interpretation could almost be seen to contain elements of child abuse, although Mitchell places Carroll in the role of kindly protector rather than predator. The theory that Carroll meant to put himself into the story as the White Knight is far from original,[67] but in this case there is a literal truth to the parallel: the same actor, Daniel Flynn, played Dodgson, Dodo, and Knight.[68]

Carroll's prime motivation, says Mitchell, would have been to entertain the three sisters; he imagines the writer's internal voice. "Will Alice like this? Will this make Alice laugh?" George McCartney's review of Cohen's biography in the *Spectator* agrees. "Dodgson knew he had to make his audience laugh . . . [his] secret was that he was enough of a child to understand his audience."

> To their delight his stories subvert adult hypocrisy. [. . .] Dodgson
> creates a child's view of adult lunacy with this difference: in the course
> of events Alice grows large enough to dismiss these denizens of Wonder-
> land for what they are, a pack of cards playing a game by arbitrary
> rules. They represent the kind of adult pretension that always deserves
> to be laughed out of court.[69]

Christopher Hampton, director of *Alice's Adventures Under Ground*—a play for adults, which ran at the National Theatre in London during

1994—agrees. "They're a brilliant realisation of how irrational the adult world seems to a child; how hemmed in it is by incomprehensible ritual."[70] Hugh Haughton's *TLS* essay on Bakewell and Thomas's biographies finds at the heart of the *Alice* stories "Dodgson's dream identification with her child heroine. The writer sees through Alice's eyes."[71] Richard Jenkyns's review of Cohen also argues that *Wonderland* is a vivid attempt to depict a child's dream. "We can agree that the Caterpillar and the Queen of Hearts display some of the snappishness and unpredictability that children experience from grown-ups, but they are nonetheless creations of Alice's sleeping mind . . . some of the early parts of the book are also quite frightening, as adults easily forget."[72] By extension, Jenkyns views any readings of the books as localised satire—"to suppose that they represent Oxford dons and their wives"—as "flat literalism", robbing the stories of their anarchic invention.

Evidence of this literal interpretation is quite rare within my sample. McCrum notes that Gardner tries to explain characters like the Hatter[73] in terms of "Victorian trivia", but he becomes impatient with this approach, groups Gardner with "anoraks (scientists, computer nerds . . .)" and complains that the annotations are occasionally tedious.[74] Will Self, we will recall, had little time for what he saw as Gardner's cover-up of Carroll's sexual urges: he describes *The Annotated Alice* in peculiar terms as "malodorous . . . like the stinking petals of a rotting bloom", and compares the author to a trainspotter who shores up encyclopaedic factoids "of little relevance".[75]

Michael Williams dubs Gardner a "weird bird" for his "forensic, quasi-literary critical analysis"; his books are "to Carroll scholarship what taxidermy is to birdwatching", while his investigation shows mad avidity "but not much wisdom": "So, if you are the kind of Alice enthusiast who wants to know where the Cheshire Cat got its grin, or what made the Mock Turtle cry, or even the Anglo-Saxon provenance of "Jabberwocky", this is essential reading."[76] The sneer is almost audible in Williams's invitation to join the Alice anoraks.

Strangely enough, it was Robert McCrum who, in an earlier review of Jones and Gladstone's *Alice Companion*, credibly accepted every mapping of the fictional text to the real world of Carroll's experience, and applauded the sourcing of every character and event in the book to "Victorian trivia".

I did not know, for example, that Bill the Lizard was a play on the name of Benjamin Disraeli or that, speaking of Disraeli, the novelist and Tory Prime Minister is unmistakably represented (by Tenniel) as the Man in the Paper Suit in the *Looking-Glass* railway carriage. Again, it's intriguing to learn that the Walrus and the Carpenter is Carroll's not-so-gentle satire on the ideals of Walter Pater and John Ruskin, and that Tweedledum and Tweedledee were possibly modelled on Hallam and Lionel Tennyson, the Poet Laureate's reportedly ghastly sons.[77]

McCrum goes on to praise the authors—"indefatigable in their identification of every last scrap of Oxford gossip"—for telling him that "the Mad Hatter's Tea Party had its origin in a buttery dispute", and so forth. This is another example of the way newspaper pieces on Carroll seem intent on condensing reasonable doubts into bite-sized but unreliable "truths".

Jones and Gladstone are, for the most part, more circumspect than the review implies: they propose only that "Bill the Lizard has components of a pun on the name of a politician who was, to many Tories and Liberals, a slippery customer."[78] To McCrum, the equation between Disraeli and Bill has become a fact he is glad to learn. Jones and Gladstone note that "Walrus comprises the 'Wal' of 'Walter' and the 'Rus' of 'Ruskin' "[79]— their link to the two Oxford aesthetes is decidedly tenuous—and McCrum takes the poem eagerly as a direct satire. The idea that Disraeli appears as the man dressed in paper is a popular one—in fairness to McCrum, *The Alice Companion* treats it as a fact[80]—but Michael Hancher's thorough research into Tenniel's illustrations for *Punch* as well as the *Alice* books makes a good case that this is simply an unfounded myth.[81]

Williams and McCrum, like Self, observe that this joining of fantasy with Oxford reality tells us little about Carroll, whom they all see as a tormented figure—"an odd, unworldly loner" with a "psychic wound" to Williams, a "tantalising and disturbing character" to McCrum and, of course, an emotionally straitjacketed "dirty old man" to Self. Williams regrets *The Annotated Alice* "does not go down this troublesome avenue" and presents a picture "unclouded by any hint of Carroll's darker or unconscious side"[82], while McCrum decides that Gardner's book does reveal "the subconscious world of these haunting stories"—dipping a hand into the "dark currents" swirling inside *Alice*, while leaving her creator untouched.[83]

The perception that the books themselves are troubling and vaguely sinister is the most noticeable single trend in this sample of articles on *Alice*. Self suggests that both books are quasi-sexual dreams, with their characteristic "distortions in scale . . . surreal elisions," and "banjaxed language"[84] resulting from Carroll's repression of his unconscious paedophilia. Geoffrey Heptonstall, arguing from the opposite position, nevertheless makes reference to this interpretation in order to expose it as reductive. "No-one denies the quality of the Alice books, but they are treated as accidents emanating from a deviant's pathology."[85]

Michael Billington's *Guardian* review of Mitchell's RSC play also identi-fies hidden desires beneath the innocent fantasy, and praises the design of this adaptation for bringing them out: "a Jabberwocky whose protruding phallic neck reminds us that both books can be seen as a form of pre-pubescent sexual fantasy . . . Sarah Redmond's shapely Tiger Lily, the stuff of more grown-up dreams."[86] Indeed, the play's designer Peter McKintosh claimed in a *Birmingham Post* interview that he saw layers of potential meaning in the text, "a viewpoint with which post-Freudians would cer-tainly connect."[87]

This is, obviously, a continuation of the psychoanalytic reading sparked off by Goldschmidt in 1933, and it is interesting to see how central it remains to these reviewers' understanding of *Alice*. In addition to the references to Freud and the unconscious above, three of the seven articles on the RSC production complain that the play wasn't dark, sinister, or ambiguous enough. "OK, so this is the RSC's Christmas treat," Ian Johns concedes,

> So you wouldn't expect Alice's dream world to be touched by post-Victorian psychological scrutiny. But . . . Rachel Kavanaugh's produc-tion assumes that we know Carroll's characters so well that it neglects to create an adequate sense of just how disconcerting they are, with their bizarre Kafkaesque logic and murderous impulses.[88]

Kate Kellaway's *Observer* review, in contrast to Michael Billington's, criticises the production design for its infantile simplicity: "McKintosh's set evokes children's television programmes (*Jackanory* or *Playdays*) rather than a subtle Tenniel universe where illogic rules."[89] In the *Independent*, Kate Bassett sees the "bright slabs of colour and cartoon trees" as no reward for a lack of any challenge or adult complexity.

> Unfortunately, what's most perverse about Rachel Kavanaugh's produc-tion is that you're left wondering where all the magic went . . . Kava-naugh seems insensitive to the vulnerability, sadness and dark predatory sides of Carroll's creatures too. Ultimately you are clinging gratefully to any fragments of delightful or dark humour.[90]

There is a shared assumption here that the original text has an inherently troubled, disturbing quality beneath its lighter wordplay and banter, and that any modern adaptation failing to recognise this deeper, darker nature has actually missed the point. This is quite a shift from the apparently unanimous nineteenth-century opinion that the *Alice* books were a healthy dose of fun and nonsense—"an antidote to a fit of the blues" as the *Reader* cheerfully called *Wonderland* in 1865.[91]

As a postscript, we might consider a letter published in the London *Metro* during November 2001, which compared *Alice* to J. K. Rowling's *Harry Potter* books. Harry, says Samantha Maske, is

> taught the power of love . . . the message is about building strong friendships and fighting the battle of good and evil." By contrast, "Alice falls asleep and has a nightmare about a stoned caterpillar, a murderous queen who dominates her wimpish husband and many more bizarre creatures. Very moral.[92]

This interpretation, turning dream unequivocally to nightmare and implying violent sexual deviancy, also touches on the psychedelic readings of the 1960s for good measure: the idea that the Caterpillar's hookah contains mind-altering substances was touted in Thomas Fensch's essay "Lewis Carroll—The First Acidhead".[93] While they have triumphantly survived the twentieth century, Carroll's fantasies have changed shape since 1898. Rather than offbeat speculation, the idea that *Alice* has adult overtones and a dark heart seems to have become key to the way the story resonates in the broader public imagination.

The next chapter returns first to the batch of recent biographies, to ask how these scholarly texts construct *Alice* rather than Carroll. It then moves on to the books themselves—a sample of fresh editions that appeared at the turn of the twenty-first century—and looks at the way they introduce Alice to a modern readership. In Chapter 4, we at last see Alice, in the form of Helen Oxenbury, DeLoss McGraw, Lisbeth Zwerger, Mervyn Peake, and Arthur Rackham's illustrations. At least two of the picture-book editions were marketed for children, much as they were in 1865; but after all this controversy around her creator—now that her own adventures are assumed to be loaded with torment and bullying, with melancholy and malice—can Alice hope to retain, or perhaps regain, her innocence?

Notes

1. Lewis Carroll to his sister Mary (21 September 1893), quoted in Cohen, *Biography*, p. 189.
2. Review of *Alice in Wonderland*, *Aunt Judy's Magazine* (June 1886), quoted in Jones and Gladstone, *Alice Companion*, p. 224.
3. Uncited review of *Alice in Wonderland*, no date given, quoted in Jones and Gladstone, ibid.

4. Review of both *Alice* books, *The Athenaeum* (16 December 1872), quoted in Cohen, *Biography*, p. 133.

5. From *Punch*, (29 January 1898), quoted in Thomas, *Portrait*, p. 355.

6. Collingwood, quoted in Thomas, ibid. p. 354.

7. Anonymous friend, quoted in Bakewell, *Biography*, p. 337.

8. Beatrice Hatch, obituary of Carroll in the *Guardian*, no date given, quoted in Bakewell, ibid. p. 336.

9. "One Who Knew Him," obituary of Carroll in the *Daily Chronicle* (15 January 1898), quoted in Bakewell, ibid. p. 337.

10. *Lucy's Little Wonderland*, http://www.geocities.com/WestHollywood/Village/7974/MainPage.html.

11. The page became unavailable between my research of and writing of this chapter.

12. *Alice's Wonderland*, http://www.geocities.com/WestHollywood/Stonewall/6626/.

13. I am, of course, using the term in its modern sense of "child abuser", not as merely "lover of children".

14. *Lady Moonwise*, http://www.geocities.com/ladymoonwise/alice.html.

15. See *WiredPatrol*, http://www.wiredpatrol.org/news/archive/ukpaedophiles.html.

16. David Barrett, "The Ring of Evil," *Western Daily Press*, Bristol (14 February 2001), p. 4.

17. Ibid.

18. Jonathan Watts, "Japan Tackles Child Porn," *The Guardian* (27 April 1999), n.p.

19. Mary Kenny, "What Makes a Paedophile?" *The Express* (6 December 2000), n.p.

20. Matthew Sweet, "Malice in Wonderland," *The Independent on Sunday* (24 March 2002), p. 7.

21. Sweet, *Victorians*.

22. Jim Harding, "*The End of Alice* is a Cruel and Perverted Novel," *Daily Mail* (27 October 1997), p. 8.

23. Waldemar Januszczak, "Victorians and Nudity are a Dubious Mix," *Sunday Times* (4 November 2001), n.p.

24. Will Self, "Dirty Old Man," *New Statesman* 129, no. 4518 (25 December 2000), p. 88.

25. Ibid.

26. Cohen, *Biography*, p. 158.

27. See Cohen, ibid. pp. 68–69.

28. Leach, *Dreamchild*, p. 164. Edward Wakeling disputes the notion that Carroll owned any adult nudes, but agrees that he enjoyed looking at them. Wakeling, personal correspondence (12 October 2002).

29. Self, "Dirty Old Man."

30. Cohen, *Biography*, p. 530.

31. William Langley, "The Real Sin of Alice's Creator," *Mail on Sunday* (7 March 1999), p. 12.

32. Ibid.

33. Ibid.

34. Ibid.

35. Graeme Woolaston, "In the Shadow of the Dreamchild," *The Herald* (8 April 1999), p. 18.

36. Geoffrey Heptonstall, "The Real Lewis Carroll," *Contemporary Review* 275, no. 1603 (August 1999), pp. 104–6.

37. Ibid.

38. Ibid.

39. Langley, "The Real Sin of Alice's Creator."

40. David Robinson, "Letter Shows Alice Author Enigma," *The Scotsman* (21 November 2001), p. 3.

41. Fiachra Gibbons, "Looking Through A Glass Darkly," *Guardian* (28 November 2001), n.p.

42. Ibid.

43. Ibid.

44. Karen McVeigh, "2 Million Pounds for a Piece of Wonderland," *The Scotsman* (23 March 2001), p. 8.

45. Ibid.
46. See Cohen, *Letters*, p. 213.
47. Leach, *Dreamchild*, p. 172. The letter in question refers to Reginald Hargreaves as "the husband of one I can scarcely picture to myself, even now, as more than 7 years old.".
48. Robert McCrum, "Alice Under the Magnifying Glass," *Observer* (3 June 2001), n.p.
49. Ibid.
50. Ibid.
51. *Lewis Carroll, Photographer.*
52. McCrum, "Annotated Wonderland."
53. Cohen, *Biography*, p. 123.
54. Ian Fitzgerald, "Death of Lewis Carroll," *History Today* 48, no. 1 (January 1998), p. 36.
55. Ibid.
56. "Wilhelm von Schmitz" and "The Lady of the Ladle" in the *Whitby Gazette* (1854); see Cohen, *Biography*, p. 44.
57. Ibid., p. 59.
58. Leach, *Dreamchild*, p. 213.
59. Fitzgerald, "Death of Lewis Carroll."
60. Stoffell, *Life and Times*, p. 82.
61. Fitzgerald, "Death of Lewis Carroll."
62. Ibid.
63. Langley, "The Real Sin of Alice's Creator."
64. McVeigh, "2 Million Pounds for a Piece of Wonderland."
65. Robert McCrum, "Annotated Wonderland," *Observer* (19 November 2000), n.p.
66. Maureen Cleave, "Adrian's Adventure with Alice," *Evening Standard*, London (23 October 2001), p. 30.
67. "Many Carrollian scholars have surmised . . . that Carroll intended the White Knight to be a caricature of himself," Gardner, p. 249.
68. Adrian Mitchell, *Alice in Wonderland and Through the Looking-Glass* (London: Oberon Books, 2001), p. 9.
69. George McCartney, "Charles Dodgson through the Looking-Glass," *American Spectator*.
70. Cressida Connolly, "Dangerous Liasons," *Observer* (23 October 1994), p. 2.
71. Hugh Haughton, "The White Knight's Cult of Little Girls," *Times Literary Supplement* (8 August 1997), pp. 23–24.
72. Richard Jenkyns, "And Quiet Flows the Don," *New Republic* 215, no. 5 (29 January 1996), pp. 39–42.
73. I am indebted to Edward Wakeling for pointing out that the term "Mad Hatter" was never used in *Alice's Adventures in Wonderland*.
74. McCrum, "Annotated Wonderland."
75. Self, "Dirty Old Man."
76. Michael Williams, "Down the Rabbit Hole," *Observer* (21 October 2001), n.p.
77. Robert McCrum, review of *The Alice Companion*, *Observer* (12 April 1998), p. 15.
78. Jones and Gladstone, *Alice Companion*, p. 21.
79. Ibid., p. 32.
80. Ibid., p. 65.
81. Michael Hancher, *The Tenniel Illustrations to the Alice Books* (Ohio: Ohio University Press, 1985), p. 87.
82. Williams, "Down the Rabbit Hole."
83. McCrum, "Annotated Wonderland."
84. Self, "Dirty Old Man."
85. Heptonstall, "The Real Lewis Carroll."
86. Michael Billington, Review of *Alice in Wonderland*, *Guardian* (15 November 2001), n.p.
87. Richard Edmonds, "A Stylish Fantasy Weekend," *Birmingham Post* (22 December 2001), p. 37.
88. Ian Johns, "Little Wonder," *The Times* (15 November 2001), n.p.

89. Kate Kellaway, "The Looking Class," *Observer* (18 November 2001), n.p.

90. Kate Bassett, "Alice Loses the Plot," *Independent* (18 November 2001), n.p.

91. Review of *Alice in Wonderland*, *The Reader* (18 November 1865), quoted in Cohen, *Biography*, p. 131.

92. Samantha Maske, "Is Alice a more moral story than Harry Potter?" *Metro* (13 November 2001), p. 13.

93. Thomas Fensch, "Lewis Carroll—The First Acidhead" (1968), reprinted in Phillips, *Aspects of Alice*, p. 421.

3

ANALYSING ALICE

"Words mean more than we mean to express when we use them."
–Lewis Carroll[1]

Perpetually hovering between seven and seven-and-a-half,[2] yet over a hundred forty years old in real terms,[3] the fictional Alice has been adopted many times for causes that would have surprised, even shocked her creator. Carroll was aware that his books were being imitated during his lifetime, and regarded these pastiches charitably: he reported in 1891 that he had

> Got *Mabel in Rhymeland* . . . as part of the collection I intend making of books of the *Alice* type. Besides this, I have *From Nowhere to the North Pole* by young Tom Hood; *Elsie's Expedition* by F. E. Weatherly, and *A Trip to Blunderland*, by Jambon; and *Wanted—A King* by Maggie Browne.[4]

A selection of these stories is reprinted in Carolyn Sigler's collection *Alternative Alices,* and if nothing else these rather bland and flat nursery-rhyme tales help the reader appreciate the sparkle and sheer intelligence of the *Alice* books. Two years after Carroll's death, "Saki" (H. H. Munro) poked fun at Lord Salisbury's government in "The Westminster Alice", a satire published in the *Westminster Gazette.* "What did they learn?" Alice asks the Salisbury-Dormouse.

> "Painting in glowing colours, and attrition, and terminology (that's the science of knowing when things are over), and iteration (that's the same thing over again), and drawing—"

"What did they draw?"
"Salaries . . ."[5]

The political climate of 1910 called for a new Alice by "Loris Carllew", with Lloyd George as the Welsh Rabbit:[6] " 'quite the cheese' in fact, and where I live isn't Wonderland but Plunderland, except when I take my summer holidays in Blunderland . . ."[7] As Maggie Parham discusses in "What We Choose It To Mean", an article written for the 125th anniversary of *Wonderland*'s publication, both the First and Second World Wars saw a range of political parodies.

> Dyrenforth and Kester published *Adolf in Blunderland*, and had Hitler, an unattractive schoolboy, cowed by an encounter with the Red Queen. Michael Barsley produced a yet more sinister version of Jabberwocky: "Twas danzig and the swastikoves / Did heil and hittle in the reich. / All nazi were the linden groves, / And the neu-raths julestreich."[8]

Donald Thomas lists a mordantly satirical group of Alices around the time of Lewis Carroll's centenary in 1932, including Alice as Hitler playing croquet across Europe in the *Daily Express* of 31 October 1934, *Alice in Rationland* of 1939, and a Hitler-Goering Walrus and Carpenter in 1942; eight years later, a *Punch* series sympathised with "The Voter in Wonderland", who had to choose between identical Tweedle-twins at the 1950 General Election.[9]

As Stephanie Lovett Stoffel's *The Art of Alice in Wonderland* shows, this satirical use of Alice continued far beyond the end of World War II; the "Blunderland" pun was wheeled out again for an American comic book poking fun at government waste, with Alice swimming in a sea of red ink.[10] The Dodgson Family Collection at Woking includes various related artefacts such as a 1963 newspaper cartoon of Harold Wilson spouting "the time has come . . . to talk of many things, of dividends, and profit tax, and land, and clipping wings"[11], and Alice remained a regular inspiration for British political caricature in the late 1960s and 1970s, particularly in the work of the *Guardian*'s Leslie Gibbard.[12] Stoffel's most recent example, *Alice in Documentland*, dates from 1989.[13]

The French Surrealists of the 1920s and 1930s championed Alice and Carroll as honorary exemplars of their ideals. Louis Aragon translated Carroll's books, Max Ernst illustrated them, and André Breton likened Wonderland to "the more or less fragmentary phrases which, when one is alone and about to fall asleep, begin to run through the mind . . ."[14] The Surrealist Alice resurfaced in Salvador Dali's wildly vivid lithographs of 1969, published as a limited edition; their connection to Carroll's text is sometimes as hard to fathom as Max Ernst's depiction of the Hatter's Tea Party as a group of figures around a mustard-coloured triangle and a circle. It almost seems fitting that Louis Aragon had described Lewis Carroll as a "professor with a fair pointed beard."[15]

Meanwhile, Alice had been co-opted into advertising, where she "stared out from birthday books and biscuit-boxes."[16] BP petrol announced "the time has come, the mot'rist said",[17] while "Alice in Holidayland" promoted the North-East Railway, "Alice's Adventures in the New Wonderland" plugged the Yellowstone National Park,[18] and Guinness appropriated Father William:

> You are old, Father William,
> Without any doubt,
> Though your hair is persistently blond.
> Your vigour and vim you attribute to stout,
> Of a brand you're particularly fond.[19]

Stoffel's handsome volume of Alice art reproduces a poster from this Guinness campaign, with the Queen of Hearts ordering the head off a pint of stout ("Come and play croquet! Guinness builds strong muscles for sport!") and shows that Alice's career in advertising was still going strong during the late 1960s, in a Wonder Bread campaign. "My dear," announces the Duchess, "everyone knows Wonder Bread helps build strong bodies 12 ways! I approve!"[20]

By 1933 Alice had appeared in six film productions, if we include the seventy-five second newsreel *Alice in U.S. Land*, covering Mrs Hargreaves's trip to the States. The first cinema adaptation was a Cecil Hepworth short, only five years after Carroll's death, and two further silent productions in 1910 and 1915 were followed by the first talkie *Alice in Wonderland* of 1931: Martin Gardner reports that "the thump of the camera can often be heard."[21] A more distinguished Paramount feature was released two years later, with W. C. Fields as Humpty Dumpty, Gary Cooper as the White Knight, and Cary Grant as the Mock Turtle. Alice's popular image today owes most, perhaps, to the Walt Disney starlet of 1951, a stylised version of Tenniel's blonde in the blue dress: this particular take on Alice will be explored further in Chapter 9, while her more recent career in movies is discussed in Chapter 6.

We have had a taste of the psychoanalytic interpretations, both tongue-in-cheek and grimly sincere, in the Introduction. In 1936 Paul Schilder, taking his lead from A. M. E. Goldschmidt—whose reading is now suspected to be fraud rather than Freudian—detected "astonishing cruelty" and "oral sadistic traits of cannibalistic character" in *Alice*.[22] Like the Surrealist reading, this interpretation was no mere fad; in 1966 Kenneth Burke was still describing Alice as a "prim, well-trained potty-girl" and unsmilingly pointing out that the "cloacal ambiguities" in the picture of the dormouse in the teapot are "startlingly clear".[23]

On another note, the Red Queen and White Knight were lifted into scientific and mathematical theory, with the latter appearing in both Arthur Stanley Eddington's *The Nature of the Physical World* and Bertrand Russell's *The ABC of Relativity* during the 1920s. As Martin Gardner's *Annotated Alice* indicates, the inhabitants of Wonderland and Looking-Glass Land still prompt, or are used to illustrate, debates in science, mathematics, philosophy, and linguistics, from the issue of what the White Knight's song is really called[24] to whether Alice, counting "four times five is twelve", as actually working in base 18.[25]

The great modernist novelists paid their own idiosyncratic tributes to Alice. Virginia Woolf wrote her ethereal homage to the author in 1939, musing

> to become a child is to be very literal; to find everything so strange that nothing is surprising; to be heartless, to be ruthless, yet to be so passionate that a snub or a shadow drapes the world in gloom. It is so to be *Alice in Wonderland*. It is also to be *Alice Through the Looking-Glass*.[26]

Mark Burstein's invigorating online study "To Catch A Bandersnatch"[27] flies back and forth between Carroll and Joyce, revealing the linguistic threads between *Alice* and *Finnegans Wake* as Joyce takes the portmanteau theory of "Jabberwocky" to extremes:

> Alicious, twinstreams twinestrained, through alluring glass[28]

> All old Dadgerson's dodges one conning one's copying and that's what wonderland's wanderlad'll flaunt to the fair[29]

> Though Wonderlawn's lost us for ever. Alis, alas, she broke the glass! Liddell lokker through the leafery, ours is mistery of pain.[30]

That last phrase is knowingly used by Karoline Leach as the title for her chapter on Carroll's anguished prayers, and Martin Gardner points out further examples such as Joyce's "hatters hares" and "humptadump".[31]

Alice was translated into Russian by Vladimir Nabokov, inviting inevitable parallels between Carroll and Humbert Humbert, and placing Alice Liddell in the unwelcome role of Lolita. Martin Gardner assures his readers that while the "nymphets" of Nabokov are "creatures to be used carnally . . . Carroll's little girls appealed to him precisely because he felt sexually safe with them."[32] However, the comparison is still irresistible to some commentators; Will Self's review, discussed in the last chapter, rehashes Nabokov's remarks about Carroll's "wretched perversion and . . . those ambiguous photographs he took in dim rooms."[33] As Bakewell reminds us, Joyce had been wilier and wittier on the same topic, jibing at both "Lewd's carol" and the amateur analysts who tried to poke at his dreamchild's psyche: " . . . we grisly old Sykos who have done our unsmiling bit on 'alices, when they were yung and easily freudened, in the penumbra of the procuring room and what oracular comepression we have had to apply to them!"[34]

I mentioned the psychedelic reading of the *Alice* books at the end of the last chapter. It seems to have been sparked by Grace Slick and the Jefferson Airplane's woozy drug anthem "White Rabbit" (1967), with its menacing invitations: "one pill makes you larger and one pill makes you small . . . go ask Alice when she's ten feet tall."[35] The Beatles, particularly John Lennon, claimed to be influenced by both Carroll and Joyce, and identified an Alice theme in both "I Am The Walrus"—with its Humpty Dumpty egg-man—and "Lucy in the Sky with Diamonds".[36] The refrain "Goo goo g'joob", at the end of the former track, is supposedly taken from *Finnegans Wake*.

This approach to the books was enthusiastically taken up by Thomas Fensch in "Lewis Carroll: The First Acidhead" (1968), which Donald Thomas sceptically decides "bloomed into self-parody before the ink was dry on the paper."[37] Although it may seem comically far out to us now, Fensch throws himself energetically into the analysis, declaring of the Drink Me bottle, "when you take something that tastes like cherry tarts, custard, pineapple, roast turkey, toffee, and toast at the same time and makes you grow and shrink—baby, that's tripping out. Lewis Carroll told it like it is—and he told it in 1865".[38]

Perhaps surprisingly, this reading survives into the twenty-first century on at least one Web site—*Alice in the Shadows*, a "psychedelic rock and roll shadow play", promotes "a campfire gathering, a rock concert, and a story of nether dimensions. Featuring natural flame, translucent color characters, a projected light show and pyrotechnics, *Alice in the Shadows* animates the exotic literature of Lewis Carroll live on screen."[39] We might expect that the Carroll, who complained about the use of "damn" in the theatre,[40] would have been horrified by the association of Alice with LSD, but Thomas points out that he owned a study of *Stimulants and Narcotics*,[41] and as a man who at least toyed with the ideas that humans could communicate with fairies through an "eerie", trancelike state "such as we meet with in 'Esoteric Buddhism' ",[42] he may even have been charmed by this use of his work.

Interpreting Alice

Of the recent biographies discussed in Chapter 1, only some offer a concerted reading of the *Alice* books—usually favouring *Wonderland* and treating *Looking-Glass* as more of the same, but less spontaneous. Stoffel restricts herself largely to retelling the plot, which results in making the books sound pointlessly inane: "the White Rabbit sends her on an errand to his house, where she changes size, gets stuck inside, and scuffles with a lizard called Bill."[43] Christina Bjork chooses to focus more on Carroll and Alice's relationship than on the texts, mentioning the books only as they intersected with Alice's experience.

Gladstone and Jones offer a compendium of asides and explanations related to the books as well as to Carroll's life, often reliant—as we saw from the review in Chapter 2—on connections between Wonderland characters and "real life" individuals. These parallels range from the inarguable—that the Duck represents Robinson Duckworth—to the annoyingly tenuous: "The Cheshire Cat's long claws and teeth and insider's knowledge of the royal court, suggest that the Cat may have been inspired by the real-life figure of Canon (later Dean) Stanley (1815–51)."[44]

Karoline Leach has little time for *Wonderland* and *Looking-Glass*, devoted as she is to dampening the myth of Alice as muse and lost love; she thanks Alice Liddell for inspiring one of the greatest children's stories ever told and for pestering Carroll to write it down, but insists "the only book truly written for Alice Liddell was *Alice's Adventures Under Ground*."[45] Beyond that point, she argues, Carroll purposefully distanced his fictional Alice from the real girl.

> He never confused Alice with "Alice" as we do. She was never his "dreamchild", and he never pretended that she was. *His* Alice, the dreamchild, shared her name, but she enjoyed an entirely independent existence; "my dream-child (named after a real Alice, but none the less a dream-child)", a creature of his fancy, whose separateness he guarded jealously, almost pointedly. Even when he wrote the first draft of the Wonderland story his "little heroine" was already carefully differentiated

from the real child whose name she shared . . . Alice Liddell soon became largely irrelevant.[46]

Her interest in sketching a relationship between Carroll and Mrs Liddell leads Leach to concentrate on *Sylvie and Bruno*, where she finds an embodiment of the Dean's wife in both the divine Lady Muriel and the hateful Tabikat: in her enthusiasm she makes claims as bold and ultimately unprovable as those advanced by Jones and Gladstone.

> These two intensely drawn portraits are the two allegorical aspects of what one woman meant to Dodgson . . . they are both images of Lorina Liddell. [. . .] Since the Sub-Warden is Sibimet, and Sibimet is Henry Liddell, the conclusions for the initiated would not be difficult to draw.[47]

Leach only returns to *Alice* when it throws up some hint of Carroll and Lorina Liddell's relationship; the Duchess and Alice are considered as another possible allegory of the two illicit lovers.[48] Of this crop, then, only Morton Cohen, Michael Bakewell, and Donald Thomas try to get to grips with the *Alice* books afresh.

Cohen begins with the more obvious layers of meaning before moving onto what he sees as the deeper, universal themes. He states outright—and somewhat bafflingly—that Carroll wrote both *Wonderland* and *Looking-Glass* with "Alice Liddell . . . her sisters and Robinson Duckworth in mind."[49] Given that Carroll's friendship with Alice and the other Liddell girls had changed and cooled dramatically by the time he was writing *Looking-Glass* in 1866 and 1867, it is difficult to establish a basis for this theory; it seems simply to result from Cohen's desire to have both books represent Carroll's Oxford in disguised form for a readership who would recognise the in-jokes.

His opening interpretation, then, is in the Jones and Gladstone vein. "The actors in both *Alice* books are transplants from real life, as are the episodes . . . the landmarks, the language, the puns, the puffery—it was all rooted in the circumscribed enclaves of their Victorian lives."[50] To some extent, it would be foolish to dispute these connections—the treacle well has its source in a real medicinal well at Binsey, "Twinkle Twinkle Little Bat" parodies "The Star"—but some of Cohen's claims ring more hollow. There have been many theories as to the origin of the Cheshire Cat[51] but Cohen is certain that the only explanation lies in the "leopards from Cardinal Wolsey's coat of arms". He is equally certain that the Bat of the song was Carroll's colleague Professor Bartholomew Price—the notion was proposed by Gardner in 1960, but only as a possibility—that the Hatter's Tea Party was a direct parody of Alice's birthday celebrations and that Humpty Dumpty, in a vague piece of deduction, was "some egghead don pontificating".[52]

Cohen's next line of discussion is more general and perhaps more interesting than this literal translation.

> Underlying the characters, however distorted and exaggerated, is the cast-iron foundation of Victorian society, its shibboleths, class hierarchy, manners, conventions, proprieties, taboos and, perhaps most of all, its foibles and follies. The Victorian idea . . . of the child is at the heart of both stories, as are the child's observation of the adult world and the adult world's insensitive, abusive treatment of the child.[53]

We saw this reading of *Alice* as a child's view of adulthood in a selection of the newspaper articles, but Cohen develops it further until the books become a full-blown allegory of growing up to emotional maturity. Cohen maintains that the fable is a "double-layered metaphor"[54], both rooted in the specifics of Victorian culture and universal enough to explain its appeal to children all over the world, a century after Carroll's death.

> For Charles, intentionally or not, got at the universal essence of childhood and captured the disappointments, fears and bewilderment that all children encounter in the course of daily living. He wove fear, condescension, rejection and violence into the tales, and the children who read them feel their hearts beat faster and their skin tingle, not so much with excitement as with an uncanny recognition of themselves, of the hurdles they have confronted and had to overcome. Repelled by Alice's encounters, they are also drawn to them because they recognize them as their own. These painful and damaging experiences are the price children pay in all societies in all times when passing through the dark corridors of their young lives . . . [55]

"Dark corridors" is heady, heavy stuff to draw from a book that was originally reviewed as an airy, nonsensical confection. However, Cohen becomes even more intense as he describes the reader and Alice embarking on "a survival course . . . determining whether their resources are strong enough to get them through. Does Alice have the wit necessary to master the maze of childhood and emerge a tried and tested teenager?"[56] His breathless analysis at this point—Alice is given "the means of dealing with a hostile, unpredictable environment"[57]—has odd but unmistakeable similarities to the following passage: "Embark on a twisted journey to save a Wonderland gone bad . . . undaunted by the diseased atmosphere, confusion, and mortal danger that surrounds her, Alice commits to set it right."[58]

Far removed from Cohen's scholarly biography but very much alike in tone, this is the back-cover blurb to American McGee's violent, horror-genre PC game, which will be discussed at length in Chapter 7. Cohen's reading of *Alice* as the story of a child's struggle against the incomprehensible cruelties of adult life—with far more of dark nightmare about it than whimsical dream—is not an isolated interpretation. It finds company in many of the analyses from Chapter 2's newspaper sample, and may even have helped to shape the understanding of people like Adrian Mitchell, who intended his dramatic adaptation of *Alice* to show "a child among grown-ups" in a "bewildering and frightening" environment.[59]

However, Cohen provides no empirical evidence for his hugely sweeping conclusion—there is no suggestion that he actually asked any children for their opinion of the books, or even established that young readers still bother with Carroll—and there is a troubling contradiction in his claim that, while supposedly firmly rooted in Victorian society of the 1860s, the *Alice* adventures also "affect all children of all places at all times in a similar way."[60] Finally, his view of the books as reflections of a bleak and terrifying journey to maturity are countered by his firm opinions, a couple of pages on, that they are also perennially hilarious to children "young or old"[61] and broke the mould of the Victorian fairy story by offering something "lighter and brighter."[62] Again, there is no evidence supplied for his assertion that the punning in *Wonderland* is "as funny today as it was in 1866, and it will continue to amuse for centuries."[63]

When we bear in mind that Cohen also wants the books to function on one level as Carroll's autobiography—"the *Alice* books become, in this metaphor, a record of Charles's childhood"[64]—and yet maintains towards the end of the chapter that "sense and meaning" in the text is perhaps not as important as "sound and feeling" in the language[65], it is hard not to feel that he is juggling incompatible readings, unwilling to settle for one alone. It would be foolish to proclaim that the books only have one valid interpretation, but Cohen seems to like all of his equally, and to be unaware that they clash.

Michael Bakewell begins his analysis by touching on the "child's view of adults" interpretation—"in Wonderland it is the adult world, as represented by the weird array of characters that Alice encounters, which is badly behaved"[66]—but moves swiftly on to stress the story's localised, personalised meanings. Unlike Cohen, Bakewell insists that "the *Adventures*"—by which he seems to mean both *Under Ground* and *Wonderland*—were told "*to* three little girls, but . . . *for* only one of them."[67] From this reasonable standpoint, he launches into a theory that would almost fit with the psychoanalytic readings.

> What gives the *Adventures* their remarkable flavour is the way in which Dodgson so absolutely identified with Alice as to become her. Because of the intensity of his feelings for Alice Liddell, Dodgson assumed something of her personality, while at the same time the Alice of his story assumed his. The dream child and the child-adult merge into one personality—the personality of Alice.[68]

This tangled network of links between girl, man, and fictional character depends on an understanding that Alice Liddell was Carroll's obsession, that Carroll was locked into a child-like emotional state, and that the "Alice" of the story is closely linked to the Alice of the river trip. We have already seen that each of these assumptions is contentious; the idea that Carroll was a "child-adult" is especially old-fashioned, and could have been lifted from Woolf's assessment of 1939 that "childhood remained in him entire."[69]

So Lewis Carroll "becomes" Alice Liddell, at least in part, and he channels this persona—a thirty-year-old's idea of a ten-year-old girl—into his fictional creation. Then, however, Bakewell informs us, Carroll also "becomes" Wonderland itself. Or rather half of him does, because Bakewell splits the man in two here and proposes that while Dodgson is Alice, Carroll is the world she walks through.

> Dodgson/Alice is being taken on a tour of Lewis Carroll's imagination. On the one hand we have the spinsterish, meticulous, nervous don who, even when in a state of free-fall down a rabbit hole, would always take the precaution of putting an empty marmalade jar where it could not fall and hurt anyone; on the other we have the anarchic, subversive eccentric who rejoiced in setting improbable conundrums for his colleagues (rather like the Mad Hatter . . .) or delighted in running the risk of offending Mrs Grundy.[70]

Again, this supposition depends on a specific understanding of Lewis Carroll: most notably, that he was a Jeykll-and-Hyde type whose "spinsterish" persona conflicted with his "anarchic", creative side. It is hard to make this theory work. Even Bakewell's passage above makes it plain that Carroll enjoyed puzzles while in his "Dodgson" mode at Christ Church. Carroll's letters to child-friends are equally playful and teasing when signed "your loving friend, C. L. Dodgson"[71]; it was "C. L. Dodgson" who wrote to Gertrude Chataway to delight in his visits from eighteen-year-old girls and to boast that " 'Mrs Grundy' has made no remarks at all."[72] Charles Dodgson was clearly a complex man whose behaviour and attitudes often seem bewilderingly inconsistent, but there is surely no need to give him an alter ego: Lewis Carroll was a rigorously defended pen-name but not a separate persona.

Bakewell agrees with Cohen, and with many of the journalists from Chapter 2, that Wonderland is a "nightmare world", with death-jokes waiting for the heroine like hidden traps; "Alice wonders what it would be like to be snuffed out like a candle and twice comes near to shrinking out of existence."[73] The "void" Bakewell identifies at the heart of Wonderland comes from Carroll's own troubled psyche—the "anxious thoughts" he tried to fight with pillow problems, the torments at his own lack of self-worth. Within this metaphor, Carroll is creating Wonderland as an allegory for his own spiritual crises, and walking himself through it as Alice. However, Bakewell also maintains that the fictional Alice contains aspects of Alice Liddell, and that she would have been "justifiably alarmed", reading or listening to the story, "at the prospect of what was going to happen to her next."[74]

The analysis then shifts feet and takes off again with the assumption that the character Alice was an avatar of Alice Liddell, transported from 1860s Oxford directly into the fantasy world.

> Alice is an inquisitive, lively, highly self-possessed little creature who is very much the product of the Deanery and of Miss Prickett's instruction . . . what Wonderland does is to subvert and undermine the Miss Prickett world . . . even the sanctimonious improving rhymes she has learned at Miss Prickett's knee begin to take on a wholly individual new existence . . . [75]

While Bakewell offers an interesting account, similar in some ways to Cohen's, of Alice's struggle with Wonderland's inhabitants—from an initial clinging to familiar meanings to an acceptance of the new rules and an aggressive conquering of the tyrannical Queen—he shrinks the book into something more trivial than it really is by insisting that the fantasy world's threats are all linked to Carroll's "own vertiginous doubts"[76] and that the heroine represents a specific little girl. This reading of the text as the story of Alice Liddell/Charles Dodgson in Carroll's subconscious results in both looping flights of psychological speculation and ploddingly literal conclusions: Bakewell winds up calling the fictional Alice's sister "Lorina", as if there were no distinction between the girl in the boat and the one in the book.[77]

Donald Thomas shies away from broader, universal meanings—in contrast to Cohen, who builds much of his argument on the books' perennial appeal whatever the context—and tries to ground Carroll's writing in a specific cultural surrounding or literary tradition. He initially relies on a combination of the Jones and Gladstone approach, seeking real-life personalities behind every fabulous beast, and the Gardner method of hunting down "factoids". He accordingly opens his discussion by comparing the Caterpillar to the Broad Church don Benjamin Jowett, sourcing the Cheshire Cat to a *Notes and Queries* debate of the 1850s and finding the Mouse's dry lesson in Havilland Chepmell's *Short Course of History* of 1862.[78]

At this point Thomas pauses to remark, in common with Cohen and Bakewell, that the *Alice* tales contain "much that was macabre, cruel and . . . sadistic", locating them in a mode of "corrupted romanticism" and "the art of the grotesque" with a debt to de Sade.[79] "Most people who are underground", he reminds us with reference to *Wonderland*'s original title, "are dead."[80] It is "beyond proof" that Carroll intended a parallel to Homer and Virgil's accounts of a trip to the underworld in the *Odyssey* and the *Aeneid*, and the creatures of Wonderland find ancestors or cousins in the Chimera, the Gryphon, and the Furies. Alice survives a perilous journey, as she did in Bakewell and Cohen's interpretations, but here it is presented as a specific echo of classical epics.

> Alice, like Aeneas, emerges unscathed from the dream, he by the gate of horn and she to the Oxford river bank. The horrors and predictions which Virgil's hero encountered were implacable and unalterable. But Alice triumphs. However cruel their humour or authoritarian their manner, the figures of tyranny are, at last, "nothing but a pack of cards," and the Red Queen as Fury "really *was* a kitten after all."[81]

The sources and echoes Thomas finds are often unexpected and original. Having demonstrated some correspondence between *Alice* and the *Aeneid*, he then takes the reader through the criminal law of 1850–1865 and argues that the trial of the Knave of Hearts "presented a burlesque version of the system whose reform was a major topic of news and discussion in English society at mid-century." He is as sure of this link as he was about the classical analogy: "art, in Dodgson's courtroom, followed life."[82]

Carroll followed developments in criminal psychiatry, so his fascination may have spilled out into the "psychopathic royalty and the mentally alienated bourgeoisie" of Wonderland.[83] Carroll had discovered, in photography, "a world where time stands still", and he transferred it to the eternal six o'clock of the Hatter's Tea Party.[84] In turn, Carroll's philosophical questions about perception and existence in the Red King's dream were taken up, as noted above, by Bertrand Russell, while the White Knight's distinction between his body and mind was used by Roger Holmes to illustrate Cartesian Dualism. Furthermore, "Dodgson's treatment of time and space was to prompt comparisons with Einstein and Eddington."[85]

Towards the end of his analysis, Thomas returns to the Jones and Gladstone paradigm and looks for references to Carroll's contemporaries in the *Alice* books. To his credit, he remains cautious about the connections, asking "was Queen Alice a representation of Victoria Triumphans? Was the Red King a spectre of Archdeacon Dodgson?" but for the most part sticking to questions rather than statements. He is certain that the Lion and the Hatter of Tenniel's illustrations were based on *Punch* cartoons of Gladstone, and makes a persuasive argument that the extinct or mythical creatures of Wonderland—Dodo, Gryphon, the doomed Bread-and-Butter Fly—reflect "the Darwinian debate of 1859–60" and "the pre-historic exhibits at the University Museum."[86]

The *Alice* books, Thomas concludes, "have a claim to be the cleverest fiction ever written in English," and Thomas's explanation of the various parallels across academic fields is very clever in itself. However, he spends more space and time reconstructing the context than he does looking at the actual text—a page and a half on the legal system is followed by half a page on its relevance to one scene from *Wonderland*—and the detail of his background continually threatens to swamp the foreground figures of Alice and Carroll. The books themselves are pulled in briefly for examination, then pushed away again.

Introducing Alice

Three major new editions of the *Alice* books were published around the turn of the twenty-first century: the centenary Penguin *Wonderland*, *Looking-Glass*, and *Under Ground* in a single volume (1998); the definitive third edition of *The Annotated Alice* (2000); and the Bloomsbury versions of each book with illustrations by Mervyn Peake (2001). Each was a prestigious release, offering up an old favourite for the new millennium with fresh packaging and extra features; each, to some extent, included a modern reassessment of these Victorian children's stories. The Bloomsbury *Alices* showcased short introductions by novelists Zadie Smith and Will Self, Martin Gardner added new annotations and reproduced his prefaces from the previous editions, and the Penguin volume included a substantial essay by the writer and academic Hugh Haughton.

Haughton's is certainly one of the most accomplished engagements with *Alice* I have personally encountered: sharp, deft, and glittering with wordplay, it casts the net wide, drags in details from the two adventures and nimbly carves them open. Haughton is fully aware of the interpretive heritage he inherits here, from Nabokov through Woolf to Disney, and begins by establishing two schools of thought on the books: those who choose to enjoy them merely as a pretty nonsense (broadly speaking, the nineteenth-century approach) and those who insist the text has hidden meanings that they want to shake out (to generalise, the twentieth-century method). Which path we opt for depends partly on whether we see the *Alice* books as stories for children or adults, and at this point Haughton agrees with all the analyses in the previous section that what they provide on one level is "a child's view of adulthood . . . dismayingly bizarre and perverse."[87] The ability to see *Alice* as delightful whimsy certainly seems to have been lost; whatever age the books are assumed to appeal to, there is an overriding agreement—both in this chapter and in the newspaper reports of the last—that this appeal is "dark" and based on the recognition that growing up is an assault-course.

He then takes a detour into biography, and into the least sparkling section of his introduction. The life of Carroll given in these sixteen pages is conventional enough in its details, but Haughton wholeheartedly subscribes to the theory that Carroll was fixated on little girls and, more specifically, was romantically infatuated with Alice Liddell. This is a familiar part of the Carroll myth, but it is surprising that the man introducing *Alice* to a new century embraces it so warmly and uncritically, with less equivocation than either Bakewell, Thomas, or Cohen. The falling back on a pat notion of the repressed paedophile and his child-muse seems strangely old-fashioned, and Haughton's decision to treat the secondary evidence at face value results in a conveniently but misleadingly straightforward account. This may simply be another example of space-time compression, with the uncertainties we would expect in a book-length biography flattened into facts when an entire life has to be crammed into sixteen pages.

Carroll is portrayed here as a rather dull man with one intriguing abnormality: "a dream of childhood, focused on the figure of a beautiful young girl. [. . .] The anomaly's first name and incarnation was Alice Liddell, and it was in the shadow of Alice's name . . . that Dodgson lived his later life."[88] While "the nature of Dodgson's love of Alice remains a subject of speculation"[89]—"he never explained the nature of their friendship"—there is no doubt in Haughton's mind that he loved her; not just regarded her with affection, but "was head over heels in love" with her.

This is a pretty solid statement that leaves little room for further guesswork; neither is there much ambiguity in the description of the "haunting, yet subliminally creepy photographs" of the Liddell girls. The images themselves are easily read: Haughton agrees with Bakewell that they "tell us, if nothing else, he was in love with Alice."[90] She was the "only begetter" of *Wonderland*,[91] and the social break from the Liddells—a "dramatic rift"[92]—prompted a lovestruck Carroll to write an elegy for her in the prefatory poem to *Looking-Glass*, "as if she was dead." Haughton mentions all the usual clues to a possible love-relationship between the little girl and the don—the diary entry about A. L.—"presumably Alice Liddell", he explains—the gossip from Lord Salisbury, and the anguished prayers at the time of his "banishment" from the Deanery.

As already implied, Alice Liddell is represented here as just the primary incarnation of Carroll's internal ideal; his love for her was symptomatic of his "mysterious paedophile sexuality."[93] Like many other commentators, Haughton's makes sly insinuations that whisper of an erotic aspect to Carroll's child-friendships: he had an "obsessive fascination with girls before puberty,"[94] he was "the Casanova of the Victorian nursery", his diaries are a "roll-call of conquests", he used Eastbourne for "cruising."[95] The last word in particular carries connotations of "queer" deviance—"cruising" still implies a gay pick-up—and conjures the stereotype of the predatory loner seeking anonymous sex. The *Alice* books—and here Haughton echoes Morton Cohen's analysis—allowed Carroll to channel this weird erotic drive by placing himself in the persona of a young girl, exploring "his identifications with his child heroine"[96] and combining this intense passion for prepubescent females with his equally fervent investment in questions of mathematical and linguistic meaning.

When he moves on to this latter area, Haughton's findings are far more original and provocative. While not going to the literalist extremes of Gladstone and Jones—or, in places, Donald Thomas—he argues that Carroll's dream worlds were built "out of the details of Alice Liddell's actual environment"[97] and perceptively notes that although Carroll himself presents the stories "as if Alice travels to some fairyland of pastoral childish innocence,"[98] both fantasies are constructions of "culture, not nature".

> . . . Alice is confronted by grave travesties of most of the institutions which govern her and her author's life—the monarchy, the rule of law, education, grammar and social etiquette. [. . .] Having discussed growth and reproduction with a caterpillar and pigeon, and madness with a brainy disembodied cat, Alice finds herself in the more complex rituals of Wonderland society—first the endlessly rotating Mad Tea

Party, with its parodies of a parlour-song recital, children's story . . . and tea-time etiquette; then the shambolic royal croquet game . . . then, to cap it all, the Mock Turtle and Gryphon's nostalgic Old Boys' duet about their schooldays.[99]

There is no attempt to say that the Gryphon was inspired by Ruskin, as Jones and Gladstone characteristically suggest;[100] the point made here is that Wonderland is a stylised Victorian realm on a level that goes beyond specific links between fictional creature and real-world individual. Looking-Glass Land, Haughton observes, is "if anything, more systematically constricting than that of the earlier book . . . less anarchic than Wonderland but no less threatening as a mirror of modernity."[101] Holding up this fictional world like a snow-globe, Haughton examines its juxtaposition of the mythic British past with "the communication networks of Victorian England". His language becomes beautiful.

> In the tonally bleaker, more elegiac *Through the Looking-Glass*, the winter sequel to the Maytime trip to Wonderland, Alice's sense of self hardens in the colder, more political climate she finds six months later . . . the air grows cold in the region of mirrors. The looking-glass . . . leads into the world of Victorian mediaevalism and the "dark wood" of Spenserean Romance, albeit in a comically warped form. It is a world where modern railways, newspapers and postal systems interlock with Quixotic knights, lions and unicorns.[102]

In this light, Tenniel's artwork is the only possible match for Carroll's monstrously warped version of 1860s culture:

> His graphic idiom, however fantastic and allegorically grotesque, is as pedantically referential as an exhibition catalogue of Victorian social types, settings, furniture and costume—just like Dodgson's own. When Alice travels underground and through the glass, it is not only her unconscious dream world that she finds—but Victorian England, and the world of the Oxford establishment she shared with Dodgson.[103]

Again we are reminded that this is a harsh world for a child to wander through; Haughton sees various horrors in the dream landscape: "terror and appetite", a "lovely garden" but also a "pool of tears", a "random violence and competitiveness", "a disconcerting madness." And yet this analysis offers a satisfying reason why Alice should be forced to struggle. *Wonderland* and *Looking-Glass* deal with the biggest issues in her life, and perhaps in the lives of all her peers: "food and the food-chain, growing and ageing, manners and madness, childhood and adulthood, freedom and rules, authority and identity."[104] These concepts do not merely apply to children, or to the Victorians, and they are huge themes to grapple with: it makes sense that the dreamworlds should involve loneliness, loss, and the threat of death.

While playing down the influence of direct satire, contemporary debates and Oxford squabbles as "muted and indirect", Haughton convincingly locates the books as projections of their specific period in a broader sense. However, their appeal has to be explained beyond a Victorian social allegory, and Haughton maintains that their deeper, most central theme is the construction of identity and meaning. Alice is, measuring herself against what she remembers from the real world ("I ca'n't be Mabel . . . "), "very much a child of her time and class,"[105] but questions of who we are and what words signify are, of course, broad-ranging enough to apply beyond Alice's schoolroom. "Who am I?" is, Haughton suggests, "the question that the best novels . . . return to again and again,"[106] and it recurs constantly in the *Alice* books, from "I'm sure I'm not Ada"[107] to "who are *you?*"[108] to "you're only a sort of thing in his dream!"[109] The context of the question may be specific to Lewis Carroll, Alice Liddell, and their contemporaries, but the question itself is, arguably, part of what makes us human.

So far, then, some form of consensus is emerging as to what recent commentators feel the *Alice* books are "about". They are grounded in their specific social context, although there is disagreement about the extent to which they intentionally reflect or parody individuals, debates, and locations in Alice Liddell and Lewis Carroll's lives. They are concerned with the child's experience in an adult environment and with the process of growing up, with finding a sense of self. This environment is frequently brutal and cruel; Wonderland and Looking-Glass Land are commonly seen as nightmarish rather than light-hearted dreamworlds. The stories contain something of Lewis Carroll's intense attitudes towards childhood, whether he is understood to have invested himself in the character of Alice or projected his own ideal of Alice Liddell into the protagonist. In any case, they are far from nonsensical: they are packed with heavy-duty, "adult" meanings about language, identity, maturity, and death.

Martin Gardner's contribution to this discussion is probably more influential than any other. Though reissued for 2000 as the final word in Alice encyclopaedia, Gardner's *Annotated Alice: The Definitive Edition* reproduces the introduction from his original *Annotated Alice* of 1960 and follows it with the *More Annotated Alice* preface of 1990, which contradicts a number of points from the first essay. The only brand-new introduction is a brief note on the text, a page long. The dominant voice here, then, is from 1960.

Gardner explains his project almost apologetically, anticipating objections to any book that threatens to ruin the innocent fun of *Alice*; "but no joke is funny unless you see the point of it, and sometimes a point has to be explained."

> . . . we are dealing with a very curious, complicated sort of nonsense, written for British readers of another century, and we need to know a great many things that are not part of the text if we wish to capture its full wit and flavor. It is even worse than that, for some of Carroll's jokes could be understood only by residents of Oxford, and other jokes, still more private, could be understood only by the lovely daughters of Dean Liddell.[110]

So the books' dependence on a specific context is established, although a more universal meaning is also implied; Gardner does not say we cannot appreciate or enjoy the *Alice* stories at all without knowing the background, only that certain levels of reference will remain obscure. Unlike Cohen, he fears that children of the late twentieth century, especially American children, do not read and enjoy the books; young readers are "bewildered and sometimes frightened by the nightmarish atmosphere of Alice's dreams."[111] The stories' immortality, to Gardner, lies entirely in the fact that they are still studied by adults, by "scientists and mathematicians in particular", and so his own annotations are addressed to this audience. As such he roundly confirms the notion that *Alice* is a dense text for grownups, to the point that he places the hopes for the books' future in wholly adult hands. I might point out here that I first read Gardner at age nine, and adored him.

On the whole, *The Annotated Alice* avoids the Jones and Gladstone method of seeking direct parallels between every character and an Oxford notable; his explanations are generally more dependably solid, noting for instance that a fender is a kind of fireguard,[112] that "washing—extra" meant a boarding school that sent out the laundry,[113] and that whiting did appear to have their tails in their mouths when laid out in a fishmonger's window.[114] Gardner warns that he has no truck for psychoanalytic readings, which at the time of his writing qualified as "recent". "We do not have to be told what it means to tumble down a rabbit hole," he rumbles, "or curl up inside a tiny house with one foot up the chimney."[115] There will be no room for the "oral sadistic traits of cannibalistic character" here, for Gardner prefers the explanation that "small children are obsessed by eating and like to read about it in their books."

However, Gardner's Carroll does not escape analysis. "The point here is not that Carroll was not neurotic (we all know he was) . . . " The account of the author's life that follows is dated, though with some justification given the period in which it was written. His external self was "dull"—this is in keeping with the Virginia Woolf theory that Carroll, as Dodgson, "had no life"[116]—"he was a fussy, prim, fastidious, cranky, kind, gentle bachelor whose life was sexless, uneventful, and happy."[117] Photography was one of his "hobbies", on the same level as making a mouse from a handkerchief or folding a pistol from paper. He had a "fixation upon little girls" yet "professed a horror of little boys, and . . . avoided them as much as possible."[118] He took photographs of nude little girls, of which "none seems to have survived"; Gardner amends this note in the preface to *More Annotated Alice* below, but lets it stand here.

"A long procession of charming little girls . . . skipped through Carroll's life, but none ever quite took the place of his first love, Alice Liddell."[119] There is no "hint of impropriety" to his relationships or indication that Carroll consciously approached girls with anything other than "the purest innocence"; there is no evidence that he wanted to marry Alice or "make love to her", but "his attitude towards her was the attitude of a man in love."[120] At this point Gardner offers his parallel with Humbert Humbert, contrasting the carnal passion for "nymphets" with Carroll's feelings of sexual safety in young female company; this idea that Carroll felt his passions comfortingly neutralised by children is, we might remember, the line that was later taken by Donald Thomas.

"It is easy to say," Gardner observes, "that Carroll found an outlet for his repressions in the unrestrained, whimsically violent visions of his *Alice* books."[121] Indeed, this is precisely what Cohen and Haughton conclude. Gardner, however, declines to come down on either side of the question, and leaves it hanging here. As to the broader meaning of *Alice*, he approaches the issue by comparing the books to Kafka and G. K. Chesterton. The ultimate moral in all three, whether expressed through grim fable or "metaphysical nightmare,"[122] is that life is nonsense. It is a tale "told by an idiot mathematician . . . we all live slapstick lives, under an inexplicable sentence of death."

In the preface to *More Annotated Alice* that follows directly on the tail of this essay—correcting, contradicting, and sometimes overlapping with the previous piece—Gardner reconsiders the question as to whether the stories channelled Carroll's repressed energies, and wavers towards the conclusion presented by Hugh Haughton. The *Alice* books were, he decides, a flood of creativity produced by the twinning of Carroll's two internal streams—the passion for logic, linguistics, and numbers and the enthusiasm for the company of young girls. The question as to whether Carroll was in love with Alice is reconsidered in the light of more recent data, and we get a sense here of the shifts that occurred in Carollian studies between the 1960s and 1990s: the cut diary is mentioned as part of the proof that "Mrs Liddell sensed something unusual in his attitude towards her daughter,"[123] and Gardner includes a lengthy quotation in which Morton Cohen changes his mind.

> Actually, I didn't change my mind recently; I changed it in 1969 when I first got a photocopy of the diaries . . . I believe now that he made some sort of proposal of marriage to the Liddells, not saying "may I marry your eleven-year old daughter," or anything like that, but perhaps advancing some meek suggestion that after six or eight years, if we feel the same way that we feel now, might some kind of alliance be possible?[124]

The definitive edition of this influential text, then, very strongly gives the impression that Carroll was not just in love with Alice but that he "expressed marital intentions to Alice's parents." There is no more interpretation of the actual books offered in the introduction, but of course Gardner's analysis continues throughout the extensive notes (he admits to rambling) that run in columns of tiny print alongside the text. His comments on *Alice* fall into several categories, yet for the most part offer inarguable explanations and background rather than speculation; he is true to his word about steering clear of psychoanalysis. Some of his contextualising betrays an American perspective and imagined readership: "treacle" is translated as "molasses,"[125] "barley sugar" is described in plod-dingly pedantic terms,[126] and "take care of the sense, and the sounds will take care of themselves" is given its origin in the familiar British proverb about pence and pounds.[127]

There are occasional ventures into the Jones and Gladstone field, with a firm statement that the "drawling-master" is "none other than the art critic John Ruskin"[128] and "little doubt" that the man in white paper is Benjamin Disraeli.[129] This confident, possibly overconfident assumption that the dream worlds contain thinly disguised figures from 1860s England intersects with Gardner's theories about Carroll and Alice when he tells us the White Knight's farewell is a secret message from the author to his love: "This scene, in which Carroll clearly intends to describe how he hopes Alice will feel after she grows up and says good-bye . . . "[130] The Wasp, from the suppressed Chapter Eight-and-a-half of *Looking-Glass*, is also presented as a mouthpiece for Carroll's appraisal of Alice—"there never was such a child!"—but not as another authorial self-portrait; Gardner accepts that the class-conscious Carroll would not have allowed himself to guest-star as a mere drone.

Other notes fulfil Gardner's promise to provide Victorian references for the satire, such as the source for "Father William,"[131] the possible birthplaces of the Cheshire Cat,[132] and the potential causes of the Hatter's insanity.[133] There are occasional discoveries of accidental inconsistency in the text and Tenniel illustration, as when the Cheshire Cat appears in the same tree despite the fact that Alice has "walked on"[134] or the milk-jug fails to appear either in the description or drawing of the Tea Party, yet gets tipped over two pages later.[135] For the most part, though, the notes are content to point toward trivial and intriguing side roads from the main route of Carroll's story; it is entirely possible to ignore them and the detours may distract, but the off-track rambling is often fascinating.

Finally, the two briefest and most recent introductions from this group: Will Self and Zadie Smith's prefaces to the Bloomsbury *Alice* books are essentially "celebrity" cameos, intended as a showcase for two contemporary, relatively young and high-profile novelists to do a turn about *Alice*. The point, presumably, is more about linguistic flair and idiosyncratic authorial stamp than scholarly analysis, and so these are quite different from either Haughton or Gardner's essays. Self's prose is garnished with arcane, swallowed-a-dictionary vocabulary—"the pun is . . . a numinous fulcrum", "these few short scenes . . . are wholly ensorcelling"[136]—while Smith's often slips into a grating arm-round-the shoulders familiarity, musing "Oh man, darker, yes" and nodding "yeah, that's what I thought."

Both take a personal, unashamedly subjective view of the books—Smith admits she "couldn't quite remember"[137] *Looking-Glass* when she came back to it after a number of years, and recalls being "more *afraid* of Tenniel's drawings than amused"[138]—but Self is unique in devoting his five opening pages to memories of *Wonderland*.

> The boy sits among a slew of records, 45s and LPs, some in their sleeves, some out. In front of him is a portable record player, a heavy, foursquare cabinet, with grey cloth stretched over its wooden sides, a black lid, and a rubber mat on the turntable . . . the LPs are dramatisations of *Treasure Island* and *The Count of Monte Cristo*, there's also a London Symphony Orchestra recording of Prokofiev's *Peter and the Wolf*, with Peter Ustinov doing the narration.[139]

One of the 45s is an adapted dramatisation of *Alice in Wonderland*, and through "these few short scenes" the young Will Self is drawn into the sticky May afternoon with Alice on the riverbank; "he wanders in her train, through the hypercast of the fervid imagination itself . . . "[140] Although the record lasted only fourteen minutes, Self claims that it included the opening scene and rabbit hole, the Pool of Tears, Bill the Lizard, the meetings with the Caterpillar, Duchess, and card-gardeners, and the Hatter's Tea Party. It is pretty hard to see how all these episodes, complete with dialogue and songs, could be crammed into a quarter of an hour, but as the experience is constructed as a precious and unreachable gem from distant childhood, we should perhaps allow for idealisation.

Although he touches on the various cultural uses of *Alice* in the twentieth century—"from James Joyce to Jefferson Airplane"—and makes a topical snipe at the "child abusers on the internet"[141] who stole Wonderland, the remainder of Self's introduction is about what the books mean to him personally. We learn about his first encounter with the pages as opposed to the vinyl of *Wonderland* ("a particularly luxurious edition"[142]), about the role of Carroll's language in his own childhood and in the lives of his children (an "inter-generational epiphany"[143]), and about the part *Alice* plays in his career as a novelist.

> When people ask me (as they often do) what books have influenced me most as a writer I almost always detail the same three: Swift's *Gulliver's Travels*, Kafka's *Metamorphosis* and Carroll's *Alice's Adventures in Wonderland*. What these three share is a marvellous confidence in the primacy of the imagination, and a conviction that the fantastic is anterior to the naturalistic.

Here Self comes closest to pinning down the "meaning" of *Alice* in his own terms—and comes closest to Martin Gardner when he implies that the books are about the fundamental chaos of the real world, exaggerated and revealed through a parallel universe:

> . . . the juxtaposition of the quotidian and the fantastic; the transposition of irreconcilable elements; the distortion of scale and a means of renouncing the sensible in favour of the intelligible; and most importantly, abrupt transmogrification conceived of as integral to the human condition. [. . .] The word "curious" appears so frequently in Carroll's text that it becomes a kind of tocsin awakening us from our reverie. But it isn't the strangeness of Alice's Wonderland that it reminds us of—it's the bizarre incomprehensibility of our own.[144]

Zadie Smith's approach to *Looking-Glass* is also a closer cousin to Gardner's analysis than to any other—interesting, given that his thoughts on the book are more than forty years old. Like him, she brushes aside "Mr Freud and the rest",[145] while proving unable to resist a comparison to Humbert Humbert and Lolita; the difference to her is that Lolita was possessed by Humbert, constructed through the adult gaze, and "seen through his glass", while Alice "remains untouched", "always and every-where herself."[146] Carroll, she suggests, loved his child-friend and dreamchild "without at all *impinging* on them"; she calls this hands-off adoration a "noble instinct" in the author, which comes as a refreshing contrast to the whispering campaigns in recent journalism about his preda-tory perversions.

As in Haughton, Gardner, and the biographies discussed above, Car-roll's real-life relationship with Alice Liddell is seen to shape the text intimately. *Looking-Glass* is to Smith, as *Wonderland* is to Cohen, a story about Alice Liddell's growing up to maturity, "from eternal seven-year-old to fully grown woman."[147] In common with Gardner, Smith subscribes to the belief that Carroll inserted himself as the White Knight to say goodbye and wave her off into womanhood: "I think it was very hard for Carroll to watch her go." The real Alice and fictional Alice are confusingly merged in this interpretation, which seems to assume the two are one and the same: the name is used indiscriminately to describe the Dean's daughter and the Carroll character in adjoining sentences.

Smith, like Self, runs through some of the text's broader meanings and cultural significance, although she has little more time for the linguistic uses of *Alice*—"neither big, I fear, nor clever"[148]—than she does for the Freudians, the "sexologists", or the logicians.[149] She spends a while on her own personal feelings about portmanteaus, making rather strained connections with early-1990s culture such as Nirvana's "Smells Like Teen Spirit" and Normal Schwartzkopf's pronouncements on the Gulf War[150]; Carroll's humour is traced vaguely down through P. G. Wodehouse and Kingsley Amis to Monty Python,[151] and Alice's importance is compared, not altogether flatteringly, with that of Harry Potter. "We have kept her this long," Smith proclaims for her generation, "and we will not lose her yet."[152]

The main reason for these new editions, though, is not Carroll but Mervyn Peake, whose 1940s illustrations have been digitally restored. Unsurprisingly, both Self and Smith approach him through Tenniel, whose images of Alice are, in Self's words, "a given".[153] Peake himself admitted that Tenniel was "inviolate, for he is embedded in the very fabric of childhood memories."[154] However, Self compares Peake's style favourably with the "undifferentiated planes of colour, which typify Tenniel's work."

These are quite distinct from Peake's own fluidity of line, let alone his subtle interpenetrating of stippling and adumbration. The Tenniel illustrations are hieratic—many of them take the form of tableaux. Certainly Tenniel's Alice is a plangently Victorian miss, a mannish boy-woman, let loose in a crowded, bourgeois drawing-room of painfully arranged knick-knacks and taxidermy. Whereas Peake's Alice is more eroticised and more downbeat. In the opening drawing, the curve of her hip acts as an insinuating portal to the netherworld, and her eyes are dilated with dewy astonishment.[155]

This is a chunky piece of writing, convincingly recreating the stilted quality of Tenniel's images: it echoes Haughton's observation above that "however fantastic and allegorically grotesque", Tenniel's depiction of dreams remain "as pedantically referential as an exhibition catalogue of Victorian social types, settings, furniture and costume."[156] Smith's response to the two very different styles is remarkably similar, suggesting perhaps a shared cultural and generational attitude towards Tenniel as the man behind a respected but slightly stuffy establishment *Alice*. She too praises Peake's technique with line, judging it more suited to the "encroaching darkness" of *Looking-Glass* than Tenniel's static, unchanging style from *Wonderland* to the altogether colder world of the sequel: " . . . perfectly textured background cross-hatching imbues many of the drawings with a certain foreboding; the delicate shadowing on faces, in forests, in wool shops, on walls, creates a kind of scotopia in the reader—everything you're looking at is fading, pretty much, or dying, or *leaving* . . . "[157]

This vision of *Looking-Glass* as elegiac, a fable of loss, is familiar from Haughton's commentary, and it can also be found in Bakewell, who finds "images of decay, mutability and fading beauty haunt[ing] the pages of the book."[158] However, Smith's real enthusiasm is reserved—oddly, perhaps, after she has hymned his darkness—for Peake's sense of fun.

Though only a fool would cast any serious cloud over Tenniel . . . as a child I remembered being more *afraid* of Tenniel's drawings than amused—such severe-looking birds, such aggressive flowers, such a frowning, school-marmish Alice! It makes a nice change, then, to see a wide-eyed beatific Alice in her crown, not to mention a wide-eyed positively *camp* March Hare (in ballet pumps? And a *skirt?*)[159]

These latter two introductions are most valuable not in what they say about Carroll—apart from the personal reminiscences, their observations can be found in expanded form elsewhere—but in what they suggest about Tenniel's role; what Tenniel makes of Alice and her world, and how it changes when his stage-setting, costuming, and casting is replaced with someone else's vision. And that's another chapter in itself.

Notes

1. Lewis Carroll, letter (1896), quoted in Gardner, *The Annotated Snark* (Harmondsworth: Penguin, 1979), p. 22. Cohen dates the letter as August 18, 1884; see Cohen, *Biography*, p. 409.
2. As she is seven in *Wonderland* and seven and a half in *Looking-Glass*, the age of the fictional Alice fluctuates depending on which book we refer to, and so, arguably, cannot be fixed.
3. That is, from the moment of her origin during the river trip of July 1862.
4. Carroll, diary entry (11 September 1891), quoted in Hugh Haughton, "Introduction" to *Alice's Adventures in Wonderland and Through the Looking-Glass* (London: Penguin, 1998), p. lix.
5. Saki, *The Westminster Alice* (London: John Lane, The Bodley Head, 1927), quoted in Thomas, p. 358.
6. This satire may have inspired Gilbert Adair's Welsh Rabbit in *Through the Needle's Eye*; see Chapter 5. See also Chapter 9 for Lloyd George's further association with the White Rabbit.
7. "Loris Carllew," *Alice in Plunderland* (London: Eveleigh Nash, 1910), quoted in Thomas, *Portrait*, p. 359.
8. Maggie Parham, "What We Choose It to Mean," *New Statesman and Society* (1 November 1991), p. 36.
9. Thomas, *Portrait*, p. 361.
10. Stephanie Lovett Stoffel, *The Art of Alice in Wonderland* (New York: The Wonderland Press, 1998), p. 90.
11. DFC F/35/14, cartoon by Illingworth (4 October 1963) document in Surrey History Centre, Woking.
12. The *Centre for the Study of Cartoons and Caricature* Web site has examples online. http://library.ukc.ac.uk/cartoons/collections/database.php.
13. Stoffel, *Art of Alice,* p. 10.
14. Thomas, *Portrait*, p. 366.
15. According to Bakewell, *Biography*, p. 345.
16. Parham, "What We Choose It to Mean." p. 37.
17. DFC F/34/2 (1928) document in Surrey History Centre, Woking.
18. Stoffel, *Art of Alice*, p. 18.
19. Parham, "What We Choose It to Mean."
20. Stoffel, *Art of Alice*, p. 18, p. 91.
21. Gardner, *Annotated Alice*, p. 330.
22. Schilder, in Phillips, ed., *Aspects of Alice*, p. 286.
23. Kenneth Burke, from "The Thinking of the Body," in Phillips, ibid. pp. 342–43.
24. Gardner, *Annotated Alice*, p. 256.
25. Ibid., p. 23.
26. Woolf, in Phillips, *Aspects of Alice*, p. 48.
27. Mark Burnstein, "To Catch a Bandersnatch," http://www.lewiscarroll.org/bander.html.
28. James Joyce, *Finnegans Wake* (New York: Viking, 1959), p. 528.
29. Ibid., p. 374.
30. Ibid., p. 270.
31. Gardner, *Annotated Alice*, p. 70, p. 228.
32. Ibid., p. xx.
33. Ibid., p. xxx.

34. Joyce, *Finnegans Wake* (London: Faber & Faber, 1939), p. 115, quoted in Bakewell, *Biography*, p. 345.

35. Grace Slick, "White Rabbit," Phillips, *Aspects of Alice*, p. 419.

36. See Bakewell, *Biography*, p. 344.

37. Thomas, *Portrait*, p. 365.

38. Fensch, in Phillips, *Aspects of Alice*, p. 422.

39. *Alice in the Shadows*, http://balibeyond.com/alice/index4.html.

40. See Cohen, *Biography*, p. 307.

41. Thomas, *Portrait*, p. 365.

42. See Cohen, *Biography*, p. 369.

43. Stoffel, *Art of Alice*, p. 69.

44. Jones and Gladstone, *Alice Companion*, p. 35.

45. Leach, *Dreamchild*, p. 178.

46. Ibid., p. 175.

47. Ibid., pp. 187–88.

48. Ibid., p. 197.

49. Cohen, *Biography*, p. 135.

50. Ibid., p. 136.

51. See Gardner, *Annotated Alice*, pp. 62–64; see also Chapter 9 for further claims to the Cat's origin.

52. Cohen, *Biography*, p. 136.

53. Ibid., p. 137.

54. Ibid., p. 138.

55. Ibid., p. 138.

56. Ibid., p. 139.

57. Ibid.

58. Cover blurb, *American McGee's Alice* (Rogue/E.A. Games, 2000).

59. Quoted by Maureen Cleave, "Adrian's Adventures with Alice."

60. Cohen, *Biography*, p. 140.

61. Ibid., p. 140.

62. Ibid., p. 143.

63. Ibid., p. 140.

64. Ibid., p. 139.

65. Ibid., p. 143.

66. Bakewell, *Biography*, p. 139.

67. Ibid., p. 140.

68. Ibid.

69. Woolf, in Phillips, *Aspects of Alice*, p. 48.

70. Ibid., p. 140.

71. See for instance the letter to Edith Blakemore of 27 January 1882, signed "Dodgson" and including a cartoon of himself eating a cannonball of a plum pudding. Reproduced in Cohen, *Letters*, p. 114.

72. Lewis Carroll to Getrude Chataway (7 September 1890), quoted in ibid., p. 198.

73. Bakewell, *Biography*, p. 141.

74. Ibid.

75. Ibid., pp. 141–42.

76. Ibid., p. 143.

77. Ibid., p. 144.

78. Thomas, pp. 155–56.

79. Ibid., p. 156.

80. Ibid., p. 157.

81. Ibid., p. 160.

82. Ibid., p. 162.

83. Ibid., p. 163.
84. Ibid., p. 164.
85. Ibid., p. 165.
86. Ibid., p. 166.
87. Haughton, "Introduction," p. xiii.
88. Ibid., p. xix.
89. Ibid., p. xxi.
90. Ibid., p. xx.
91. Ibid., p. xxiii.
92. Ibid., p. xxi.
93. Ibid., p. xxii.
94. Ibid., p. xix.
95. Ibid., p. xxvi.
96. Ibid., p. xxv.
97. Ibid., p. xlii.
98. Ibid, p. xlvi.
99. Ibid.
100. Jones and Gladstone, *Alice Companion*, p. 113.
101. Haughton, "Introduction," p. xlvii.
102. Ibid., p. xliv.
103. Ibid., p. xliii.
104. Ibid., p. lx.
105. Ibid., p. xli.
106. Ibid., p. xl.
107. Carroll, *Alice's Adventures in Wonderland*, reprinted in Gardner, *Annotated Alice*, p. 23.
108. Ibid., p. 49.
109. Carroll, *Through the Looking-Glass*, reprinted in Gardner, *Annotated Alice*, p. 199.
110. Gardner, *Annotated Alice*, pp. xiii–xiv.
111. Ibid., p. xiv.
112. Ibid., p. 20.
113. Ibid., p. 102.
114. Ibid., p. 109.
115. Ibid., p. xv.
116. Woolf, in Phillips, *Aspects of Alice*, p. 47.
117. Gardner, *Annotated Alice*, p. xvii.
118. Ibid., p. xviii.
119. Ibid., p. xix.
120. Ibid., p. xx.
121. Ibid., p. xxi.
122. Ibid., p. xxiii.
123. Ibid., p. xxviii.
124. Cohen, quoted in Gardner, *Annotated Alice*. p. xxix.
125. Ibid., p. 80.
126. Ibid., p. 94.
127. Ibid., p. 96.
128. Ibid., p. 102.
129. Ibid., p. 182.
130. Ibid., p. 262.
131. Ibid., p. 51.
132. Ibid., pp. 61–62.
133. Ibid., p. 69.
134. Ibid., p. 71.
135. Ibid., p. 74.

136. Will Self, "Introduction," Lewis Carroll and Mervyn Peake, *Alice's Adventures in Wonderland* (London: Bloomsbury, 2001), p. viii.
137. Ibid., p. ix.
138. Ibid., p. xv.
139. Self, "Introduction," pp. vii–viii.
140. Ibid., pp. viii–ix.
141. Ibid., p. xii.
142. Ibid., p. xi.
143. Ibid., p. xii.
144. Ibid., p. xiii, p. xvii.
145. Smith, "Introduction," p. vii.
146. Ibid., p. viii.
147. Ibid., p. ix.
148. Ibid., p. xi.
149. Ibid., p. x.
150. Ibid., p. xiv.
151. Ibid., p. xii.
152. Ibid., p. xvii.
153. Self, "Introduction," p. xv.
154. Quoted in Self, ibid.
155. Ibid., p. xv.
156. Haughton, "Introduction," p. xliii.
157. Ibid., p. x.
158. Bakewell, *Biography*, p. 173.
159. Ibid., p. xv. Her liberal use of italics for indignant or astonished stress could be paralleled with the pastiche of Carroll's style I identify in Adair, Noon, and Roiphe's novels in Chapter 5, and with fan "performance" in Chapter 9.

4

ILLUSTRATORS OF ALICE

"Enchanting Alice! Black and white has made your deeds perennial;
And nought save 'Chaos and old Night' can part you now from
Tenniel."

—Austin Dobson[1]

When John Davis wrote the introduction to Graham Ovenden's *Illustrators of Alice in Wonderland* in 1972, the books had already been interpreted by "well over a hundred artists."[2] As the introduction to Peake's edition suggested, all these artists worked in the shadow of John Tenniel, whose slightly sulky miss is still the girl we call to mind when hearing the name Alice. Even the blander version from the Disney studios owes much to his template; the stockings and black strapped shoes, the waisted dress and white apron, the blond hair held back with what became known, in her honour, as an Alice band.[3]

Tenniel enjoyed, or rather tolerated, a close working relationship with Carroll that at times approached joint authorship. The artist ordered the first edition of *Wonderland* to be withdrawn because of inferior printing[4] and recommended that the Wasp in a Wig chapter be cut because it was "beyond the appliances of art"[5] and "does not interest me in the least".[6] In turn, Carroll specified the size and position of each drawing, offered his own sketches as a guideline, and apparently encouraged Tenniel to use a life model as the basis for Alice—an invitation Tenniel declined. While the identity of this girl has become a matter of myth and rumour—some say she was Mary Hilton Badcock, daughter of the Dean of Ripon, but there is a rival claim from Kate, daughter of the *Punch* editor Mark Lemon[7]—the fact that author and artist debated the issue is clear from

Carroll's indignant report to Gertrude Thompson that "Mr Tenniel . . . resolutely refused to use a model."[8] In any case, *Wonderland* and *Looking-
Glass* saw an unusual level of collaboration and creative dispute between
the two men who first imagined Alice.

> Dodgson gave very specific instructions as to the shape, dimension and
> content of each illustration and its exact place on the page in relation
> to his text and provided his own drawings as a guide. Tenniel was
> simply required to contribute his professional skills as a draughtsman.
> He had never been treated like this in his life, and, very naturally,
> resented it . . . [Carroll] had carefully studied the way in which other
> stories for children had been illustrated, and in producing his own
> drawings for *Alice's Adventures Under Ground* he had seen exactly how
> text and picture could be most effectively integrated.[9]

However, the towering precedent set by Tenniel has not deterred other
artists from trying their hand.

> Clearly these books have fascinated artists in the same way as they have
> appealed to readers. The treatment of Carroll's characters has varied
> from the surrealistic to the mundane: contemporary events and attitudes
> are frequently reflected—the cost of the Mad Hatter's hat fluctuating
> with current prices, the Playing Cards wearing Prussian helmets in pre-
> 1914 illustrations, demarcation-conscious Trade Unionists disputing over
> the painted rose tree in 1957.[10]

These topical variations, similar to the culturally specific readings
discussed in the last chapter, tend to belie Davis's surprising assertion that
the *Alice* characters "are meticulously described by Carroll, who left little
scope for the artist to do much more than embellish the story."[11] In fact,
Carroll rarely describes the characters at all in visual terms. The reader
who wants to know what a Gryphon is receives the curt instruction "look
at the picture."[12] That Alice has long hair is only suggested by the fact
that it drips into the water as she leans to catch the scented rushes in
Looking-Glass;[13] there are very few details of her appearance given in the
text.[14] Iconographic traits like the Hatter's price tag and the Hare's crop
of straw were invented by Tenniel, not Carroll; and when Carroll does
specify an aspect of the characters' appearance, it is ignored as often as
it is acknowledged. The Duchess's chin is described as "uncomfortably
sharp",[15] but both Peter Newell and Mervyn Peake, two of *Wonderland*'s
most distinguished illustrators, turn a blind eye to the direction.

Davis notes that while only three alternative illustrated editions were ventured during Carroll's lifetime—indifferent spin-offs such as *Alice and Other Fairy Plays* (1880), illustrated by Mary Sibree[16]—a flood of new *Wonderland*s followed the author's death in 1898, and the end of the book's copyright in 1907 prompted "an almost indecent rush by publishers to produce editions with new illustrations; at least eight being published in the autumn of that year."[17]

> From 1908 onwards new illustrators tackled Alice in Wonderland almost every year. Each obviously contributed his own style and expertise but few produced a really original approach and many seemed prosaic in performance as if under instructions from their publisher to illustrate Lewis Carroll's book after *Robinson Crusoe* and before *Grimm's Fairy Tales*.[18]

Cooper Eden's gorgeous edition of *Wonderland*, compiling the work of more than thirty illustrators, includes plates from 1907–1908 that match this description. W. H. Walker's Mock Turtle is precisely like Tenniel's—bear in mind that the calf head and tail were the artist's invention, never specified in Carroll's text—and his vision of the croquet ground is cluttered with what look like badly drawn versions of Tenniel's court cards.[19] Even in more accomplished illustration like that of K. M. R. from 1908 or Maria Kirk from 1907, Tenniel's images of the Duchess, Hatter, and Hare have clearly influenced the character design.[20] As we shall see below, Tenniel's 1865 conception of *Wonderland*'s cast continued to influence illustrators of *Alice* at the end of the twentieth century.

Davis singles out Arthur Rackham, "the first artist to bear comparison to Tenniel", for the "haunting quality" and sombre atmosphere of his 1907 Wonderland, with "browns and greys predominating" and backgrounds "which occasionally dominate the characters".[21] We should note that even Rackham, whose interpretation is now regarded highly enough to be reprinted in a lush new edition,[22] was condemned for daring to challenge Tenniel, and turned down an offer to illustrate the sequel because he was so "shaken by the negative reviews."[23]

Some might also value the eerie monochrome of Peter Newell's 1901 illustration,[24] or Mabel Lucie Atwell's cute but occasionally creepy cartooning of 1910,[25] or the confident, elegant draughtsmanship of Harry Furniss (1926), who had valiantly illustrated *Sylvie and Bruno* some thirty-seven years previously.[26] They do not move John Davis; after Rackham, he finds nothing but a "barren wilderness" until 1929 and Willy Pogany's Art Deco Alice, "a '30s American bobbysoxer with a page boy hairstyle."

This "milestone in the artistic characterisation of Alice" featured club cards "as West Point cadets, the diamonds and hearts straight from the

Willy Pogany's Alice.

Ziegfield Follies chorus line, whilst the spades are obviously members of the painters' and decorators' union."[27] Davis passes no comment on the fact that Pogany's Cook is an African American "Mammy" stereotype, or on the unmistakeable connotations of pubertal change when his Alice, looking like a teen fashion drawing in a department store catalogue, twists her hands in her lap and meekly offers, "I can't help it . . . I'm growing."[28]

From the following decades, Davis enjoys Edgar Thurstan's "mature" Alice of 1931, with apparent references to the Wall Street Crash—"his Humpty Dumpty reminds one of an insecure business executive just about to fall off his chair"—and Phillip Gough's "rococo" illustrations (1949), including the Tweedle twins as "minor French courtiers."[29] D. R. Sexton's Alice from 1933 is even more mature—a pouting, heavy-lashed nymphet who looks more suited to a candy bar wrapper[30]—and J. Morton Sale's dreamchild of the same year looks like a poised, self-possessed young woman in her late teens or early twenties, wearing lipstick, heels and an evening gown for her adventure and showing the clear suggestion of a bust.[31] When she perches next to the White Queen, they could be taken for sisters.

The "most memorable interpretation,"[32] in Davis' eyes, is that of Mervyn Peake. Graham Greene's comment to Peake, in a personal letter, is now well-known; it is reproduced on the back cover of the Bloomsbury

J. Morton Sale's Alice.

editions, and Davis quotes it here. "You are the first person who has been able to illustrate the book satisfactorily since Tenniel, though I still argue as I think I argued with you years ago that your Alice is a little bit too much of a gamin."[33] Why Greene used the masculine form for Alice, rather than *gamine*, is not clear. Davis, prefiguring Will Self and Zadie Smith, describes Peake's pen-and-ink drawings as "weird, almost macabre" and like Smith, sees them as even more suited to the autumnal *Looking-Glass*.[34] Recent commentary on Peake's *Alice* tends to agree: Hilary Spurling in the *Observer* remarks that it was "too subversive for immediate acceptance" of this "strange, skewed vision."[35] She quotes Henry Tube's description of this Alice as "an infant Bardot . . . peering through the grasses like a sultry puma" and Malcolm Muggeridge's Cold War comparison of the Mad Tea Party to "an international conference at the highest level."[36]

Ralph Steadman's interpretations of *Wonderland* and *Looking-Glass* are the next landmark, although Davis neglects them in his introduction.

Ralph Steadman's Alice.

Steadman's *Alice in Wonderland*, published in 1967, won the Francis Williams Memorial behest in 1972 for the best-illustrated book of the previous five years; the award coincided with his centenary edition of *Through the Looking-Glass*. While aggressively contemporary in many ways—Steadman's March Hare performs a John Cleese-style Nazi goosestep, his Jabberwock is horned with mushroom clouds and adorned with the Union Flag, and the Tweedles are bowler-hatted businessmen[37]—this stark, op-art vision of Carroll's world can also be seen as strangely loyal to the original.

This White Knight is clearly drawn from Carroll's self-portraits and his farewell to Alice is spread over four pages of illustration, stressing its supposed importance as a fictional goodbye from the author to Alice

Liddell. If the references sometimes seem more suited to political car-tooning—the Lion as a sulky English sportsman, the Hatter dressed like one of Alex's droogs from Kubrick's *Clockwork Orange* (1971)—precisely the same could be said of Tenniel's caricatures of a century before. Alice herself wears the dress, bow, striped stockings, and long hair Tenniel gave her, although her leap into adulthood is marked by a sudden acquisition of breasts. The most unnerving thing about these pictures, however, is how strikingly the heroine resembles the young Lady Diana Spencer, who would not enter the public eye for almost another decade.

Between Steadman's *Wonderland* and its sequel came Peter Blake's 1970 series of watercolours. Celebrated by Davis as "superb", these are uncanny snapshots from a world of grotesques; a photorealistic Alice, pouty and freckled, mixes with a Mad Hatter who resembles the young Mick Jagger crossed with Roald Dahl's Willy Wonka, dressed in chocolate cords, bottle-green socks, and psychedelic shirt. The 1980s and 1990s saw no slowing in the tide of new interpretations; Davis and Ovenden's guide stops with the 1970s, but two excellent websites demonstrate that a score of international versions appeared during the last decades of the twentieth century, from Barry Moser's looming, luminous creatures of 1982 through Greg Hildebrandt's rich, deep paintings of 1990 to David Frankland's oddly old-fashioned, scratchy art for the 1996 Ladybird book.[38]

The five books under discussion during the rest of this chapter were all published around the year 2000, and, like the new introductions above, they present an interesting picture of Alice entering a new millennium. All are interpretations of *Wonderland* rather than *Looking-Glass*, the latter having received less attention. Arthur Rackham's 1907 illustrations were reissued in a lavish SeaStar edition of 2002; Mervyn Peake's, as we have seen, were published as two Bloomsbury volumes in 2001. The other three are Lisbeth Zwerger's picture book *Alice in Wonderland* of 1999, Helen Oxenbury's *Alice's Adventures in Wonderland* from the same year, and DeLoss McGraw's *Alice's Adventures in Wonderland*, published in 2001.

McGraw, based in Los Angeles, trained as a fine artist in the 1960s. Before approaching *Alice* he had already illustrated a number of books for children, including Edward Lear's *The New Vestments* (1995). His Wonder-land is depicted in eye-poppingly gaudy gouache and an abstract style. Zwerger, born and trained in Vienna, came to *Alice* after having won praise for her *Wizard of Oz* (1996); her illustration of *Wonderland* is described by the *Sunday Telegraph* as "wonderfully quirky", but was overshadowed by Oxenbury's hugely popular version.[39] Her "playful watercolours", in the words of another journalist, "have the clarity and luminosity of a Dutch interior; her wit and finesse of line is reminiscent of Bruegel."[40]

Demurely clad in white with a distinctive swoosh of brown hair, Alice has a watchful, introspective manner. With subtle textures, translucent colours and ethereal shadows, Zwerger treads softly in the curiously detailed, but selective logic of Alice's puzzling dream world.[41]

Oxenbury's *Alice* is more generously illustrated than usual, with a picture decorating most of the creamy pages. It was exceptionally well received, winning the Kurt Maschler Award in the year of its publication and the Kate Greenaway Medal in 2000; my search through the British press turned up twenty-one enthusiastic reviews (compared with only a few for Zwerger) from 1999–2001. The *Guardian* sets the tone by describing her heroine as "an Alice for the new millennium",[42] "very contemporary . . . a very modern little miss in a blue shift dress . . . much more accessible to this age group".[43] *The Scotsman* celebrates "a fresh look for a treasured heirloom"[44] and praises the "simplicity and relevance" of the watercolour and pencil drawings;[45] the *Sunday Telegraph* says it "brings Alice to life for the modern child in a totally fresh and accessible way."[46] It is time, finally, to look more closely at the dreamchild in her recent incarnations.

Alice

Though Tenniel may have refused to base his drawings on a real little girl, the blonde in the waisted dress and pinafore had a life prior to the publication of *Wonderland*. She was one of Tenniel's prototypical representations of a nice middle-class girl, and she appeared in *Punch* at least once during the 1860s, as did variations on the White Queen, the Carpenter, the Tweedles, and the Leg of Mutton. Michael Hancher reproduces a Tenniel title page from *Punch* that shows Alice, or a girl so alike that it could be her twin, placing a garland round the neck of the British Lion.

Of course, no reader in the middle of 1864 . . . could have recognised Alice in this her first appearance. And by the time, a year and a half later, she finally appeared as herself in *Alice's Adventures*, the old image from *Punch* would have slipped from memory. Yet, like the absent-minded White Rabbit, the Victorian reader might well suppose that he already knew who Alice was.[47]

As Hancher shows, the Victorian reader would recognise Alice as a social type even if he or she was unfamiliar with Tenniel's illustrations. A "little darling" looking very much like Alice—prim and slightly tetchy, with long

Tenniel's proto-Alice from *Punch*.

blonde hair, pale dress, and neat, strapped black shoes—appears in Leech's cartoon of 1864.

> Grandpapa: Heyday! What makes my little darling so cross!
> Little Darling: Why, Grandpa, Mama wants me to go to a pantomime in the day time, as if I was a mere child![48]

Beyond the pages of *Punch*, her style finds other echoes. Alice's outfit in the *Looking-Glass* railway carriage is remarkably similar to that of the girls in Augustus Leopold Egg's painting "The Travelling Companions" (1862) and to John Millais' "My First Sermon" (1863).[49] The hat with its dainty feather and the barrel muff were in keeping with high fashion for little girls in the late 1860s and early 1870s, as was Queen Alice's formal dress;[50] Hancher includes an 1871 photograph of three miniature aristocrats in identical outfits, and remarks quite rightly that "the girl on the left"—she has her feet neatly turned out—"could be Alice herself."[51]

He also points out that while there may have been no life model for Alice, one of the key influences on Tenniel's heroine was Carroll's own impression of how she should look. Carroll's drawings for *Under Ground*

113

Leech, "Little Darling" from *Punch*.

feature a girl who, with her long wavy hair and clinging tunic, looks only a little like Alice Liddell and has far more in common with Carroll's broader ideals of pre-Raphaelite beauty. Jones and Gladstone make a direct comparison between the soft muslin smock of Arthur Hughes's painting "Lady with the Lilacs"—which Carroll owned and displayed in his room—and the "diaphanous, tape-trimmed tunic" worn by the *Under Ground* Alice.[52] In one Carroll illustration, Alice's head-tilted pose and thoughtful expression seem to directly echo those of Hughes's model.[53]

> Tenniel combs Alice's abundant hair back, instead of parting it, and he minimizes the pre-Raphaelite wave . . . aside from the long hair, the most important trait that Tenniel takes from Carroll's drawings of Alice is the impassive, almost pouty expression. Another mark of pre-Raphaelite style, it suits the sober child described in the text.[54]

The most noticeable trait in all the reviews of Helen Oxenbury's *Alice* is the need to contrast this early twenty-first century heroine with Tenniel's girl of the 1860s. The *Independent*'s breezy comment is typical. "Gone is the Alice in prissy petticoats and a pinafore. This Alice is casually dressed, a child of today—and of tomorrow."[55] Intriguingly, Oxenbury's Alice was,

Carroll's Alice.

unlike Tenniel's, based on a real person: a young guest at a wedding party in 1995. "I'd been struggling to come up with a modern Alice," Oxenbury confessed, "because her traditional image, from John Tenniel's illustrations, is so strong."

> But as soon as I saw the girl by the stream I knew I had found the new Alice. She had lovely long slim arms and legs, and a wonderful mass of long, curly hair. She was wearing a slip dress and white plimsolls. I watched her playing with some balloons and on the swings. Her movement was so free, so easy, she was a child of today. Little girls were not supposed to jump and play around in Alice's day.[56]

Madeleine Salvage, who was fourteen by the time this *Alice* was published, made it clear, "I'm not angelic any more, that's for sure. I'm stubborn and I like to get my own way, but Alice is a bit like that too." "She's lost the amazing look of blonde innocence that you can have when you are ten," her father added.[57] Madeleine is eighteen at the time of writing; it would be interesting to see how she compares to the grave, sulky Alice Liddell who sat for Carroll's final portrait of her in 1870.

Oxenbury's protagonist was received as "a thoroughly modern Alice in a mini dress",[58] a "sunny, Home Counties-style Alice in her sundress and sneakers . . . meeker than the argumentative seven-year-old we know from the text",[59] "a more relaxed, casual child, attractive and accessible."[60]

> Tenniel's Alice is famous for her straight-faced, straight-laced, buttoned-up demeanour. By doing away with the buttoned shoes and the starchy skirts, and allowing just the occasional smile, Oxenbury gives us a cheerful, slightly younger child with an unruly mop of hair . . . This Alice scampers about bare-legged in plimsolls, and her liberatingly skimpy cotton shift allows her a much more physical involvement in her adventures.[61]

While this is generally agreed to be a lighter, airier Alice, with none of the "darker subtexts detected by modern critics",[62] one reviewer does introduce a note of juvenile sexuality by observing that this "young Alice is less sophisticated than many previous representations, though flashes of her knickers show her to be less innocent than she looks."[63] This projection of knowing sensuality upon a ten year-old in a short dress is the only reminder of the "paedophile" rumours around Carroll; otherwise, the book is received so warmly as a joyful, innocent tale for children and their parents—much as it was in 1865—that the contemporary ambivalence about its author seems to have been entirely forgotten.

As we saw in Chapters 2 and 3, the *Alice* books are so closely associated with "darkness" in the modern mind that it would hardly be thought possible to market them as children's literature. However, Oxenbury's fresh vision has apparently washed the page clean of all puberty allegory, political satire (except for one cheeky caricature, discussed below), death traps, and dilemmas of identity. Only a single review complains that something has been lost: Susie Maguire describes this "contemporary alternative to Tenniel's original illustrations" as "missing an essential humour and madness." Oxenbury's Alice is "boot-button-eyed, bland by comparison."[64]

> Lizbeth Zwerger's Alice, a little older, is quite different. With her thoughtful introspective gaze, it's clear that this child is psychologically well equipped to deal with the spiralling illogicalities of the plot. Zwerger combines a delicate watercolour technique with a robust and unusual sense of composition: cropping the images with great bravado to reflect the topsy-turvy dislocations of the story; and making eloquent use of white space.[65]

Zwerger's protagonist is a pensive-looking schoolgirl with long, almost waist-length mousy hair, wearing a sleeveless maroon top over a white shirt and matching skirt. Like Tenniel's Alice, she wears neat black shoes; her stockings are bright scarlet, adding a touch of rebellion to an otherwise sober outfit. She responds to her adventures with mild bemusement; she barely raises her eyebrows as she shoots down the rabbit-hole with hair

Zwerger's Mad Tea Party.

flying up behind her,[66] smiles with faint interest as she grows until her head hits the ceiling[67] and seems to be sunk in her own thoughts at the Hatter's Tea Party.[68]

She appears to wander sadly through Wonderland, unworried but resolutely immune to entertainment. The Tea Party becomes a desultory affair as she stares at the tablecloth; she turns the same unmoved gaze on the Pigeon,[69] showing no sign of distress at the fact that her neck has stretched to serpentine lengths, and is once again lost in her own inner world as the jurors note the evidence against the Knave of Hearts.[70] She only seems to enjoy herself once, when she runs a Caucus-Race with the animals to dry off, and here she is very small in the picture.[71] As Sarah Johnson points out in the *Times*, Alice is "often only half-seen or dwarfed by architecture";[72] she is frequently cropped out of the frame and appears only as a pair of legs, or a hand, or a departing back.

This is not a nightmarish world, perhaps, but it seems a very bleak one; a long, unnerving, and thankless dream. Small figures are dotted about the white pages, adding to the sense of fragmentation and dislocation.

Sometimes the only illustration on a double-spread is a little thimble,[73] or a forlorn fish and seahorse with no relation to the text.[74] The Mouse's Tale is embellished with a small tableau of an impassive cat and dog with rodents hanging from their mouths—unprompted by any detail in the story itself, but arguably true to its tone. While Zwerger doesn't seem directly to echo any of the recent critical discourses around *Alice*, she captures the sense—expressed by many of the commentators in the previous two chapters—that the books depict a child's journey through a not especially pleasant adult environment. Most striking is the cold, rigid atmosphere created by her unnatural creatures frozen in white space: an atmosphere usually associated with *Looking-Glass*, not *Wonderland*.

By contrast, Oxenbury's Alice wears her emotions close to the surface. For the most part, she shows an unfazed interest in her new surroundings, approaching the Cheshire Cat and the Hatter's party with an open-minded, "impress me then" attitude[75] and responding to her changes in size with mild curiosity. Being too small for the glass table or cramped in the White Rabbit's house[76] are temporary inconveniences, and she seems to know something else will come along to restore her to normal or entertain her in the meantime.

However, unlike Zwerger's heroine—and Tenniel's for that matter—this Alice also enjoys the extremes that Wonderland offers. Her face and body language are unselfconsciously expressive; she clasps her fists to her mouth in concern as the Duchess flings the baby,[77] clutches herself as she shivers beside the Pool of Tears,[78] sits with her head in her hands when "The Voice of the Sluggard" comes out wrong,[79] and sulkily resists the Duchess's sharp chin when they meet again.[80] She also smiles a great deal more than the Tenniel Alice—at the plate of tarts, at her flamingo, at the story of the Duchess boxing the Queen's ears. This Wonderland is almost a theme park, with splashes into pools, thrillingly upside-down conventions, an opportunity to dance, an anarchic game, and the possibility of jam tarts at the end. Alice finds herself with a day of free rides, and loves even the scary parts.

One intriguing aspect about Oxenbury's version is her depiction of Alice's sister. Unnamed in the text, this character actually frames the story—by ignoring Alice, she prompts the dream of Wonderland, and she appears again at the end with a whole postscript to herself. This short epilogue, told with a touching hindsight like the *Looking-Glass* passage where Carroll says Alice will always remember the White Knight's song, leaps through a series of surprising perspectives. Alice's sister dreams "after a fashion" of Alice and her endearing habits, then of herself in Wonderland, but only half believing it, and then of "the after-time" when

Oxenbury's Mad Tea Party.

her little sister will grow up and tell the story of the dream to a new generation. "And how she would feel with all their simple sorrows, and find a pleasure in all their simple joys, remembering her own child-life, and the happy summer days."[81]

This sequence, with its implication that Alice's older sister can only place one foot in the innocent dream-world—she knows she has only to open her eyes "and all would change to dull reality"—and its final, remarkable shift to decades in the future when Wonderland is "long ago", aches with loss despite its apparent optimism. Alice's childhood is imagined as past before she has even grown up; Alice's sister is nostalgic for the present, painfully aware of how quickly it will fade into history. It is a passage that surely expresses some of Carroll's personal feelings about childhood in general and his mixed emotions about the process of growing up.

Yet Alice's sister, such a key character as the bearer of this adult perspective, is very rarely shown in illustrations. Rackham begins with the rabbit and ends with the pack of cards; Peake opens with Alice alone on the bank and ends with the Queen; Zwerger starts with the rabbit hole and ends with Alice leaving the trial. Of this group, only McGraw finds room for the older sister; she sits at the edge of his penultimate illustration, a larger clone of Alice who still seems absorbed in her book. Mabel Lucie Atwell shows her as a young blonde in the background of one drawing,[82] but there is no other sign of her in Cooper Eden's anthology of illustration. Tenniel omits her, although Carroll's *Under Ground* includes her at the start as a rather severe, beaky brunette with a domed forehead, apparently older than Lorina, who would have been around thirteen when the story was written.[83]

Oxenbury, however, shows her in three pictures. She looks between eighteen and twenty, dressed in a white t-shirt and skirt, with hair a shade darker than Alice's. At the end of the adventures, recognising that Alice is sorry to have woken up, she puts her book down and kisses her little sister on the cheek; and then she has a final page to herself. It is sunset, and the young woman is sitting, silhouetted, under the tree where Alice fell asleep. Her chin is in her hands. Leaves are beginning to fall around her. The image conveys perfectly the air of contemplation in Carroll's final paragraphs, and also the sense of a bittersweet ending: the light is a delicate pink, the evening is obviously still warm, but the summer day, and Alice, have gone. The way is paved for "Long has paled that sunny sky: / Echoes fade and memories die: / Autumn frosts have slain July", and *Looking-Glass*'s winter.

Peake contributes fewer illustrations than Tenniel or Zwerger, and far fewer than Oxenbury; moreover, Alice appears in only eight of them. We do not, therefore, get a strong sense of her as a character. Described—as we saw—as puma-like, gaminesque, eroticised and downbeat, this is a slender girl with tangled shoulder-length hair, wearing a simple short-sleeved dress. Although she shows a doe-eyed distress at being confined to the Rabbit's house,[84] looks very downcast at her long neck,[85] and smiles at the Mock Turtle's dance, there is a sense of aloofness about her; she doesn't join the dance as Oxenbury's Alice does, but stands with her arms folded, watching.[86] In more than one of the pictures a sensual quality could be read from her pose and expression; she holds her long, slim limbs with poise, sleeps with a faint smile as if she knows she's being

Oxenbury's Alice and her sister.

Peake's Alice.

watched,[87] and in the opening illustration plays her little finger around her full lower lip.[88]

But we rarely see her interact with Wonderland—we don't see her chatting with the Hatter and Hare, standing up to the Queen, protesting

Peake's Mad Tea Party.

her identity to the Pigeon, or resenting the Duchess' sharp chin. Instead, the characters are shown separately, in isolation, and often in close-up cameos as if we share Alice's perspective. The Duchess, for instance, appears from the neck up, the picture roughly corresponding to the line "she had quite forgotten the Duchess by this time, and was a little startled when she heard her voice close to her ear".[89] Though depicted in profile, the matronly aristocrat peers sideways at the reader as though we were walking next to her.

Similarly, the Queen glares out at us, the Cat sneers straight ahead rather than down, and the Tea Party guests glance knowingly out of the picture as if we were placed in the spare armchair. We are positioned centrally in Wonderland and see the inhabitants as the heroine would;

but their environment is very sketchy, as if they are appearing briefly from the mist, and the overall effect is like a series of postcards or a slide show from a Wonderland holiday. This is the Queen she met, who was most unpleasant—and here is the funny little Fish-Footman—but the pictures were taken in fog, with few signs that Alice was there at all, and even fewer that she engaged the people in conversation.

Arthur Rackham's Alice is, like Oxenbury's, based on a real girl—in this case, Doris Dommett, known as Jane. "I was so pleased he copied my print frock exactly," said Jane, "because it was one my mother had allowed me to design myself."[90] This Alice is not so distant historically from Tenniel's—she appeared forty years after the publication of *Wonderland*—and she clearly shares her manners and composure with the original rather than with Oxenbury's little girl. Rackham's Alice stands with demure grace on the frontispiece, her light brown hair behind her ears, hands behind her back, and one striped-stockinged leg slightly forward. The rose print on her white dress matches her slightly flushed cheeks.

She greets Wonderland with the same reserve, sitting hands in lap and listening politely to the Turtle,[91] struggling quietly with the flamingo-mallet[92] and pig-baby,[93] and remaining straight-faced, bolt upright in her armchair at the Hatter's party.[94] She smiles only once, after the Caucus-Race;[95] her expression shows the same civil display of interest whether she is talking to the Caterpillar, the Mouse, the Rabbit, or the Pigeon—and in the last instance, the fact that her neck is tangled like elastic round branches hardly seems to bother her, though the image is more than a little disturbing. She seems distressed by her sudden growth in the early scene, by the flying plates in the Duchess' house. and by the rising up of the pack of cards, but her face when surrounded by huge animals and swimming the pool of her own tears is telling—she looks bored.

Rackham's Wonderland is crueller than any other example in this group. The colours are muted; shades of earth, stone, and bark. The animals have fierce beaks and claws and angry little black eyes, like the work of a spiteful taxidermist;[96] the humans, or human-grotesques, also have sharp features and weirdly elongated fingers.[97] Even the trees look malicious, with knotty trunks and twisted branches. In a typical piece of detail, a second glance at the Knave in the court scene reveals that the executioner's bony hands are gripping his neck.[98] It is a nasty, vicious-looking world that fully suggests a journey through hell or a struggle against the odds to reach adulthood; yet ironically, this Alice treats it as a rather tiresome social visit.

Finally, McGraw's *Alice* comes closest to visualising the "psychedelic" readings of Carroll that emerged during the late 1960s. His one hundred

Rackham's Mad Tea Party.

odd illustrations are bold, splodgy, splashy paintings in sometimes lurid, almost fluorescent colours. Alice and her fellow characters are reduced to templates, symbols, and cyphers rather than the more naturalistic and detailed figures of Tenniel, Rackham, and, in a more relaxed style, of Oxenbury. The beasts and birds of the Pool of Tears become ghostly white shapes,[99] the Gryphon and Mock Turtle dance across a frieze like hieroglyphs,[100] and the Caterpillar is a huge green face with a spatter of blood-brown across it.[101] Most of the backgrounds are white or flat colour, with only a few childlike houses to break up the view of desert yellow and plain green.

McGraw's Alice.

Here the protagonist is identifiable in every picture mainly by her canary yellow hair, which glares out of the navy blue Pool of Tears[102] yet threatens to blend in with the mustard colour of the Hatter's armchair.[103] Her face, generally shown in flat profile, is pale white with circles of rose on the cheeks, and she wears a party frock similar to that provided by Tenniel—with a bow and apron sometimes clearly visible[104]—except that it tends to change colour from one scene to the next, shading through ochre in the rabbit hole to pink at the croquet game and turquoise with the Gryphon and Mock Turtle.

Blotted down to her bare essentials, we can hardly read personality off McGraw's protagonist—she comes to signify Alice in much the same way as the silhouetted figures on road signs signify people. McGraw's cut-out little girl can be identified fairly confidently as between five and ten years old, with a specific ethnicity and, from her pretty dress and occasional heels, level of wealth, but it is fruitless to guess at her emotional response to Wonderland. This Alice's profile is stuck almost invariably in the same open-mouthed expression of dumb wonder, which could be interpreted as constant incredulity or stupidity: she has the same look of vague enjoyment about her whether falling down the rabbit hole,[105] watching the Lobster Quadrille,[106] or growing "a mile high" in the courtroom.[107] Character is, in McGraw's *Alice*, swamped by visual spectacle.

Wonderland

Just as these Alices are very different little girls, so the creatures of Wonderland take diverse forms from one artist to the next, with varied connotations. There is a vast difference between Tenniel's fat, googleeyed and grinning Cheshire Cat to Oxenbury's cuddly, complacent old ginger tom, McGraw's stunt-limbed, striped green reptile, Zwerger's weird creature with a white body and red head, and Peake's sinister, manky beast with tombstone teeth and narrow eyes; and the Cat says something about the kind of Wonderland we are in, from Oxenbury's sunny play park to Peake's uncertain, misty world.

As already suggested, the illustrators who came to *Alice* after Carroll's death had far more freedom than Tenniel, and chose to illustrate aspects of the text that he, under the author's close direction, left to the reader's imagination. Zwerger's multiple miniature paintings dotted round the pages include the dead mouse picture described above, a picture of a flamingo, and a toothy pot of mustard—illustrating the Duchess's theory that they "both bite"[108]—and a sweet vignette of the three sisters in the treacle well.[109] In the same spirit of illustrating stories-within-stories, Peake provides an image of the crocodile welcoming fishes into his "gently smiling jaws"—we know he lives in the Nile, because there's a pyramid in the background[110]—and McGraw contributes a bizarre visual of the Hatter's adversary "Time", a figure made of giant numbers, leaping through space.[111] Oxenbury, on a more modest scale, shows the guinea-pigs nursing Bill,[112] a scene that Carroll depicted in his own drawings[113] and Tenniel left out.

More surprising than the differences are the similarities, in terms of the common incidents these illustrators choose to highlight, the composition of the pictures, and the shared iconography. When we bear in mind that these artists will surely have been trying explicitly to move away from the familiar Tenniel images and carve out a different, distinctive visual style for their own Wonderlands, the points of overlap are even more intriguing. Tenniel's template may have deeper hooks in them than they realised, or perhaps there is a sense, equally subconscious, that certain elements must be retained for the story to remain and be recognised as *Alice*. For instance, Oxenbury states outright that she wanted to distinguish her work from previous illustrations, but she still draws the heroine with shoulder-length blonde hair and a blue dress. As we know, her little girl was based on a real-life source, but nevertheless she chose the colour scheme, and it is striking how immediately that blue and blonde says "Alice" to a readership used to Tenniel and to Disney's simplified adoption of his design.

The same, of course, is true of McGraw's artwork—his yellow-haired heroine's party dress goes through most colours of the visible spectrum, but we might remember that Tenniel also drew her with a pale lemon-coloured frock, in the *Nursery Alice*. The remarkable influence of the 1865 character design extends, as Stephanie Lovett Stoffel's *The Art of Alice in Wonderland* shows, to Greg Hildebrandt's near-photorealistic paintings of 1990 and to a recent, anonymous Japanese manga Alice: though the styles are very different from each other and from Tenniel, both artists depict a girl with straight, shoulder-length blonde hair wearing a blue Victorian party dress with bow and apron.[114]

The overall look of Wonderland, though—the styling, and the incidents that are actually selected for illustration—goes even further back than Tenniel. Carroll submitted his own drawings as guides, and Michael Hancher demonstrates that Tenniel's far more accomplished pictures do owe a great deal to Carroll's originals. It is interesting to note that while Zwerger's dead mice, McGraw's flying Time, and Peake's crocodile have no precedent in *Alice's Adventures Under Ground*, Oxenbury's guinea-pigs are not just featured in the original illustrations but seem modelled on Carroll's naïve art, with the animals' stance and arm positions similar enough to suggest a deliberate homage.[115]

Despite the very different styles and the variation in the number of illustrations, six of the seven versions under consideration here—Carroll's, Tenniel's, McGraw's, Peake's, Oxenbury's, and Zwerger's—choose to show Alice's growth in the White Rabbit's house.[116] Carroll crams her within the frame of the page itself,[117] while Tenniel modifies the image but keeps to the same composition, as Hancher shows.[118] Peake has her still growing, not yet confined by the walls but worryingly cramped;[119] Zwerger shows just a pair of red stockings and skirt-covered knees, with Alice too huge to fit in the picture.[120] McGraw has a haunting four panels in Warholian colours, with Alice turning uncomfortably in the confined space like a bloated foetus,[121] and Oxenbury gives the scene a double-spread, closely following the text in its detailed directions that Alice's foot was in the chimney and hand out of the window.[122]

Carroll's guinea pigs and Oxenbury's similar creatures.

Six of these artists—all but Tenniel—show Alice with her elongated neck, the result of eating the mushroom.[123] Six of them—all except Rackham—show the three card gardeners painting the Queen's rose tree red, exhibiting striking similarities in the composition.[124] Five of them—Carroll, McGraw, Oxenbury, Peake, and Tenniel—have a head-to-tail picture of Bill the Lizard shooting vertically into space.[125] All seven depict the Caterpillar, all but Carroll feature the Duchess with her baby and the Hatter's Party,[126] and intriguingly, all but Rackham illustrate the song "You Are Old, Father William", which introduces an entirely different story-space, fictional even within Alice's fictional world.

Father William and the young man do not qualify as characters in Wonderland, yet Carroll gave them four full-page pictures in *Under Ground* and for whatever reason, most of the others follow suit: Tenniel provides four, as does Oxenbury, while Zwerger has eight Father Williams in the margins, and even Peake, who is sparing with his illustrations, offers them a whole page. McGraw's images of Father William standing on his head and balancing the eel bear an uncanny resemblance to Tenniel's, bearing in mind the differences between the former's splashy primary colours and the latter's exacting line.[127]

If it seems predictable that all these illustrators should show the Duchess with her baby and the Hatter at table—they are major characters, with chapters of their own, and these are perhaps the obvious choices for a

128

picture—then consider the points of overlap within the depictions them-selves. Carroll barely describes either Duchess or Hatter: he tells us only on her second appearance that the former was "very ugly", with a "sharp little chin",[128] and that the latter has a pocket watch,[129] shoes,[130] and a hat he doesn't own, when he attends court at least.[131] There is nothing to inform us that the Hatter actually wears a hat to the Tea Party, yet each one of these illustrators includes the detail. Zwerger's Hatter looks strangely debonair wearing a peach-coloured hat box, Oxenbury's is a cockney chancer with pencil moustache and three examples of his own wares perched on his head, Peake's sports a flower pot with a brim, and Rackham's is a very close cousin of Tenniel's Hatter, complete with price tag in his topper.[132] Once more, McGraw's illustration, though leagues away from Tenniel in style and execution, nods back to the character's original design: his schoolboyish, rosy-cheeked figure wears the label "8$^1/_2$"—a meaningless price in modern American or British currency—in the brim of his bowler hat.

It could be objected that to depict a Hatter wearing a hat is an obvious, even inevitable choice in terms of visual possibilities and ease of identification—not that anyone would be likely to confuse him with the Hare and Dormouse if he were bareheaded. Even if we accept this point, though, there is no reason why the Hatter in all these illustrations should be dressed in shabby-eccentric formal wear, except that Tenniel established him thus in the 1865 pictures. Each one of these artists gives the Hatter a cravat or tie—Peake's wears his with an open-necked shirt, Rackham's is a blue and white polka dot, Zwerger's a white bow tie, McGraw's a multicolored dotted affair, and Oxenbury's a pink one—and each of them, apart from McGraw, whose style is too vague to discern most items of clothing, gives him a jacket or waistcoat. The only relevant textual detail Carroll offers about the hatter's dress is that he has a pocket for his watch. Given that there were very few hatters in Oxenbury's Britain of the late 1990s, she at least had free reign to make him a young market-tradesman in a t-shirt, or a middle-aged specialist in a sweater; that she did not surely has more to do with Tenniel's influence than it does with any considerations of "realism", visual interest, or textual fidelity.

There is, equally, nothing to tell us that the Duchess is overweight or what her age might be, yet almost all these illustrators show her as plump and mature, from Peake's solid society dame through McGraw's blue, blobby-hipped woman to Zwerger's formidable lady in a voluminous green dress. Rackham's fur-clad hag could be skinny under her robes, but in other respects, such as her ermine and headdress, his design once more closely follows Tenniel.[133] It was Tenniel who established that the character should be full-figured and middle-aged—from the text, she could be an unattractive but slim eighteen year-old, just as the Hatter could carry his merchandise in a bag, rather than wearing an example—and all these more recent illustrators, for all their efforts to plough new ground, seem to have internalised his portrait of the characters. Though they may deliberately react against their own mental pictures, they still make assumptions about the Hatter and Duchess's appearance that come from the 1865 illustrations, not from the text.

As we heard from Michael Bakewell above, Carroll was finicky about the location of the images on the page and their relation to specific lines of dialogue and description. In one instance he even made the words into a picture—as the Mouse's Tale, where the story twists and the font shrinks to the tail's tip.[134] This concrete poem, with the shape of the verse suggesting the subject, was introduced in *Under Ground* with different words but a very similar form. Rackham's version reproduces it faithfully, as do Peake and McGraw—the latter echoing the textual shape with a kaleidoscopic, snakelike swirl of an appendage that must extend some twenty meters from the back of the Mouse.[135] Zwerger, however, opts for the strange and not entirely satisfactory middle ground of having the Mouse's introduction—"mine is a long and sad tale"—winding down a drawing of the tail itself, but laying out the poem as if it was straight dialogue.[136] Oxenbury's design is more successful but still a halfway house; she gives the poem layout a few tweaks so it echoes her adjacent drawing of the Mouse but chooses not to make the words twist and taper quite so dramatically as they do in Carroll and Tenniels' original.[137] This is a case where the 1865 design served a specific purpose, and where variations like Zwerger's seem genuinely to lose something.

Hancher points out that the Tenniel illustrations were intended to subtly mesh with certain points of the text. The picture of Alice drawing back the curtain to find a tiny door is "let in" on the page so it corresponds directly with the words "she came upon a low curtain she had not noticed before, and behind it was a little door about fifteen inches high."[138] The design here directly echoes Carroll's own arrangement in *Under Ground*, where "low curtain" and "tried the little key" fit the picture almost as exactly as a written caption in a comic strip.[139]

Similarly, Tenniel's illustration of the elongated Alice, opened up like a telescope, reaches from head to foot of the page with the words "little feet" right next to her shoes;[140] and the same clever convergence of text and picture recurs in both *Under Ground* and *Wonderland* when she pushes her hand through the Rabbit's window.

upon a low curtain
she had not noticed
before, and behind it
was a little door
about fifteen inches
high: she tried the
little golden key in
the lock, and to her
great delight it fitted

Alice opened the
door and found that
it led into a small pas-
sage, not much larg-
er than a rat-hole: she
knelt   down   and
looked along the pas-

Tenniel's Alice and the little door.

The references to "a snatch in the air" and "a crash of broken glass" in what might be "a cucumber frame," run in parallel with the depiction of these things. There are other examples in both books of such nice matching of marginal illustrations with the text. This finesse suffers more or less in later editions.[141]

It suffers in Peake—none of these three illustrations are even there, let alone choreographed with the words—and in Rackham, where the image of a stretched Alice is a full page away from any reference to feet.[142] McGraw's image of the extended Alice is opposite, and so at least roughly linked to, the description of her hitting the ceiling, but the address to "Alice's Right Foot, Esq." actually falls at the head of the page.[143] Zwerger does well with this one, echoing Tenniel's layout by having Alice's head at the top of the page and shoes very near the words "Alice's Right Foot, Esq.",[144] and despite a perspective that shows Alice from slightly above, Oxenbury's illustration of the scene also roughly matches the text.[145] She also reproduces Tenniel and Carroll's correspondence between word and image around the "cucumber-frame" incident, showing Alice's chubby hand more or less adjacent to the phrase "a snatch in the air",[146] and McGraw,

her hand, and made a snatch in the air. She did not get hold of anything, but she heard a little shriek and a fall, and a crash of broken glass, from which she concluded that it was just possible it had fallen into a cucumber-frame, or something of the sort.

Next came an angry voice—the Rabbit's—"Pat! Pat! Where are you?" And then a voice she had never heard before, "Sure then I'm here! Digging for apples, yer honour!"³

"Digging for apples,

Tenniel's Alice and the cucumber-frame.

despite the apparent looseness of his style, also has the "grab through the window" picture directly opposite the "snatch" line.¹⁴⁷

These points may seem trivial, but Hancher argues convincingly that the "precise bracketing" of the Tenniel pictures by the text adds to their "dramatic immediacy".¹⁴⁸ Carroll, with characteristic attention to detail, intended the illustrations to depict a particular moment in the story, and labelled them accordingly as, for instance, "cucumber-frame"—which could only refer to a single line of description—and "Queen of Hearts (off with her head)".¹⁴⁹ As an extended example, Hancher focuses on the Tea Party scene, and demonstrates that Tenniel's familiar picture of Alice slumped in the chair is meant to show the second that passes between two lines of dialogue.

> "You should learn not to make personal remarks," Alice said with some severity: "it's very rude." The reader next sees, at the top of the opposite page, the tea-party illustration: there Alice is still glowering at the Hatter, her left hand gripping the arm of her chair. And then, immediately below the illustration: "The Hatter opened his eyes very wide on hearing this, but all he *said* was, "Why is a raven like a writing-desk?" Apparently the illustration depicts the precise moment when, wide-eyed, the Hatter put his famous riddle to Alice.¹⁵⁰

"*That* you won't!" thought Alice, and, after waiting till she fancied she heard the rabbit just under the window, she suddenly spread out her hand, and made a snatch in the air. She did not get hold of anything, but she heard a little shriek and a fall, and a crash of broken glass, from which she concluded that it was just possible it had fallen into a cucumber-frame, or something of the sort.

Next came an angry voice – the Rabbit's – "Pat! Pat! Where are you?" And then a voice she had never heard before, "Sure then I'm here! Digging for apples, yer honour!"

"Digging for apples, indeed!" said the Rabbit angrily.

Oxenbury's Alice and the cucumber-frame.

Tenniel's Mad Tea Party.

All the artists under discussion here provide at least one picture of the Tea Party, but not of the same moment. Oxenbury gives the scene one full-page painting, a double-page spread, a black-and-white image of the Hatter, and a little vignette of the Dormouse. The first comes at the start of the chapter and shows the Hare complaining while the Hatter listens and the Dormouse curls up like a cushion between them; it seems to illustrate Alice's first view of the characters, and the description "the other two were resting their elbows on it, and talking over its head."[151] The second image appears directly between the Hatter asking "Have you guessed the riddle yet?" and Alice replying "No, I give it up", but the picture clearly serves the slightly earlier line about the Hatter pouring "a little hot tea" on the Dormouse's nose.[152]

The third is a gorgeously sun-dappled scene showing the entire table loaded with scattered cups, sandwiches, and cakes—there is also a milk jug, although not close enough to the Hare for him to tip it over into his plate. As Alice is gazing with interest at the Dormouse, the picture cannot relate directly to the next line, where she exclaims "very angrily".[153] The only visual clue is that the Hare is pulling on one of the Dormouse's ears, although this can only correspond to a paragraph a page and a half away, with Hatter and Hare pinching their friend to wake him up.[154]

Peake has only one illustration of the scene; this full-page image shows the Hatter and Hare resting their elbows on the Dormouse's head, as in Oxenbury's first picture, but here the characters are turned towards the visitor rather than each other. As the Hare seems to be grinning at the Hatter, and the Hatter is smiling out at the reader—who, as noted above, takes Alice's position—the most obvious explanation is that the Hatter has just remarked "Your hair wants cutting", and is waiting for a response.[155] However, the dialogue that bookends the image is the Hare's tormenting of Alice—"Do you mean that you think you can find out the answer to it? . . . then you should say what you mean"—and there is certainly no directly evident connection between the picture and the surrounding or immediately facing text.

McGraw, unusually, incorporates dialogue into his illustration—the words "NO ROOM!" drift from the Hatter and Hare's mouths and float in the air above the table as Alice approaches.[156] Perversely, though, the actual dialogue occurs on the preceding page and the image appears out of sequence. The illustration facing the line " 'No room! No room!' they cried out when they saw Alice coming" shows Alice plumped securely in the armchair,[157] so that the pictures suggest a narrative whereby Alice initially sits down, then stands and walks towards the table against the Hare and Hatter's protests. The images are certainly linked to the text,

McGraw's Mad Tea Party.

but in the wrong order; a decision probably made for the sake of layout, and one that produces an inverted logic.

Rackham also uses a full page for his single illustration, which seems to correspond to the Hatter's last remark—"It *is* the same thing with you"—before the party lapses into uncomfortable silence; the Hare is already staring blankly ahead, and Alice sits in miserable isolation.[158] Zwerger's picture, in turn, clearly shows the Hare as he dips his watch "into his cup of tea"; however, the position of the characters does not allow Alice to look "over his shoulder with some curiosity", as the text specifies.[159] Again, while there is some continuity between what Carroll describes and what the illustrators show, neither of them demonstrate the same attention to detail that Tenniel does in his depiction of the Hatter's wide eyes and Alice's angry glare.

Overall, these artists take less care or interest over the relation of image to word—in terms of precise lines of description and dialogue—than Carroll did with Tenniel's illustrations. However, this is partly a result of their opting for full-page images. The Tea Party picture used in Hancher's main example only takes up half the page, and so can be bracketed neatly by specifically chosen paragraphs; the large-scale scenes in all the above examples would make it far more difficult to ensure a tight match of this kind. On the other hand, Oxenbury's second picture of the Hatter is

Tenniel's Queen of Hearts.

small enough to fit in a gap just as Tenniel's image did, and no precise correspondence is managed here: it may simply be the case that Carroll was attempting something more ambitious than these more recent artists can be bothered to emulate, even if they notice it in the original.

Finally, I want to use one of Michael Hancher's more sustained examinations of Tenniel's pictures as the basis for a case study across the five twentieth-century examples, to draw both specific and general conclusions about the common ground and differences between all these versions. Hancher devotes an entire chapter to the Tenniel illustration of the Queen jabbing her finger wildly at an impassive Alice and screaming "Off with her head!" His analysis goes through several stages.

Firstly, he discusses the composition—the Queen taking up a quarter of the picture space, and the "umbral halo" that surrounds and protects Alice[160]—and then the various degrees of three-dimensionality in Tenniel's artwork, from the realistically shaded Alice through the half-flat portrait of the King and the pasteboard figures of the lesser cards to the rounded curves and depth of the landscape in the distance.

> The hierarchy of reality according to which Tenniel ranks the figures
> in the foreground corresponds to the degrees of complexity that the

figures present in Carroll's story in general, or at this particular point of the story. Alice is the only character in the book who might be called a "round" character in E. M. Forster's sense; that is, one who is "capable of surprising in a convincing way." The Queen is relatively inflexible and predictable . . . yet she has a certain capacity to surprise, and so gets a degree of modelling. The Knave is even more completely defined by his simple knavish role in the history of the tarts . . . [161]

Hancher goes on to compare Tenniel's illustration to Carroll's version of the scene, demonstrating that while the latter is technically inferior, many of its elements—fountains, a low fence, a crown on a cushion—were carried over into Tenniel's more accomplished art;[162] he suggests that the decorative topiary in Tenniel's picture was borrowed from *Punch* illustrations, the hemispherical glass observatory in the picture's background from the Crystal Palace of 1851,[163] and the Queen's crown from the St Edward's crown that appeared on every Ace of Spades playing card during the eighteenth and nineteenth centuries.[164] Allowing that the Queen owes something to Tenniel's illustrations of Queen Victoria,[165] Hancher argues that her menace is at least partly due to the fact that she wears the robes not of the Queen of Hearts, but of the Queen of Spades, the queen of death.[166]

Rackham does not illustrate this precise scene, but he opts for a moment very near it: the Queen is turning away from the King and commanding the Knave to flip over the prostrate gardeners.[167] There is some play with flat and "rounded" characters here, as in Tenniel; although Alice does not appear, the Knave and Queen are subtly shaded and moulded as solid figures, while the King appears more faded and flat and the other court cards merge into a single plane of grey shuffle at the back of the picture. Rackham's character designs closely follow Tenniel's as they did in the Tea Party illustration, with the Queen dressed in a black-edged bonnet and sombre robes and the Knave sporting a cap, blonde bobbed haircut, and dark moustache. There is, however, very little background—unusually, considering the bleak but detailed landscapes of knobbled trees and the claustrophobic interiors we see in Rackham's other *Alice* illustrations. The rose bush is characteristically twisted and thorny, and the colours are muddy as ever, but the space behind the cards is merely thick, dirty smog.

Peake chooses to give this scene a long-shot perspective, rather than his usual close-ups: the relevant line is "It's a friend of mine—a Cheshire Cat", and the Cat's head is hanging in the sky like a hallucinatory moon, casting the little figures of Queen, King, and Alice in stark light.[168] There

Rackham's Queen of Hearts.

is no sign of any other cards, although a hedgehog is visible by the King's feet and a flamingo writhes in Alice's grip. Peake's Queen has been shown previously, in more detail,[169] but here we can scarcely make out any features besides the crown tied to her starched pigtails and the cards that form her train. There is little direct relation to Tenniel's original, although like the Duchess she is shown to be middle-aged and portly without any such instructions from Carroll.[170] She and the King are given the same rounding of shadow as Alice, with no distinction made between human being and playing card: the croquet-ground is marked only by unruly, lumpy hedges. Of all the illustrations in this set, Peake's—with its looming, malicious Cat-head bleaching the world like a bomb blast—is most likely to give a child nightmares.

McGraw splits the scene into several lesser images, choosing not to focus on the moment of the Queen's arrival or her direct engagement

Peake's Queen of Hearts.

with Alice. The gardeners are shown painting the roses alone, and their design is used as the basis for all the card characters—flat, muddily pale rectangles, clearly two-dimensional as we can see their thin edges when they turn. In keeping with McGraw's unruly approach, they wear clubs on one page and spades on the next, and are topped with decorative party hats.[171] The Queen herself first appears in a vignette at the centre of a page, directly under her line "What's your name, child?"[172] and loses her temper two pages on in a half-page image of her yelling; whether she is calling for Alice's or the gardeners' execution is unclear. The closest line to the picture is Alice's "you shan't be beheaded", which takes place after the royal procession has moved on and only the soldiers, not the monarchy, are left behind.[173]

Here the Queen appears against a plain white background, with a row of crimson lollipop trees, all black stalk and round head, providing some landscape at the base of the opposite page. Unusually, McGraw draws her identically to the lesser cards, as a flat rectangle with features rather than as a semi-human character. She wears tiny heels and a Christmas-cracker crown, and her little outstretched hands are gloved, but she clearly remains

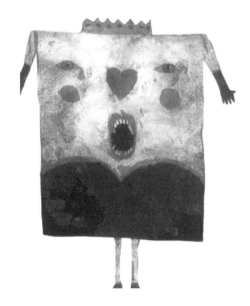

McGraw's Queen of Hearts.

part of a pack of cards, a cardboard figure with a red heart for a nose, and as such is on a different level of "realism" even to the flat but recognisably humanoid Alice and the other living creatures such as the Hatter, Rabbit, and Gryphon.

Zwerger's illustration has the Queen and Alice together staring down at the gardeners, with no King or Knave in attendance despite their appearance in the text. "And who are *these?*" reads the appropriate line, a few seconds before the Queen orders Alice's head off.[174] There is a "hierarchy of reality" at work in that the Queen is literally rounded—wrapped in playing cards that form a tube around her body, a curved cloak on her back, and a cylindrical crown for her head—while the courtiers behind her are crammed into two dimensions, their exposed faces becoming flatter the further away they get, and the gardeners have no heads or limbs at all. The setting is a vague wash of blue and beach, its suggestion of seaside taken up in many other Zwerger illustrations (the Caucus-Race, the sleeping Gryphon, and the Lobster Quadrille are all positioned next to water). The Queen, unusually, is not especially forbidding: adorned with scarlet hearts, matching shoes, and lipstick, she merely looks baffled and slightly lost, as Alice does throughout.

The arrival of the King and Queen gets a double-page spread in Oxenbury, complete with all the soldiers, attendants, and, uniquely, the

Zwerger's Queen of Hearts.

darling little royal children mentioned in Carroll's description.[175] As in Tenniel, the grouping of flat cards, semi-rounded court characters, and a real little girl involves a mixed perspective: the soldiers' backs are collaged from actual playing cards and march on a single plane, while the lesser courtiers are more realistically drawn but have less solidity than the White Rabbit, Alice, and the Queen herself. Unlike Tenniel's, Carroll's, and Rackham's monarchs, this one wears a crown; her dress is modelled on the conventional playing card, with simple patterns of red, gold, black, and blue and a flower held decoratively like a sceptre.

Oxenbury draws the court characters with white, blue-outlined faces, cleverly suggesting their lack of solid realism by contrast to Alice's healthy tan and prefiguring her dismissal of them as nothing but cards. The Queen

Oxenbury's Queen of Hearts.

therefore seems cartoonish and halfway towards mirage even when she folds her arms and stamps her feet in fury; she also provides the only outstanding instance of political caricature from the examples here, as she bears a distinct resemblance to Queen Elizabeth II in a grumpy mood. The grounds behind her are pale and pencilled despite the ornamental topiary and pillars—this may be simply for visual convenience, as a previous picture shows them as a lushly green, overgrown paradise[176]—and again owe something to Carroll and Tenniel's designs of a Victorian pleasure garden.

Overall, of these five post-Tenniel Wonderlands, the most intriguing aspect is how much they draw from Tenniel; while they tend to lack the close interaction between word and image that resulted from Carroll's unique relationship with his artist, the twentieth-century depictions of Alice and her world owe far more to the original version than they have to. For a text that contains relatively few instructions about how characters and settings should look, *Alice in Wonderland* has inspired consistently similar designs, especially when we consider that the artists in this chapter were actually trying to escape Tenniel's shadow. The more recent illustrated *Wonderlands* may no longer be a precise inventory and bestiary of Victorian values, but as noted above, Oxenbury's "beautiful garden" could have sprung from 1865 and McGraw's Alice, with her shoulder-length blonde hair striking a familiar note even in the most abstract images, clearly wears a party dress very similar to the one Tenniel gave her.

That these artists, even the most recent and experimental among them, retain so many aspects of the original 1865 illustration must be due to their own internalised images of Tenniel's art, because they could hardly have been guided by cues and specifications in the text itself. The book is, as we have seen, surprisingly vague about the appearance of its characters and settings, and was designed from the outset to rely on illustrations rather than written description. Ironically, where Carroll does specify a physical feature or reaction, it tends to be overlooked; as is the case with the Duchess' sharp chin or with the croquet-ground scene where Alice gives a "scream of laughter" and "could not help bursting out laughing", yet is shown stoney-faced by Tenniel, Zwerger, and Rackham. The contemporary illustrator is allowed an enormous amount of power over the appearance of Wonderland and Alice, and by extension the context and connotation of Alice's encounters. However, not one of the five illustrators discussed in this section fully escapes the visual stamp that Tenniel first imposed in the mid-1860s.

The paradox then, is that illustrators of *Alice* have a great deal of free rein to transform the text, but that they rarely take full advantage of it, not because of Carroll's controlling influence but because of the cultural authority of Tenniel's original designs. That said, these artists do each give the book an individual slant, shaping the mood of Wonderland and the nature of its inhabitants; the same world, based on the same words, becomes threatening and alienating in Rackham, or jolly and harmless in Oxenbury. Wonderland is a coldly bewildering dream in Zwerger, a bizarre first-person tour in Peake, and a gaudy hallucination in McGraw.

Apart from Oxenbury's version, all these Wonderlands tally to some extent with the contemporary reading of *Alice* as dark, twisted, and fraught with potential danger: even McGraw's fluorescent parade of abstracts was described warily by the US *School Library Journal* as "nightmarish."

> The images of Alice with the bottle of poison in front of her face and
> the executioner as a masked club card clutching an ax are particularly

jarring. The story can be read on many levels. McGraw has chosen to portray the deeper, darker side of Alice's adventures. This is definitely a sophisticated and special interpretation that will appeal to a very limited, mature audience.[177]

This contemporary idea that the original text has a "dark" side—and that drawing out hints of the sinister in *Alice* shows fidelity to Carroll's intention—was also evident in the *San Diego Union-Tribune*'s review of McGraw's interpretation:.

> Wonderland may be full of whimsy, but it is also a place with its dark edges. McGraw is attuned to this facet of Carroll's writing too. Some faces disturb more than delight; he renders the Queen as a signboard with shrivelled limbs and a small, ferocious mouth.[178]

However, none of these illustrators taps to any noticeable degree into the reading of *Alice* as steeped in sexual overtone, or conveys any sense of the discourse around Carroll as a man of dubious sexual tastes. The former interpretation has, as we saw, been around since the 1930s, and the "paedophilia" notion currently trails Carroll like a stalker through scholarly and journalistic discussion. But although Peake, Zwerger, Rackham, and McGraw all depict Wonderland—in very different ways—as an intermittently spooky or disturbing place, none of them hint that Alice is ever subject to a sexual threat.

Carroll's text would not actually prohibit such an imposed meaning in the illustration—there is nothing in the book to say that the White Rabbit doesn't have pornographic drawings of children on his wall, or that the Hatter isn't pawing at his young guest under the table—but even in these "darker" visualisations of Wonderland, the artists prefer not to acknowledge the rumours about Carroll's supposed obsession with young girls or to incorporate Freudian readings of the text explicitly into their imagery. McGraw's illustrations may be reviewed as suitable for a "mature audience", but they are surely not "adults only": the most unnerving of these *Alice*s could still be given to children.

What twentieth-century artists do occasionally recognise is the notion that *Alice* is a metaphor of growing up: we have seen that some illustrators, like Ralph Steadman and J. Morton Sale, depict the heroine as a girl of ambiguous age, potentially a teenager, and of course Peake's protagonist was noted for her sensuous potential. More generally, the artists who show Wonderland as an unnerving, almost nightmarish place support the reading that *Alice* is about a child's struggle in an adult world as she herself goes through the changes that lead to adulthood.

However, none of these versions of *Alice* are truly horrifying, however grotesque the inhabitants become; and this is surely because we take our cues from Alice. In all these Wonderlands the backgrounds and characters can be dismal or menacing, but the heroine never seems troubled by them. There is no sign that she is terrified, that she fears she won't escape Wonderland alive, that she is ever praying to get out of this place and go back home to the river bank. If Alice was shown to scream in any of these pictures the book would immediately become very much more disturbing; as it is, she remains calm, and so the adventure never sinks fully into the "darkness" that some contemporary critics see in the text. We could argue, though, that this basic level of reassurance is faithful to Carroll's tone: while Alice is subject to numerous death jokes, threats, and even physical attacks, she tends to respond by tossing her head and changing the subject.

If we identify with Alice, as Carroll is supposed to have done, then her reactions provide us with a guide to how we should feel, and in most of these illustrations she looks variously inquisitive, bored, and long-suffering: the responses of a polite child, not a knowing nymphet. Even in the most nightmarish imaginings of Peake and Rackham, it would be hard to find any suggestion of predatory sexuality; and as Oxenbury's version shows, *Alice* can also be made entirely innocent again. For all the Freudian interpretation of her plunge into holes, her long neck, and her key in little doors—for all that her creator has been pushed into the waiting-room of contemporary respectability, his case up for question while he lingers halfway between heritage celebrity and paedophile *persona non grata*—the books can still be held away from adult debates and renewed as a carefree, sunlit adventure for children. Carroll, however horrified he would be if he learned of his current reputation, might be gladdened by the continued success of Oxenbury's Alice.

Notes

1. Austin Dobson, from the prefatory "proem" to Arthur Rackham's illustrated edition of *Alice in Wonderland*, 1907), also misquoted by Gardner, *Annotated Alice*, p. 328.
2. Graham Ovenden and John Davis, *The Illustrators of Alice in Wonderland* (London: Academy Editions, 1972), p. 5.
3. See Jones and Gladstone, *Alice Companion*, p. 75, for a fabulously detailed account of Alice's outfit.
4. See Bakewell, *Biography*, pp. 147–49.
5. See Gardner, *Annotated Alice*, p. 294.
6. Tenniel, letter to Carroll (1 June 1970), quoted in Gardner, ibid. p. 183.
7. See Bakewell, *Biography*, p. 147, and Hancher, *Tenniel Illustrations*, p. 102.
8. Lewis Carroll, letter to Gertrude Thompson, no date, quoted in Bakewell, ibid.

9.   Ibid., p. 146.
10. Ovenden and Davis, *Illustrators of Alice*, p. 5.
11. Ibid., p. 18.
12. Carroll, *Alice in Wonderland*, reprinted in Gardner, *Annotated Alice*, p. 98.
13. Carroll, *Through the Looking-Glass*, reprinted in Gardner, ibid., p. 214. I owe Karoline Leach for this canny observation: see Leach, *Dreamchild*, p. 175.
14. We know she doesn't have ringlets, for instance, and that she has "wandering hair," but indications of what Alice looks like are very rare. See Carroll, *Alice in Wonderland*, reprinted in Gardner, *Annotated Alice*, p. 18, p. 109.
15. Carroll, *Alice in Wonderland*, ibid., p. 95.
16. Ovenden and Davis, *Illustrators of Alice*.
17. Ibid., p. 11.
18. Ibid., pp. 12–13.
19. See Lewis Carroll, Cooper Edens, ed., *Alice's Adventures in Wonderland* (San Francisco: Chronicle Books, 2000), p. 100, p. 115.
20. Ibid., p. 63, p. 72.
21. Ovenden and Davis, *Illustrators of Alice*, p. 11.
22. Lewis Carroll and Arthur Rackham, *Alice's Adventures in Wonderland* (Singapore: SeaStar Books, 2002).
23. Peter Glassman, "Afterword," ibid., p. 169.
24. See Edens, ed., *Alice in Wonderland*, p. 58; Newell's illustrations were also used in Gardner's *More Annotated Alice* of 1990.
25. Ibid., p. 107, for a particularly uncanny Mock Turtle.
26. Ibid., p. 67.
27. Ovenden and Davis, *Illustrators of Alice*, p. 13.
28. Ibid., p. 33, p. 45.
29. Ibid., p. 16.
30. Ibid., p. 33.
31. Ibid., p. 74.
32. Ibid., p. 17.
33. Graham Greene, letter to Mervyn Peake, quoted in Ovenden and Davis, ibid.
34. Ibid., p. 18.
35. Hilary Spurling, "A Subversive World of His Own," *Sunday Telegraph* (23 January 2000), n.p.
36. Ibid.
37. See Lewis Carroll and Ralph Steadman, *Through the Looking-Glass and What Alice Found There* (London: Hart-Davis, MacGibbon, 1975).
38. See *Illustrators of Alice*, *http://www.lewiscarroll.org/illus.html,* and the superb *Alice Illustrators* compendium by Lauren Harman, *http://laurenharman.tripod.com/alice/illustratorsal.html.*
39. Dinah Hall, "Christmas Books," *Sunday Telegraph*, 28 November 1999, n.p.
40. Elaine Williams, "The Joke's On Them," *Times Educational Supplement Primary Magazine*, 26 January 2001, p. 49.
41. Joanna Carey, "Different Strokes," *Times Educational Supplement*, 29 October 1999, p. 9.
42. *Guardian Education*, 16 May 2000, p. 67.
43. "Off the Shelf," *Guardian*, 9 May 2001, p. 9.
44. Catherine Lockerbie, "How Doth The Little Crocodile . . . " *The Scotsman*, 16 October 1999, p. 10.
45. Giles Gordon, "Christmas Light Reading," *The Scotsman*, 23 November 2000, p. 30.
46. Dinah Hall, "Christmas Books.".
47. Hancher, *Tenniel Illustrations*, p. 20.
48. Reprinted in Hancher, ibid., p. 116.
49. Ibid., p. 91, p. 93.
50. Ibid., p. 104.
51. Ibid., p. 94.

52. Jones and Gladstone, *Alice Companion*, pp. 247–48.
53. See Charlie Lovett, *Lewis Carroll's England: An Illustrated Guide for the Literary Tourist* (London: White Stone Publishing, 1998), p. 54, for more details on the painting.
54. Hancher, *Tenniel Illustrations*, p. 103.
55. "The 50 Best Books: Once Upon A Time," *Independent*, 27 November 1999, p. 4.
56. David Harrison, "A Thoroughly Modern Alice," *Sunday Telegraph*, 29 August 1999, p. 6.
57. Ibid.
58. Nicolette Jones, "From Circus Clown To Publisher," *The Times*, 9 August 2000, n.p.
59. Sarah Johnson, "Alice is Cool and Cuddly," *The Times*, 21 October 1999, n.p.
60. "Book Review," *Financial Times*, 20 November 1999, p. 4.
61. Carey, "Different Strokes." p. 9.
62. "Children's Books," *The Sunday Herald*, 21 November 1999, p. 31.
63. Julia Eccleshare, "New Faces in Wonderland," *Guardian*, 27 May 2000.
64. Susie Maguire, "The Perfect Draw," *Scotland on Sunday*, 18 June 2000, p. 13.
65. Carey, "Different Strokes."
66. Lewis Carroll and Lisbeth Zwerger, *Alice in Wonderland* (New York: North-South Books, 1999), p. 7.
67. Ibid., p. 13.
68. Ibid., p. 55.
69. Ibid., p. 41.
70. Ibid., p. 89.
71. Ibid., p. 25.
72. Johnson, "Alice Is Cool and Cuddly." n.p.
73. Carroll and Zwerger, *Alice in Wonderland*, p. 23.
74. Ibid., p. 85.
75. Lewis Carroll and Helen Oxenbury, *Alice's Adventures in Wonderland* (London: Walker Books, 1999) p, 103, p. 118.
76. Ibid., p. 22, pp. 60–61.
77. Ibid., p. 98.
78. Ibid., p. 40.
79. Ibid., p. 172.
80. Ibid., p. 149.
81. Ibid., pp. 206–7.
82. Edens, ed., *Alice in Wonderland*, p. 2.
83. Lewis Carroll, *Alice's Adventures Under Ground* (London: Pavillion, 1998), p. 23.
84. Carroll and Peake, *Alice in Wonderland*, p. 41.
85. Ibid., p. 63.
86. Ibid., p. 131.
87. Ibid, frontispiece.
88. Ibid., p. 3.
89. Ibid., pp. 116–17.
90. Lewis Carroll and Arthur Rackham, *Alice in Wonderland*, p. 168.
91. Ibid., p. 135.
92. Ibid., p. 103.
93. Ibid., p. 75.
94. Ibid., p. 85.
95. Ibid., p. 29.
96. See Ibid., p. 29.
97. See Ibid., p. 71, p. 85.
98. Ibid., p. 143.
99. Lewis Carroll and DeLoss McGraw, *Alice's Adventures in Wonderland* (New York: HarperCollins, 2001), p. 25.
100. Ibid., pp. 142–3.

101. Ibid., p. 60.
102. Ibid., p. 25.
103. Ibid., p. 86.
104. Ibid., p. 149.
105. Ibid., p. 2.
106. Ibid., p. 142.
107. Ibid., p. 169.
108. Carroll and Zwerger, *Alice in Wonderland*, p. 72.
109. Ibid., p. 59.
110. Carroll and Peake, *Alice in Wonderland*, p. 19. Cf. Gred Hildebrandt's unusual decision to depict the Owl and the Panther, picture reproduced in Stoffel, *Art of Alice*, p. 5.
111. Carroll and McGraw, *Alice in Wonderland*, p. 93.
112. Carroll and Oxenbury, *Alice in Wonderland*, p. 67.
113. Carroll, *Alice's Adventures Under Ground*, n.p.
114. See Stoffel, *Art of Alice*, p. 84, p. 112.
115. Carroll and Oxenbury, *Alice in Wonderland*, p. 67.
116. See also Oliver Hereford (1917) in Edens, ed., *Alice in Wonderland*, p. 31; a dishevelled Alice sprawled across the Rabbit's dining room.
117. Carroll, *Under Ground*, n.p.
118. Carroll, *Alice in Wonderland*, p. 41. See Hancher, *Tenniel Illustrations*, p. 31.
119. Carroll and Peake, *Alice in Wonderland*, p. 41.
120. Carroll and Zwerger, *Alice in Wonderland*, p. 29.
121. Carroll and McGraw, *Alice in Wonderland*, pp. 42–43.
122. Carroll and Oxenbury, *Alice in Wonderland*, pp. 60–61.
123. See also Charles Robinson and Margaret Tarrant in Edens, ed., *Alice in Wonderland*, p. 51, p. 53, and the manga version in Stoffel, *Art of Alice*, p. 57.
124. See also A. E. Jackson, in Edens, ed., p. 83, again with a similar layout, and Henry Morin in Stoffell, *Art of Alice*, p. 32.
125. See also the very similar picture by Mabel Lucie Atwell in Edens, p. 36.
126. Neither event featured in *Alice's Adventures Under Ground*.
127. See also his lobster from "The Voice of the Sluggard," Carroll and McGraw, *Alice in Wonderland,* p. 138, which seems directly informed by Tenniel's illustration of the creature.
128. Carroll, *Alice in Wonderland*, pp. 95–96.
129. Ibid., p. 74.
130. Ibid., p. 118.
131. Ibid., p. 117.
132. See also Maria Kirk, Charles Folkard, A. A. Nash, and A. L. Bowley in Edens, ed., *Alice in Wonderland*, p. 71, p. 72, p. 73, p. 77, and Jourcin, Frank Adams and Gwynedd M. Hudson in Stoffel, *Art of Alice*, p. 28, p. 42. p. 48. All seven base their visualisation of the Hatter unashamedly on Tenniel's, down to every detail of the outfit: bow tie, waistcoat, jacket, and top hat with price label.
133. See also Peter Newell, K.M.R. in Edens, ed., *Alice in Wonderland*, p. 58, p. 63; also Jourcin and Gordon Robinson in Stoffel, *Art of Alice*, p. 8, p. 43. Newell's Duchess is actually comparatively presentable as Duchesses go; K.M.R.'s and Robinson's are very close to Tenniel's. All four draw her headdress and robes according to the Tenniel model.
134. Carroll, *Alice in Wonderland*, p. 35.
135. Carroll and McGraw, *Alice in Wonderland*, p. 35.
136. Carroll and Zwerger, *Alice in Wonderland*, p. 24.
137. Carroll and Oxenbury, *Alice in Wonderland*, p. 49.
138. See Hancher, *Tenniel Illustrations*, p. 126.
139. Carroll, *Under Ground*, n.p.
140. Ibid., p. 127. There is no such correspondence in *Under Ground*.
141. Ibid.

142. Carroll and Rackham, *Alice in Wonderland*, p. 15.
143. Carroll and McGraw, *Alice in Wonderland*, p. 14.
144. Carroll and Zwerger, *Alice in Wonderland*, p. 13.
145. Carroll and Oxenbury, *Alice in Wonderland*, p. 26.
146. Ibid., p. 62.
147. Carroll and McGraw, *Alice in Wonderland*, p. 45.
148. Hancher, *Tenniel Illustrations*, pp. 121–22.
149. Ibid., p. 121.
150. Ibid.
151. Carroll and Oxenbury, *Alice in Wonderland*, pp. 108–9.
152. Ibid., pp. 112–13.
153. Ibid., p. 120.
154. Ibid., p. 116.
155. Carroll and Peake, *Alice in Wonderland*, p. 86.
156. Carroll and McGraw, *Alice in Wonderland*, pp. 88–89.
157. Ibid., p. 86.
158. Carroll and Rackham, *Alice in Wonderland*, pp. 85–86.
159. Carroll and Zwerger, *Alice in Wonderland*, pp. 54–55.
160. Hancher, *Tenniel Illustrations*, p. 58.
161. Ibid., p. 59.
162. Ibid., p. 60.
163. Ibid., p. 63.
164. Ibid., p. 61.
165. Ibid., p. 63.
166. Ibid., p. 64.
167. Carroll and Rackham, *Alice in Wonderland*, p. 101.
168. Carroll and Peake, *Alice in Wonderland*, p. 110.
169. Ibid., p. 107.
170. In fact, Carroll drew her as thin and angular: see *Under Ground* and Hancher, *Tenniel Illustrations*, p. 59.
171. Carroll and McGraw, *Alice in Wonderland*, p. 102.
172. Ibid., p. 107.
173. Ibid., p. 109.
174. Carroll and Zwerger, *Alice in Wonderland*, p. 64.
175. Carroll and Oxenbury, *Alice in Wonderland*, pp. 128–29.
176. Ibid., p. 123.
177. Heide Piehler, *School Library Journal*, quoted on reviews page for Carroll and McGraw on *Amazon.com*.
178. Robert L. Pincus, *San Diego Union-Tribune*, 28 October 2001, n.p.

5

THE FURTHER ADVENTURES OF ALICE

> I do not know if "Alice in Wonderland" was an *original* story—I
> was, at least, no *conscious* imitator in writing it—but I do know
> that, since it came out, something like a dozen story-books have
> appeared, on identically the same pattern.
>
> –Lewis Carroll[1]

*T*he Sandman was a monthly comic book scripted by the British author
Neil Gaiman and published by DC; it ran during the 1990s. The
protagonist was called Morpheus, or Dream, and his home territory
was the mass unconscious, centered around a castle. The castle contained
a library. In issue #22, from January 1991, the curator explained:

> It's a very unusual library . . . somewhere in here is every story that
> has ever been dreamed. You'll find none of them on earth. In this
> section, for example, are novels their authors never wrote, or never
> finished, except in dreams.[2]

On the shelves, in one small panel, we can see the spines of these books.
P. G. Woodhouse, *Psmith and Jeeves*; G. K. Chesterton, *The Man Who Was
October*, J. R. R. Tolkien, *The Lost Road*. At the far end, the curator is
taking a book down: peering closely, we can just make out Lewis Carroll's
Alice's Journey Behind the Moon.

Previously in Wonderland

The prospect of imagining a new adventure for Alice tempted writers
even before Carroll wrote his sequel; Carolyn Sigler's *Alternative Alices*

includes Jean Ingelow's *Mopsa the Fairy* and Juliana Horatia Ewing's *Amelia and the Dwarfs* from 1869 and 1870 respectively. Sigler structures her collection into various categories, from subversive through didactic to sentimental and political; all the stories, however, are pre-1930, from what she calls the "golden age of Carroll's influence on popular literature". These examples take on the structures and themes of the *Alice* books "and respond to the issues they raise" rather than using them as a vehicle to explore or parody distinct contemporary issues, as was, she says, the tendency after 1930;[3] her anthology ends with a section of satires from the early twentieth century, such as Saki's *Westminster Alice*, Caroline Lewis's *Clara in Blunderland*, and Edward Hope's *Alice in the Delighted States*. We have already seen examples of how this trend continued with *Alice in Blunderland*, *Alice in Rationland*, and their like. The earlier stories are in a different vein, attempting simply to reproduce the pleasures of Carroll's original.

> They thus share specific characteristics with Carroll's *Alice* books and with one another: an *Alice*-like protagonist or protagonists . . . who is typically polite, articulate, and assertive; a clear transition from the "real" waking world to a fantasy dream world . . . rapid shifts in identity, appearance, and location; an episodic structure often centering on encounters with nonhuman fantasy characters and/or characters based on nursery rhymes . . . nonsense language and interpolated nonsense verse, verse-parodies, or songs, an awakening or return to the "real" world . . . and, usually, a clear acknowledgement of indebtedness to Carroll through a dedication, apology, mock-denial of influence, or other textual or extratextual reference.[4]

References to Alice in comic books constitute an unwritten history. In the superhero comics of recent years—the more adult-oriented mainstream stories of the graphic novel period, following the success of Alan Moore's *Watchmen* and Frank Miller's *Dark Knight Returns* in 1986—Alice, her supporting cast and author have been a recurring motif. The overlap of the Lewis Carroll "mythos", as comic fans would call it, with Batman titles alone would be worthy of a chapter to itself. A costumed villain known as the Mad Hatter—dressed as Tenniel designed him, right down to the "In This Style, 10/6" label—has been a regular since 1949,[5] and the debt to Carroll is made explicit in Jeph Loeb and Tim Sale's *Haunted Knight* (1996), where the character's first appearance sees him snarling, in jagged lettering, "twinkle, twinkle, little bat!"

Batman's reaction to the Hatter in this story is interesting in terms of its construction of Carroll and Alice as innocent nostalgia, something precious that the homicidal schizophrenic Tetch—for so the story diagnoses him—has corrupted. This cherishing of Carroll and his work as untainted stands in contrast to the "dark" discourse, prevalent in the 1990s as we saw from Chapters 2 and 3, which sees the *Alice* books as coded allegories and their author as a dubious individual with suspect motives. For Bruce Wayne/Batman, who was orphaned at a young age by a petty criminal, childhood is especially sacred; *Alice* is clearly positioned for him here as an artefact associated with his beloved mother—again, Carroll would approve—and fiercely protected. "In taking his identity from *Alice in Wonderland*," Batman muses, "Jervis Tetch unknowingly perverts a happy childhood memory . . . of which I have so few . . . and reminds me of her . . . which I cannot afford to have happen."[6]

It is Tetch's appropriation of Carroll as props for his criminality—with overtones of child molestation—that outrages Batman, although it seems clear that Tetch is on one level only reading into Carroll what some critics have been identifying for decades, and seeing Alice as inherently disturbing. The clash between superhero and villain in this story, then—which is self-consciously strewn with echoes from *Wonderland*—could be seen as a clash of interpretations. Tetch kidnaps a group of Gotham City's children, including Commissioner Gordon's daughter Babs, and forces them to act out his fantasies by dressing them in masks of the Dodo, the Duchess, and the Cheshire Cat. "Some sort of insane tea party," Gordon mutters. "Keeps them sedated . . . making them drink drugged tea. The one dressed as Alice . . . matches the description of my daughter." Inside Babs is slouching in the armchair at the end of Tetch's table, in a double-page spread explicitly pastiching the Tenniel illustration. "I don't mean to be rude," she scowls. "Really. I just . . . don't like tea."[7]

Batman, however, is also acting out his own reading of Carroll, finding himself semi-consciously reciting lines from the text. When he meets the runaway masked as the Cheshire Cat, the child tells him he's mad. "How do you know I'm mad?" asks Batman. "You must be," is the inevitable reply, "or you wouldn't have come here."[8] Following a rat towards Tetch's hideout, Batman ponders "O Mouse . . . do you know the way out of this pool?"[9] Their face-to-face confrontation, then, is partly a battle to decide who will be master of what *Alice* means, as well as the more prosaic matter of rescuing kidnapped children from a predator. Tetch panics, seeing his approaching nemesis as the Jabberwock, and Batman marks his victory by smashing the Hatter's head into a mirror, knocking him out of the *Wonderland* text and into its sequel. "Jervis Tetch lost his mind . . . " runs his internal commentary, "swallowed up in the book . . . but this madness ends . . . through the looking glass."[10]

The final scene shows Bruce Wayne retiring to his library and confirming his own interpretation of the text as a comforting, though bittersweet artefact. "On rainy days in particular . . . I miss my mother."[11] As in *Sandman*, we see the spine of a Carroll book on the library shelf, and Batman curls up, out of costume and huddled in a dressing gown. The final words of the story are "Alice was beginning to get tired of sitting by her sister on the bank . . . " *Alice* has been reinstated as a safe, innocent text, although the adventure shows that this meaning has to be fought for and defended.

Batman stories, like most mainstream comic book narratives, are underscored with laws, sometimes explicit and sometimes unwritten, of "continuity"—the names, dates, meetings, events of the superheroes' lives that have to be kept in consistent order to retain a sense of a credible fictional world and avoid the wrath of fans. Of course, some landmarks in Batman's career, or features of his character, are more important to readers than others. It is understood that Wayne started out as a solo crimefighter, for instance, and so a story that contradicted continuity by showing Robin during this period would be "wrong". The notion that Wayne's mother read him *Alice in Wonderland* shortly before her murder would feature far lower down the hierarchy of continuity, and yet the inclusion of this subplot in *Haunted Knight* is probably due to the fact that Carroll and Alice are woven into an earlier Batman volume, *Arkham Asylum*, with very similar connotations.

This hardback graphic novel, written by Grant Morrison, also features the Mad Hatter, and his appearance is again marked by a recitation, in a similar spiky font, of "Twinkle, Twinkle, Little Bat." The coincidence of finding a bat in the Mad Tea Party rhyme is obviously irresistibly tempting to both Morrison and Loeb—and *Arkham Asylum* also quotes the Cat's "We're all mad here . . . you must be, or you wouldn't have come here" line as an opening epigram[12]—but the similarities between their melding of Carroll and Batman run deeper. Morrison also links the *Alice* books to Bruce Wayne's childhood and relationship with his mother, while portraying the Hatter as a corrupting agent and associating him with child molestation. Leering as he puffs on a hookah and fingers a Barbie doll—Dave McKean's illustrations of the character are clearly based on the British comedian Sid James, famous for his lewd chuckle—the Hatter tells Batman

> . . . that's why children . . . interest me. They're all mad, you see. But in each of them is an implicate adult. Order out of chaos. To know them is to know myself. Little girls, especially. Little blonde girls. Little

shameless bitches! Oh God. God help us all! Sometimes . . . sometimes I think the asylum is a head. We're inside a huge head that dreams us all into being. Perhaps it's your head, Batman. Arkham is a looking glass. And we are you.[13]

Morrison is clearly riffing on the Red King syndrome, the question "which dreamed it?" and playing up the notion that Batman, an adult in fancy dress driven by his parents' murder, may be no less insane than those he puts in the asylum. There is also, more obviously than in Loeb's story, a knowing, nudge-nudge awareness of the Carroll-as-paedophile rumour and an understanding that readers will recognize the reference: the Hatter is clearly drawing his love-hate affair with "little blonde girls" from a reading of the *Alice* books as disguised expressions of obsession, and from the popular perception of the Carroll-Alice Liddell relationship as romantic or quasi-sexual.

Batman, on the other hand—as in Loeb's story—is repeatedly linked to his mother; he cries "mommy?" when in pain, visualizes her variously as a nun at prayer or dressed in pearls on the day of her murder, and is taunted by one of the inmates as "mommy's boy". The quotation at the end of the book links this motif with the alternative reading of Carroll's *Alice* as a comforting text of childhood.

And is that not a Mother's gentle hand that withdraws your curtains, and a Mother's sweet voice that summons you to rise? To rise and forget, in the bright sunlight, the ugly dreams that frightened you so when all was dark.[14]

The passage is from "An Easter Greeting to Every Child Who Loves 'Alice' ", which Carroll added to *Looking Glass* in 1876, and the sentimental lines offer a very different representation of Carroll and *Alice* to that suggested by the Hatter in the asylum. This is the innocent, reverent Carroll, and the view of *Alice* as nostalgic fairy-tale, as opposed to the twisted, sinister version voiced by the Hatter. This take on the books and their author is given a double authority; it is associated through the memories of an idealized mother with Batman, who plays the role in this narrative of upright and even prudish crimefighter contrasted to the deviance of the asylum, and it comes with the relief of the story's end, as a last word.

As in Loeb, we are presented with the two key readings of Carroll/ Alice that I identified in the Introduction and have been tracing through the previous chapters—the vision of *Alice* and her author as "dark", perverted and disturbing, and as "light", precious and nostalgic—and while the former interpretation is given a temporary space to dominate, it is ruled out by the end in Batman's victory and reaffirmation of the Carroll who whispered the praises of the Victorian mother and offered pious advice to his beloved child-readers.

Morrison's fascination with Carroll extends into his other superhero work of the same period—in *Zenith*, written for the British weekly comic *2000AD*, a woman vanishes in stages, leaving first a grinning face and then a Cheshire grin;[15] in a later episode, a classic paradox puzzle is solved through reference to Lewis Carroll.[16] Carroll's world of nursery-rhymes-gone-wrong, adults in animal form, and looking-glass logic seems to offer intriguing possibilities for crossover into the superhero universe of grown-ups in animal costume, clowns-turned-killers, and dual identies. The extent of this borrowing could be explored at far greater length—*Worlds Finest*, for instance, compares Lex Luthor and the Joker with the Lion and Unicorn, and Superman and Batman with White and Black Knights in a "deadly quadrille".[17]

One further intriguing example, distinct from the superhero genre although written by one of the giants of the field, is Alan Moore's *Lost Girls*. This independent comic book series, with art by Melinda Gebbie, explores the later lives of child-heroines Dorothy, Wendy, and Alice, who find themselves staying at the same hotel near Lake Constance, on the Austrian border. The date is given on the back cover as 1913, but Alice is "on the verge of sixty", which, if we work from the fictional Alice being seven years old in 1865, would actually point to 1917.

Although the character in *Lost Girls* has parallels with Alice Liddell, Moore—whose meticulously researched graphic novel *From Hell*, about the Ripper murders, shows that he can reconstruct period and biography when he chooses to—is imagining the future of the book-Alice, not the real daughter of the Dean. This Alice is Lady Fairchild, who part-owns a mine in Pretoria and also keeps a house called "Greylawns", presumably in the UK.[18] Alice Liddell, of course, became Alice Hargreaves, and in 1913, at the age of sixty-one, was living at "Cuffnells" in Hampshire with her husband; by 1917 her circumstances were unchanged except that two of her three sons had been killed in action.[19]

This elderly aristocrat, then, presumably holds the same relationship with Alice Hargreaves as Tenniel's blonde did with the young Alice Liddell: half-sisters with some similarities of personality despite the difference in appearance.[20] A couplet from "Child of the Pure Unclouded Brow", the verse that opens *Through the Looking-Glass*, serves as epigram—"We are but older children, dear, who fret to find their bedtimes near"—and Alice's chapter is called "The Mirror". Moore's Alice would not please purists, as she has been given the more suspect traits that some critics ascribe to Carroll. Her dressing table holds a bottle of laudanum, recalling the theories that Carroll must have been on some kind of hallucinogenic drug—Katie Roiphe has him using the same substance in her novel *Still She Haunts Me*—and the first page finds her seducing a young girl. The scene is shown through reflections, with only part of the room visible, but the speech balloons are unambiguous. One voice demands "tell me a story." The other, which we deduce to be Alice Fairchild's, replies, and the two alternate across the remaining panels.

Oh, I don't know any stories. Your little white breasts, they're so lovely. They'll never be as beautiful once you're grown. Will you touch them for me?

Most certainly not. First, you really ought to tell me a story. That's manners.

Well, at least let me see you properly. Open your legs just a little, and I'll do the same. Yes, there. Like that.

May I have my story now?

Goodness, child, were you always this impatient? I haven't forgotten your story. It's just that I want to touch myself . . . [21]

In Moore's fiction it is Alice who is haunted, phantomwise, by half-memories of the mirror. Trying to tell her young girlfriend the story she demands, Alice rambles, clutching for fragments from the tale Carroll related in the 1860s.

I recall there was something very important, very fragile, but then a terrible thing happened and it got broken, forever. Nobody could ever mend it, but what? . . . The mirror never breaks, the mirror never melts. Not anymore. [22]

Later, Alice relates to the looking-glass image of herself as a lover, performing naked in front her reflection and exchanging sweet nothings. "Oh, that was good. Just watching you, it thrills me so much."

Again, there is a reference to Carroll that would be obvious to many readers, and strike a subconscious chord with others—"I know, the barrier between doesn't melt anymore doe's [sic] it, like silvery mist? It doesn't break." [23] In *Looking-Glass*, the barrier into the dreamworld melts away, "just like a bright silvery mist." [24] While its rewriting of Alice as a narcissistic paedophile and drug addict might well be distasteful to lovers of the original books, Moore's series can be seen as an interesting example of contemporary fiction that taps into the reading of Carroll and his children's stories as "dark "and laden with hidden, adult perversions, but projects these elements onto the figure of his heroine."[25]

Obviously, we are already talking about different types of story here. The tales in Sigler's collection—especially those with an explicit basis in Carroll's mythos like Anna M. Richards's *A New Alice in the Old Wonderland*, John Rae's *New Adventures of Alice*, and Howard R. Garis's *Uncle Wiggly in Wonderland*—attempt to continue the *Alice* series or at least provide a similar fairy-tale adventure peppered with linguistic quibbles and topsy-turvy verses. *Lost Girls* is also a continuation, in a very different way, of the fictional Alice's life after *Looking-Glass*. *Haunted Knight* and *Arkham Asylum*, on the other hand, incorporate themes and motifs from *Alice* for their resonance with the psychology of Batman and his regular cast, but treat Carroll's books as fictional references within the Batman mythos.

The body of this chapter deals in detail with three novels, all published within the last twenty years; two of them fit within the first category, and one takes a different angle by reconstructing not the fictional Alice but the real Liddell girl and her relationship with Carroll. Gilbert Adair's *Alice Through the Needle's Eye* and Jeff Noon's *Automated Alice* are both "third adventures", taking very different approaches while displaying similarities not just in their attempts to pastiche Carroll's style but in their plot devices and imagery. Katie Roiphe's *Still She Haunts Me* is an exploration of Carroll's relationship with Alice Liddell, set in a fairly faithfully recreated period environment and based largely on the available documents of their lives during the 1860s.

As we have seen, there is a precedent for Noon and Adair's experiments in style that dates back before *Looking-Glass*, but Roiphe was not the first to recreate Carroll as a character in fiction. Anne Thackeray, according to Karoline Leach, depicted him as the confident, rather cold "George Hexham" in *From An Island* (1877), her roman a clef of the social circle around Tennyson's Isle of Wight residence.[26]

> Hexham was, as I have said, a young man of an impatient humour. He was a little hard as young men are apt to be. But there was something reassuring in his very hardness and faith in himself and his own doings. It was reassuring because it was a genuine expression of youthful strength and power. No bad man could have had that perfect confidence which marked most of George Hexham's sayings and doings. His was, after all, the complacency of good intentions . . . [27]

As Leach notes, this is a distinctly "un-'Carrollian' " portrait, failing to match up with the received ideas of the man as a shy, stuttering recluse or a dreamy, overgrown child. However, as she points out, Thackeray was actually acquainted with Carroll, and her fictional version of him deserves attention as a record, however elaborated or disguised, of how Dodgson came across to at least one observer of the time. By contrast, Pat Barker, writing over a century later in *The Ghost Road*, includes a far more familiar cameo.

> At dinner one evening Mr Dodgson had leaned across to mother and said, "I l-l-l-love all ch-ch-ch-ch-"
> "Train won't start," Charles had whispered.
> "Children, M-Mrs Rivers, as l-l-l-long as they're g-g-g-girls."
> He had looked down the table at the two boys, and it had seemed to Rivers that the sheer force of his animosity had loosened his tongue. "*Boys are a mistake.*"[28]

Edward Wakeling, who discussed this passage in a lecture at the Lewis Carroll Society in April 2003, investigated its veracity by writing to Pat Barker. The novelist generously pointed him to Katharine Rivers's "Memories of Lewis Carroll", which, as Wakeling observed, was far from an entirely reliable document; it was written long after Katharine actually met the author, and contained a number of instances of pure wishful thinking. As Wakeling notes, the depiction feels "right" and fits our perception of Carroll's personality—or rather, "the myths concerning his personality."[29]

The three novels I have chosen to study in more depth, it will be noticed, only fall into two of the three categories I identified above. The third—novels from the last few decades that refer to the *Alice* books in some way but do not incorporate Carroll as character or attempt to continue Alice's adventures—do not really warrant such extensive discussion. The most obvious examples are the anonymously authored *Go Ask Alice*, a supposedly genuine account of a teenage runaway's involvement in drugs and prostitution, and A. M. Homes's *The End of Alice*, the story of a paedophile and his epistolary relationship with a teenage girl that, as we saw in Chapter 2, prompted outrage from the *Daily Mail* reviewer Jim Harding.

Harding fumed that "the cynical reference to Lewis Carroll's creation is quite deliberate."[30] In fact, there is little more than a reference here—another Carroll quotation as epigram, this time "A stopped clock is right twice a day."[31] The line has no obvious relation to the novel itself, except in its implication that even a self-confessed pervert like the book's narrator can, on occasion, engage us and invite our complicity; otherwise, it seems only to be there to trigger the reader's "knowledge" about Lewis Carroll's relationship with young girls and give the story a wry literary echo. The quotation from Carroll would clearly be mystifying and pointless if the whispers about his paedophilia were not familiar to most readers; that its relevance to a story about the seduction of children seems obvious—even if we reject the association—is testament to how widespread and well-known this discourse has become.

Homes need offer no more explanation for the quotation; no paragraph from Carroll's writing about the perfect age for child-models, or affection-ate letter to a young friend. The mere name "Lewis Carroll" and the idea of sexual relationships with pre-adolescents, she demonstrates, walk hand in hand in the public imagination. Even a critic like Harding, who recoils from the cynical use of "Alice" and the novel's deliberate brutalising of that name's connotations—it still conjures up a sense of childhood inno-cence despite all the readings of Carroll's work as sophisticated or sinister allegory—understands full well what Homes is playing at.

Go Ask Alice, which claims to be based on the diary of a middle-class girl, is also deliberately titled to recall Carroll; here once more "Alice" evokes a reassuringly safe childhood, making the protagonist's downward spiral through exploitation and addiction more striking. The name cannot help but call to mind Carroll's heroine, and just as the juxtaposition of "Alice" with sexual murder seems like a violation, so this Alice's decline is brought home as a fall from innocence partly because of what the name so strongly implies. However, while Homes assumes we know the rumours about Carroll's paedophilia, *Go Ask Alice* just as obviously nods to the 1960s reading of Carroll as drug user. The title alone makes this explicit through its link to Carroll through the Jefferson Airplane song "White Rabbit", which implies that all Alice's shape-changes were the result of various recreational drugs:

> One pill makes you larger
> And one pill makes you small,
> And the ones that mother gives you
> Don't do anything at all.
> Go ask Alice
> When she's ten feet tall.
> . . .
> When the men on the chessboard
> Get up and tell you where to go
> And you've just had some kind of mushroom
> And your mind is moving low.

Go ask Alice
I think she'll know.[32]

The book's title was presumably chosen by the editors of the supposedly genuine diary, but the link to Carroll is made by the author herself in an entry shortly following her first experiments with LSD.

It's a completely new world I'm exploring, and you can't even conceive the wide new doors that are opening up before me. I feel like Alice in Wonderland. Maybe Lewis G. Carroll was on drugs too.[33]

The addition of a middle initial is comically baffling—unless it's a variant on the pattern that adds an "H" to "Jesus Christ"—and gives the impression that the narrator's theories were not really based on an intimate knowledge of the *Alice* books. As with *The End of Alice*, the references here are brief and used for the immediate triggers that "Alice" and "Carroll" can produce—the contrasting kick of innocence and psychedelia, childhood and corruption.

"How sad no third adventure lies in wait . . . "

I am approaching *Alice Through The Needle's Eye* and the other two novels in this study much as I have previously examined Internet-based fanfiction.[34] This comparison may meet with some resistance from those who see published novels as considerably superior to stories posted on a Web site—particularly those stories within the genre of "slash fiction", which typically explore sexual or romantic relationships between pop culture characters. Of course, a book like *Still She Haunts Me*, imagining Carroll and Alice's relationship, written by Katie Roiphe and published by an imprint of Hodder Headline, does not hold the same cultural status as "Secrets of the Heart", imagining Qui-Gon Jinn and Mace Windu's relationship, written by Anastasia and published on the *Star Wars* fan site *Master Apprentice*.[35] I wouldn't seek to argue that these particular stories have identical literary merit, although I do believe that we shouldn't assume professionally published novels are by any means inherently "better" than online fiction; it would be easy to find examples from both ends of the cultural hierarchy that contradict this idea. However, I think the three *Alice* novels I am examining here have a great deal in common with the fan fiction I have encountered; on a formal level, in their relationship with the "official" texts of Alice and Carroll, and in the dynamic they build between familiar, accepted elements of the mythos and invented, imagined additions that still have to feel "right".

As I shall explore more fully in Chapter 8, Carrollians engage with Carroll and Alice in ways extremely similar to those of popular media fans relating to their favoured texts and icons. Rather than seeing a comparison of Adair and Roiphe's novels with fanfiction as a provocative manoeuvre, a cheeky debasing of the former or an unwarranted elevation of the latter form, I think we should get over the prejudices attached to the word "fandom" and accept that if these fictional elaborations around the official Carroll/Alice mythos can be productively examined through theories from fan studies, there is no point resisting for the sake of snobbishness. After all, could, or would anyone write an Alice novel without being a Carroll fan of some description?

Any sequel—or "trequel", as Noon calls his third adventure—aims to combine the familiar with the new; to reassure the reader they are in the same world as before, with the same pleasures, but to still excite and surprise. Fanfiction that attempts to continue someone else's fictional world, especially when that world is extremely dependent on an individual language, tone, and prose style, like the Alice mythos—it would be almost unthinkable to write a third adventure for Alice and not try to reproduce Carroll's distinctive "voice"—does the same, but doubly so. Adair's challenge is to make the reader feel he or she is back in Carroll's hands, to reassure us and encourage us to trust him as we settle comfortably into the illusion that we really are experiencing a third adventure—or at least, a good enough simulation of it. Of course, a new story requires novelty, but Adair has to ensure that his invented elements are the kind of elements Carroll "would have" invented, according to our sense of his persona. In addition to recreating Alice as a character, then, Adair has to recreate Carroll as an author, and then inhabit that imagined authorship—in Noon's terms, a kind of automated Carroll, or replicant—to write what Carroll "would have written". He enters into a complex conjuring act with the reader—we want to be complicit in the illusion, because we want a new adventure for Alice by "Carroll", but too many disruptions will destroy our pleasure. How he pulls it off, for the most part, is worth examining carefully.

Firstly, Adair constructs a careful pastiche of Carroll's style; that is, the style in Alice, because the Carroll of *Sylvie and Bruno* or of poetry like "Faces in the Fire" (1860) is not what the reader expects or wants. Presumably Adair has achieved this effect by both consciously studying and noting distinctive traits and motifs—linguistic, typographical—and less consciously, internalizing a feeling for Carroll's rhythm and tone. The first page is obviously the most important in terms of gaining the reader's trust and allowing him or her to relax into an authentic fake.

We open *in media res*, immediately recalling—whether we remember it or not—*Through the Looking-Glass* with its abrupt "One thing was certain, that the *white* kitten had had nothing to do with it".[36] Adair cleverly echoes this with "Even if Alice didn't know for certain how long she had been trying to thread the needle, she couldn't help but notice that the sand in the hour-glass which stood on the chimney-piece was slipping away at an alarming rate."[37] Before going further, I want to suggest a distinction between two different types of readers of Carroll-related fiction; this will inevitably be a broad categorisation, but I think it enables a meaningful point to be made about potential responses.

Any reader of Adair's novel, let us assume, will have read the two existing *Alice* books and know something about Carroll's life—for the sake of sketching a sense of this reader, let's imagine he or she has read some of the newspaper articles from Chapter 2, but none of the biographies from Chapter 1. We could think of this reader as the interested layperson, with a general level of knowledge about Carroll and Alice gained from journalism, but no inclination to attend Lewis Carroll Society meetings or to read *Sylvie and Bruno*. The second type of reader I would call the Carrollian, for shorthand—the fan, the specialist. This reader will be intimately familiar with the *Alice* books from repeated readings and will have read, even written, commentaries on them; he or she will own more than one biography of Carroll's life and will see most journalistic accounts on Carroll as comparatively loose and inaccurate.

These are, again, very broad types, meant to imply a general distinction between Carroll fan and non-fan; the categories are problematised in this case because a reader with a casual but not committed interest in Carroll would still have picked up a great deal of information or misinformation about him from less specialist sources. The individual who likes Carroll's *Alice* books but has never felt inclined to read a biography would be likely to have a fairly certain idea about where he worked, what his personality was like, and what relationship he had with young girls. There is also a range of potential distinctions between and around these two proposed reading positions. As we shall see, though Roiphe and Adair seem to have undertaken considerable research, there are still points in their fictions where a reader with even more knowledge would catch them out and lose faith in their authority; similarly, though Noon is a self-confessed fan, he reproduces discourses around Carroll and Alice that others, perhaps more invested in protecting Carroll's reputation, would see as unfounded myth, lazy, or even slanderous.

We are talking about a continuum, then, rather than binary categories with no overlap or middle ground in between. If my definition of the "interested layperson" as being someone familiar with Chapter 2's newspaper stories seems rather loose, the concept of the "Carrollian" is informed by my study of the Lewis Carroll Society and by questionnaire responses from a sample of its members; so there is a basis in real people behind this working definition, and we shall meet them in Chapter 8.

In this instance, to go back to my two general types, I would draw the distinction that while the "Carrollian" probably knows the opening line of *Looking-Glass* more or less by heart and immediately recognises what Adair is doing, the "layperson" feels a sense of rightness and familiarity about Adair's sentence without knowing precisely why. Similarly, the layperson will pass over "chimney-piece", merely allowing the word to cushion his or her reassuring sensation that this is the Victorian interior we expect from Carroll; the Carollian may well be nudged to remember that Carroll revised his texts a number of times between 1866 and 1897, and made numerous fiddly, almost pointless changes, most of which involved adding hyphenation. In the 1897 edition of *Wonderland*, for instance, "schoolroom" became "school-room" and "Cheshire Puss" was transformed to "Cheshire-Puss".[38] This more specialist knowledge adds an extra level of wry pleasure as we observe and appreciate Adair's attention to detail, and perhaps congratulate ourselves on spotting it, too.

The remainder of Adair's opening paragraph runs " 'If I don't succeed *very* soon,' she thought, 'poor Dinah's jacket wo'n't be ready till next winter but one!' " Of course, here we have Dinah, a recurring secondary character in the "real world" of *Wonderland* and *Looking-Glass*,[39] as a landmark to orient ourselves back in the familiar fictional universe. We are also hearing Alice's reported thoughts for the first time—her rather rambling little musings, which crop up in quotation marks in the first paragraph of *Wonderland* with the famous " 'what is the use of a book,' thought Alice, 'without pictures or conversations?' "[40]

A little more subtly, the italics on "*very* soon" are unnecessary to the actual meaning of Adair's sentence, but invaluable in establishing the right tone and our confidence in the simulation of Carroll's voice. "*Very* remarkable" appears in the third paragraph of *Wonderland*, and "*white* kitten" right in the first line of *Looking-Glass*; the slightly prissy, precise effect of italics is a key element in Carroll's narration and, more broadly, relates to our idea of his character as a little finicky and just-so. "Wo'n't" is, however, a more surprising choice on Adair's part. According to Hugh Haughton's notes, Carroll changed "can't" and "won't" to the more pedantically correct "ca'n't" and "wo'n't" in his 1897 edition of *Wonderland*,[41] but this spelling doesn't seem to have survived to every recent edition of the book—it is in the Penguin Classics version and the *Definitive Annotated Alice*, but not the original *Annotated Alice* or the Bloomsbury *Wonderland* with the Mervyn Peake illustrations. To some readers, then, Adair's "wo'n't" may sound "false", too over-correct, and will jar with the *Alice* of their acquaintance.

Adair wastes no time in laying on the traits we expect from Carroll, perhaps knowing that the illusion must be built quickly and convincingly. The first two tricks of wordplay begin in the next line, as we learn that Alice would boast of Dinah's

> oh, *ump*teen kittens, perhaps even twice that mysterious number. (For Alice, no matter how slowly and carefully she counted, somehow never managed to find a place for umpteen, "though I can certainly count up to twenty, and umpteen *must* come before that.") Now the kittens had kittens of their own. "What ought one to call *them*, I wonder? Grand kittens?" Yes, thought Alice with a dreamy smile, the word would do nicely. For hadn't they all been grand kittens, every last fluffy one of them . . . [42]

The inclusion of a wry, parenthetical aside is, again, neatly in keeping with Carroll's style and as important to his storytelling persona as the italics;[43] but this passage seems, frankly, to be overdoing the tweeness. The authorial voice is clearly patronising towards Alice in a way that invites indulgent adult smiles, rather than speaking to a child's understanding of the world. Alice's limited ability with figures makes her seem rather less sharp than she was in *Looking-Glass*, where she smartly works out 365 minus 1 immediately in her head, and only writes it out in her memorandum book when Humpty doesn't understand the sum.[44] In Carroll's scene it is, by contrast, Alice who "couldn't help smiling", and the joke is on the adult egghead. Similarly, Adair's Alice seems rather fluffy and silly, going off into reveries about kittens: this doesn't seem quite the same girl who decided "*that* you wo'n't!" and deliberately pushed the White Rabbit into a glass cucumber-frame,[45] or held her own—"then it wasn't very civil of you to offer it", "you should learn not to make personal remarks"[46]—with a Hatter and Hare she'd only just met.

In fairness to Adair, though, we could remember that the opening to *Looking-Glass* features Alice in a quite sickeningly sentimental mood—

> " 'I wonder if the snow *loves* the tress and fields, that it kisses them so gently? And then it covers them up snug, you know, with a white quilt;

and perhaps it says 'Go to sleep, darlings, till the summer comes again.' "[47]

We might also make the allowance that, had Carroll written a third adventure for Alice, it would probably have taken another five or six years to appear—*Looking-Glass* was published six years after *Wonderland*—and that Carroll's writing for children grew more pious and sentimental as he grew older.

The same pattern of familiarity and the right kind of novelty, balancing the reassuringly recognisable and the reassuringly not-too-different, continues to weave through Adair's introduction. *Looking-Glass* took place before Guy Fawkes Night and *Needle's Eye* is set in December, which gives a sense of continuity although it disrupts Carroll's structure of exactly six months passing between episodes, and also, surprisingly, doesn't seem to add Alice's age up correctly: she is seven and six months in *Looking-Glass* but a full four months older in Adair's fiction.[48]

Alice's sister, who plays an important part in both of the original adventures as an offscreen presence, the one Alice reports back to later,[49] is mentioned on page 2 of Adair's story. Equally early on, we get Alice coining the word "vexingest", which most readers would surely recognise as a creation along the lines of "curiouser", and which both confirms our sense of her character—happy to make things up when she's not entirely sure—and provides a convincingly "Carrollian" wordplay. Alice's nurse appears on the same page, effectively ticking-off another box in the list of minor characters—she is mentioned in the first scene of *Looking-Glass*,[50] and Adair diligently inserts a reference for added authenticity. Finally, Alice's attempts to thread her needle—"the thread would happily have gone through *the time before* or *the time after*—but never at the right time"—are an example of another motif which, I think, would immediately strike the Carroll fan as a self-conscious play on "jam to-morrow and jam yesterday—but never jam *today*" from *Looking-Glass*,[51] and to the reader less intimately familiar with the originals, simply feel appropriate and fitting in its whimsical logic.

A few more brief examples will show how carefully and thoroughly this opening sequence is crafted from an armoury of *Alice* motifs, tweaked until they become just different enough. The anthropomorphism of Alice's needle and thread—which seems to quiver "exactly as if it were wrinkling up its nose"[52]—is in keeping with her cutesy attitude towards the snow and indeed the kittens in *Looking-Glass*. Her whimsical imagining that Dinah's "maeiou-ing" constitutes an attempt to learn the alphabet[53] reminds us—again, perhaps semi-consciously—of her fancy that Kitty, in *Looking-Glass*, purred at a clever chess move.[54] Buttercup, the name Adair gives to one of the kittens, is a clever variant on Snowdrop from *Looking-Glass*. The notion that Dinah and Alice might be able to chatter together, in *Needle's Eye*, is in the silly spirit of Alice's scolding of the *Looking-Glass* Kitty—"you little mischievous darling! . . . I'm going to tell you all your faults."[55]

Adair's Alice plans to teach Dinah "what the French is for mouse, you know",[56] echoing her musings on how to address the *Wonderland* mouse based on a Latin grammar—"to a mouse—a mouse—O mouse!"[57]—and we get the sense that Alice is learning the language from the Red Queen's "speak in French when you ca'n't think of the English for a thing"[58] and "what's the French for fiddle-de-dee?"[59] As she tumbles through the needle's eye, Alice considers that she might be consulted as an expert on bird's-eye views—" 'an Orni-theologist, I think it's called—' (she *thought*, but she was by no means *certain*)".[60] Compare Carroll's account of her fall down the rabbit hole:

> "I wonder what Latitude or Longitude I've got to?" (Alice had not the slightest idea what Latitude was, or Longitude either, but she thought they were nice grand words to say.) . . . "How funny it'll seem to come out among the people that walk with their heads downwards! The antipathies, I think—" (she was rather glad there *was* no one listening, this time, as it didn't sound at all the right word)[61]

One interesting twist is that some of Adair's motifs seem drawn not from the existing *Alice* books but from intertextual material—Carroll's letters and, as we shall see below, elements from his and Alice Liddell's biographies. The imagined conversation with Dinah in *Needle's Eye*, including its mention of French, is a little like Carroll's letter to Xie Kitchin, reprinted in Morton Cohen's selected collection and widely available: "the little dog thought for a minute, and then he said "She's very 'bonne', you know: that means 'good' in French. But she's not so good as a bone!"[62] Adair's play on "maeiou-ing" and on Dinah's ability to produce the consonants "m" and "s" is reminiscent of a letter to Edith Jebb in the same anthology: Carroll describes a curious gentleman who said, " 'SSSS.' I thought at first he was only hissing like a snake . . . [he] said in rather a cross tone, 'Don't hiss at me like that! Are you a cat or a steam-engine? SS.' "[63] These echoes are, arguably, mere coincidence, but when Adair makes a sentence into the shape of a maze on the page later in his novel[64] there is little doubt that he lifted the device from Carroll's labyrinth-letter to Agnes Hull.[65]

With Adair's approach to replicating and pasticheing Carroll's style and tone now, I hope, clearly dissected, we can turn to other aspects of the narrative. In structure, Adair keeps closely to the framework that Sigler identifies in *Alice* and *Alice* variants. "A clear transition from the 'real' waking world to a fantasy dream world . . . rapid shifts in identity, appearance, and location; an episodic structure often centering on encounters with nonhuman fantasy characters and/or characters based on nursery rhymes . . . "[66] His Alice is first at home in the domestic setting familiar from *Looking-Glass*, then transported to the world within the needle's eye. There is, generally, one new setting or character per new chapter—a Country Mouse in an A-stack; a beach with Siamese-Twin Cats; an Election that features, most prominently, a Grampus and an Italian Hairdresser; Jack and Jill; a Llabyrinth. The journey through the dreamworld, which is broadly similar to that of *Wonderland* and *Looking-Glass* in its combination of English pastoral settings and contemporary institutions like a railway, country inn, and village shop—frequently involves sudden changes of scene, with jumps and juxtapositions. A storm of cats and dogs ends "as abruptly as it had begun" on page 41—following a row of *Looking-Glass* asterisks—and by page 42 a crowd has gathered on a previously deserted beach. An even more dreamlike transition occurs on page 84, when Alice suddenly realises she is not in a train carriage anymore, but a study in brown; the shift is a conscious copy of the sheep/shop dissolve in "Wool and Water".

The characters Alice meets do not seem to follow a clear system like those in *Wonderland* and *Looking-Glass*, where the dominant idea is of course playing cards and chess pieces respectively. Jack and Jill are from a nursery rhyme and the Country Mouse from a fable; the Grampus and the Hairdresser have the same rhythm to their names as the Walrus and Carpenter, especially when they feature in a poem, "of ale—and ants—and ambergris animatedly talking"[67]—but the main theme throughout is simply encounters with talking animals, some of whom take their names and characteristics from a play on words.

The Siamese-Twin Cats were clearly created in this way,[68] for instance, as was the Welsh Rabbit;[69] the precedent for this kind of invention in Carroll would be the Looking-Glass insects such as the Rocking-horse fly and Bread-and-butter-fly. The Country Mouse could be cousin to the Mouse in *Wonderland*, and the Welsh Rabbit a relation of his White counterpart. There is also, oddly, a non-talking animal—"a puppy . . . *only* a puppy", as Alice remarks in surprise[70]—who seems to have wandered in from *Wonderland*.[71] We meet the Red and White Queens again, which is actually another clever move within the established "rules" of Carroll's *Alice* mythos; Hatter and Hare from *Wonderland* reappear as Hatta and Haigha in *Looking Glass*, so character cameos from the previous adventure—

which Alice remembers in *Needle's Eye*—are not just allowed but almost expected.

The lack of obvious defining concept behind the secondary characters in *Needle's Eye* comes down to the fact that they are chosen for their initial letters—the structural system here is the alphabet, running from A-stack through Beach and Bees to Cats and Sea, and so on until Alice finally realises over a cup of capital tea what kind of world she's inhabiting. As such, *Needle's Eye* is perhaps more of a puzzle book than Carroll's *Alice* adventures—we hardly need to be told that *Looking-Glass* is built around a chessboard, but Adair tries to keep his system subtly concealed until a late stage, which gives him the opportunity for a wry turning to the reader at the point of revelation to ask, "what do *you* think?" The line takes up all of chapter 10, which both recalls the final line of *Looking-Glass*—"which do *you* think it was?"[72]—and the one-line chapter "Shaking", when "it really *was* a kitten, after all."[73]

Studying Adair's intelligent fake helps us realise what we expect from an *Alice* book; the traits we anticipate, or half-remember and enjoy when we see again, and those without which we would feel dissatisfied. In terms of characters, Alice will be treated with rudeness by most of the people she meets, and at one point will be misrecognised as another creature or object entirely: in *Wonderland*, by the Pigeon—"Serpent!"[74]—and in *Needle's Eye*, by the Country Mouse, who thinks the tumbling blonde is a comet and takes her protests that she's called Alice as confirmation. "Just what I thought . . . 'Alley's Comet."[75] At least one of the characters in an *Alice* book will have a comedy working-class accent—the Country Mouse, obviously, who is in the same tradition as the Irish labourer Pat, from *Wonderland*, and the "suppressed" Wasp from *Looking-Glass*, who is clearly a drone with his mutters of "Dreary me" and "worrity, worrity!"[76]

And of course, there will be songs; songs that come out wrong. Moreover, Alice will find the songs, which almost everyone she meets seems obliged to perform, a bit of a social chore. She forces herself to look misty-eyed as the Cats give her "The Sands of Dee", or a version thereof involving hippopotami, and is commanded to recite "Jack and Jill" backwards. The Swan's song, which seems to pastiche Carroll's own "Gardener's Song" from *Sylvie and Bruno* as much as it does any other source, brings in another familiar motif: a meal that disconcertingly introduces itself to the diner, like the Mutton in *Looking-Glass*. "*Will* you be able to eat me all, that's what I'd like to know?"[77] Alice, on the other hand, almost puts her foot in her mouth when talking to potential food; her near-faux pas with a Frog-Waiter in *Needle's Eye*, when she has to cover up her distaste for frog's legs, is a reminder of her hasty comment about *Wonderland* whiting, "I've often seen them at dinn-"[78]

Penultimately, the pictures. Jenny Thorne's illustrations are pastiches of the Tenniel style, but on the whole less rich and detailed; however, there are a few instances where her contributions support the overall simulation in a more interesting way. Carroll—as the previous chapter showed—explicitly uses Tenniel's picture as support for his prose when he doesn't feel like describing a Gryphon. Adair and Thorne duplicate this interaction and in fact almost overdo it by including it twice—once when Adair tells the reader to look at the Emu picture and discover that its feathers are in fact the concrete poem "emu", repeated many times, and again when he archly remarks that the artist has not suddenly become very lazy in drawing Jack and Jill; they really are stick figures.

Page 131 shows the phenomenon of two parallel lines meeting, and while there is no prompt in the text, we are expected both to recognise them as Disraeli and Gladstone and to wryly appreciate that this is a nod to Tenniel modelling the Lion on Gladstone and the Unicorn[79] on Disraeli. The most intriguing point about this reference is what it suggests about the implied reader. It would be possible to just accept the illustration in *Needle's Eye* as depicting two Victorian gentlemen, with no loss to the story. The illustration is there, though, for the sake of a political reference in the style of Tenniel—so we are meant to get the double joke that this is Gladstone and Disraeli, and that this is what Tenniel did with the Lion and the Unicorn. Thorne is performing what she thinks Tenniel "would have done", just as Adair is doing with Carroll, and the joke is intended as a little, hidden treat for those familiar enough with the background of *Looking-Glass* to appreciate it. The complication is, though, that a dedicated Carollian, steeped in debates and quite possibly well-read beyond Adair's level, might well be aware of Michael Hancher's persuasive argument that Tenniel's Lion and Unicorn were stock figures from Tenniel's *Punch* cartoons, and not intended as political caricatures.[80] If the received wisdom is wrong in this case, then Thorne's replicated "Tenniel" is based on a misconceived notion and therefore rings false, too clever for its own good.[81]

Finally, as mentioned above, there are elements in *Needle's Eye* that, rather than being based on anything in the *Alice* books, are attempts to invent something new, yet familiar—novelty within the mindset that Carroll would have occupied. Again, Adair's attempt to inhabit this intellectual and emotional space, which he constructs from evidence of Carroll's life and motives, is interesting in the relationship it creates with the reader. That Adair includes a satirical election scene, for instance, and a Parliament of letters, is surely because his research uncovered Carroll's active interest in British politics.[82] To the reader who shares this knowledge of Carroll, the inclusion of such scenes seems "right" and offers the further satisfaction of recognising why Adair did it. Adair's most significant invention in this sense is the addition of Welshness to the Alice mythos—the Welsh Rabbit, the Llabyrinth, and the Welsh town name writhing with "l"s.

A reader knowing little of Alice Liddell—the name itself may partly have inspired Adair's extended puns on "l" and "eels"—would associate her with Oxford, if anywhere. The more expert Carrollian would recognise, accept, and smile at the Welshness as a reference to Llandudno, where the Liddells customarily spent their family holiday. Carroll is supposed by local tradition—although, as I shall explore in Chapter 9, the story is much disputed—to have visited Alice there and dreamed up the start of *Wonderland* on the shore. Be that as it may, it seems to make perfect sense that Carroll would draw on the culture surrounding Alice's holiday home to amuse and please her when it came to a third adventure.[83]

However, I would suggest that a reader with yet more specialist involvement in Carroll and his work—that is, a third level of fandom—would, while recognising what Adair was aiming for, feel superior not just because of an understanding of the intended reference, but because of a reading of Adair's Welsh motifs as flawed in their reconstruction of what Carroll "would have written". Not only is the Carroll-in-Llandudno theory associated with received popular wisdom as opposed to scholarship—a plaque on a statue, rather than the result of engaged research[84]—but the idea of Carroll writing a third *Alice* adventure to entertain Alice Liddell also seems founded on myth rather than on a more critical and scholarly approach.

The idea that Alice Liddell was Carroll's muse and obsession is, as we saw, commonly found in journalism. It would be an easy assumption to make that as Carroll is known to have told the original *Alice* story to the Liddell girl, and written it up painstakingly in his own handwriting for her, incorporating in-jokes about her life and private references to their outings, he would do the same with a second and third Alice adventure. However, as Karoline Leach convincingly argues, Carroll was distinguishing Alice Liddell from his "dreamchild", the fictional Alice, even during the writing of *Under Ground*, and by the time he gave her long flowing hair in *Looking-Glass*, he was carefully fencing his own creation off from the girl he now found "less than congenial".[85]

If we imagine that he would plausibly have been writing *Needle's Eye* in the mid-1870s, would he really have been trying to insert little treats and secrets for a lady aged around twenty-three? We commonly hold the vision of Alice clamouring for more stories from dear Mr Dodgson, but think of the sullenly reserved Alice Liddell in Carroll's last portrait of her, from 1870; would she really be running to thank him for jokes about Welsh Rabbits and Llandudno? And that portrait was taken a year before the publication of *Looking-Glass*. There would be no reason for Carroll to play to Alice Liddell's tastes in *Needle's Eye*—he would be more likely to have his own eye cannily on the market and on the responses of newer child-friends—and in this instance, Adair's simulated Carroll appeals to a popular idea of the man, turning out the kind of book we might think he should have written, rather than what he would have written.

"The *wonder* of life, the *mirror* of life, the *future* of life"

Jeff Noon claims he re-read only one page of the *Alice* books, "just to get an idea of the rhythm"—before beginning *Automated Alice*. "I did very little research . . . the last thing I want to do is copy Carroll."[86] Noon is, then, by his own admission, not attempting the same precise and complete illusion that Adair tries to construct, and his third adventure is more of an experiment with Alice than an immersion in pastiche. However, he is a long-term fan, and provides an enthusiastic account of his teenage epiphany through the *Alice* books.

> I remember walking through the college library, wondering what strange novel to read next, when my eyes fell up on a combined edition of *Alice in Wonderland* and *Through the Looking-Glass*. I don't know what made me take it off the shelf, but I flipped it open at random.
>
> I was 16 years old, ready for any adventure, but tremendously shy and unconfident at the same time . . . that accidental encounter in the college library transformed my way of viewing the world. I began to allow the childish, the whimsical, into my own work, my paintings of the time . . . years later, writing my first novel, *Vurt*, I would create a world where the doors between dream and reality are worn thin and can be stepped through. It seemed only natural to incorporate elements from Carroll's work into my own.[87]

Interestingly, Noon explicitly recognizes the twin, polarized contemporary discourses around Carroll that are the main object of my own study.

> The two *Alice* books continue to sell all over the globe, to adults as well as children. Is the popularity of Carroll's work merely the result

of nostalgia, or do the stories hold uncomfortable secrets we still need to this day? Thoughts such of these were uppermost in my mind when, a few years ago, I became fascinated with the idea of writing a third Alice book of my own . . . [88]

Noon, therefore, is entirely aware of what Carroll and Alice have come to mean in modern culture, and, like Adair, is familiar with the critical commentaries around the author and his heroine, as well as with the primary texts. He chose his title when gazing blurry-eyed at *The Annotated Alice*; Gardner's book mutated into *The Armour-Plated Alice*, and from there Noon forged his Automated protagonist.

However, as the title alone suggests, this is not a straight homage to Victorian fantasy. Generically, "automated" cues us to recognize Noon's book as a form of steampunk, the branch of science fiction whose most famous vehicle is *The Difference Engine*, Bruce Sterling and William Gibson's collaborative novel.[89] Essentially, though it comes in variant guises and subgroups, steampunk's schtick is Victorian science fiction, pushing the technology of the time—the Babbage engines I mentioned in Chapter 2—to a more advanced point while retaining the elegant styling, the manners, and the imperialist ambition of the age. Steampunk is a what-if, parallel universe game, and it seems to come closest to what Noon is doing with his protagonist by sending her forward in time to 1998, but retaining a skewed, slightly Victorian culture in "present-day" Manchester. One paragraph in Noon's adventure even seems to pay explicit homage to Gibson and Sterling:

> Alice screamed out Celia's name as they fell into the yawning gulf of an ellipsis in the marble . . .
>
> Ce . . . li . . .
> a . . .
> !
> !
> ![90]

Gibson and Sterling's climax runs

> Dying to be born.
> The light is strong,
> The light is clear;
> The Eye at last must see itself
> Myself . . .

I see:
I see,
I see
I
![91]

Rather than imagining what Carroll would have written in the mid-1870s, and constructing a simulated Carroll as Adair does, Noon's speculation seems based on the notion that Carroll was presciently imagining the late 1990s but through a Victorian perspective. The vision doesn't quite add up, and can't be consistently rationalised. There is no explanation, for instance, for the book being set in 1860,[92] two years before the "Golden Afternoon"—which would presumably set this third adventure prior to *Wonderland*, if anything[93]—and the conceit that Carroll could, towards the end of his life,[94] write a novel that involves puns on Jimi Hendrix and Quentin Tarantino is, of course, riddled with holes. However, the overall feel of the technology is in keeping with the way Carroll might conceivably, in a whimsical mood, have imagined the mathematical engines of the future. Computers are powered by termites, or computermites,[95] automatons like the Alice-replica of the title, Celia, have a mound of termites scurrying in their skulls,[96] and the streets are crowded with "metal horses."[97]

Noon is only half-heartedly retaining the consistency in this imagined "Carroll" perspective, though, and seems more interested in asking, light-heartedly, what Carroll would have made of various cultural phenomena of the 1990s. Rather than the near-watertight illusion of Adair's work, Noon's "Carrollian" take on modern life mainly comes down to puns and logical puzzles, some of which would shame a Christmas cracker, but the approach is basically similar—what would Carroll have written if he'd written about this?

As part of the computermite discussion, then, we are introduced to the "beanery" system,[98] based on a bean's presence or absence, and a little later to "Randomology", a form of chaos theory that the Civil Serpents, the villains of Noon's piece, want to suppress. "The Universe makes the trouble; I'm just the watcher of the trouble," explains Captain Ramshackle.[99] Alice later encounters Professor Chrowdingler, who has performed, as the reader alert to corny wordplay will guess, a Schrödinger's Cat experiment explained in tongue-twisting terms. "A quark is a set of hypomental elementary particles, postulated to be the fundamental and invisible units of all carryons and chrownons."[100]

Popular culture gets the same treatment as science, with Alice running into a jazz-playing slug called Long Distance Davis,[101] Chimera-maker

Quentin Tarantula,[102] and axe-man automaton James Marshall Hentrails.[103] Noon puts a satirical spin on twentieth-century art and critical movements—zoodism, fludism, chewedism, foodism, pseudism, and, in one of his better jokes, all the young dudism[104]—and subsequently turns to literature with shelves containing *Butcher in the Pie*, *Hatch 22*, *Withering Kites*, and *Fooligan's Wake*.[105] This last is perhaps a nod to Joyce's influence on Noon, and his debt to Carroll—after all, Joyce actually invented the word "quark", in *Finnegans Wake*, as well as fooling around with his Alis, alas and Dadgerson's dodges. Otherwise, the puns are not especially inspired, and not really up to the inventive standard of Carroll's "Drawling, Stretching, and Fainting in Coils",[106] but we should note out of interest that Noon's library of never-written books parallels that of *Sandman*, and that he, like Adair, includes a maze—a librarinth here, not a llabyrinth—something missing from Carroll's originals. Disneyland Paris, we shall see, also builds its Alice features around a maze; an interesting common feature to these modern reworkings.

On a less obvious level, Noon incorporates some nods to debates around popular culture. The police response to Chimera/cinema—"a blatant pandering to the sickly needs of the common herd"[107]—is a version of the moral panics that greeted most new media of the twentieth century. The automata Alice encounters in Noon's second maze, a not-garden or knot garden, are described as "*monstrous, perverted images* of the subject"—an oddly extreme phrase unless we see it as an homage to very similar passages in Jean Baudrillard's work on simulacra.[108]

Similarly, Alice's automated double Celia is discussed in terms that recall the replicants of Ridley Scott's *Blade Runner* (1982)—"I've improved myself so much . . . I've become rather more intelligent than a human being"[109]—and the book's final page, with Alice unsure if she is she, or Celia the Automaton, is very reminiscent of *Blade Runner*'s ambiguous ending, with the question "is Deckard a replicant" left deliberately unsolved. On a related note, some of Celia's speeches—"we are the not-quite twins, the sisters of the corkscrew"—sound rather like the prose of cyberfeminist Sadie Plant's *Zeroes and Ones*, which, perhaps not coincidentally, explores the relationship between digital technology and the analytical engines of Charles Babbage and Ada Lovelace.[110]

Adair resists the temptation to comment with twentieth-century hindsight on critical discourses of Carroll, or wryly nudge about more recent interpretations. Noon, on the other hand, doesn't shy away from this kind of inside reference from a modern perspective. At one point Alice eats a "wurm", and everything goes "very slipperty-jipper indeed . . . "

Alice is now floating along a long snake of water, through a slowly turning world of golden-afternoon colours. It takes her an age to realize that she is no longer inside the prison cell, it takes her an age and a half to realize that she is now lazily reclining in a small rowing boat. Her two sisters, Lorina and Edith, are aboard the boat with her, as is her friend, the kind Mister Dodgson. It takes Alice *two whole ages* to realize that Mister Dodgson is now telling fanciful stories to the three little maidens.[111]

This return to the origin sequence of *Wonderland* is clearly figured as a drug hallucination; Alice starts seeing worms in the picnic and becomes sucked into their embrace, allowing herself to be dragged beneath the soil. It self-consciously dips into the "Alice as drug metaphor" reading, and like some of Adair's additions, implies a reader who would also be aware of this perceived meaning and enjoy the reference. As such, it addresses a reader on the less specialist, interested-layperson level, because the notion that Alice has some relation to hallucinogenic drugs is common enough in journalism and popular culture[112] to provide a satisfying moment of recognition.

I would suggest, though, that the drug implications of this passage would be rejected by more dedicated afficionados of Carroll on two counts: because of the lack of any reliable evidence that Carroll had experience of such substances, and because of the way it seems to slur, or at least inaccurately represent, Carroll's character. Already the text would meet with a distinctly split response based on the reader's level of familiarity with Carroll's life and fan investment in his reputation.

The same can be said of Noon's approach to the Carroll/Alice relationship, which is equally knowing and clearly informed by rumours and theories circulating during the twentieth rather than the nineteenth century. Alice wanders into "DONE WONDERING", an idyllic cottage where the elderly Carroll is waiting to offer her dinner. Rather than remain stuck in this afterlife, Alice pleads for Carroll to send her back to the real world.

The Reverend's tears fell like puddles onto his unfinished roast beef. "I was rather hoping we could spend some time together, Alice," he choked, "but perhaps you really must leave me now . . . " And then the Reverend Dodgson leaned close to Alice's face and said these final words, "Will this young Alice kiss me goodbye?"
Alice kissed him, and the old man's lips were salty with life . . .

It hardly needs to be said that this scene relies on an understanding and acceptance of the idea that Carroll had some kind of lifelong infatuation, whether quasi-sexual or purely romantic, with Alice Liddell. For it to ring true and feel "right" we have to buy into the idea that Carroll was a slightly queer fish, kindly but with a fixation on Alice—who in this scene is "both a *real* and an *imaginary* character"[113]—that crossed the lines of comfortable taboo. The dubiousness of their relationship is underlined by a Joycean exchange in the next scene: Alice explains "Mister Dodgson must have kissed me here," and a Chimera rabbit replies "Misterly Dod-gily!"[114] Again, I suggest that Carrollians with a "purist" investment in Carroll, rejecting any suggestion of a romantic or sexual relationship between him and Alice, would see full well what Noon was aiming for, but would resist the insinuations, seeing the passage as a perpetuation of unfounded myths.

Some readers would, meeting these aspects of the novel, be put in an ambivalent position with regard to Noon's authorship and authority. While there seems little question from his interview, cited above, that Noon is a fan of Carroll and Alice—the books have heavily influenced his work—these two scenes, the "drug" passage and the strong implication of paedophilic desire in the "Dodgson" passage, would, I believe, seem distasteful to readers with a specific type of critical and emotional invest-ment in Carroll. Noon's indulging of these received wisdoms would be seen by these readers as displaying a lack of deeper and more critical knowledge about Carroll, and a reliance on half-truths circulated in popular culture. We cannot fully know the extent of Noon's research or scholarly involvement in Carroll's life and work—it could be the case that he was deliberately including the motifs of psychedelia and paedophilia because he knew the popular audience would expect it in a modern Alice—but this is another case where I think we have to draw distinctions between degrees of Carroll fandom. Noon, despite his long-time enthusiasm for the books, is revealing himself here as less "purist", and arguably less well-informed, than some of his readers.

Despite all the departures from Alice "continuity", Noon does make an effort—far more effort than his interview suggests—to replicate the Carroll style and the Alice structure. Looking at *Automated Alice* in this respect, following the detailed examination of *Needle's Eye*, allows us to build a clearer sense of the elements that seem to constitute the essential template for a third Alice book—those features without which it wouldn't be recognisable even as an attempt to replicate Carroll and extend Alice's adventures. Although his novel is far wilder and looser than Adair's, Noon still follows the same pattern outlined above in much of his prose style, invention, and narrative; introduce novelty but keep touching base with the familiar.

Automated Alice also takes its opening from *Looking-Glass*, with Alice indoors, vaguely bored, rambling to herself and inventing theories. The first sentence is almost identical to *Wonderland*'s "Alice was beginning to get very tired of sitting by her sister on the bank, and of having nothing to do . . . ";[115] Noon announces, "Alice was beginning to feel very drowsy from having nothing to do."[116] Already, the claim that he only read a single page to get a sense of the rhythm is sounding disingenuous. The second sentence introduces italics—"doing absolutely *nothing at all* could make one so tired"—underlining the sense that Carroll's finicky stress on certain words is one of the most important tools in recreating his style.

By the end of the paragraph Alice is wondering "how you *do* make Heaven-knows-what? . . . Perhaps they get the recipe from somebody who's only recently died?"[117] This would be a very early death joke even for Carroll, who waits until Alice is falling down the rabbit hole before his first morbid crack.[118] It provides us with Alice's airy trains of thought, which appear in inverted commas in Noon as in Carroll and Adair, and to an extent confirms our memory of her character as inquisitive but given to flights of fancy. The interrogation of an everyday expression is reminiscent of similar moments in Carroll, such as the Hatter's challenge that Alice doesn't know Time personally and shouldn't talk so freely about wasting it.[119]

The use of parentheses also occurs several times on the first three pages, with the same sense of authorial stage whispering. "Great Aunt Ermintrude had three daughters of her own (triplets in fact) but they were all much older than Alice (and Alice always had trouble telling them apart), so they weren't much fun at all!"[120] The tone sounds authentic enough and gives a feeling of reading aloud, with the grown-up making wry asides; in this sense *Wonderland* and *Looking-Glass* remain true to the original telling of *Alice's Adventures Under Ground*. However, the exclamation mark is jarring, over-enthusiastic, and out of keeping with Carroll's drier, more deadpan manner.

As the reference to Great Aunt Ermintrude suggests, Noon has already, by page 3, introduced characters and settings that lie far outside Carroll's depiction of his Alice's "real life". Alice is now—for reasons that have little to do with Carroll and much to do with Noon's intention to produce a satire of his home town—living in Didsbury, Manchester, and the reader looking for a reassuring simulation of the original will have become disillusioned by this point. The result of this devil-may-care forcing of local references and careless approximations into his pastiche—Great Aunt Ermintrude is too cartoonish a name to really convince as a Carroll invention—is a mish-mash of sentences that sound almost right next to sentences that sound blatantly wrong.

" 'I've got something even betterer, even sharperer!' (In her excitement Alice had forgotten all about her grammar.)"[121] sounds fine as a variant on "curiouser". "Alice was a serpent-surfer!" sounds lamely out of Carroll's character.[122] And Alice's discussion with Celia, based on mishearing the town name Rusholme as "Rush Home", sounds like a poor man's version of Humpty's *Jabberwocky* interpretation:

"Why do they call this village *Rush Home?*" asked Alice . . . "It seems to me that the people of Manchester are rushing away from their homes."
"Exactly so, Alice. And in eight hours' time they will commence to rush home after finishing their day's work. They call these twin times the rush-hours."[123]

"It's called '*wabe*', you know, because it goes a long way before it, and a long way behind it—"
"And a long way beyond it on each side," Alice added.
"Exactly so."[124]

Nevertheless, from the first scenes of Noon's book alone we can pick out a number of moments that either explicitly emulate the original books or, conceivably, result from Noon's successful internalisation of Carroll's style and tone. Alice's polite "Oh, Mister Ant" is close to her plaintive "O Mouse" in *Wonderland*.[125] Her subsequent mistaking of the Ant's gender and species, and its outraged reaction—"How dare you, young miss! . . . I am not an *ant*. I am a termite"[126]—reminds us of Humpty's stern "It's *very* provoking . . . to be called an egg—*very*!"[127] The entry into the dreamland, this time, is through a clock, and Noon gives the transition a page to itself, marked only with " . . . Alice *vanished!*"; the single line on a blank sheet is an early echo of Carroll's "Waking" chapter. The invention of "squoking" as a word "exactly halfway between speaking and squawking"[128] is in the *Jabberwocky* mode, Alice's tumble "down, down, down" lifts the phrase exactly from *Wonderland*,[129] and three rows of authentic-looking asterisks pop up on page 20 to mark Alice's entry into the fantasy.

The structure of *Automated Alice* also follows that suggested by Sigler and identifiable in Adair. We have already seen the transition from the waking world to the dream, effected when Alice follows her parrot, Whippoorwill, into a grandfather clock. The quest for the parrot propels her through the story, paralleled by her search for twelve missing pieces in a jigsaw puzzle of London Zoo. Along the way there are, as Sigler requires from an Alice story, surreal and sudden transitions, such as Alice's shooting up a microscope, with a corresponding shift in size; and there are nonsense songs like Ramshackle's ode to Randomology, although these don't seem to parody existing verses.

As in Carroll and Adair, each chapter tends to feature a new character or scene—Captain Ramshackle in chapter 2, Celia and the knot-garden in chapter 3, Pablo and Jimi Hentrails in chapter 4. The character names alone suggest that there is no kind of common root uniting the cast by this point; no source in nursery rhymes, parlour games, or even alphabets, although Celia is an anagram—like "Lacie", in *Wonderland*[130]—and Jimi Hentrails is a play on words along the lines of the Welsh Rabbit.

The common theme uniting most of the secondary characters emerges on page 82, when Pablo explains about Newmonia, a disease that mixes animals and humans into new combinations. We only encounter this phenomenon on full display when we reach page 105—"Goatboys and Sheepgirls, Elephantmen and Batwomen"—and it reaches a more intense level on page 144 with Squirrelmen, Ostrichmen, Pianogirls, Soapboys, and a man with a kitchen sink for a head. The overarching theme behind the characters and plot, then, is this disease that causes mutation and bricolage; creatures welded awkwardly together from two halves of animal and human, human and object. Ramshackle, we realise, falls into this category, as a Badgerman, and so do the Snailman Long-Distance Davis and Dr Chrowdingler, the Crow-woman.

The actual narrative structure interlocks Alice's search for the jigsaw with a crime mystery, as she becomes suspected of involvement in the Jigsaw Murders—which are distinguished by the victim's body, already a cross-breed, being cut up and grotesquely rearranged. Rather than taking an existing framework or cultural image like playing cards, then, Noon is building this adventure around notions of the fragmented self, a theme that culminates in the final confusion over whether the real Alice, or her twin twister, the termite-powered automaton Celia, has escaped back to 1860.

> I must add that (just *occasionally*) Alice would feel a terrible itching feeling inside her skull. Why, it was as though a thousand termites were running hither and thither with tickling messages! And sometimes (just *sometimes*) Alice would feel a certain stiffness in her limbs, as though her legs and arms were not quite fleshy enough.[131]

Noon ends his novel "which do *you* think she was?" in deliberate reflection of the last line of *Looking-Glass*; a return to Carroll after a diversion into themes that, as noted above, have as much in common with Rick Deckard's "unicorn dream" in *Blade Runner* as they do with Alice's dream of the Red King.

A final, intriguing factor in Noon's book is its authorial attitude towards Alice. He seems unable to resist sometimes childish scatological or quasi-sexual references in connection with the heroine, and furthermore inserts himself as a character, Zenith O'Clock, in a scene that allows him to dote on her and reveal himself as her only friend. This sentimental tendency reveals itself quite early on, as Noon breaks off the narrative to announce that "it is getting rather late, and this is quite enough writing for one day. I will see you in the morning, dear sweet girl."[132] The drug hallucination scene involves coy references to Alice expelling the wurm through her "nether passage: the passage that can never be written about,"[133] and a chapter title involves the double entendre "Alice Looks Up Herself."[134] Adair may cross a boundary from which Carroll would have flinched by including a joke on "dam" / "damn",[135] but the toilet humour in Noon—such as Ramshackle mishearing "social *faux pas*" as "social fart pants"[136]—would have disgusted Alice's creator.

The Zenith O'Clock scene is particularly odd in its parallel with the White Knight passage in *Looking-Glass*: just as Carroll is supposed to have been depicting himself as Alice's faithful helper and saying farewell as she crosses the brooks to adulthood, so Noon self-indulgently writes himself into the novel as the only normal and endearing man his Alice comes across. He proceeds, after holding court about the negative critical reaction to his books *Solumn* and *Shurt*—puns of a sort on Noon's *Pollen* and *Vurt*—to recite a "love poem" to Alice. The two enter into a paradoxical discussion about whether Zenith is now writing *The Automated Alice* and creating them both as characters, and then he has to leave her.

> . . . the writer's hand came down to stroke once again at Alice's pinafored shoulder. It was noon. It was that very softest of touches, the breath of friendship, amidst strangers . . . and then he was gone . . . [137]

It is hard to know what to make of this scene. Noon could be playfully pastiching Carroll's approach, putting himself in the text merely to reproduce the White Knight motif, but the extensive complaint about misreadings of *Pollen* and *Vurt* implies that the Zenith scenes are meant as a genuinely personal expression, and that Noon felt some desire to engage with Alice directly on an emotional, albeit fictional, level. While he presents Carroll as having a slightly unnerving obsession with his heroine, then, Noon as Zenith—although he does carefully keep his contact to a mere caress rather than a kiss on the mouth—is displaying the same kind of tendencies himself. Like many modern commentators, he suggests Carroll was in love with the real Alice; Noon is unusual in that he seems also have fallen in love with the fictional one.

"Alice sans Habillement"

Katie Roiphe's *Still She Haunts Me* falls into a different genre of Alice fiction, as an exploration of the imagined relationship between Carroll and Alice around the time of the "rift" with the Liddell family. Despite the difference in its subject matter, its project and the pattern of its approach is still very much the same as the previous two novels—building a relationship of trust with the reader by establishing known, verifiable, or authentic-sounding details, then using that basis to make a creative departure. *Still She Haunts Me* is effectively—bearing in mind the provisos I stated above about cultural status and the different gatekeeping processes behind publishing print novels and amateur stories—a work of slash fiction. It uses the familiar as a framework for supposing a sexual and romantic relationship between two characters whose actual relationship remains unknown; it builds on cues in the "official" text to construct an unofficial one, which nevertheless has to seem plausible.

The key difference between Roiphe's novel and the vast majority of slash fiction is that most slash is based on fictional characters. However, as I suggested in the Introduction, Lewis Carroll and Alice Liddell have to a great extent become bound up in myth and rumour, mixed up with fiction—Carroll is obviously Dodgson's own invention anyway, a deliberate creation of a persona, and Alice, in her last years, at least deliberately allowed the blurring of boundaries between herself and the book character. Carroll's life, as Chapter 1 showed, is still a web of facts with gaping openings between them, a network of quite extensive documentation that still leaves tantalizing blanks and empty spaces for speculation; the diaries and letters are an invaluable record of his more private side, but fundamental aspects of the man like the precise nature of his attitude to women and girls remain a mystery.

As with Adair, I am taking a close survey of Roiphe's text to identify and draw out how she achieves her effect, or at least attempts to convince the reader of her interpretation; I am arguing that it follows the same dance between the reassuringly familiar and the new yet plausible. Roiphe has to weave the invented into the accepted, gaining our confidence and credibility before branching out. She begins "the letter came by the afternoon post just as he was putting the finishing touches to his Euclid lecture."[138] The detail of the lecture's topic is there for authenticity. Any reader familiar with a modern biography of Carroll would find this detail clicking smartly into place against their own knowledge—that Carroll published several books on Euclid is mentioned various times, for instance, in Cohen's account of his life.

Tearing open the letter, Carroll "felt himself vanishing, skin, hair, mouth, until all that was left was a single point of pain."[139] The purpose of this sentence is to nudge us towards a memory of the Cheshire Cat's disappearance and bring this channelling of Carroll's internal imagery home to something we at least half recognise. Carroll wrote the Cat, the logic runs, so this is the kind of picture he might call up when imagining himself emotionally shrinking. The biographical detail supported Roiphe's sketching of Carroll's external life, and the reference to his fiction, his created worlds, supports her speculation about the way he would think.

The technique of reading Carroll back from what he actually wrote is used repeatedly throughout the novel. On page 69, he confesses to his speech therapist Dr Hunt that his dreams "involve a great d-d-deal of growing and shrinking." Page 147 sees him dreaming of Alice in a canopy bed: "a kitten was chanting softly, then louder and louder: *Off with her head!*" On page 154 he sees a baby with a turned-up nose, "almost like a pig"; the next page has Carroll applying Alice's encounter with the caterpillar to his own identity torments.

> All kinds of creatures are constantly asking Alice who she is and she is constantly demurring. And that was how Dodgson felt as he sat in the library: the constant nagging question, the absence of answer.

We have two checks against authentic and "official" texts, then, by the time Roiphe introduces her first real invention, still on the first page of the novel. "*It is no longer desirable,*" the letter reads, "*for you to spend time with our family.*" This message is later revealed to be from Mrs Liddell, although any reader who had come across the kind of potted history featured in Chapter 2's newspaper articles would already guess what it signified. This is the start of and explanation for the "rift" that, as we saw, fills the space between diary entries and can be interpreted as a scandal, the aftermath of a proposal, evidence of a love affair between Carroll and one of three Liddells, or simply a mannered and proper response to poorly founded rumour. The letter is fictional, but of course sounds suitably formal-Victorian; it is interesting that even in a novel about Carroll, Roiphe makes use of those characteristic italics.

Leaving the letter "folded like a closed door"—an image that, again, rings faintly familiar from *Wonderland*'s early sequences—Carroll surveys his stack of albums.

> 1,031 photographs, each labelled in scratchy print on the bottom right-hand corner. His point of view made visible. The past sliced into stills.

Roiphe is creating a sense of Carroll's approach to life that subtly fits our expectations—that is, it fits most popular and indeed scholarly conceptions of his manner and attitude. We may not realise that she is tailoring her Carroll to the dominant, received idea until we imagine how jarring the effect would be if we made just slight changes. What if Carroll tossed the letter aside "like a handkerchief"? What if the photographs were "scattered at random, some with a scrawled label, some without . . . frivolous moments from the summers of his life."

It wouldn't work: we would feel something wrong about this Carroll. Even a reader whose image of the man comes from popular newspaper stories rather than more in-depth research would, I believe, have a sense that Carroll is methodical, precise, slightly cold. We think of him as contained and as applying mathematical or logical methods to keep his life within safe boxes; and this is what Roiphe provides.

As with the references to *Alice*, the approach to Carroll as calculating—literally, in that he controls the world through mathematics—is used repeatedly throughout the novel. On page 34, imagining Alice getting older, he "added and multiplied her by herself. He thought of her turning fourteen, then forty-nine, then three hundred and forty-three . . . " On the same page, he works out "his importance to the Liddells by the number of people seated closer to them"[140]; a later scene has Alice and Carroll divided by rigid quantities of matter, romantic longing reduced to something neater and numerical.

> The nursery window looked blurred through the snow and impossibly far away. An inch of glass, a thousand kilograms of snow, a hundred feet of night, eight inches of wall.
>
> Hours later, he was still bent over his writing table toying with quantities. He felt the same pleasurable ache he had when working on a particularly hard logic problem. How to simplify the situation? Alice was now ten. How to get beyond the limitations of space and time?[141]

We are already a point, though, where some readers might reject her construction and dispute her authority. Roiphe's suggestion that Carroll was uptight and abnormally obsessed with detail, which is strongly implied by the "1,031" photographs—not even 1,030, but the precise number— could be regarded as a perpetuation of a myth given that Carroll's diaries and letters offer another side to him as a socialite and confident mover in London's artistic circles.

More specifically, Roiphe's credibility would be undermined for any-one who checked the number of photographs against the dates. Carroll never, as far as we know for sure, received a letter of this kind from Lorina Liddell, but if he did, it would have been at the start of the period of social separation. That would be around the end of June 1863; he wrote to her on the twenty-seventh asking if the children could be photo-graphed and the following pages, as we saw in Chapter 1, were razored out. Edward Wakeling and Roger Taylor's record of Carroll's photographs record that picture 953 was taken on 27 June 1863, and 954 to 956 on the thirtieth.[142] Roiphe's figure sounds plausible until it runs up against this kind of research—and any author writing on Carroll unfortunately has to be prepared for a reader whose knowledge and taste for investigation are pedantically thorough.

For the less rigorous reader, Roiphe confirms the authenticity she has been building in the first paragraphs with her description of three photo-graphs that do exist and are relatively widely known—we saw that these images, or images much like them, were discussed and reproduced in recent newspaper articles. "Alice in the straw Chinaman's hat that tied under her chin; Alice pretending to be asleep on a fur throw outside; Alice sitting with her ankles crossed next to a fern."[143] This credibility is necessary in the bargain Roiphe is making with the reader—I tell you something you know is true, so you believe me next time when I tell you something along the same lines—because the next reference to a photograph is creative invention. Carroll did not take a photograph of Alice crying and label it "neg. 206 1/3";[144] according to Wakeling's record, picture 206 is a Tunny Fish.[145] He did take a photograph of Alice as a beggar girl though, as mentioned on page 40; which is important as again, the well-known image barters for our trust at a later stage, when Roiphe describes Carroll taking nude pictures of Alice.

Roiphe's account on page 2 of Carroll taking a diary and slicing out "each offending page" will correspond with half-remembered accounts of his life, and again plays on the sense of him as coldly methodical: "it cut with a pleasing violence, slicing through the tiny cottony threads, neat but somehow fleshlike. A surgeon of himself."[146] However, the details she provides of the diary and its censorship are oddly out of synch with the available evidence.

> On the mahogany writing table were the diaries, fawn-colored leather scratched, spines broken, pages warped. He pulled out the fourth volume and flipped to the month of April.

This is the month from which he then amputates several pages. The famous missing pages from the diary, covering the reason behind the split with the Liddells, are from late June 1863, the "present day" of Roiphe's fictional scene. We can be pretty sure that Carroll did not cut these pages himself, because a note was made of their contents long after his death, and furthermore, Wakeling records that it was the eighth, not the fourth volume of Carroll's diary that covered this period of 1862–1864.[147] This cannot, then, be the cut that Roiphe is describing.

The fourth volume ran from January 1856 to December 1856, and April was the month when Carroll first met Alice. It makes some sense that he should cut this scene from his life, except that there is only one page cut from volume 4, and it falls on 31 December. "Carroll is reflecting on the past," opines Wakeling in a note on this censorship, "and may have said more than he intended, removing the page himself."[148] At any rate, we have his record of the first meeting with Alice: "the three little girls were in the garden most of the time, and we became excellent friends . . . I mark this day with a white stone."[149]

There seems, then, no factual basis for this depiction of Carroll's excising multiple pages from April in his fourth volume; again, it passes muster on one level and would satisfy a reader without a close knowledge of the diary history, without the inclination to check against dates and records, and without the critical demands of the devoted Carrollian, who might also protest wryly that the diaries were covered in dark green, not fawn.[150] Once more, we see the degrees of hierarchical knowledge and approach within Carroll fandom—Roiphe has without doubt done her research, but for some, on this evidence, it would not be enough.

It is worth observing, as a sidenote, that Roiphe's American identity regularly shows through her careful tapestry of 1860s Victorian Britain—not just in spelling variants like "colored" and "the sky was yellow gray"[151]—but in "knit together" as the past tense instead of "knitted together,"[152] "ladybug" instead of "ladybird,"[153] and, most glaringly, "a piece of candy."[154] The first two may be excusable in a book that was published for a United States as well as a United Kingdom readership, but "yellow" rather than "yellowy" sounds wrong for the voice Roiphe is adopting, which as we have seen seeks to convey Carroll's clipped and measured thought process. Even in the scenes where Carroll is absent, Roiphe's description adopts a formal English manner suitable to the period and social milieu. "Knit together" is even harder to forgive because it actually appears in one of Carroll's diary entries, purporting to be written by him, and "piece of candy" is an awful error of judgement. Like "ladybug", it effectively breaks the reader—the British reader at least—out of the illusion, like an alarm clock ringing in the middle of a dream.

Despite the overall plausibility of Roiphe's recreated Oxford and its small cast of inhabitants, there are, as we have already seen, moments where the fabric of her fiction unfortunately wears thin or snags. I have suggested that some of these points would only catch the attention of a dedicated Carroll fan with an extensive reference library and a penchant for checking facts; others, like the oddities of language, would stand out for the more general reader.

Ironically, there are further passages where it is Roiphe's research, rather than any lack of it—or rather, her heavy-handed use of that research—that disturbs the mood. One of these examples occurs early on, just after the sequence with the cut diary. "He had first met Alice seven years earlier. Late afternoon, April 25, 1856."[155] This is fine as exposition, but the previous paragraphs have, despite the use of the third person, effectively channelled Carroll's internal state. On the diaries, for instance: "He was creating a sympathetic companion, a phantom thrown up by his own words, an illusion cut and formed out of vacant hours . . . "[156] This, like the image of vanishing to a point of pain, like "the past sliced into stills", is Carroll's voice through the medium of Roiphe. However, Carroll would not have to tell himself, in flat tones, the history of his relationship with Alice. His surrounding thoughts, as represented in Roiphe's prose, are fragmented, frigid but imaginative. The line about Alice sounds like a recitation from a biography, because essentially that's what it is.

A more glaring intrusion of background research into the fiction comes with the introduction of Mrs Liddell.

> Her own insecurities clustered around the single issue of social origin. William Thackeray, who was a classmate of Henry Liddell, wrote to a mutual friend when the Liddells married: "Dear brave old Liddell . . . has taken a 3rd rate provincial lady (rather first rate in the beauty line, though, I think) for a wife . . . " Though the nineteen-year-old Lorina Hannah Liddell could not have known about this remark, she woke up the morning after her wedding with the uneasy feeling that this exact sentiment was being discussed over breakfast by remote acquaintances.[157]

There is, I think, an extremely awkward shift in approach here as Roiphe shoe-horns in an authentic quotation—after the academic-style ellipsis, we almost expect to see a footnote—then seems to remember she is telling a story, and pulls herself back with the very flimsy link that Lorina couldn't have known this, but somehow felt it. The same syndrome recurs on page 119, as we sit through a lengthy and detailed retelling of John Ruskin's relationship with Effie Gray, interspersed and supported with quotations from his letters—the latter giving the prose a sense of a lively lecture, rather than bringing Ruskin's character to life. Again, there is a flimsy relevance offered—"Dodgson knew the bare outlines of Ruskin's romantic history. Everyone did"—to justify the introduction of extensive documentary evidence. Roiphe steps outside the world to tell us about it, then at the end of the passage shifts back to the more impressionistic language that signifies one of her male subjects' thought processes:

> And what about Alice? Ruskin wrote of his confusion in her presence on one specific occasion: "It was like being in a dream." And "dream" seemed to be a sort of code word. Ruskin and Dodgson both used it constantly to describe the time they spent with Alice. It was a pretty way of saying beyond the reach of conventional possession: Unreal because I do not want it to be real. Beautiful and impotent in the way dreams are impotent.[158]

Elsewhere, Roiphe reaches even greater heights of contrast between the internal and external, producing one paragraph of Carroll's surreal nightmare—"He rushed into the room and in one motion twisted off Alice's head, which, to his surprise, came off like a cork"[159]—right next to a paragraph that coolly discusses the introduction to his *Pillow Problems* and quotes six lines from that publication. Roiphe tells us that Carroll put the nightmare from his head by turning to Euclid, "his thoughts . . . gathering themselves. Focussing on the numbers", and we are then taken briskly from the theatre to the schoolroom as she seems to feel a need to justify the descriptive passage above. "In the introduction to a mathematical tract, *Curiosa Mathematica* . . . Dodgson once wrote about mathematics as escape."[160]

On a different note, there is an interesting tendency in Roiphe's novel, given its basis in documentary evidence, to invent material not where gaps need filling, but where the real documents don't come up to scratch in entertainment value. She therefore "improves" on the reality, boosting brightness and contrast to make Carroll in particular more immediately striking than his diaries suggest—more like the "Carroll" we would expect and want to read about based on the kind of news stories discussed in Chapter 2. This shift into a kind of hyperreality is signalled early on, when Roiphe has the author himself comment on his journal entries "so much of what he was writing was monotonous. So much of it boiled down to red potatoes for dinner alongside his mutton."[161]

This is absolutely true for the most part, but ironically, the diary entries Roiphe includes—the invented ones—are very different. They include authentic detailing like "Ch.Ch." for Christ Church, which might well inspire trust in a reader unfamiliar with Carroll's diaries, but their language is pure invention.

> August 15, 1859
> Four o'clock. Bronze light. [. . .] I wanted to see her, not through the accidental sag & drape of clothing, but truly see her—A little piece of walking art—Nymph in the garden—Fairy in the woods—Innocent frolicking—Smelling of grass & river wind & cat hairs—A stretch of milky stomach—Dark, dirty Alice . . .

As we saw in Chapter 1, even when plunged into despair about his unworthiness in the sight of God, Carroll recorded his feelings in quite formal terms alongside records of his dining companions and the direction of his daily walks. Compare this entry from 1863:

> Dec: 12. (Sat) End of Collections. I have been hard at work all the week looking over honour papers.
> Dec: 14 (M). After five and a half hours consultation, we got the list out about half-past four.
> Dec: 16 (W) Oh God help me to begin a holier and better life! For thy Son Jesus Christ's sake. Amen.[162]

Roiphe's problem is that even at his most open and emotional, Carroll's diaries do not read like Virginia Woolf or Joyce, which is what she seems to want: so she does the job for him, making him write like a modernist. In an odd twist, she does include an entry rather like the one from December 16 above—it is a little more poetic in form, but it suggests she has read some of his diaries or is at least familiar with their style.

> June 18, 1863
> Please God Give me a new heart.[163]

When we look to Carroll's actual diary to compare the entry from this date, though, we find only that he took a photograph "with Horne and

Thornethwaites's Collodion", and helped with a raffle.[164] The gulf between the real, disappointingly banal Carroll and the fictional, thrillingly tormented Carroll is comical.

This rewriting of the history and its participants into what Roiphe feels it should have been like—and to be fair, the reader without an immersion in the details of Carroll's life and private documents might be dismayed or at least bored by a more accurate picture—extends to the *Alice* book and the explanation of the Liddell-Carroll social split. We saw at the start of Chapter 2 that *Alice in Wonderland* was not, at the time, reviewed as a coded message about forbidden love or an allegorical expression of a man's inner demons. Roiphe is taking one of the dominant twentieth-century interpretations of the book and projecting it back to the 1860s, giving us a reading that fits with the way Carroll and his work are seen now, but that would probably have baffled readers in 1865. Visiting Tenniel, Carroll is relieved to find that the illustrator has failed to bring out the "darkness" in the manuscript, and has disguised the personal desires and fears hidden in the work.

> Has he understood me? With a bewildering combination of relief & disappointment I see that he has not—His Alice is not my Alice—she is blond, vapid, lovely, of the type that people are so fond of these days. He has made the story sweet & whimsical, and erased almost all signs of darkness . . . his Wonderland is less wild & menacing, his Alice washed out & pretty & not at all like my black-eyed, sparkling little creature. He will never see Alice. He has transformed my dreams into a pastel fantasy populated by harmless creatures & blond girls. Perfect.[165]

This is quite a surprising reading. Whether we like Tenniel's illustrations or not, to call the heavily cross-hatched tableaux "pastel" and see them as a reduction of Carroll's story to a twee playtime in fairyland seems to be another example of nudging the evidence aside when it doesn't fit. The account of *Wonderland*'s dark undercurrents and inherent menace is very similar to the journalistic slant we encountered in Chapter 2, and this is also how Hunt reads the text—not as "hearty and healthy fun" at all.

> You are nothing but a pack of cards, Alice says, and then they all fly at her, and she screams, and it is only a dream, and leaves are falling gently on her head. Hunt was surprised to feel himself perspire. The terror so delicate and realistic.[166]

The story clearly reveals to him that Alice is Carroll's muse, but "there was something more . . . the feeling made him jittery. Falling off a cliff, like one of the pages of Dodgson's story."[167] Again, this is a late twentieth-century projection of attitudes towards the Alice-Carroll relationship; it has more to do with late twentieth-century conceptions of and expectations of these two figures than it does with social mores of the time, when the idea of a man falling for a girl of eleven would not have prompted a stomach-churning fear of the "paedophile" as it does in twenty-first-century Britain.[168]

The reaction to Carroll's nude pictures of Alice—which Roiphe invents, having sought to gain the reader's trust through her mention of genuine, existing photographs—is similarly a product of the 1990s more than the 1860s. Edith Liddell, who discovers the shocking evidence, "had never seen a naked photograph";[169] Hunt can only remember having seen one "nude photograph of children . . . several naked children, seen from the back . . ."[170] The images of Alice are like a grenade thrown into the Deanery, rocking the balance of primly repressed society and sending out shockwaves of scandal. A grown, "relatively open-minded"[171] man like Hunt has to retire home in trauma, trying to wash the memories away.

> Hunt thought he should have seen the faint shadow of the naked child in the earlier series of photographs. He should have been able to isolate and anticipate the precise nature of Dodgson's interest. And then he realized it was even worse. He *had* seen it. [. . .] There was something tyrannical about these images that would not allow any other way of looking. That was what horrified Hunt the most, and he could only imagine how Mrs Liddell must have felt. The danger of this sort of fantasy was that it imposed itself on you. Creating new avenues and channels that you had not known existed in yourself. Hunt wished the picture did not exist. He wished he had never seen this little girl standing naked . . .

Roiphe's depiction of the aftermath depends on her reader responding to the idea of nude child photography as sick and inherently sexual. It works only if we view the Victorians as sharing our values, and if we ignore, or are ignorant of, the kind of historical context helpfully spelled out by Karoline Leach.

> Naked little girls adorned the picture postcards sold in tea shops and bought by decent people on their holidays to give to one another. The respectable middle-class moral majority sent Christmas cards decorated with straight-limbed smiling Venuses baring their hairless pubic mounds. Men and women who might shrink from the supposed indecency of adult nudity felt free to smile and coo and rapturize over naked little girls.[172]

Hunt's revulsion at the feelings Carroll's images inspire in him—the idea that they are somehow exceptional and speak only of sexual desire—does not tally with a society that regularly saw images of the nude child and regarded them as appealingly innocent. More specifically, Lorina Liddell's hatred of Carroll following this incident—she draws back from hounding him out of Oxford only to save Alice's reputation—fails to interlock with the diary record of their later meetings. If Mrs Liddell felt, in June 1863, that Carroll "should not be living next to decent families",[173] and consoled herself with the thought that her social interaction would be limited to "smiling at him at large breakfasts and dinners",[174] why was he invited to the Deanery on December 19 of that year? "Mrs Liddell was with us part of the time," Carroll records, but there is no evidence here that the lady of the house detested their guest—he marks the day with a white stone and stresses a *very* pleasant evening."[175]

It will be clear by now that Roiphe is writing the Carroll that she sees from a perspective some 140 years later. Her 1860s Oxford, despite the sometimes showy research, judges Carroll by late twentieth-century standards; this is a recreation of middle-class Victorian society only on the surface, in the formal dialogue, the supporting cast, the historically accurate novels that the characters happen to be reading. It is occupied by people with late twentieth-century attitudes who feel sullied by a nude photograph of a child, who shudder at the thought of a man becoming friends with a young girl, who suspect sexual motive in every relationship and seek hidden "darkness" in children's stories. It may come as little surprise to find that Roiphe, having explored the Carroll-as-paedophile reading for most of her novel, brings in the Carroll-as-drug-user reading in the final act.

The hallucinatory fantasy near the very end of the book is prompted by Carroll's experiment with laudanum, in accordance with the 1960s theory that the *Alice* books could hardly have been written without recreational drugs. It leads to a parade of warped characters from *Wonderland*, who tease and torment their creator much like the monstrous versions of the Hatter and Hare in Dennis Potter's *Dreamchild*. "You are correct in nothing," announces the Dodo, while Humpty Dumpty—"massive and egglike and grotesque, rolls of fat under his chin"—challenges Carroll's death joke about leaving off at age seven. That Carroll had not written Humpty Dumpty's *Looking-Glass* scenes in 1863 is perhaps the most blatant discrepancy in the entire novel, but any reader who wishes for consistency between the fiction and such details as the dates of Carroll's published work will have realised by now that Roiphe's priorities are different, and either accepted or rejected her terms.

I have been arguing that Roiphe's Carroll is a product of the late twentieth-century discourse around Carroll—broadly speaking, the image of a paedophile, whether repressed or not, with possible experience of hallucinatory drugs. This kind of shorthand is necessary for convenience, but of course this is only one way that Carroll is constructed in contemporary culture, and I have suggested throughout this study that there is another, equally powerful discourse of the author as an innocent, kindly eccentric. This portrait of Carroll is vital to retaining his role in English heritage and, by extension, *Alice*'s place as an innocent classic of children's literature—the notion of the author as a pervert and his books as an expression of that perversion threaten their places in respectable culture— and so those who believe Carroll should retain this position have to defend him against perceived slurs.

Roiphe's novel came up against this defensive reaction in more than one review. The *Guardian* described her approach as "celebrity scandals of yesteryear" and cautioned against her treatment of Victorians according to modern beliefs, her attitude of "feeling these accomplished people are stupid."[176] Meg Sorensen's article in a Queensland newspaper also describes as "scandalous" Roiphe's "attenuation of the solid facts of Dodgson's life . . . adding her own little squiggles and curlicues to the straight line of his apparently celibate and undeniably repressed life."[177]

> Only the 21st century, with its media-induced lust for intimate details of the rich and famous, could have spawned this ludicrous work of fiction. For the very private Charles Dodgson, the result, one suspects, would be as hallucinogenic as caterpillar breath.[178]

An echo of both articles can be found again in Michael Eck's review for the New York *Times Union*, where Roiphe is accused of "silver-spoon muckraking" and told "next time . . . take on someone who's still alive, someone with a chance of biting back."[179] These reviewers are all well aware of the "paedophile" discourse—"it's no great revelation," says Eck, "to point out that Lewis Carroll's classic . . . was inspired by a less than lily-white relationship with the young Alice Liddell."[180] "It's . . . repeatedly suggested," Sorensen acknowledges, that the *Alice* books were written "to sublimate his Nabokovian love for the pre-pubescent child."[181] The rumours are entirely familiar even to those who reject them, and now cling so closely to Carroll that an author like Noon seems to feel he has to incorporate them in his depiction; Adair wrote an *Alice* novel with no hint of knowingness about child-love from a twentieth-century perspective, but then, his book was published in 1984, when popular fears and loathing about the paedophile were perhaps less rampant and Carroll's name was, possibly, able to circulate more freely without the winks and nudges about nude photographs and inappropriate obsessions. However, as the critical response to *Still She Haunts Me* shows, the meanings around his name are still open to debate, and the whispers of scandal denied. The innocence or otherwise of Wonderland and its author are still being struggled for.

Alice does, as Noon cannily suggests, have a "twin twister" in today's culture, a version of herself with similar but distorted features. In fact, the situation is more complex because the name "Alice" already implied twins: the Dean's daughter, and the fictional dreamchild. Our concepts of both the real girl and the fictional counterpart now circulate alongside alternate visions of them as innocent or cynical, light or dark. Roiphe reverses more familiar contemporary interpretations by depicting Alice Liddell as knowingly manipulative and Alice in Wonderland as a pale pastel disguise; the image of Carroll as seducer, rather than seduced, is also cast in negative. Carroll, too, of course, has a twin shadowing him in the form of the "paedophile", and another, related stalker in the image of him as "drug user". Like Noon's Alice, the Carroll of the popular imagination is a neither-nor, a Shrödinger's Cat, shifting between potential identities. We look at one reworking and see a repressed molester and a sultry little tease; we look again, and see a kindly, intelligent man and a quick-witted little girl briefly illuminating each other's lives.

Notes

1. Lewis Carroll, introduction to *Sylvie and Bruno* (1889; New York: Dover Publications, 1988), p. xxxvi.

2. Neil Gaiman, Kelley Jones III et al., "Season of Mists," *The Sandman* #22 (New York: DC Comics, January 1991), p. 2.

3. Sigler, *Alternative Alice* (Lexington, KY: University Press of Kentucky, 1997), p. xi.

4. Ibid., p. xvii.

5. According to a Batman fan site, "a love for the Mad Hatter character . . . mixed with an infatuation for his secretary, Alice, caused Jervis to become an odd and bitter man. Donning the guise of the Mad Hatter, he tries to win Alice's affection by [making her] believe he was suave and debonair." *Batman: Shadow of the Bat*, http://thebatman.bravepages.com/comics/villains/hatter.htm (May 2003).

6. Jeph Loeb and Tim Sale, "Madness," *Haunted Knight* part 2 (New York: DC Comics, 1996), p. 96.

7. Ibid., p. 118.

8. Ibid., p. 131.

9. Ibid., p. 113.

10. Ibid., p. 135.

11. Ibid., p. 138.

12. Grant Morrison and Dave McKean, *Arkham Asylum* (New York: DC Comics, 1989), n.p.

13. Ibid.
14. Carroll, quoted in Morrison and McKean, ibid.
15. Grant Morrison and Steve Yeowell, "Zenith," in *2000AD* #595 (London: Fleetway, 8 October 1988), n.p.
16. Morrison and Yeowell, "Zenith," in *2000AD* #602 (London: Fleetway, 26 November 1998), n.p. The puzzle concerns a crocodile who steals a baby from the banks of the Nile, and tells the distraught mother she can have her child "if you say truly what I will do . . . otherwise I will devour it." Peter St John smiles "Lewis Carroll. Child's play," and replies that the woman must tell the crocodile "you will devour my child."
17. Dave Gibbons, Steve Rude et al. *World's Finest* (New York: DC Comics, 1993), n.p.
18. Dorothy has become Dorothy Gale, and Wendy's surname is now Potter.
19. See Cohen, *Biography*, pp. 517–8.
20. Alice Fairchild is white-haired but the cover, showing her younger self, makes it clear that she used to be blonde; that is, like Tenniel's drawings of Alice, rather than Carroll's photographs of Alice.
21. Alan Moore and Melinda Gebbie, *Lost Girls* (Northampton: Kitchen Sink Press, 1995), n.p.
22. Ibid.
23. Ibid.
24. Carroll, *Through the Looking-Glass*, p. 149.
25. The second volume of Moore's series *The League of Extraordinary Gentlemen* (Titan Books, 2003) also makes extensive and fascinating mention of Alice in its Almanac sections.
26. Leach, *Dreamchild*, pp. 261–65.
27. Anne Thackeray, *From an Island* (Newport: Hunnyhill Publications, 1877), quoted in Leach, ibid., p. 264.
28. Pat Barker, *The Ghost Road* (London: Penguin, 1995), p. 26.
29. Edward Wakeling, "The Real Lewis Carroll: As Revealed in his Private Diaries," lecture to Lewis Carroll Society, 11 April 2003.
30. Harding, "*The End of Alice* Is a Cruel and Perverted Novel."
31. Quoted in A. M. Homes, *The End of Alice* (New York: Scribner, 1996), p. 9.
32. Jefferson Airplane, "White Rabbit" (1967).
33. Anonymous, *Go Ask Alice* (1971; London: Arrow, 1997), p. 28.
34. Will Brooker, "Slash and Other Stories," in *Using the Force: Creativity, Community and Star Wars Fandom* (London: Continuum, 2003).
35. http://www.masterapprentice.org/archive/s/secrets_heart.htm l.
36. Carroll, *Looking-Glass*, p. 143.
37. Gilbert Adair, *Alice Through the Needle's Eye* (London: Pan Books, 1985), p. 1.
38. See Hugh Haughton, "A Note on the Text," in *Alice's Adventures in Wonderland and Through the Looking-Glass* (London: Penguin, 1998), p. lxxii. Although this information is now available in a popular Penguin Classics edition, until 1998 it would have only been known to a more specialist audience through Selwyn Goodacre's article in *Jabberwocky* 11 no. 3 (Summer 1982).
39. Although she only appears for the first time in *Looking-Glass*; in *Wonderland*, whose real world is outside rather than in, Dinah crops up in Alice's thoughts and conversation, with Carroll's parenthetical explanation "Dinah was the cat." Carroll, *Alice in Wonderland*, p. 14. Adair cleverly echoes, "Dinah was the cat, now quite old and sleepy."
40. Carroll, ibid. p. 11.
41. Haughton, "Note on the Text."
42. Adair, *Needle's Eye*, p. 2.
43. Another important stylistic motif in *Alice*, the asterisks that mark the crossing of a brook, first appears in Adair's novel on p. 41.
44. Carroll, *Looking-Glass*, p. 223.
45. Carroll, *Alice in Wonderland*, p. 41.
46. Ibid., pp. 72–73.

47. Carroll, *Looking-Glass*, p. 146.
48. Adair, *Needle's Eye*, p. 90.
49. This reporting-back appears later in Adair, p. 73: "as Alice afterwards described it to her sister." Cf. *Looking-Glass*, p. 278, "when she was telling her sister the history . . . "
50. Carroll, *Looking-Glass*, p. 147: "Nurse! Do let's pretend that I'm a hungry hyaena . . . "
51. Ibid., p. 206.
52. Adair, *Needle's Eye*, p. 3.
53. Ibid., p. 5.
54. Carroll, *Looking-Glass*, p. 145.
55. Ibid.
56. Adair, *Needle's Eye*, p. 5.
57. Carroll, *Alice in Wonderland*, p. 26.
58. Carroll, *Looking-Glass*, p. 176.
59. Ibid., p. 268. Note that Alice's learning of French recurs both in Noon's adventure and in Roiphe's novel.
60. Adair, *Needle's Eye*, p. 8.
61. Carroll, *Alice in Wonderland*, p. 13.
62. Carroll, letter to Alexandra Kitchin (21 August 1873), in Cohen, *Letters*, p. 54.
63. Carroll, letter to Edith Jebb (18 January 1870), ibid., pp. 46–47.
64. Adair, *Needle's Eye*, p. 112.
65. Carroll, letter to Agnes Hull (22 October 1878), in Cohen, *Letters*, p. 84.
66. Sigler, *Alternative Alices*, p. xvii.
67. Adair, *Needle's Eye*, p. 123.
68. They also work on our knowledge that Carroll was interested in twins and mirror-images, most obviously in the Tweedle brothers.
69. Though the Lloyd George satire mentioned in Chapter 3 could have provided the germ of this creation.
70. Adair, *Needle's Eye*, p. 102.
71. Carroll, *Alice in Wonderland*, p. 46.
72. Carroll, *Looking-Glass*, p. 285.
73. Ibid., p. 282.
74. Carroll, *Alice in Wonderland*, p. 56.
75. Adair, *Needle's Eye*, p. 12. Cf. Jeff Noon, *The Automated Alice* (London: Doubleday, 1996), p. 21: the Termite thinks Alice is "a lice". "We don't want no lice in this mound!".
76. Carroll, "The Wasp in A Wig," in Gardner, ed. *The Annotated Alice: Definitive Edition*, p. 310.
77. Adair, *Needle's Eye*, p. 162.
78. Carroll, *Alice in Wonderland*, p. 107.
79. And the Man in White Paper, according to Martin Gardner.
80. See Hancher, *Tenniel Illustrations*.
81. The same is true of the "Peg-Leg Ned" drawing on page 121, which pastiches Millais" "The Boyhood of Raleigh"—we are meant to smile at the copy, and appreciate that Tenniel's illustration of Alice on the Looking-Glass train was a copy of another Millais painting, "My First Sermon," but the resemblance may be coincidental.
82. See Cohen, *Letters*, pp. 423–31. Of course, Carroll also included a courtroom in *Wonderland*.
83. Note also that Carroll referred to a Welsh landmark, the Menai Bridge, in the White Knight's Song.
84. Michael Senior's book on the subject is an exception: see Michael Senior, *Did Lewis Carroll Visit Llandudno?* (Wales: Gwasg Carreg Gwalch, 2000).
85. Leach, *Dreamchild*, pp. 173–75.
86. Stephen Jewel, "Britain's Urban Spaceman," *Sunday Star-Times*, Auckland (4 May 1997), n.p.
87. Jeff Noon, "All Kinds of Alice," *The Guardian*, 7 January 1998, n.p.
88. Ibid., n.p.

89. It is interesting to observe that China Miéville, one of the leading writers in the subgenre, included an in-joke reference to "The Wasp in A Wig" in his recent novel: it is a book in the library of Armada, the floating city. China Miéville, *The Scar*, London: Pan (2003), p. 186.

90. Jeff Noon, *The Automated Alice* (London: Transworld, 1996), p. 207.

91. William Gibson and Bruce Sterling, *The Difference Engine* (London: Gollancz, 1990), p. 383.

92. Noon, *Automated Alice*, p. 45.

93. Gardner suggests that *Looking-Glass* is probably set in 1862; Gardner, *Annotated Alice*, p. 144.

94. Noon, *Automated Alice*, p. 88. Carroll is supposed to have written this future-fiction in his "old age".

95. Ibid., p. 44.

96. Ibid., p. 69.

97. Ibid., p. 96.

98. Ibid., p. 32.

99. Ibid., p. 48.

100. Ibid., p. 189.

101. Ibid., p. 117.

102. Ibid., p. 109.

103. Ibid., p. 79.

104. Ibid., p. 89.

105. Ibid., p. 167.

106. Carroll, *Alice in Wonderland*, p. 102.

107. Noon, *Automated Alice*, p. 109.

108. For instance, the second phase of the image "masks and perverts a basic reality": Jean Baudrillard, "Simulacra and Simulations," in Peter Brooker, ed., *Modernism/Postmodernism* (London: Longman, 1992), p. 152.

109. Noon, *Automated Alice*, p. 70.

110. See Sadie Plant, *Zeroes and Ones: Digital Women and the New Technoculture* (New York: Doubleday, 1997).

111. Noon, *Automated Alice*, p. 122.

112. See the reviews of American McGee's *Alice* game in Chapter 7, and its knowing play on "LSD" for the commands Load, Save, Delete.

113. Ibid., p. 222.

114. Ibid., p. 223.

115. Carroll, *Alice in Wonderland*, p. 11.

116. Noon, *Automated Alice*, p. 11.

117. Ibid.

118. Alice boasts that she wouldn't say anything if she fell off the top of the house; Carroll observes that this is "very likely true." Carroll, *Alice in Wonderland*, p. 13.

119. Ibid., p. 75.

120. Noon, *Automated Alice*, p. 13.

121. Ibid., p. 63.

122. Ibid., p. 208.

123. Ibid., p. 101.

124. Carroll, *Looking-Glass*, p. 227.

125. Noon, *Automated Alice*, p. 13; cf. Carroll, *Alice in Wonderland*, p. 26.

126. Noon, *Automated Alice*, p. 23.

127. Carroll, *Looking-Glass*, p. 218.

128. Noon, *Automated Alice*, p. 14.

129. Ibid., p. 19; cf. Carroll, *Alice in Wonderland*, p. 13.

130. Ibid., p. 78.

131. Ibid., p. 249.

132. Ibid., p. 49.

133. Ibid., p. 126.

134. Ibid., p. 157.
135. Adair, *Needle's Eye*, p. 127. Cf. Carroll's dismay at the words "damn me" in *HMS Pinafore*, Cohen, *Letters*, p. 307.
136. Noon, *Automated Alice*, p. 199.
137. Ibid., p. 156.
138. Katie Roiphe, *Still She Haunts Me* (London: Hodder, 2001), p. 1.
139. Ibid.
140. Ibid., p. 31.
141. Ibid., p. 65.
142. Wakeling and Taylor, *Photographer*, p. 254.
143. Roiphe, *Still She Haunts Me*, p. 2.
144. Ibid., p. 35.
145. Wakeling and Taylor, *Photographer*, p. 244.
146. Ibid.
147. Wakeling, *Lewis Carroll's Diaries*, vol. 4.
148. Wakeling, "What Happened to Lewis Carroll's Diaries," *The Carrollian* 8 (Autumn 2001), p. 57.
149. Quoted in Cohen, *Letters*, p. 60.
150. Wakeling, "What Happened to Lewis Carroll's Diaries," p. 52.
151. Ibid., p. 7.
152. Ibid., p. 175.
153. Ibid., p. 77.
154. Ibid., p. 75.
155. Ibid., p. 3.
156. Ibid., p. 2.
157. Ibid., p. 13.
158. Ibid., p. 120.
159. Ibid., p. 147.
160. Ibid.
161. Ibid., p. 3.
162. Wakeling, *Lewis Carroll's Diaries*, p. 265.
163. Roiphe, *Still She Haunts Me*, p. 174.
164. Wakeling, *Diaries*, p. 210.
165. Roiphe, *Still She Haunts Me*, p. 163.
166. Ibid., p. 173.
167. Ibid.
168. See for instance Cohen, *Letters*, p. 102, for details of successful marriage proposals to girls of ten, eleven, and twelve around the time of *Wonderland*'s publication.
169. Roiphe, *Still She Haunts Me*, p. 186.
170. Ibid., p. 202.
171. Ibid.
172. Leach, *Dreamchild*, p. 65.
173. Roiphe, *Still She Haunts Me*, p. 215.
174. Ibid., p. 218.
175. Wakeling, *Diaries*, p. 266.
176. Anna Shapiro, "Books: First Novels," *The Guardian*, 4 November 2001, n.p.
177. Meg Sorensen, "Taking the Wonder out of Wonderland," *Courier Mail*, Queensland, 29 December 2001, n.p.
178. Ibid.
179. Michael Eck, "A Lukewarm Victorian Fantasy," *Times Union*, 13 January 2002, n.p.
180. Ibid.
181. Sorensen, "Taking the Wonder out of Wonderland."

6

ADAPTING ALICE

At a private screening at her home in 1933, Alice Hargreaves watched Gary Cooper as the White Knight, W. C. Fields as Humpty Dumpty and Bing Crosby as the Mock Turtle. She died the following year.[1]

In preparation for this chapter, I read eight academic anthologies on the process of adapting a work from literature to cinema.[2] In total, these anthologies contained 108 essays. Only one of them focused on the *Alice* books and their adaptations; and this was odd, because as Donald Thomas points out, Carroll had "been dead only five years when Cecil Hepworth's *Alice in Wonderland* appeared on the cinema screens of England in 1903 in a ten-minute version,"[3] with many more to follow. There were well over twenty film or television versions of *Wonderland* or *Looking-Glass* in the twentieth century, including looser adaptations like Dennis Potter and Gavin Miller's *Dreamchild* (1985) and oddities like *The Care Bears Adventure in Wonderland* (1983), which paired Carroll's heroine with the cuddly crew of Tenderheart, Grumpy, and Good Luck.[4]

A complete list would also include films with extensive reference to *Alice*, such as Terry Gilliam's *Jabberwocky* (1977) or the Wachowski brothers' *The Matrix* (1999), which repeatedly uses motifs like the white rabbit and the mirror portal; the *Animatrix* spin-offs include an even more direct homage, Shinichiro Watanabe's *Detective Story* (2003), which name-checks Dinah, the Jabberwock, Red Queen, and White Pawn.[5] At the time of writing, exactly a century after Hepworth's short film, two major productions are in development—Wes Craven's provisionally titled *Dark Wonderland*, based on the PC game that forms the basis of my next chapter, and an MTV rock opera rumoured to star Britney Spears. These particular prospects may not delight purists, but they indicate that the challenge of adapting the *Alice* mythos to cinema, however freely, holds an ongoing appeal in the twenty-first century.

In this chapter I am discussing six film and TV adaptations of *Alice in Wonderland*, some of which include elements from *Through the Looking-Glass*. Although my field of close study throughout most of this book has primarily been the 1990s, the importance of Disney's *Alice* film in fixing Alice's image as cultural icon—not to mention its obvious relationship to the Disney theme parks discussed in Chapter 9—demands that I extend that field back to 1951 in this instance. The other versions under discussion are Jonathan Miller's black-and-white, rather grown-up TV film of 1966, Harry Harris's all-star CBS production of 1985, Jan Svankmajer's surreal Czech animation of 1989, and Nick Willing's effects-laden effort of 1999.[6]

The almost total lack of reference to *Alice* adaptations was not the only surprising feature of the essays mentioned above. In some chapters an old-fashioned hierarchy seemed to be at work, treating the film adaptations as inherently and inevitably second-rate next to their literary originals, and judging an adaptation as praiseworthy only inasmuch as it matched "faithfully" up to the ideal of the novel—or rather, up to the commentator's individual notion of what the novel was about. Of course, the reverse is also true and adaptations were condemned for failing to coincide with the critic's interpretation of the novel's themes, or with the letter of the text in terms of character appearance and behaviour. This is Ian MacKillop and Alison Platt on the BBC's 1994 *Middlemarch*:

> We think the BBC missed the point about Ladislaw. He is after all a dilettante, a figure whose point of view is relative to the particular moment of his development. He grows up during the course of the novel. On the screen, however, he dominates: he is fully formed, glowing and glowering. In the [TV adaptation] Ladislaw loses the playfulness he shows in the novel . . . he sings only in Italian and the ditty he improvises walking to church, during which he resembled "an incarnation of the spring", is omitted. [. . .] As for Dorothea, we want to stress that Juliet Aubrey is completely excellent in her own handling of the role . . . [7]

Richard Barsam puts Joseph Strick in the dock for his adaptation of *Ulysses*, scathingly reeling off the director's perceived errors in departing from the text:

> "Aeolus" takes place in the offices of the *Freeman's Journal and National Press*, not the *Irish Times* as Strick believes; an inexpensive sign would

have solved that problem . . . Strick adds his own touch of moral con-
demnation—something Joyce never does—by having the bookseller spit
in contempt after Bloom has purchased an erotic novel for Molly. These
few examples are not picayune indications of Strick's faithlessness, but
rather primary evidence that Strick, when in doubt, persecutes Bloom,
Stephen, Molly and Joyce. [. . .] The film demands that the audience
accept Strick instead of Joyce, ignore continual violations of the elementary principles of cinematic theory and practice, and sit impassively
while a complex, ambiguous comic masterpiece is interpreted clumsily
in a one-sided manner.[8]

Mary Ellen Bute does no better with her 1969 adaptation of Joyce;
she is accused of making a film that "fails to do what it attempts . . . while
retaining ideas and images from Joyce's *Finnegans Wake*, it gives them a
radically different, indeed opposed meaning; it misrepresents the work."[9]
This approach, which strikes me as a quite absurd combination of the
absolute and the subjective—Joyce and Thackeray simply "are" this way
because that's how I read the novel, and any variation from the way I see
it is "wrong"—reaches a high point of self-indulgence in Julian Moynahan's
essay on David Lean's *Great Expectations*, which offers "notes taken at the
time" as analysis, enthuses wildly about the director's successes when his
vision happens to overlap with Moynahan's, and finds the film testing his
patience when it strays from the exact detail of Dickens's work:

> INSTANTLY the convict, fearful to behold, pouncing! Abruptness, vio-
> lence, pitifulness, all there just right. Joe Gargery, the blacksmith, should
> be brawnier though Bernard Miles a fine actor. [. . .] The other convict
> has "a big scar on his face." In the book it is a "badly-bruised" face.
> Lean is planting a detail for quick identification later on. Allowable.
> [. . .] He is halfway down the stairs when she combusts and he hears
> her screams. All wrong. In the book she ignites immediately . . . beating
> out the flames, tearing at the rotted drapes to cover her—terrific![10]

Suffice it to say that I do not think this a useful approach to film and
TV adaptations of *Alice*. Just as "Alice" as a character, text, and cultural
concept has gathered a rich and interesting cluster of interpretations since
1865—even if we don't agree with the readings, they have kept her active,
alive, relevant to the shifting concerns of several decades—I believe that
the many faces of Alice as envisioned by Disney, Miller, Svankmajer, and
others only make her more fascinating and vibrant. These *Alices* do more
than simply express a single director's individual interpretation; they seem
to channel a broader way of seeing and responding to the book and its

central character, relating to the readings discussed in Chapter 3. The film versions examined here all draw to some extent on the cultural understandings of Alice as dark fable, innocent children's fantasy, Freudian dreamwork, English heritage treasure, or drug hallucination—often incorporating more than one reading in the same film, despite the fact that some seem mutually exclusive.

I am not interested in putting black marks against these adaptations wherever they choose not to depict a scene just as Carroll described it or Tenniel drew it, or in praising them for their fidelity to the letter of the text. What good would a slavishly faithful *Alice* be, anyway—one that gave us moving versions of the Tenniel illustrations, put every line of Carroll's dialogue in the characters' mouths and used his prose descriptions as stage directions? Why should we look to a film for a precise acting out of the book, when we have the book for that? What I am interested in is what each production has included, what it has dropped, what it has changed, and what effect this has in giving us a specific vision of Alice and her world.

I am also interested in what these five very different productions have in common. Despite their differences, and their differences from the original, they all share a skeletal narrative structure, a core of key scenes that also involves a shared bank of dialogue and basic templates of character and setting. From this sample we can draw some sense of the essential Alice—the elements that these directors all see as vital to an adaptation of *Alice in Wonderland*. In this approach I am borrowing and modifying an idea used productively by Imelda Whelehan, who borrows it in turn from Roland Barthes.[11] In his essay "Structural Analysis of Narratives", Barthes splits narrative into various categories and subcategories—functions, indices, cardinal or nuclei functions, catalyser functions, and so on.[12] One effect of this is to make storytelling as coldly complex as the study of protons and neutrons, and I am not adopting his full system of terms here. However, the idea of primary, cardinal functions, elements with "direct consequence for the subsequent development of the story"[13] as opposed to elements that fill in detail and tone, is useful in this survey of five *Alices*.

In my analysis (see Appendix A) I shall be looking for the key narrative elements in each film and mapping them against each other to gain an understanding of what they share and how they differ, taking from this an idea of essential functions without which, these filmmakers seem to agree, the story would not work successfully as *Alice*. From this shared framework I will be considering the elements that make each adaptation so distinct—discussing the setting, costume, lighting, music, and performance styles that shape each film's sense of what *Alice in Wonderland* is "about" and considering how this relates to the broader cultural readings of the books we encountered in previous chapters. Finally, I want to focus more closely still on a specific scene—the Mad Tea Party—and apply the same analysis (see Appendix B), based around shared elements and variations, to explore further the adaptations' relationship to the original book and the way in which they construct their individual readings of Alice.

Structures

We can see in table form, in Appendix A at the back of this book, the way that each of these five films structure *Alice in Wonderland*.

What do all these adaptations share? We are introduced to Alice in the real world, with either an older sister or other adult characters. She follows a White Rabbit into some form of tunnel or hole, and entering Wonderland finds a small door she wishes to get through. She drinks a magic potion that shrinks her, and then eats a magic cake. Animals swim in a pool of tears. The Rabbit mistakes her for his maid, Mary Ann, and sends her to his house, where she makes herself big again, then small again as the animals try to evict her from the house. She leaves the house and encounters a Caterpillar who asks "Who are you?" She joins a Mad Tea Party, and meets the Queen of Hearts with her court; they play croquet. There is a trial culminating in her waking from the dream.

This is a very basic story, and its reduction to this bare bones outline is due partly to the fact that Svankmajer's version strips the encounters with Wonderland creatures to a minimum of Rabbit, Mouse, Hatter, Hare, Dormouse, and Queen, with the White Rabbit playing other roles such as Duchess, Cook, and Executioner. Svankmajer spends far longer exploring the earlier sections, with an extended sequence in Alice's bedroom at the start and a number of extra scenes based around the Rabbit and his nightmarish animal assistants. Two of the adaptations—Disney's and Willing's—also include scenes from *Through the Looking-Glass*, both choosing the Tweedles and the Live Flowers, although they shoehorn in extracts from the sequel at different points, Disney early on and Willing towards the end. Of course, these extra scenes cannot be included as key elements as they only occur in two of the five examples, and the same goes for the sometimes bizarre additions such as the monkey and goat cameo in Harris's film and the singing tree invented by Willing.

Other characters have also to be excluded from the list of shared narrative elements—despite their memorable role in the original book—

because they fail to appear in all the adaptations. The Duchess, Gryphon, and Mock Turtle are only in three of the five; the rose painters are in all but Svankmajer's version; the Mouse is in every film but Disney's. On the other hand, certain lines of dialogue recur across these very different productions—"who are you" and, in all but Willing's, "keep your temper"; "curiouser and curiouser", in every film but Svankmajer's. Even the detail of the Queen's "Rule 42" crops up in three of the five versions. We shall see later that the five Tea Party scenes also share many elements of dialogue despite their very different tone.

The common narrative functions that emerge from this comparison are surprising. We can agree that we have to see Alice in the real world for Wonderland to figure as a dream; she has to fall down a hole or climb down a tunnel to enter the dream world; she has to wake up at the end. Without these elements, *Alice in Wonderland* really would be a different kettle of fish, and so these can surely be classed unproblematically as cardinal functions with "direct consequence for the subsequent development of the story". Does Alice have to shrink, then grow, then go through the same procedure reversed in the Rabbit's house of ingesting magical food and drink that makes her grow then shrink? In a way, these sequences are redundant, because she would have done better to avoid all the bottles and cakes and stay the same size. Once she has made the mistake of trying the potion, true, she has to correct it with the cake or she would be trapped—first as a helpless miniature Alice at the foot of the table, and subsequently as a giant in the Rabbit's house. The cakes serve a cardinal function, then, but only when they follow the drink.

Is her encounter with the Caterpillar, which appears in all these adaptations, a cardinal function in Barthes' sense? Arguably, yes, because the mushroom brings her to a more normal height. In the book, she is three-inches tall when she meets the Caterpillar, then goes to the extreme of growing a serpent neck, nibbles her way to her conventional size, but then works back down to nine inches because she realises the Duchess's house is only four-feet tall.[14] However, not only is this level of complex detail missed out of all the film adaptations considered here, but the magical properties of the mushroom itself are not mentioned in every version. What about the Tea Party and the croquet game? They actually serve no purpose other than to frustrate and offend Alice, and slow down her progress through Wonderland. The only other scene from all these versions that truly advances the narrative is the trial, because Alice's argument with the Queen leads to the emotional climax that breaks her out of the dream and back to the real world.

Why, then, do all these adaptations, despite their variation, feature the Tea Party, the White Rabbit, the Caterpillar, the croquet game and— although they are unlabelled in Svankmajer—the "Drink Me" bottle and the "Eat Me" cake? The only reasonable explanation is that these are regarded as iconic elements without which the story would seem lacking, that each director sees them as necessary to and expected of *Alice in Wonderland*, whatever other changes are made to the plot and detail. The Tea Party in particular is featured almost as regularly as Alice herself in tourist and heritage attractions, as Chapter 9 below discusses more fully: Alice's Shop in Oxford sells a wide range of tea-making accessories branded with the Hatter and Hare, for instance, and the Disney parks in Anaheim, Paris, and Orlando all feature a Mad Hatter's Tea Cups ride.

It seemed odd to me that the Caterpillar appears in all versions and not the Duchess, but this may be because of my close acquaintance with Carroll's original. Disney's adaptation in particular has, I suspect, played a significant role in shaping the popular conception of Alice's iconography, and the omission of the Duchess may not come as such as a surprise to the "interested layperson" I was referring to in Chapter 5. Zadie Smith writes of *Looking-Glass* as "the repository where missing stories you *thought* were in *Wonderland* turn out to be . . . ",[15] indicating that without regular reference to the books themselves, things get mixed up between the two. I would suggest that the powerful and pervasive influence of Disney's retellings has something to do with this; it is surely not unlikely that some readers, their memories of Alice shaped by the 1951 animation, are surprised when they find the Duchess in Carroll's original book. Deborah Ross makes a similar point:

> By the time our eight year-olds have developed the vocabulary and syntactical sophistication to appreciate the humour and style of Milne or Grahame or Carroll (if in fact they ever do) they reject their works as "baby stuff". Since these stories will then be known to our children only in the Disney version, Disney has gained a monopoly on the next generation's fantasies . . . [16]

So much for the similarities, but despite these common elements the five films are very different. How do they create a distinct and individual tone and approach—a whole way of seeing and telling *Alice in Wonderland*— around this shared skeleton plot?

Disney: "my world would be a wonderland."

The Disney *Alice* is dismissed by Donald Thomas as owing "more to the culture of popcorn and bubble-gum than to the genius of either Dodgson or Tenniel. For the first time, the self-confidence of Alice was touched by the vulgar assertiveness of Lolita."[17] His disdain combines a snobbishness about American commercial culture with the implication that this Alice is brashly sexualized; a little surprising given that Disney is commonly thought of as a sanitizing influence, reducing classic tales to tweeness, but in any case it is clear that he regards it as a travesty barely worth commenting on. Reviews in the English press at the time of the film's release ran along similar lines in terms of the perceived brashness; "cheaply pretty songs" said *The Times*, while the *Illustrated London News* turned up its nose and blocked its ears at the "indescribable hullabaloo" and "sheer din".[18]

Dedicated studies of Disney and his work suggest he had a fascination with Carroll's heroine that was first expressed in *Alice's Wonderland* (1923) and endured through a series of Alice comedies, although these were only loosely related to the original books.[19] He planned to make a full-length adaptation in 1933, starring Mary Pickford, but was put off by the Paramount film of that year and had to postpone the idea; instead, he registered the title in 1938 and released *Alice in Wonderland* in 1951.[20] The *Alice* ride at Disneyland debuted in 1958, only three years after the park's opening.[21]

One reason Disney's adaptation might be thought crudely overplayed is the addition of several new songs; unlike the verses in Carroll's original, these are played straight rather than as parodies, and offer a commentary that may seem coyly sentimental when compared to the wry, sometimes grim twists in Carroll's "How Doth the Little Crocodile" and "You Are Old, Father William". This is Alice's song to herself as she wanders across the meadow with Dinah at the opening of the film:

> All the flowers, would have very extra-special powers,
> They would sit and talk to me for hours,
> When I'm lonely in a world of my own . . .
> [. . .]
> I could listen to a babbling brook and hear a song that I could understand.
> I keep wishing, it could be that way
> Because my world would be a wonderland.

This introductory scene presents an idyllic English summer, with a vague Oxford hazy in the background, swans drifting by, and butterflies fluttering across the grass. Alice's sister, reading the "William the Conqueror" passage aloud from her book, is wearing a rather old-fashioned bonnet; if Alice's voice, provided by Kathryn Beaumont, is cut-glass haughty, hers is even further up the scale of reserved refinement.[22] Dinah is a fluffy, wide-eyed bundle and the Rabbit a tubby, flustered flibbertigibbet; both are drawn in a more stylized manner than the girls. It would be easy to conclude that this version reduces the sophisticated address and the dry irony of Carroll's prose to a soppy heroine in a blandly stereotyped English pastoral, and Tenniel's detailed creatures to crude slapstick cartoons.

Robin Allan points out that much of the comedy in the film is inspired by the twentieth-century American tradition—Ed Wynn and Jerry Colonna's Hatter and Hare evoke radio comedy badinage, the Cheshire Cat is "like Harpo with a voice", and Alice, despite her accent, comes up with slang like "I'm through with Rabbit." The overall effect is "burlesque . . . vaude-ville . . . effect piled upon effect and gag on gag."[23] The characters Alice meets follow the stylized design introduced with the White Rabbit—the Cheshire Cat is pink and lilac-striped, the King of Hearts is an ineffectual midget next to his giantess of a Queen, the Dodo wears a wig and tricorner hat in a similar eighteenth-century mode to Alice's sister. Again, the impression is of a silly dolly-mixture of over-sugared songs and anachronistic American stylings.

In terms of the broader discourses around Carroll and Alice I have been referring to, this version would seem a washed-out interpretation that sanitises and censors the more morbid and violent elements of the original along with much of the knowing, intelligent appeal to adults—where Tenniel's images are almost eerie in their depiction of grotesques on the same level of realism as Alice, Disney clearly distinguishes Wonder-land as fantasy. It promotes *Alice* as innocent family fun, but cleans up the text—a little like Carroll's notion of a bowdlerized edition of Bowdler's Shakespeare—replacing the creatures' rudeness with zaniness, and their wordplay with music-hall pratfalls.

However, this would be to ignore the fact that *Alice in Wonderland* was produced soon after Salvador Dali's residence at the Disney studio, and shows signs of his influence. Karal Ann Manning sees the film as "full of surreal suggestions, most notably the Daliesque deconstruction and reconstruction of the Mad Hatter's watch . . . "[24] More notable yet in my view is the chase sequence at the end of the film, where Alice flees across a bleak landscape with stark shadows—it is a brief shot, but startlingly like *Spellbound*, Hitchcock's 1945 collaboration with Dali, and it makes Wonderland look at least as hostile and threatening as something from Rackham or Zwerger.

Finally, the innocence of the Disney Wonderland is complicated by the potential for drug readings. Of course, the Caterpillar's hookah and mushroom, Alice's shifts in size and dreamlike scene transitions are present in the original text, but there does seem a possibility that the connotations with pot-smoking, hallucinatory fungi, and their effects are deliberately played up in Disney's version. The Caterpillar's appearance is accompanied by languid, exotic music and his voice is lazily drifting, with smoke shapes accompanying and illustrating his dialogue. Alice's final escape from Wonderland is, as noted, a literal trip through surreal distortions, culminating in a slow-motion, nightmare struggle towards the little door and a vision of herself asleep under the tree. To read these elements as linked to drug experience might seem arbitrary were it not for the fact that Disney actually promoted the film along these lines after *Fantasia*, on a 1969 re-release, had proved a hit with hippy college audiences.

> . . . in 1971 *Alice in Wonderland* was the top renting 16mm film in every college town across the country, playing to capacity crowds in heavy smoke-filled fraternity houses, university theaters, discos and private homes, where it sometimes ran over and over again for an entire weekend.
>
> After the smash cult revival of *Fantasia*, Disney withdrew the 16mm prints of *Alice* and targeted a 1974 theater re-release. The studio prepared ads with copy such as "Down the rabbit hole and through the talking door lies a world where vibrant colors merge into shapes of fantasy, and music radiates from flowers," "Nine out of ten Dormice recommend Walt Disney's *Alice in Wonderland* for visual euphoria and good, clean nonsense," and "Should you see it? Go ask Alice," a reference to Jefferson Airplane's song "White Rabbit."[25]

Though it may not have been intended at the time of the original release, the drug association was apparently officially recognized and subtly used for marketing purposes within a later context. Like Carroll's, Disney's *Alice* now manages a balancing act—still sold as healthy stuff for kids, it nevertheless carries less innocent meanings for knowing adults. Officially, *Alice in Wonderland* is now a Disney Classic to be treasured by families; yet the unofficial drug reading still clings, winked at and enjoyed though never explicitly confirmed.[26]

Miller: "the things which I have seen I now can see no more."

Jonathan Miller's adaptation opens with a close-up of Anne-Marie Mallik as Alice, seen through leaves; the motif of tangled undergrowth, coupled with the lettering style of the title and the pouty, pre-Raphaelite, tousle-haired stare of the pubescent heroine, recalls the manuscript and illustrations of *Alice's Adventures Under Ground*. The end credits confirm the quotation by using Carroll's actual drawings. Already, then, from the first shot there is a sense—as with some of the references in Adair and Roiphe, it requires a degree of specialist knowledge to recognize—of going back to the ur-text, the very original and the version regarded as "less *cooked* . . . it has its own dreamy, associative integrity, and it's altogether more *primi-'tive* . . . "[27] This adaptation is being signaled as something more grown-up than usual, and the meditative, mature air continues with Alice's voice-over, a quotation from Wordsworth's "Intimations of Immortality from Recollections of Early Childhood".

> There was a time when meadow, grove, and stream,
> The earth, and every common sight,
> To me did seem
> Apparell'd in celestial light,
> The glory and the freshness of a dream.

The quotation that bookends the film and closes the verse leaves Alice's adventure with a reflective melancholy. The girl recites:

> It is not now as it hath been of yore;—
> Turn wheresoe'r I may,
> By night or day,
> The things which I have seen I now can see no more.

Miller's film seems quite clearly to be exploring the reading of Alice as a fable of growing up, with Alice passing through and engaging with the customs of the adult world on her route to maturity. The final lines quoted above capture the complex nostalgia evoked by Carroll's end sequence, with Alice's older sister already feeling a sad fondness for the present of "happy summer days" before they are even passed—Anne-Marie Mallik's Alice wakes beside her sister having spent only minutes in Wonderland, but already feeling that freshness and glory of vision is something she has left behind in childhood.

Miller's book *Subsequent Performances* supports this impression. His way into adapting the text was by seeing it as a parallel of Kafka's *The Trial*—Carroll's book, he says, gives us the paranoid idea that "*people had been talking about A . . .* "[28]

In most of the previous adaptations of *Alice* there had been slavish replicas of rabbit-headed men and courtiers dressed like playing cards. [. . .] It was necessary to turn in a different direction altogether to find the visual details appropriate to a Victorian dream. The hallucinatory realism of the Pre-Raphaelites gave me the appearance and effect that I wanted in the film . . . by recognizing rather than ignoring the book's Victorianism, and by stripping off the traditional disguises of the characters, other themes began to surface from the novel that I thought I knew so well. The nineteenth-century preoccupation with childhood, and the glorious freshness of infant vision before it becomes clouded and obscured by the duties and responsibilities of growing up, helped me to think about Alice's changes of size. These can acquire interesting meanings for a child who is not yet an adult but on the edge of becoming one.[29]

Questions of identity are raised early on in Miller's film—though in a manner entirely faithful to Carroll's text—by Alice's breathy internal voice-over as she first explores Wonderland.

I wonder if I've been changed in the night? Let me think. Was I the same when I got up this morning? I almost think I can remember feeling a little different. If I'm not the same, the next question is, who in the world am I? Ah, that's the great puzzle. Who am I?

Wonderland itself—filmed at Spike Island military hospital, months before it was torn down[30]—is a place of peeling walls, of curtains blowing at open windows. Anatomy posters and religious oil paintings hang in the background; inconsistencies and absurdities are accepted by Alice with dream logic as common sense. "When it came to representing the Pool of Tears, the film showed fully clothed figures seen floundering in water through a hole in the floorboards. The camera must treat all of these events with a perfunctory casualness . . . "[31]

That the animals of Wonderland appear in civilian dress, unmasked, emphasizes the sense of Alice's encounters with an adult world that sometimes seems ridiculous, sometimes threatening. The Mouse's reading and Caucus-Race are like a social meeting or after-dinner conversation, with Alice as a bored guest, which disintegrate into lunacy. She does not race herself, and observes coolly, detached like a teenager from her embarrassing parents and their friends. The audience with the Caterpillar, though, places her in the position of a schoolgirl with a master, told to recite and troubled to find the words mangling on the way from her mind to her mouth. When she tells him "I think you ought to tell me who you are first," Miller's persuasive construction of Victorian society, and the fact that this is an adult world rather than a fantasy of huge animals or men in costume, makes her challenge seem bold and daring.

Her retorts in the face of rudeness and her loss of respect for authority mark her passage from childhood, but there is still a subtle awareness that she recognizes social structures and hesitates to overstep the mark. She informs the Footman, "I think you're absolutely idiotic," but he is working-class and she may well feel she has the right; when it comes to one-upmanship with the Mock Turtle about their schooling and he asks if her establishment had "washing", she audibly holds back before unleashing an indignant rejoinder of "certainly not!"

In its unnerving rendition of dream logic through understated devices that marginally skew the realism—dialogue where Alice or her companion don't move their lips, a shot of her walking into a new location that doesn't clearly connect to the last—Miller's *Alice* also echoes *Spellbound*, Alain Resnais' *Last Year at Marienbad* (1961), and Maya Deren's *Meshes of the Afternoon* (1943)—and like these films it cannot avoid associations with Freud's theory of dreams. While there is no explicit suggestion here that the Wonderland props of keys, holes, little cakes, and long hallways are symbols of more taboo areas like sex or birth, Miller's version, because of its mature tone, its highlighting of the more disturbing or uncanny elements of Carroll's story, and its attempt to render a dream rather than a song-and-dance fantasy, seems reminiscent of the Freudian articles on *Alice*.

It also evokes at least a suspicion of the drug reading, although whether this is intentional or not is hard to tell. To a great extent, the trippy atmosphere is the result of Ravi Shankar's sitar soundtrack; George Harrison trained with Shankar, and the distinctive sound calls to mind the Beatles' more psychedelic tracks such as "Within You, Without You" (1967). The croquet game takes the form of a lazy, all-day garden party, with men in military costume apparently collapsed in a daze or afternoon sleep. A soldier reaches out ever so slowly for a plate of tarts . . . a maid runs a brush repeatedly through Alice's hair . . . Alice sits still, holding a croquet ball . . . Alice gathers wildflowers in a bouquet. To a modern eye, Miller seems to be depicting a 1960s music festival in Victorian dress, and the soldier outfits only help to reinforce memories of Sergeant Pepper: but it is hard to say whether this is merely the imposition of received ideas about "the 1960s" onto a text that was merely trying to evoke a dream using an exotic yet increasingly popular form of music, and contemporary aesthetics of performance, costume, and cinematography.

Harris: "one of the worst feelings in the world is to be homesick."

I have already observed that Harry Harris's production includes a scene missing from Carroll's original and the other adaptations. After the Queen has scared off the Duchess, Alice wanders down a forest path—by the looks of it, the same forest path she has wandered down in several previous scenes—and finds a baby goat trapped under a fallen tree. Freeing the animal, she cradles it and coos "Bye little goat . . . go back to your mother. I'm sure she misses you . . . I'm sure mine does too." She then notices a chimp sitting on a nearby tree trunk, clapping her clumsily; as she approaches, it takes and kisses her hand. "And you hurry back to your mother too," she tells it. "Bye!" The story then continues more conventionally with the Gryphon and the Mock Turtle. Like Miller's *Alice*, this scene has a Beatles style. Unlike Miller's *Alice*, the connection here is not George Harrison's sitar but Ringo Starr in a turtle suit, singing

> Nonsense, nonsense, that's what we're terribly short of. If you don't love nonsense, I'll knock off your head . . . 'Tis nonsense will save . . . the blooming human race.

It will be clear that Harris's *Alice* takes a rollicking pantomime approach, with guest-star cameos round every corner—the titles are like an '80s American soap opera, with each actor's beaming face appearing above his or her name—and heavy slatherings of cute sentiment. The scene with the monkey and the baby goat is slightly less bizarre than it initially seems if we regard it as a variation on Alice's *Looking-Glass* encounter with the Fawn, which is also featured in this production and includes a real baby deer. However, while Carroll's scene is bittersweet, ending with the Fawn remembering its identity and bounding away from Alice in fear, Harris plays the meeting for pure schmaltz. Alice strokes the little animal, announcing "You're the only normal person I've met here," and sings to it:

> Why do people act as if they're crazy?
> Why do they live the way they do?
> Don't they understand that the things I've planned are dreams that
> I demand
> Come true . . .
> Will there come a day, we'll all know how to say
> I love you.

She croons the final line again to the Fawn, "I . . . love . . . you," and lets it run off "so you can find your mother, and I can find mine." Obviously, there is a theme emerging here. From early on in the story, as Harris tells it, Alice's motivation is not to get into the beautiful garden or to follow the White Rabbit out of curiosity—as it is in Svankmayer and to some extent in Disney and Willing—but to get out of Wonderland. Even in the room with the little door, near the start of her adventure, this Alice—played by nine-year-old American Natalie Gregory—is worrying "how'm I ever gonna get home?" The secret garden is attractive only because "this must surely be the way home." Meeting the Cheshire Cat, Carroll's Alice muses "I don't much care where . . . so long as I get *somewhere*," with a laid-back cool that, according to Martin Gardner, inspired the Beats[32]—Harris's Alice is insistent that she needs to get "home, I need to get home. I know my mothers already begun to miss me." This stubborn desire to break out of the dream and return to reality even informs her defence of the Knave in the trial scene.

> Why don't you let the poor prisoner go, you can see he's a nice man. Let him go home . . . his family probably misses him very much. And one of the worst feelings in the world is to be homesick.

Alice's rejection of Wonderland is a little ungracious given that we saw her at home in the real world wishing she could join her mother and sister's adult social sphere, and that the fantasy is such a jolly place, populated by adults who, for the most part, entertain and welcome her. The Mouse sings "I Hate Dogs and Cats" accompanied by other gaudily costumed animals, the Hatter serenades her with a cheery "Laugh . . . and we shall all perform for you", and the Caterpillar engages her in a full-blown song-and-dance routine that transforms him into Father William and her into the Young Man. As the number ends with an explosion, the Caterpillar, exuberantly played by Sammy Davis Jr, exclaims "that was excellent!" The tone is *Muppet Show* rather than Freudian nightmare. Even the animals' attempts to evict Alice from the Rabbit's house prompt her to chuckle "I wonder what they're gonna do next. You better not do that again!"

Overall, this is an *Alice* where Carroll's few sentimental moments are emphasized and multiplied until they swamp the sharp banter of the original and the confident reserve that its heroine generally displays. Natalie Gregory was praised in reviews as "self-assured, very expressive and oh, so innocent";[33] "a very self-contained young miss who . . . demonstrates the assurance and aplomb of a seasoned veteran."[34] "Gregory is more than a talent," enthused the *Chicago Tribune* at the time of the adaptation's release. "There is, in her performance, an intelligence that stops just short of being spooky . . . you sense that she is plugged into the storyline, that all the word play, the double meanings and illogical inside pitches are within her realm."[35] Gregory's manner, though, is that of a bright nine-year-old actress from the 1980s United States, energetic and willing to perform tears or tapdance on command; her type of intelligence is not that of a Victorian seven-year-old child from Oxford's privileged classes.

Despite the use of "innocent" as an adjective of praise in one of the reviews above, and the stress that this is a children's version, there are aspects of this *Alice* that feel a little unnerving. Telly Savalas in a cat suit is strange enough, but when he creeps up on Alice in the forest and tells her "listen closely, little girl . . . there's no way home", it is hard to avoid a sense of unease. During his song, with its doom-laden and threatening lyrics, we cut between his smile of grim enjoyment and Alice's anxious expression.

> There's no way home from this strange land,
> Don't even try to understand.
> You're lost in time without a trace,
> Resign yourself to your disgrace!
> Somehow you've strayed, lost your way
> And now there'll be no time to play
> No time for joy
> No time for friends
> Not even time to make amends . . .
> You are too naïve, if you do believe,
> Life is innocent laughter and fun
> There are things to fear, so you see my dear
> Your adventures have only begun.
> The worlds a mess, but sad to say
> It makes no sense in any way!
> So what care I, if you should cry
> There's *no way home!*

"I think you're a mean old cat!" Alice cries. The Cat breaks out of character into his Kojak persona and grins "miaow, baby!" before vanishing. Even if we discount any overtones of the sexual predator as entirely unintentional—Savalas's leering that the little girl's adventures have only begun is fairly creepy, but a connotation of child molestation could hardly be deliberate—the song is shockingly bleak. It does raise the question as to whether young audiences enjoyed the film as a nonstop ride of fun and frolics, or found themselves troubled by this kind of lapse into pop-nihilistic philosophy.

Svankmajer: "now you will see a film. Made for children. Perhaps!"

This teasing voice-over, interrupted by intertitles, opens Jan Svankmajer's adaptation. We have already met Alice on the riverbank, petulantly throwing stones into the water as her sister reads; the spoken introduction accompanies a close-up of the little girl's sulky pout. Kristyna Kohoutova is younger than Ann-Marie Mallik, so the sensuality of her features and the playfulness of her address are already potentially uncomfortable in a culture that veers clear of child sexuality. The discomforting intimacy evoked by the close-up shots of Alice is heightened when we learn that Svankmajer was infatuated with his young actress: "I finally chose Kristyna . . . the whole crew, including the director, was as in love with her as Professor Dodgson had been."[36]

This is not just a children's film, as Alice's wry "perhaps!" makes fairly clear, but it is dominated by a child. After every line of dialogue we cut back to Alice's mouth in close-up as she, or rather her dubbed English counterpart, ploddingly narrates "sighed the White Rabbit" or "cried the Mad Hatter". Alice, rather than Carroll, is telling the story. The opening scenes—as discussed, the first scenes of the book are expanded and elaborated upon in Svankmajer's film with the result that many other chapters are compressed or lost—subtly demonstrate that Alice is also creating Wonderland for herself. The camera moves unhurriedly around the girl's bedroom, sliding across apple cores, a mousetrap, jars of pickled fruit, dead flies, and faded drawings; among the props it picks out are skulls, beetles, and dolls that will later appear in her dreamworld.

The idea that Wonderland is comprised of real-life elements is also used in Nick Willing's version, which employs a surprisingly similar device of showing a puppet theatre, a house of cards, toy Tweedles, and a stuffed Hare in Alice's bedroom; but the implication in Svankmajer's film is a good deal more disturbing. Willing's Alice, as we shall see, dreams Wonderland to help her overcome her shyness. If Svankmayer's Alice dreams up such a nightmare from her surroundings, what does that say about her life, and if it's a deliberate daydream as the voice-over suggests, how much worse is the reality she's escaping?[37]

In dispensing with most of Carroll's dialogue, Svankmajer significantly changes the tone of the story; it becomes far less reliant on the pleasures of unconventional conversation and tricks with language and far more on striking visual imagery. Svankmajer develops a vocabulary of repeated motifs that echo many of Carroll's themes through pictures rather than words: Alice's many struggles to open school desks and the appearance of protractors and slide rules in the tunnels recall Carroll's mathematical puzzles and his puns on education in the Gryphon and Turtle scenes. The White Rabbit's greedy scoffing of sawdust to replace the stuffing that bleeds from his stomach exaggerates the eating and drinking motifs already present in *Alice*. The representation of the Rabbit and his animal crew—a vicious canine and a team of ill-assembled skeletons, clacking their limbs as they drag mismatched tails behind toothy skulls—only emphasizes the sadism and violence present in the original story. Svankmajer's most horrific scene, where the rickety collection of skeletal birds and beasts hunt Alice down and bully her into a pot, is his invention, but remember that in Carroll's tale the animals hit Alice's face with pebbles, the Pigeon beats her "violently with its wings",[38] and Alice takes the Duchess's baby because "they're sure to kill it in a day or two . . . wouldn't it be murder to leave it behind?"[39]

Svankmajer is a long-standing member of the Czech Surrealists and explicitly takes inspiration from Dali and Luis Buñuel;[40] unsurprisingly, his *Alice*, like Miller's, recalls the psychoanalytic readings of Carroll's books. Some scenes strongly resemble Magritte paintings: food sprouts nails, skulls hatch from eggs in spills of yolk, a key is hidden in a tin of sardines. Alice tumbles into what looks like a cauldron of milk—or some other white liquid—and becomes a giant doll-sarcophagus, a shell she has to break out of. The Caterpillar is a sock with false teeth, in a room of holes where stockings stiffen and plunge in and out of tunnels. If Freudian theorists made a meal out of Carroll's original, there are far richer pickings here: Roger Cardinal comments of Svankmajer's adaptation that "the treatment of objects within Wonderland corresponds to the fantastical procedures of dream-work, codified by Freud . . ."[41]

It is interesting to note that Svankmajer defines his work against Disney's.

> Disney is among the greatest makers of "art for children." I have always held that no special art for children simply exists, and what passes for it embodies either the birch or lucre. "Art for children" is dangerous in that it shares either in the taming of the child's soul or the bringing up of consumers of mass culture. I am afraid a child reared on current Disney produce will find it difficult to get used to more sophisticated kinds of art, and will assume his/her place in the ranks of viewers of idiotic television serials.[42]

As we saw, Disney's *Alice* has more in common with Svankmajer's than he is aware of or prepared to admit—both fall under the influence of Dali, although in Disney the moments of truly uncanny surrealism may be fleeting. There is a further irony in the fact that while Svankmajer has documented his experiences with LSD in the early 1970s at a military hospital in Prague,[43] it is Disney's psychedelically multicoloured *Alice* that seems most blatantly to invite the reading of Carroll's story as a drug hallucination.

Willing: "you don't need us anymore."

Like Harris's version, Nick Willing's adaptation of *Alice* gives the heroine a motivation absent from the original. Where Harris's Alice wanted to go home and Carroll's wanted, for the most part, to penetrate Wonderland more deeply, Willing's is trying to escape. Rather than falling asleep as a response to her boredom on the riverbank, the Alice of Willing's production is first shown—like Miller's—in the bedroom having her hair brushed by a maid in preparation for her formal recitation of a song at her parents' garden party. As noted, the credits sequence takes us on a swooping camera journey over and under Alice's floor, allowing us to identify the items that feed into Wonderland; as the scene shifts to outside the house, it would take a very dull or naïve viewer not to realize that the adult guests—Martin Short in a boater, laughing as his companion holds loaves up as ears; Ben Kingsley puffing a hookah—are also set to cross over into Alice's dream.

It seems entirely possible that Willing was familiar with both Miller and Svankmajer's adaptations, both of which are well-known and critically acclaimed, and incorporated visual concepts from the openings of their films. Certainly, his production models its visual style closely on Tenniel, particularly in Short's Hatter, whose authentically enlarged head and distorted features were achieved through digital effects and prosthetics,[44] and he claimed to have approached Carroll's text "reverently . . . I love the book." It may seem strange, then, that he felt he had to improve upon it by moving the locale of the introduction and giving Alice a recitation of "Cherry Ripe" to worry about, but he explains this change in terms of contemporary audience expectations.

> The main thing I insisted on is that Alice is asked to sing a song and is scared. The reason I did that is I felt the book is a collection of anecdotes, sketches written at different times and then cobbled together in a book.

It is not written as a story with a beginning, middle and end. And our modern movie sensibility has to have an emotional pull for us to stay with a character. [. . .] Singing the song becomes a metaphor for growing up.[45]

In a way, this gives Willing's *Alice* a parallel with Miller's portrait of a child dealing with adult conventions, and also with Harris's version, which links Alice's changes in size to her initial wish to join the adult tea party—"no doubt about it," says the Gryphon as she towers over the court—"you're growing up." As such, it makes more visible the fairly well-established readings of Alice as a parable of puberty. However, Willing's framework about the fear of singing affects more than the beginning and ending of the film; it entirely changes the characters' relationship with Alice, and the nature of Wonderland itself. Willing says proudly of his Mock Turtle,

. . . he's the one I picked to draw her out. He gets her to sing—coaxing her out of her shyness like a good friend. It is an enormous moment of healing.[46]

Gene Wilder, who plays the Turtle, chimes in: "I only want to do things that are somewhere inside of me, and I can create something beautiful by taking the role."[47]

Carroll's Turtle and Gryphon prompt Alice to think grumpily to herself, "How the creatures order one about, and make one repeat lessons!"; her attempt at "The Voice of the Sluggard" is greeted by the Turtle with "it sounds uncommon nonsense . . . what *is* the use of repeating all that stuff?"[48] Willing's Turtle, who calls his companion "Griff", exclaims, "so you like performing then. It's such fun!" and encourages Alice to join in with "Turtle Soup". "You're in for a treat, Alice!" cries the Gryphon, and after a series of reaction shots showing Alice's delighted but coy enjoyment of the song, she contributes a couple of "ooo"s to the last chorus. The Turtle smiles "and now my dear . . . I think you're ready to find your way."

I promised I had no interest in judging an adaptation by its fidelity, but there does seem something perverse about claiming a "reverence" for the original text and going on to so utterly change its tone. The creatures' rudeness and challenging demeanor are a significant part of Alice's developmental journey in Carroll—by taking insults, retorting with quick objections, and standing her ground, she shows an ability to deal with adult manners at their most absurd and extreme—but in Willing, the denizens of *Wonderland* are almost all dedicated to helping her out. The Caterpillar indulgently advises, "you mustn't be afraid. That's worse than not remembering." The White Knight gallops in for a brief appearance, much of his dialogue from *Looking-Glass* cut down to make room for his reassurance about singing in public. "Just be brave . . . and always get back on your horse. Just be brave!"

The most fundamental change, though, is signaled at the end of the trial, when Alice finds the inner strength to confront the Queen. The Rabbit asks, "are you so confident, young lady?" "Yes," Alice replies, "I am confident." "Then you don't need us anymore," the Rabbit concludes, and with that the dream world begins to disappear. Rather than ending in conflict, with Alice rejecting and exposing the authority of the court, Willing's production reveals Wonderland to have been a kind of symbolic counseling session, a role-play constructed by her unconscious to enable her to conquer her shyness. All the creatures were just there to encourage her in some way, and in the real-world postscript she performs "The Lobster Quadrille" to the audience—whose members she now recognizes from her fantasy—her delighted grin freeze-framing at the final moment. It may come as little surprise that this production was made by Hallmark, the greeting card manufacturers.

Six Tea Parties

As we saw, the Mad Tea Party appears consistently across this range of *Alice* adaptations despite its lack of importance in actually furthering the plot. This section examines more closely, through analysis of a single scene (see Appendix B), the pattern of variation—the additions, the aberrations, the spins that make these versions so different—balanced against the base level of fidelity that seems necessary to keep the film recognizable as *Alice*. I am introducing one further text here: *Dreamchild* (1985), written by Dennis Potter and directed by Gavin Millar, which rather like *Still She Haunts Me* examines the relationship between Carroll and Alice Liddell in the early 1860s and allows real life to mesh with the Wonderland characters. Unlike Roiphe's novel, *Dreamchild* is not set at the time of *Wonderland*'s writing, but in 1932, when Alice Hargreaves sailed to New York for the anniversary of Carroll's birth. The scenes around the Deanery and on the Isis are shown in flashback as an elderly Alice becomes bewildered by the New World and finds herself mixing her memories of Carroll with the fantasy of his creations. At one point she opens a door in her hotel suite and finds herself back at the Tea Party.

As with the comparison of the film structures as a whole, we can easily draw out the common features from the table in Appendix B. All the adaptations include Alice approaching the table where the Hatter, Hare, and Dormouse are sitting with their tea, although not all of them show her leaving—we never see her get up from the table in Millar or Miller's versions. All of them include the lines "no room!", and the "why is a raven like a writing-desk" riddle. Every film but Willing's has some business with the Hatter's watch,[49] based around it being two days slow. Four of the six adaptations include the "have some wine" dialogue from the March Hare, although Svankmajer moves it to later in the scene. Disney, Miller, Harris, and Willing include "Twinkle, Twinkle, Little Bat"; Miller, Harris, Svankmajer, and Willing include a form of "your hair wants cutting", although again, Svankmajer uses the line later in the scene. Miller, Harris, Millar, and Willing incorporate the exchange about "say what you mean", following the book quite closely in every case. Miller, Millar, and Willing use the conversation about beating Time; Miller and Harris alone include the story about the three sisters in the treacle-well.

This list may seem pedantic, but it allows us to see a kind of hierarchy structuring elements of the original text, whereby some are apparently deemed essential and others can be left out. As was the case with the larger-scale study of plot elements, there seems no immediately obvious logic behind all the inclusions and exclusions: why should "no room" be regarded as integral to the scene, and the treacle-well as incidental? Perhaps because of the latter dialogue's length—if the Dormouse starts telling his story, then it needs to be developed and used as a basis for at least some of the punning to-and-fro about "well in", "what did they draw", and so on, or it will just seem a confusing story-within-a-story with no purpose or benefit for the scene. "No room" very quickly establishes the absurdity of the situation—there is blatantly room at the table—and the rudeness of the hosts. "Have some wine" is also a brief and neat exchange that glibly turns conventional manners upside-down, as does "your hair wants cutting."

The longer passage that begins with Alice believing she can guess the riddle and ends with the Hatter and Hare mocking what she "might as well say" may be included in four of the five versions because it follows from the "raven and writing-desk" question; although Disney short-circuits this sequence, ending it abruptly with the "stark raven mad" pun, and Harris, for some reason, ends the riddle dialogue early, then starts it up again with Alice's question about how the Hare got his name. The riddle itself, another of the very few elements that occurs across all six adaptations, is arguably one of the lines from *Alice* that has acquired fame in its own right, like "curiouser and curiouser" and "the time has come, the Walrus said". It may also be the case that the adaptations themselves perpetuate and build on the sense of certain elements being "essential" to the retelling—if Disney has monopolized our understanding of *Alice*, as Deborah Ross argues,[50] then the inclusion of the writing-desk riddle in this version, not to mention its reappearance in adaptations from 1966, 1985, and 1989, may surely have shaped Nick Willing's film, which seems knowingly conscious of previous screen *Alices*.

Despite significant common features across all six adaptations, their depictions of the Tea Party are in keeping with the tone and approach of each film; that is to say, they are markedly different from each other. Some of the variations can be seen from the table in Appendix B. Svankmajer obviously uses less of the dialogue than any of the others, and conveys the insanity of the occasion not so much through linguistic twists as through repetition of short dialogue cues and visual motifs until they build up into a frantic montage cycle. Harris and Willing see fit to improve on the scene by adding new dialogue and songs—in Willing, the George Formby-like "Auntie's Wooden Leg" and in Harris, the Hatter's ballad "Smile". Disney showcases the "Un-birthday Song", which is repeated three times, and an elaborate visual sequence with the White Rabbit's pocket watch. Miller's adaptation, despite its lack of any attempt to recreate the world of Tenniel's illustrations, is most faithful to Carroll's dialogue, languidly reproducing virtually the entire scene with few additions or cuts. Millar's film, based on the Potter script, also stays very close to Carroll's text in the fragmented scenes it includes, though the Tea Party goes through shifts in time and space, with the older Alice Hargreaves replacing young Alice Liddell as guest and the acting-out of the Wonderland scene flowing into Carroll's telling of it in the boat. Other aspects that these filmmakers introduce or change—and the effects of these modifications—cannot be so easily identified from the table, or deserve a more extended analysis.

Disney's film, as mentioned, relies heavily on visual business based around a stripped-down form of the Carroll dialogue, which is filled out with brief musical numbers. Over the fifty years since its release, it is probably fair to say that the "Un-birthday Song"—which features on spin-off albums and as the soundtrack to the Disneyland Mad Hatter's Tea Cups rides—has become as familiar as the writing-desk riddle; in the scene itself it has more prominence than any one of Carroll's extended linguistic quibbles from the original chapter, as the idea of un-birthdays is explained to Alice and then brought up again when the White Rabbit mourns his watch. Ironically, the concept of un-birthdays is lifted from the "Humpty Dumpty" chapter in *Looking-Glass*,[51] so on one level Disney does show fidelity to Carroll's writing even though the idea has been moved from one book to the other and offered to different characters. The visual gags that to some extent replace the puns include the Hare drinking a half cup of tea—split down the middle with the liquid sloshing safely inside—and Alice being given a cake that explodes into a rocket, releasing the Dormouse like an ejected astronaut. Overall the effect is wacky slapstick, culminating in the Rabbit being flung out of the garden like a cabaret artist failing his audition.[52]

Miller, as we know, keeps closely to the length and detail of the original dialogue, but sets it in a more "realistic" environment—three grown men and a girl in a summer garden. The viewer's response to the scene may be shaped, at least initially, by the recognition in the Hatter and Hare roles of Peter O'Toole—what we would now see as "the young" Peter O'Toole, which prompts another kind of pleasurable fascination—and for Batman fans at least, Michael Gough, who played Alfred the butler in the 1960s TV series. O'Toole dominates the scene, lingering over much of the dialogue as if half-dazed—"Your um, your er, hair wants cutting."—and at one point standing up to perform a jig with the teapot, as he mumbles a little ditty about Adam and Eve. The other most noticeable feature of this tea party is the length of the pauses; there is a lazy gap before the Hatter perks up with "what day of the month is it?", during which the sitar music rises like a hum of bees and the camera dollies slowly down from the end of the table to Alice; the Hatter yawns and the Hare stares dolefully ahead. During a later pause the shot becomes distorted through a fish-eye lens as if even our vision has been warped by the heat, and Alice's dialogue stays on voice-over; she is too bored and tired even to bother opening her mouth. If Disney, and indeed some of the other versions, are cabaret, this comes across like a meeting of old college friends whose in-jokes and unspoken references are both tedious and rude to the outsider.

Harris's production adds bonus verbal jokes—although these embellishments, such as the Hatter's response to Alice's "are you sure your watch is running?" tend to be of a cornball variety that would be unlikely to amuse many viewers over the age of ten. The tone is far more friendly than Carroll's gathering—the sense is of well-meaning children's entertainers, rather than forbidding or insulting grown-ups—especially when the Dormouse and Hare invent rude word versions of the "Twinkle Twinkle" song, making Alice cry gleefully, "you do make me laugh", and prompting the Hatter to serenade her.

Laugh at every single thing you do.
Laugh . . . and we shall all perform for you.

Just smile and tensions will unwind
And you'll find that your mind takes a kinder view . . .
Laugh, yes even when your skies are grey
Just laugh and troubles seem to flow away . . .

As with Miller's film, one level of the viewer's attention may be taken up with the spectacle of watching Anthony Newley performing, with the characteristic barrow-boy pronunciation that inspired David Bowie's early work creeping through. Watching it in the wake of the "paedophile" theories about Alice's creator, there may also be a feeling of unease—as I suggested around the Cheshire Cat scene—at the Hatter's crooning so close to Alice's face, and the Hare's indulgent smiles. The close-ups between the adults and the child create a sense of intimacy that could seem discomforting; in "real" terms, after all, Alice is a nine-year-old who has wandered into a situation with three grown men, and allowed their leader to get quite close to her emotionally and physically. Such a reading of the scene would only be likely in a cultural context highly attuned to the risk of paedophilia and child abuse—that sensitivity heightened by the rumours around Carroll—but it is also enabled by the fact that in Harris's version, unlike most of the other adaptations, the Hatter, Hare, and Dormouse are clearly men in costume rather than grotesque creatures or animals.

Like Willing, Millar uses Jim Henson's creature workshop for the fantasy characters, but the effect is quite different. Millar's Hare and Dormouse are past their prime rather like Alice Hargreaves; while clearly resembling the Tenniel pictures, they have gone to seed and become bitter, misshapen creatures. The Hatter, too, is a puppet figure here, whereas Willing casts Martin Short and keeps him reassuringly recognizable despite the latex features and digital head enlargement. Though the dialogue is scripted closely from Carroll's text, its tone is changed by the sneer that the party hosts put into every question. When Alice is caught out by the "I mean what I say" line, all three of them snigger cruelly among themselves, deliberately mocking, and make even the self-possessed young Alice—an apt combination of fact and fiction, with Alice Liddell's hair and Alice in Wonderland's outfit—begin to doubt herself. When Alice Hargreaves, fragile and confused, replaces her younger self in the chair, she is far more vulnerable to their attacks. "You stupid, halfwit, ugly old hag," spits the Hatter, the viciousness of the insult more shocking because of its insertion among Carroll's familiar dialogue. "You should be dead, dead, dead." Carroll's creatures may be rude, but they are never this obscenely abusive.

Millar's version also raises issues of authorship, by cutting back to Carroll in the boat on the occasion of the original story. We see him intent, almost in a dream world himself, constructing the exchanges through a creative dialogue with Alice Liddell. " 'what a funny watch,' said Alice," he announces, then immediately follows up with a flat "Why." Alice's reply takes him back without a break into the story, which she seems to have some role in writing herself. This scene is part of an ongoing subplot in which the elderly Alice remembers her relationship with Carroll, his obvious fixation on her, and her rejection of him as she grew older; we get a sense from the dialogue in the boat of Mrs Liddell's emerging disapproval and Carroll's meekness when not swept up in storytelling. Again, there will be a marginal fascination for those viewers who recognize Jane Asher as Alice's mother, and remember her earlier role as Alice.[53]

I have discussed the way that Svankmajer opts to cut dialogue to a minimum and convey the manic frustration of the scene by cycling through the same visual motifs, building the sequence up more and more rapidly: pour tea, shift round the table, drink tea, butter the watch. Through these devices he also suggests a different way of seeing the Hatter/Hare relationship, because the Hare is a moth-eaten windup animal who depends on the Hatter to keep his motor running. The Hatter, then, is not perhaps the Hare's friend so much as his master, owner, or creator; but there is an added level of intrigue in that the Hatter is depicted as a carved wooden puppet with strings. Who is the Hatter's puppet-master? The only answer is Alice, because as we saw, the world is made out of her possessions and surroundings, and at the film's end she emphasizes her mastery while waiting for the Rabbit. "He's late as usual . . . I think I'll cut his head off." The whole nightmarish environment and its inhabitants seem to be her own creation, designed to entertain and perhaps temporarily frighten her. Though she sometimes seems a victim during the course of the film, the final scene shows Alice to be far more powerful than the Queen of Hearts.

Nick Willing's rendition of the scene cuts it down and then pads it out again, throwing in the elaborate "Auntie's Wooden Leg": the Hatter dances across the table while the cups become glowing footlights and the Hare thumps at a organ with fanciful spouts. The sequence is live action, but in the mode of kids' animation—the Hatter plummets from the table like Wile E. Coyote, then climbs back up unharmed to whizz back into his chair at super speed. Objects on the table change shape—cakes and pies sprouting legs and wriggling like crabs—but while the concept may seem akin to Svankmajer surrealism, the shrieking jollity of the performances and the thick golden light that bathes the scene keep the mood on the safe side of strangeness. Perhaps most significantly, as in the illustrated versions, our response to the weird elements is shaped by

Alice's reaction. In Millar's film, both the older and younger Alice look troubled and frightened, but Willing's star, Tina Majorino, is more worried about her forthcoming recital than anything else, and welcomes the Tea Party characters as an escape from the more frightening real world. Of course, the theme of learning confidence through performance is brought out again in the Hatter's extra musical number.

One aspect of Willing's interpretation that deserves note is the way the characters refer to each other by familiar abbreviations—"Dormy" and "Marchy". Combined with the Hatter's exuberant performance, this gives the scene an air of theatrical camp and hints at the idea that the Hatter and Hare may be intended as some kind of bizarre male couple. Martin Short's Hatter certainly seems to play up to a stereotype of the effeminate gay actor, screeching "Oh! Oh! Ohhh!" after his curt "get your hair cut", and the Hare's simpering response of "flatterer" when the Hatter refers to his March madness does appear to imply a flirtatious relationship between them. Of course, we couldn't expect cross-species gayness to be explicitly spelled out in a production aimed primarily towards children, but it seems possible that the actors or production team may have intended this subtle undertone as a knowing little nod to the adults watching.

The one aspect missing from almost all these adaptations—they echo the illustrated versions in this respect—is anything that could plausibly be read as an intentional reference to the "paedophilia" discourse. This is even the case in the "darker", adult-oriented versions from Miller and Svankmayer, where we find possible connotations of hippy drug culture in the former and undeniable images of physical violence in the latter. Both, as I suggested, seem particularly open to interpretations of *Alice* as a representation of unconscious child anxiety and desire, rather than mere innocent fantasy. In Miller, though, Alice tends to seem bored and frustrated by her encounters with the adult world, and in Svankmajer the threats to her body—a fire on her head, oars hitting her hand, rocks through a window, tipped into a pot—have no clear and undisguised sexual associations. Indeed, it is implied that Svankmajer's Alice has ultimate control of the whole kingdom she struggled through, and, proving at least as sadistic as her previous antagonists, is unlikely to become a victim. The lack of sexual danger in this version is particularly striking when we consider that Svankmajer's *Down to the Cellar*, regarded as a precursor of *Alice*, follows its heroine into an underworld where an old man offers her sweets. Michael O'Pray comments,

> *Down to the Cellar* is tense and menacing, and has a disturbing sexual undercurrent, due partially to the association made in our culture with

any young girl under threat. Svankmajer has made the nature of this threat more explicit, however, in the character of the old man with the sweets who returns to haunt her in the cellar—bribing her, it seems, for sexual ends. It is as if Svankmajer had rooted out the sexual subtexts of stories such as Carroll's *Alice in Wonderland*, with their barely veiled eroticism.[54]

While Miller and Svankmayer's versions depict Alice with a degree of sensuality, especially in the discomforting close-ups, she nevertheless remains as sexually innocent as Natalie Gregory and Tina Majorino's heroines in safer environments. I have suggested that the Cheshire Cat and Hatter from Harris's adaptation could be read as potential predators without too huge an imaginative leap, but this would only be the result of quirks in the performances and song lyrics meeting a contemporary hyper-awareness towards any possibility of child sexual abuse; it would be stretching credibility to argue that this was intended by Harris, Telly Savalas, or Anthony Newley in the way that the "gay" overtones of Willing's tea party might have been. Millar's film, of all those discussed here, comes closest by far to exploring Carroll's potentially romantic attraction to Alice Liddell, but then *Dreamchild* is not actually a direct adaptation of the *Alice* books, and even here the abuse leveled at Alice from the Hatter and Hare, though deliberately hurtful, has no sexual element.

This absence even from the adaptations that explore *Alice* as a sometimes brutal, sometimes frightening expression of the unconscious is surprising when we remember the extent to which the idea of Carroll as some form of paedophile—repressed obsessive, shy lover of Liddell girls, troubled deviant—recurred in newspaper stories, biographies, and novels like *Still She Haunts Me* and *Automated Alice*. Given that this image of Carroll is so pervasive, we might have expected an "adult" adaptation of the book that Alice Liddell inspired to have incorporated some hint of the Wonderland denizens seducing, falling in love with, or preying sexually on the heroine.

Perhaps this discourse is too recent to have informed Miller and Svankmajer—although as we saw, it was visible enough in 1947 through Florence Becker Lennon's "he loved little girls" theory. Perhaps writing about Alice as a potential object of sexual desire is a different matter from casting and directing a child actress in a fantasy scene where she is lusted after by adults or animals. Perhaps there is a distinction being made between Alice Liddell, who is constructed by many writers as Carroll's love-object, and Alice in Wonderland, the eternal child in a book that is still marketed for young readers and treasured as an intelligent but innocent classic.

Explicitly sexual images of Alice in Wonderland do exist, but they remain across a cultural boundary, in the category of pornography: the 1976 erotic musical version of *Alice*, for instance, directed by Bud Townsend, and the numerous online archives that depict Disney's Alice naked and engaged in sex acts with the film's other characters.[55] Townsend's film may now seem fairly dated, almost quaint, but the Web sites that strip and sexualize the Disney girl are apparently getting a kick out of the process of violation; the corruption of an icon of innocence. However, the cultural status of this kind of image is leagues away from Miller, from Svankmajer, from Roiphe's novel of sexual obsession, even from American McGee's "dark" PC game with its teenage Alice and its fast-and-loose play with the mythos: it only exists on an unofficial level, underground.

Notes

1. Bakewell, *Biography*, p. 342. I have taken a liberty with Bakewell's text and used Alice's name for clarity, where he uses the personal pronoun.
2. Robert Giddings, Keith Selby, and Chris Wensley, eds., *Screening the Novel* (Hampshire: Macmillan, 1990); Deborah Cartmell and Imelda Whelehan, eds., *Adaptations* (London: Routledge, 1999); Cartmell, Whelehan, Heidi Kaye, and I. Q. Hunter, (eds.) *Pulping Fictions* (London: Pluto, 1996); Cartmell, Whelehan, Kaye, and Hunter, eds., *Classics in Film and Fiction* (London: Pluto, 2000); Neil Sinyard, *Filming Literature* (London: Croom Helm, 1986); Robert Giddings and Erica Sheen, eds., *The Classic Novel from Page to Screen* (Manchester: Manchester University Press, 2000); Wendell Aycock and Michael Shoenecke, eds., *Film and Literature, A Comparative Approach to Adaptation* (Texas: Texas Tech University Press, 1988); Michael Klein and Gillian Parker, eds., *The English Novel and the Movies* (New York: Frederick Ungar, 1981). The exception is Deborah Ross, "Home by Teatime: Fear of Imagination in Disney's *Alice in Wonderland*", in Cartmell et al., *Classics in Film and Fiction*.
3. Thomas, *Portrait*, p. 364.
4. See the excellent reference site *http://www.alice-in-wonderland.fsnet.co.uk/film_tv_intro.htm*.
5. Available at *http://whatisthematrix.warnerbros.com/*. Thanks to Brandon Perlman for this reference.
6. I am referring to the films by their directors only for convenience. Harry Harris's *Alice* was scripted by Paul Zindel, and Nick Willing's by Peter Barnes.
7. Ian MacKillop and Alison Plant, "Television and *Middlemarch*," in Giddings and Sheen, *Classive Novel from Page to Screen*, pp. 82–84.
8. Richard Barsam, "When in Doubt Persecute Bloom" in Klein and Parker, *English Novel and the Movies*, pp. 298–300.
9. Sarah W. R. Smith, "The Word Made Celluloid," in Klein and Parker, ibid., p. 301.
10. Julian Moynahan, "Seeing the Book, Reading the Movie" in Klein and Parker, ibid., p. 147, p. 150.
11. Imelda Whelhan, "Adaptations: the Contemporary Dilemmas," in Cartmell, Whelehan et al., eds., *Adaptations*, p. 9. Whelchan is actually taking the idea from Barthes through Brian McFarlane's *Novel to Film* (Oxford: Clarendon Press, 1996).
12. Roland Barthes, trans. Stephen Heath, "Structural Analysis of Narratives," in *Image-Music-Text* (London: Fontana, 1977), p. 92.
13. Ibid., p. 94.

14. Carroll, *Alice in Wonderland,* p. 58.
15. Smith, "The World Made Celluloid." p. ix.
16. Ross, "Home by Teatime," p. 223.
17. Thomas, *Portrait*, p. 365.
18. Quoted in Robin Allan, "Alice in Disneyland," *Sight & Sound* (Spring 1985), p. 138.
19. See Alan Bryman, *Disney and His Worlds* (London: Routledge, 1995), pp. 4–5.
20. Allan, "Alice in Disneyland," p. 137.
21. See *www.thrillmountain.com* for details.
22. Heather Angel, the sister, played Mrs Darling to Beaumont's Wendy in the 1953 Disney *Peter Pan*.
23. Allan, "Alice in Disneyland," p. 138.
24. Karal Ann Manning, *Designing Disney's Theme Parks* (New York: Flammarion, 1997).
25. David Koenig, *Mouse Under Glass* (New York: Bonaventure Press, 1997), pp. 90–91, quoted in http://www.snopes.com/disney/films/drugs.htm.
26. Deborah Ross makes the point that Disney's *Alice* seems uneasily to balance between the revolutionary and the reactionary—containing moments of radical style that are ultimately made safe by conservative gender politics. See Ross, "Home by Teatime," p. 210.
27. Haughton, "Introduction," p. 244.
28. Jonathan Miller, *Subsequent Performances* (London: Faber and Faber, 1986), p. 241.
29. Ibid., pp. 242–47.
30. See Phillip Hoare, *Spike Island: The Memory of a Military Hospital* (London: Fourth Estate, 2001).
31. Miller, *Subsequent Performances*, p. 241.
32. Carroll, *Alice in Wonderland*, pp. 65–66, and Gardner's accompanying note.
33. "AP", "TV's *Alice* fantasy sure to delight kids," *Toronto Star*, 9 December 1985, n.p.
34. John J. O'Connor, "Carroll's *Alice* on CBS," *New York Times*, 9 December 1985, n.p.
35. Steve Daley, "An Alice Made for the Part," *Chicago Tribune*, 8 December 1985, n.p.
36. Svankmajer, quoted in Frantisek Dryje, "The Force of Imagination," in Peter Hames, ed., *Dark Alchemy: The Films of Jan Svankmajer* (Wiltshire: Flicks Books, 1995), p. 153.
37. Jeremy Heilman's review on *MovieMartyr.com* suggests an even bleaker prospect: that Alice has even dreamed up her boring sister from the introductory scene, such is the loneliness of her everyday existence. *http://www.moviemartyr.com/1988/alice.htm*.
38. Carroll, *Alice in Wonderland*, p. 56.
39. Ibid., p. 65.
40. His recent film *Otesánek* (2000) includes an homage to *Un Chien Andalou* (1928); see Peter Hames, "Bringing Up Baby," in *Kino-Eye, http://www.kinoeye.org/02/01/hames01.html*, vol. 2, no. 1 (7 January 2002).
41. Peter Cardinal,"Thinking Through Things: The Presence of Objects in the Early Films of Jan Svankmajer," in Hames, *Dark Alchemy*, p. 86.
42. Hames in *Kino-Eye*.
43. Jan Svankmajer, "An Alchemist's Nightmares," *Kino-Eye, http://www.kinoeye.org/02/01/svankmajer01.html#4*.
44. See http://www.alice-in-wonderland.fsnet.co.uk/film_tv_majorino_02.htm.
45. Nick Willing, quoted in M. S. Mason, "*Alice in Wonderland*: A Dreamy Cast and Fabulous Effects," *Christian Science Monitor* 91, no. 63 (26 February 1999), p. 18.
46. Ibid.
47. Wilder in Mason, ibid.
48. Carroll, *Alice in Wonderland*, pp. 110–11.
49. The White Rabbit's, in Disney.
50. Ross, "Home by Teatime," p. 223.
51. Carroll, *Looking-Glass*, p. 223.
52. Allan, "Alice in Disneyland," p. 138.
53. On a spoken-word version in 1958: see http://www.alice-in-wonderland.fsnet.co.uk/sound_only2.htm.
54. Michael O'Pray, "Jan Svankmajer: A Mannerist Surrealist," in Hames, ed., *Dark Alchemy*, p. 73.
55. *Disney Porn Collection, http://www.extreme-toons.com/disney/*, features an explicit image of this kind on its front page.

7

DARK WONDERLAND

I generally hit every thing I can see—when I get really excited.
—Tweedledee[1]

*A*merican McGee's Alice (Rogue/EA Games, 2000) is a third adventure for Lewis Carroll's heroine, set in 1874. Alice's parents were killed one night ten years earlier, when Dinah upset a gas lamp and set the house ablaze; Alice threw herself out of her bedroom window into the snow, but has been catatonic in an asylum for a decade. Her journey back to Wonderland and Looking-Glass land begins when her stuffed rabbit turns its face to her and asks for help, and her subsequent quest to rid the dream world of the Queen's monstrous influence is a symbolic battle against her own demons of grief, rage, and guilt.

American McGee's Alice is also a third-person shooter using the Quake III engine, a kind of evolution from *Castle Wolfenstein* and *Tomb Raider*. It has limited artificial intelligence in the minor enemies, which could use extra polygons in some cases, and a range of big bosses at the end of the later maps. The genre is action-adventure, with a reliance on 3D platformer strategies that nevertheless elevate the game mechanics above mere hack-n-slash. The eye candy is stunning: an atmospheric CGI-rendered introduction and incredible level design with detailed textures and models combined with a straightforward and effective HUD. Minimum specifications include 580 MB HD space and a 16 MB Open GL 3D card.

Of course, this second definition represents an extreme, almost a caricature, of the PC games discourse that surrounded *American McGee's Alice*—henceforth *Alice*, in this chapter—on its release. Some of the reviews were not far off this kind of response, though; little to no mention of

Carroll, a vague and half-remembered sense of the books and their characters, and an assessment based mainly on technical achievements, comparison to similar games, and a set of standards for satisfying gameplay. As was the case with "unfaithful" film adaptations, I am treating this response as "interesting", rather than "wrong"; interesting partly in its contrast to my immediate response. I approached the game from a position of immersion in Carroll and Alice through the kinds of books, articles, and adaptations I have been discussing so far, with far less direct experience of the TPS genre that *Alice* falls into.[2]

So this chapter begins by examining *Alice* in much the same terms I was using for the "third adventure" novels and the films, as an adaptation and extension that borrows familiar elements from Carroll and introduces new ones. Through this kind of close, step-by-step analysis of the game text—using its accompanying literature, cinematic introduction, and first scenes as the body of evidence—I also want to capture and question the experience of playing this *Alice*. What emotional and intellectual responses does the game inspire? What process of identification is involved when we control Alice, yet watch her behaving independently in cut-scenes? What unique pleasures and anxieties, specific to the form, does this kind of interactive sequel offer?

The second part of the chapter looks at the way in which the game was received from the specialist gaming perspective. How does their response differ from my "Carrollian" analysis? To what extent do they refer back to the *Alice* books as source, and is their reading of Carroll shaped by the deliberately "dark" and "adult" twist that the game gives to the Alice mythos? Is their implied readership—the community they are addressing—assumed to be familiar with the original books; and is there any suggestion that the game will lead these players to Carroll's *Alice*, either to revisit or for the first time? In addition to reviews, I look at the online fan communities around the *Alice* game, and ask again what relation, if any, this fandom has to Lewis Carroll.

"Wonderland's become quite strange . . . "

I quoted the back-cover blurb of *Alice* in Chapter 3: here it is again, in full.

> When Alice responds to a mysterious summons to return to Wonderland, the place is barely recognisable. Something has gone very wrong. Undaunted by the diseased atmosphere, confusion, and mortal danger that surrounds her, Alice commits to set it right. Embark on a twisted

journey to save a Wonderland gone bad . . . but be warned if you're gonna chase this rabbit . . . you'd best go armed . . . [3]

The headline above announces, in kooky lettering much like that used for Tim Burton's *The Nightmare Before Christmas*, "The Fairytale Is Over." Screenshots below show Alice blasting with an Ice Wand, stabbing Fire Imps while the Cheshire Cat slinks by, flinging an exploding Jackbomb across a shadowy chessboard castle: we also find game features hyperbolically listed here. "Stunning third-person, 3D action based on an enhanced version of Quake III technology . . . twisted renditions of characters from the original Alice adventures . . . defend yourself with a collection of the most deadly toys ever imagined . . . " The game is clearly being defined in relation to, but also to some extent against the original—it is "darker", "twisted", more violent, more adult. The skewing of Carroll's "fairytale" characters is presented as a selling point, perhaps along lines not so dissimilar to the pornographic cartoons of Disney's Alice; the daring appeal of breaking taboos, of forcing innocence to grow up and corrupting childhood icons. As McGee himself proudly announces on the *Making of Alice* promotional video, "Our Alice will make you rethink everything you thought you knew about Wonderland."[4]

The front cover shows McGee's Alice against a heart-shaped background of mushrooms, trees, and leaves, with the Cheshire Cat at her side. This Cat is a skinny, almost skeletal creature, like Mervyn Peake's version on a starvation diet. His neck and chest are ribbed with bones, his gravestone grin a stretch of yellow. He has acquired a pirate earring and swirling tattoos on his forehead and arm. Alice is brunette, though her hair is the length and style shown in Tenniel's drawings; her dress, too, is the familiar dark blue with white pinafore, with the addition of a necklace bearing the Greek letter "omega" and astrological symbols—representing Neptune and Jupiter—on the apron pockets. Beneath the hem we can make out black leather boots with many buckles, and from her figure—slim, small-busted—she looks at least thirteen. Her green eyes are abnormally large, almost in the style of Japanese manga girls, and she stares out with an expression between menace and melancholy, clutching a spread of cards in one hand. The balance between familiarity and novelty is cleverly achieved: there are enough cues to tell us this is the Carroll Alice, but enough additional signifiers to show she has "grown up" into a "darker" form: a child's frock customized and teamed with fetish boots, an overtone of Gothic fashion in the symbols and necklace.[5]

The game comes with two booklets; one is mainly concerned with installation and control keys, and the other is there for atmosphere, setting up background and establishing the tone. It takes the form of a journal—with vaguely Victorian ornate designs at the corners, and discoloured edges—by a doctor at Rutledge Asylum. The diary begins on 4 November 1864, when Alice arrives for treatment, and continues into 1865 before skipping past a huge gap—"after years of slumber, she chooses to speak to us with a picture, a drawing of some sort of cat"[6]—until 7 September 1873. Footnotes in italics add asides: "*Even a drawing so bizarre couldn't foreshadow the imaginings to come—29/3/74.*" The dating here is actually not implausible in terms of Carroll's chronology, and rather neater than the job Jeff Noon makes of it. November 4 is when the events of *Looking-Glass* occur, so for this adventure to begin on the same day has a fitting resonance. Martin Gardner suggests that *Looking-Glass* can be pinned down to 1862.[7] The fictional Alice was seven and a half at this point, so she is nine and a half when admitted to the asylum according to this scheme, and around eighteen and four months on the 7 September 1873. These dates do not match Alice Liddell's life—she would be twenty-one by that point—but then, the real-life Alice, aged ten in 1862, was always a little older than her fictional counterpart.

Like Noon, Adair, and Roiphe, Greg Roensch, author of this casebook, makes an effort to pastiche a Victorian—often, a Carrollian—style of writing. We have seen that the characteristic italics, coincidentally or not, are included in this text for footnotes and also for verse; apart from this device, Roensch is really just adopting a tone of formal detachment and an adjective-heavy vocabulary bolstered with thesaurus alternatives to everyday words.

> In a frenzied instant, a cankered feline pounced on Alice while she was about to be carried inside. Startled by the cat's yowl, the bearers lost their grip and dropped the wretched girl to the ground. Most curious to behold, the cat stood atop Alice as if claiming territorial right, or as if defending a rodent captured in the day's hunt from other hungry predators.[8]

This kind of over-egged prose recurs throughout the diary—"the rabbit is now sentinel to Alice's deepening dementia", "this pair was weaned from the same teat"—and it achieves a workable sense of a period voice, rather than the more accurate impression in Roiphe's novel.

The diary gives us clues to the game's contents, bridging the known world of Carroll's mythos and the as-yet unknown realms of McGee's third adventure. The twin orderlies recall Tweedledum and Tweedledee, and a sketch later in the booklet—purportedly by Alice herself—is in fact of the Tweedles as they appear in the game. Alice mutters in her sleep, "too glum" or "through him"; the doctor works it out as "boojum", which refers us back to *The Hunting of the Snark* and, again, names one of the game's villains. At least one of Alice's nightmare ramblings—"note the Centipede has a tender underbelly"—is actually a clue for game combat.

Otherwise, the purpose of the diary is simply to clarify that the fantasy world represents Alice's nightmares as she struggles internally and remains physically helpless in the asylum. The entries trace her dreamtime journey as she follows the Rabbit, witnesses chess battles, faces the Tweedles, and prepares to meet the Queen; the doctor's reports follow the structure of the game accurately and give us a taster, through sketches and snatched descriptions, of later levels.

> It's a world of sheer, chaotic terror and unmitigated bloodshed—that's the world she inhabits . . . she speaks of a nightmare realm where everything seems bent on her destruction. [. . .] It's difficult for me to connect the massively passive Alice to the aggressively assertive, powerful person she describes in her dreams. Her exploits with the knife conjure images of a musketeer's swashbuckling panache . . . [9]

The game itself, though, actually begins halfway through the journal entries. They run up to 24 August 1874, when Alice is near to conquering her internal nemesis; our point of entry is 17 April 1874, when Nurse D. stitches Alice's stuffed rabbit back together and tucks it into her bed. This moment, shown in the game's opening sequence, prompts her tumble into Wonderland.

The game's front end—the screens through which it handles loading, saving, controls, and settings—is elaborately themed. The main page has a painting of Alice looking wide-eyed as she sits on the asylum bed, clutching her rabbit—the image is minimally but effectively animated, with a thread of smoke wisping up from a candle in the foreground, and lightning flashing occasionally through the barred window. Having the "real-world" Alice—in a dirty grey smock, with bandaged, bloody wrists—as the image we start from and return to on our journeys into Wonderland emphasises the game's fundamental premise, that the realm we are adventuring in is just Alice's internal landscape. Each time we play and "die", our return to the real Alice shows that it wasn't a real death but a broken dream. The candle, meanwhile, echoes Tweedledum's mocking of Alice that she is only a creature of the Red King's unconscious: "If that there King was to wake . . . you'd go out—bang!—just like a candle!"[10]

The Settings screen shows the Alice from the game/dream, rather than the asylum—in the blue dress, like the cover picture—as a reflection in a looking-glass. Behind her is a self-portrait of Lewis Carroll, an obvious act of homage; her gaze follows the cursor as the player selects sound and picture options from a Victorian-style chart of a male facial profile. The Load and Save screen takes the form of a steampunk video monitor—this technological aesthetic is picked up throughout the game—with "bandersnatch opticals" at the top, again referring back to the *Snark* or "Jabberwocky", and the letters L, S, and D playfully arranged at the bottom. Officially, they stand for Load, Save, and Delete, but of course they also constitute a witty acknowledgement of the "psychedelic" readings. Up to six little screens representing images from previous games are shown on the left, gold-framed in a wooden casing; these are still black-and-white pictures, and when selected they shift to a main screen, whirring and flickering like early cinema. Of course, when the player actually chooses to return to this stage, the picture becomes full motion colour, so the process imaginatively represents a shift in technology from Carroll's form of photography through silent film to contemporary cinema, or CGI.

Selecting "New Game" and a difficulty level—the backdrop here shows the "SKOOL" design from an early level, The Fortress of Doors, and so provides another subtle, almost unconscious prefiguring of things to come—starts a cinematic; that is, a short introductory film giving further backstory to the game. This particular sequence is, technically, a "pre-rendered computer graphic" as opposed to the live action of "full motion video" or on the other hand a "game engine" cut-scene, which uses the same graphics as the game itself. This type of cinematic is generated using more advanced hardware than that used for the actual game and is recorded directly onto the CD-ROM, so it achieves high levels of smoothness, visual richness, and detail.[11]

It begins with what would, with a real camera, be a steadicam movement over Alice's bedroom as an ominous sequence of notes is picked out on what sounds like a harpsichord. As in Svankmajer and Willing's adaptations of *Wonderland*, this camera movement reveals both aspects of the heroine's life and elements that will subsequently reappear in the fantasy world: a chess set, playing cards, the stuffed rabbit. We see framed portraits of Alice and her parents, and discover her in bed. The representation of Alice and her family raises questions about this girl's relationship to the fictional Carroll heroine and to Alice Liddell—the Liddells were a large family and the adults bore no resemblance to the parents in these portraits, while Carroll's Alice had a brother and at least one sister. Although McGee's protagonist wears—or at least imagines herself in—the dress from Tenniel's illustrations, and has brunette hair like Alice Liddell, the game implies she is an only child.

The network between these three Alices is complicated further when we realise Alice has been reading a sequel to the *Alice* books—it is open at the chapter "A Reunion Tea-Party", and above the text we see a pastiche of Tenniel's Hatter, Rabbit, and Alice together again. The page flashes past, but it is possible to freeze and study it: chapter 11 opens

> Happily Alice had returned to Wonderland and once again was at the long table with the Hatter and the March Hare. Other friends were invited: the Gryphon, the Dormouse, the White Rabbit and of course, lots of tea.
>   "And treacle," said the Dormouse, before nodding off to sleep again.

Accompanying this rather bland addition to *Wonderland* is a shift to jollier music on the soundtrack, and the voices of the characters—the Hatter, in an eccentric English accent, announcing

> "Wake up Dormy—its time for the tea party! I've got one—why is a raven like a writing-desk?"

That the riddle is repeated even in this brief snatch from *Alice* supports my point from the previous chapter about its status as a celebrated quotation; it is particularly interesting that this Hatter echoes Willing's camp character by shortening the Dormouse's name. This may be coincidence, or Willing's film may have influenced the game's scriptwriters, providing another example of a film version shaping dominant conventions around the retelling of *Alice*.

We also see handwritten letters among the props and artifacts in Alice's room. These are extremely difficult to make out, even with the screen grabbed, saved, enlarged, and manipulated, but it is clear that one of them at least reads "Dear Mr Dodgson" at the head, and that another is "Jabberwocky" in longhand. Although these documents blur past the eye, someone has taken care to insert them for a reason. However, it is hard to know how they could add up to coherence: the family doesn't seem to be the historical Liddells, but obviously the fictional Alice would not be likely to own a third book of her own adventures or a letter to Lewis Carroll. This Alice, like Noon's protagonist, seems to exist in a middle ground, a halfway home between the real brunette and the blonde from the books.

The evening's tragic events are elegantly told. Dinah knocks over an oil lamp, which sets light to the scattered documents and books. The music becomes heightened and dramatic, and the book characters squeal

"Oh dear! We must save Alice . . . Wake up, Alice! Wake up!" Returning to the *Alice* edition, we see that the chapter has metamorphosed into "Smoke and Fire", with Tenniel's Hatter in a panic around a blaze: the text now reads " 'Fire!' " screamed the Hatter . . . 'We must save Alice!' " Their voices wake the girl, and we see from a series of photographs what happens next: she races to her parents' room but is unable to breach the flames, and as they cry "save yourself, Alice!" she flings herself from the bedroom window. The camera follows to find her sprawled in the snow; we move in on her face and pull swiftly back from her green eye to discover the older Alice rigid and unmoving in the asylum bed. Again, the game provides us with a striking image of innocence grown up, and grown "dark"; this Alice stares coldly up at the ceiling, surrounded by peeling walls and grime. "Maybe that old rabbit will bring her around," says an offscreen voice—presumably Nurse D. Alice slowly cuddles the stuffed toy to her, and it lifts its head, croaking "Save us, Alice!"

The final shot of the cinematic shows iconic objects from both the original stories and the game—a Queen of Hearts card, a chess piece, a watch with, strangely, "R. L. Rutledge and Co" on the face, the rabbit toy—slowly tumbling and turning in the air. The sequence is similar to the fall in Disney and Svankmajer's *Alice* films, both of which pick out key items from the dream as Alice plummets down into Wonderland; the visual motif of falling seems too important to the mythos for McGee's version to exclude it, even though his Alice doesn't actually find a rabbit hole.[12] This marks the end of the sequence, and while the game loads we are faced only with a painted map showing the first corner of the dream-world: Village of the Doomed, a mountain range with a wooden platform jutting out to the turquoise sea, and a tentacle poking through between the peaks. The map is marked with the Latin terms Meridies, Oriens, Occidens, and Septentrio according to the compass points, and degrees of measurement along the frame. We are left wondering what latitude and longitude Alice has got to this time.

The first shot of the game itself is the swirling violet void through which Alice falls; she screams as she plunges down the chute, but lands safely on leaves. This seems to be another interesting case of a small detail from Carroll's original—"down she came upon a heap of sticks and dry leaves, and the fall was over"[13]—being amplified by inclusion in film versions—Svankmajer and Willing, for instance—until it becomes a key iconic feature in representing Wonderland. The White Rabbit, buck-toothed, wrinkled, and google-eyed but still impatiently finicky, tells us and Alice "please don't dawdle," and scurries round a corner; the Cat appears in his absence and slinks towards Alice to begin the game's first conversation.

What we are watching now is a cut-scene; a short sequence where we merely spectate, rather than interact. The dynamic between cut-scene and game has been explored at length by contributors to Geoff King and Tanya Krzywinska's *ScreenPlay: Cinema / Videogames / Interfaces*: I will cite some of their main points here, because the first scenes of *Alice* move extensively between the two forms, with consequences for our understanding of Alice as a character, the game narrative, and our experience of participating in or merely witnessing events.

> Once the cut-scene commences, the player loses control of the character and therefore control of the camera . . . the game's shift into a more cinematic mode thus interrupts the degree of immersion . . . such a sequence causes the gamer to lose control of the avatar, thereby allowing the game-character seemingly to take on a life of its own. [. . .] When the gamer loses control of the camera / character, thus ceding control to pre-set camera positions that direct the field of vision autonomously, in accordance with a predetermined script, the game effectively enters into something closer to a cinematic mode.[14]

Sacha A. Howells discusses the various roles played by the cut-scene; the "intro movie introduces the game's fundamental conflict, while subsequent cut-scenes continue causal lines, introduce new plot elements, show character interaction and continually delineate explicit goals."[15] A cut-scene can function as motivation—"[it] shows the effects of the player's action and introduces a new goal"—or as reward for defeating a "boss", end-of-level enemy, or completing a stage, with the ultimate reward saved for the "victory movie" at the game's climax. "In narrative-driven games, cut-scenes have often come to *replace* the classic videogame reward system: points."[16] Echoing the previous authors, Howells suggests that the distinction between spectatorship and participation creates a potential obstacle in the smooth running of the game:

> The player learns the rules of interacting with the game's universe—how to move, what objects can be manipulated, how the game should be approached—and then when a cut-scene starts he or she is abruptly wrenched out of this established world and thrust into a new one, where the role of active participant is abandoned.[17]

Finally, across genres and formats, cut-scenes signify their difference from gameplay through the convention of "letterboxing", with the screen changing shape to emulate a widescreen cinema image.[18] The head-up display, or HUD—status bars, targeting reticule—will also vanish during cut-scenes.

> This, too, is all but universal; when players see that the interface has disappeared, they understand that they no longer need to be prepared to interact with the game. The spectating has begun.[19]

The Cat conversation that opens *Alice* follows these conventions, with the difference that we have still not yet entered the game proper, and so have not yet been jolted out of a different relationship with the world and its characters. This cut-scene is, as noted above, game engine-generated rather than pre-rendered like the opening cinematic. Its graphics are of the same quality that we encounter when actually playing, except that the camera becomes independently mobile, sweeping around the environment according to pre-set patterns. The scene follows cinema's storytelling and spatial conventions to some extent; Alice falls, lands, and stands up in the bed of leaves in a long shot, and we then cut directly to a reverse shot of the Rabbit at the end of the corridor hurrying her along. The eyeline between the two characters is established, and we understand that we are seeing the Rabbit more or less from over her shoulder, or from her point of view.

However, after the Cat materialises in the empty passage and pads out of shot, most of the following conversation takes place in a single shot that shows both Cat and Alice. The virtual camera starts from behind the Cat and slowly dollies around until we have a two-shot with him on the left of frame, Alice on the right. By the end of the dialogue it has circled further so we have a mid-shot of the Cat from a position nearby Alice. We have seen none of the cross-cutting of conventional mainstream cinema; rather than establishing space through editing, this camera explores it in a lengthy, free-flowing shot. In contrast to "invisible" continuity editing, this approach has the effect of drawing attention to the camera eye, almost giving it a roaming persona of its own. Tanya Krzywinska points out that the swooping camera movements down corridors in the cut-scenes of E. A's horror game *Undying* come to represent the uncanny, a feeling of the game's "deep structure" that the player is unable to control;[20] so in *Alice* the camera, more liberated and mobile than the avatar, shows us things we cannot yet see or prevent, and evokes an eerie feeling of helplessness.

"You've gone quite mangy, Cat," Alice muses, "but your grin's a comfort." The voice talent is Susie Brann, an actress from British theatre and from the TV series *You Rang, M'Lord?*; her Alice is wry, clipped, self-possessed. The Cat is Roger Jackson, a veteran of computer game and animation voice-overs, doing a very good impression of Alan Rickman's smooth, sneery tones. "And you've picked up a bit of an attitude," he drawls. "Still curious, and willing to learn, I hope."

"Wonderland's become quite strange. How is one to find her way?" Alice rocks back on her heels, playfully fascinated rather than anxious about re-entering this changed world. "As knowing where you're going is preferable to being lost, ask," advises the Cat. "Rabbit knows a thing or too, and I myself don't need a weathervane to tell which way the wind blows": an anachronistic nod to Dylan's *Subterranean Homesick Blues* that threatens to disrupt the Victorian illusion. "Let your need guide your behaviour," he concludes. "Suppress your instinct to lead. Pursue Rabbit."

"The character of Alice herself has a persona," claimed Jim Molinets, the president of co-creators Rogue Entertainment. "She has a very real characteristic about her, and we wanted to relate that to the game-player."[21] What do we learn about Alice here? She treats new situations with a bravado that may be false; she seems anxious to keep moving and never stands fully still; she speaks in an upper-middle class English accent, mixing the formality of "how is one to find . . ." with the familiarity of her address to the Cat; she is inclined to lead rather than follow. These characteristics are pretty consistent with the Alice of Carroll's books—polite yet not passive, affectionate to those she trusts,[22] generally unfazed by new challenges, anxious to keep pressing ahead towards a goal. Carroll's Alice, too, is challenging and prepared to stick up for herself when things have gone too far, yet occasionally finds it all too much and breaks down in tears: McGee's Alice fights, of course, but later in the game she also weeps.

The cut-scenes begin and end with a fade to white. The head-up display appears—antique-looking bars of red and blue signifying Sanity and Strength of Will. Some of Alice's most basic characteristics, then, have been concentrated into pure visual symbols; a pair of white footprints hovering ahead also shows the extent of her ability to jump, and when she acquires weapons, her aim is signified by a floating blue reticule in mid-air. We see Alice from behind, with the virtual camera automatically trying to retain a practical distance above and in back, with enough room for us to see her clearly. The mouse shifts this angle, allowing us to look up, down, and around her; arrow keys rotate Alice and four more directional keys let us move her back, forwards, and into a sidestep. Her default movement is a run, which again gives us some sense of persona in terms of drive, desire to escape, or discover; as does the alternative, the very prim, ladylike walk she affects when the direction keys are held down with Shift. Now Alice stands on a bed of leaves next to luminous purple mushrooms, another prefiguring of later levels. The walls are textured rock; ahead, the passage the Rabbit ran down is a tunnel lined with planks. The walls are hung with lanterns. The music, by Nine Inch Nails member Chris Vrenna, is comprised of eerie, overlapping loops: a chorus of faint voices, an underlay of violin, the sound of creaking and wind. Finally we are left alone with Alice to work out where we are and who she is.

What is our relationship with Alice? Are we Alice ourselves, or are we controlling her; or are we playing a small part in her new adventure? The relationship is ambiguous. We have already seen Alice's independent existence, her quick retorts to the Cat and before that her "real life" status in the asylum, so the switch from cut-scenes to gameplay seems like a temporary handing over of control, a donation of responsibility. For now, you hold the strings. That this first level is regularly punctuated with cut-scenes to guide and advise the player emphasises this sense that our control never lasts long; we alternate between watching and taking part, although as the game progresses this pattern inevitably changes and the ratio of gaming to spectating settles at something like nine to one.

Jason Rutter and Jo Bryce suggest that the third-person shooter genre allows us the position of "both being in control of the onscreen avatar and able to watch it. This perspective permits a highly sexualised focus on the female form . . . "[23] They are discussing Lara Croft. Whether most players would gain voyeuristic sexual pleasure from the Alice avatar— slight, stern and, in contrast to many game heroines, showing only the slightest curve of breasts—is open to question, although as we shall see, some fans have depicted her as an erotic figure. More generally, the relationship between player and character in *Alice* does take on the doubled perspective that Bryce and Rutter describe. My experience may be slightly different to that of other players, in that I grew up with Alice from the age of seven, and the icon of a girl in a blue dress with white apron has a potent significance for me, calling up memories of the books and their spin-offs from the last few decades.

Playing Alice, and especially dying as Alice, I felt a mixture of conventional gamer's pleasures, anxieties, and frustrations, and a responsibility stemming from my control over the character. What fears I felt during the game's more challenging levels were not just a reluctance to face powerful enemies and risk loss of life, or the more general, enjoyable creepiness of the horror genre, produced by the disturbing detail of the graphics and the effective soundtrack, but an empathetic fear for Alice as a character. This sense arose specifically from the third-person display, from being able to see the comparatively small and fragile avatar—a teenage girl, despite her weapons—in a large, threatening, often vertiginous environment. It depended on this dual dynamic of being and watching at the same time, of seeing a version of "yourself" who is also "her", not a sexual object but a vulnerable figure.[24]

Similarly, when Alice died, my pragmatic annoyance at having to start a level again was often secondary to my feeling, however fleeting, of guilt about what I had allowed to happen; of watching, unable to help, as Alice screamed in flames, or choked for a third time and drowned, or went down moaning with blood on her apron. Again, it took the phenomenon of both controlling a familiar character I was used to only watching, and yet still watching her as she followed my directions—of guiding her, and yet not being her—to produce this effect. At the point of death itself, the player is caught in a further twist as the game takes over for the final seconds, allowing only a helpless observation of Alice's fatal plunge or sad rise to the water's surface: the inability to save Alice is made more intense by the fact that only a second ago, she was in our hands. Of course, it also requires the richness of the soundtrack and visual setting to create this level of involvement; even the most devoted fan of Alice as a character would probably be unmoved by seeing a little blue square bump into a red X with a beep and "Game Over".

My response may, as I suggested, be partly due to my personal investment in Alice as a character, and a vague feeling of having "known" her most of my life—after following her through *Wonderland* and *Looking-Glass*, I let it end here, by failing to move her away from a giant mushroom—but the Carrollian baggage I brought to the game only enhances its internal story line of Alice confronting her own guilt and grief at what she allowed to happen to her parents. However, the experience of watching Alice die is further complicated by the visual spectacle of the game's gorier moments—though it may be painful, it is also, on one level, morbidly fascinating, and so there may be a shameful pleasure in the mix too, somewhere between sadism and masochism.[25]

"Are you the savior
Rabbit has been telling us about?"

We only have control of Alice for a short time before the deeper power of the underlying narrative wrests her away again. As Ben Sawyer, Alex Dunne, and Tor Berg argue, "the story emerges from the game . . . the player interacts with the game, which then results in the game presenting the actual underlying story back to the player."[26] In the early stages of *Alice*, the "spectator" mode dominates and gameplay, with a few exceptions, is a matter of reaching the next cut-scene trigger. As we walk down the first wooden corridor, the screen whites out and once again we are merely watching Alice, this time in conversation with a bare-chested worker half her size who is carrying a glowing rock on his back. "Our land is destroyed, our spirit crushed," he mutters. "Reminds me of the asylum," Alice comments drily. "Is there no joy here?"

"Slavery and happiness do not dwell in the same house." He continues his aimless trudging, the conversation over, but the camera keeps moving past him towards a steam-filled chasm. Again we sense the game guiding us according to its own reasons, its knowledge as a "director"—in the film sense, and in terms of a traveller's guide—superior to ours. The camera finds its mark, and the Cat appears. "When the path is problematical, consider a leap of faith. Ride the wind." His gesture at the steam geysers directs us to our first independent task; positioning Alice on an outcrop of planks and jumping her across the chasm by allowing her dress to billow with hot air.

So what has the cut-scene contributed? Pretty much what Howells described: "introduce new plot elements, show character interaction and continually delineate explicit goals." The Cat pointed us to an immediate challenge while suggesting its solution, and we had our sense of Alice as a persona—wry, a little cold—confirmed by the conversation. The dialogue is broadly in keeping with Carroll's style; the tone is formal, without any jarring twentieth-century slang or idiom, and the "slavery and happiness" maxim is consistent with elements of the original, such as the Duchess's love of trite morals. From the midget worker and his surroundings we also gained more understanding about the environment; the Queen has enslaved this section of Wonderland and runs some form of industry here. Like the worker's circular march with a load strapped to his back, the machinery in the Village of the Doomed seems to have no ultimate purpose: a rock rolls from one side of a platform to the other, then rolls back. This labour for the sake of it recalls the punishment of Sisyphus, while the technology, quite literally, is a form of steampunk—machines driven by jets of hot air. The cottage industry on the other side of the chasm confirms this; a sign reads "Drole Vel's Gas Extraction",[27] and the factory's pointless purpose seems to be making a rock hover on an air stream. The quaint village setting is broken up in places by intruding tentacles that give a hint of the Queen's reach.

A successful crossing—accompanied by Alice's slightly unladylike gasps of "uhhh!" when she leaps—cues the next cut-scene, which involves her in another conversation with a worker. This dialogue only confirms and elaborates what we have already learned—the little man warns "the Red Queen's agents are ruthless . . . defiance is useless. While the Queen reigns, only death can release us from this misery." Alice muses "Or her death, I suppose." This scene has followed conventional cinematic rules of shot-reverse shot, but once again, it doesn't end when the conversation comes to a close: the camera flies down a corridor, showing us a route deeper into the level. The Cat provides a commentary that at first seems non-diegetic voice-over, adding to the sense of a documentary rather than a participatory adventure. "Meta-essence is the life-force of Wonderland; that of your enemies is particularly potent." He materializes at the end of the corridor alongside a glowing crimson diamond—this is meta-essence, offering a boost to Alice's energy levels—and the source of his voice becomes, of course, visible in the diegetic story space. The confusion is only momentary before we are restored to gameplay and take control of Alice again, back where we left her, but it emphasizes the sense of an uncanny deeper intelligence that knows the environment and dominates our experience of it, only allowing us free rein for short periods.

At later stages, this presence does, as Krzywinska suggests in relation to *Undying*, contribute to a horror-genre feeling of helplessness: when the game takes over to pull back rapidly through a series of slamming doors on the second level; when it shows us threats to Alice, like Ants pushing a rock down a cliff or Ladybirds dropping a boulder; or, at the greatest extreme, when it makes us watch the deaths of familiar characters and the transformation of the Queen into her ultimate form. We know we are going to have to deal with these situations, but while the game chooses to hold us back, we are powerless spectators, caught in the paradox of having control taken temporarily from us but not being able to re-nounce responsibility.

Steering behind a tree root to retrieve the meta-essence is our second minor task; the next step awaits directly ahead, as we immediately see a blade hovering in luminous green glow. Arriving at it triggers another cut-scene. As the white-out fades and the letterbox format closes in, the camera glides forward again to find the mark where the Cat will appear—it could be argued that in this first sequence he almost directs the camera himself, as it always gravitates towards him and the scene ends only when he finishes speaking—and we watch as he gives Alice a tutorial in combat. "Your knife is necessary, but not sufficient." Alice stands opposite, calmly bringing up the weapon and running a finger along the edge; another confirmation of her fearlessly unfazed persona.[28] The game literature tells us this is a Vorpal Blade, cross-referencing back to "Jabberwocky"; a placard swings out below our left-hand energy gauge, showing the knife's availability.

Now it is Alice's glance to the left that directs the camera's next movement—as a character independent to us, she is responding to the scene and effectively pushing the narrative onward. Travelling up a wooden ramp, the virtual eye finds Rabbit and watches him shrink until he can vanish into a hole in the wall surrounded by pink mushrooms. Our next move is obvious, following this route to the top of the ramp, where we find "Mayor Elder", another hobbit-type character, and another cut-scene conversation. "Are you the savior Rabbit has been telling us about all this time?" he asks, his thick Irish accent in keeping with Carroll's use of comedy regional voices: recall Pat's "sure, it's an arrum, yer honour!" "I shouldn't think so," Alice replies lightly. She is, of course, used to being mistaken for others—Mary Ann, a serpent, a fabulous monster—in Adair, a comet, and in Noon, a lice. "I'm a person. And just now I wish to get very small . . . about this big." She bends and holds her fingers apart for him. When he doesn't give her a straight answer, she asks again, with amusingly patronizing patience: "I wish to become about this big."

The elder directs her to the Fortress of Doors, giving us motivation towards the next level and a sense of our task; the Cat, never far off, appears again to warn "Doors have locks, locks have keys, that you don't have." But Alice is clearly growing more accustomed to her new world, and this stage of the game, where we are nurse-maided by constant tutorials, is coming to an end. She rocks on her heels, musing, "there may be more than one way to skin a cat, if you'll pardon the expression." The exchange serves no purpose in terms of game knowledge, plot, or goals; it is merely there for the sake of character, to nod back to Carroll's exposing of the double edge in common sayings and to emphasise our sense that this is the same Alice and Cat we encountered in *Wonderland*, both fond of linguistic banter.

Back in the game, we are free to explore, like tourists,[29] the immediate environment—the front of the Rana Mushroom Shop, its roof quaintly lifting on a bed of steam much like the Dormouse's teapot in Disneyland, and the twee little leaded windows in the walls above, which also have an air of Fantasyland about them. Even in the middle of adventure, part of us admires the spectacle, caught between immersion in illusion and a more detached appreciation of the craft that went into it. Geoff King observes:

The more "contemplative" brand of spectacle emphasizes and invites the *look* of the viewer; it is designed to create a "wow" reaction that entails a subtle dialectic between awareness of spectacle *as* impressive artifice and being (or allowing ourselves to be) "taken in" by, and thus "taken into", the fictional world of which the images is [sic] a part.[30]

Even in death, part of us marvels at the spectacle; even in combat, we admire our aggressors. Alice barely has a moment to explore before her first enemy runs from an adjoining passage: a Card Guard, similar to Tenniel's depiction of the rose painters and executioner, but even more reminiscent of the card-soldiers in Disney's film and theme park. We enter a new mode of play here, clicking left or right mouse buttons to make Alice throw her knife—it flies towards the blue target reticule, taking a few seconds to return for a next shot—or swing it in hand-to-hand battle. This is a side to Alice we haven't witnessed before—a side prepared to engage in physical as well as verbal conflict, a girl who gasps in pain and deals death strikes as well as giving her all in the cut-and-thrust of conversation.

The snicker-snack of her knifeplay and her vicious attack on the Card Guard may seem to degrade Carroll's Alice, but we might remember that the Beamish Boy who defeats the Jabberwock looks, in Tenniel's illustration, rather like Alice herself; he wears her striped stockings under a tunic, and has her flowing long hair. In the original *Looking-Glass*, then, we already have seen a kind of substitute Alice, another alternate mirror version, perhaps, wielding a vorpal sword against monsters. McGee's Alice leaves the Guard dead—it is him or us—and we pick up his meta-essence, which clusters above him in a glowing gem like an externalised soul as his body conveniently fades. The path he emerged from reveals a glow of industry shrouded in steam. We run towards it, and the adventure continues.

"Self-pitying dreamers are not wanted here."

Let's look again at Sigler's definition of an *Alice*-type story. Sequels or alternatives generally feature

an *Alice*-like protagonist or protagonists . . . who is typically polite, articulate, and assertive; a clear transition from the "real" waking world to a fantasy dream world . . . rapid shifts in identity, appearance, and

> location; an episodic structure often centering on encounters with nonhu-
> man fantasy characters and/or characters based on nursery rhymes
> . . . nonsense language and interpolated nonsense verse, verse-parodies,
> or songs, an awakening or return to the "real" world . . . and, usually,
> a clear acknowledgement of indebtedness to Carroll through a dedication,
> apology, mock-denial of influence, or other textual or extratextual
> reference.[31]

We have already seen some of these features in McGee's *Alice*. The Settings screen includes a visual dedication to Carroll, and the opening cinematic lets us glimpse a letter to Mr Dodgson. The Pale Realm, home of the white chess pieces, also hides a portrait of Carroll and a Tenniel picture of the White Rabbit on one of its walls. Alice's character is well-established from the evidence so far as wry, confident, and intelligent, and the relationship between her real life and the fantasy is actually developed more in this adventure than in Carroll's original or in the film adaptations: the doctor's journal, the introductory sequence, and the end-of-game returns from Wonderland to the front page of Alice in the asylum emphasise that the two realms are distinct yet linked. That Wonderland is an embodi-ment of Alice's unconscious anxieties and desires is strongly suggested in Svankmajer and Willing's film versions, but McGee's *Alice*, as I shall demonstrate, makes it explicit.

As for shifts in identity, appearance, and location, McGee's game provides them in abundance, sometimes with a self-conscious sense that he is lifting and modifying tropes from Carroll. The first stage, as we saw, gives Alice the motivation to get "very small . . . about this big" in order to follow the Rabbit. When she does acquire the right ingredients and shrinks, she enters an environment where mushrooms and grass tower over her, and a leaf becomes a raft; an experience very much like that faced by Carroll's Alice when she escapes the Rabbit's house and wanders towards the Caterpillar. This level is called the Vale of Tears, and a statue of a weeping Alice suggests that what we are seeing is her Pool of Tears from *Wonderland*, ten years on. Saltwater has swamped the landscape and once again she finds herself swimming in her own self-pity.

The Pale Realm includes Alice's transformations into a Bishop and a Knight, requiring her to learn their moves across the chessboard: this kind of total metamorphosis was too odd even for Carroll to subject his heroine to, but he certainly implies it by having her take the metaphorical role of the White Pawn and then become a Queen. McGee repeats this motif by having Alice entrusted with the White Pawn, which she then uses on behalf of the white pieces, dropping it on a strategic square where it can replace the old White Queen and shift the balance of power between the two sides. In terms of transitions, this move, ending the Looking-Glass level, prompts the sudden arrival of the Hatter, who knocks Alice out and takes her to the next stage. Cut-scenes like this one, as already discussed, produce a sense of nightmarish helplessness as we can only watch the game acting upon Alice. No wonder Alice approaches the Queen of Hearts and asks "Who am I?" The Caterpillar's question to her from *Wonderland* has been tragically reversed—Alice is now so desperate to rediscover her identity that she will beg her deadliest enemy.

This leads us to structure and character, which can be discussed in the same way as Noon and Adair's third adventures. The basic narrative that governs McGee's *Alice* is a journey from Dementia to the Heart of Darkness level, a journey through lands lifted vaguely from both Carroll books—the chess realm, the Vale of Tears, the Hatter's den, the Caterpillar's Plot—on a quest to destroy the Queen and her agents. Other levels are more conventionally themed according to horror and adventure genres—the Land of Fire and Brimstone, a rollercoaster runaway mine cart, an *Indiana Jones*-style sprint in front of a tumbling boulder—while at least two, the giant tea cups of the Hatter's Crazed Clockwork and the hedge labyrinth of the Majestic Maze, seem intended as "dark" versions of Disney's theme park attractions.[32] The design of the Pale Realm, its red chess counterpart, and the Hatter's asylum in particular shows a visual quoting from Escher, and the impossible machinery, the endless doors, and the realistic depiction of implausible locations in the earlier levels recall Magritte. Once more, it seems that McGee's team could well have become aware of film adaptations such as Miller and Svankmajer's respective *Alices*, and allowed these previous visualizations of her world to shape their work.

The underlying structure of McGee's *Alice* is less coherent than in Carroll, Adair, or even Noon, as there is no existing system at work—alphabet, chess, cards, Newmonia halfbreeds—and the characters are either taken loosely from Carroll's work—Boojums from *The Hunting of the Snark*, an eponymous ghost from *Phantasmagoria*—or dreamed up without any unifying rationale: Lava Man, Nightmare Spider, Fire Imps. Some of the minibeast enemies such as Ladybugs and the Centipede may recall "Looking-Glass Insects" with its Snap-dragon-fly and Rocking-horse-fly, but McGee's Army Ant has a more obvious connection to Jeff Noon's termites than to anything in Carroll. However, although on a superficial level McGee's game lacks a structure beyond the conventional game arrangement of a quest to the big boss through a series of smaller bosses, a more subtle underpinning emerges during later levels.

During much of the game, the only rationale and motivation for Alice is progressing further with the aim of defeating the Queen and freeing Wonderland's denizens. As we progress, the situation becomes richer in detail and more complex in its workings—we learn that the Jabberwock and Hatter are now the Queen's key operatives, while other creatures like the Gryphon and Turtle are either victims of or rebels against the system—but our tasks are still determined by the fantasy world, with no direct link to the real world of Alice's asylum. The characters, as noted, are mainly adapted from Carroll and given the same "dark" twist Alice and the Cat received. The Hatter has become obsessed with automata and clockwork, and has trapped his former friends the Hare and Dormouse in a vivisection chamber. Humpty is empty-shelled, brain-dead, sitting on a wall with one eye permanently closed as he mechanically lifts a cigar to his lips. The murder of the Rabbit and finally of the Cheshire Cat are ultimate shock tactics, taking the familiar and ripping it apart—the scenes have emotional impact for the Alice avatar and probably for most players, but they also hammer home McGee's threat that "The Fairytale Is Over."

However, the encounter with the Jabberwock marks a departure from the previously hermetic game world. It takes place in a two-storey house of brick and white wooden cladding, perched at the top of a lava mountain but still potentially familiar from the opening cinematic: Alice's house. Inside, the windows and doors are blackened, alive with flame, and the Jabberwock stalks before Alice, tormenting her with his understanding of her real-world history.

> You're habitually late, aren't you? Between your dim-witted day-dreaming and your preening vanity the hours just fly by; there's barely time for anything else. Your family was expecting you to come to them, weren't they? Perhaps they thought you might warn them of the danger . . . being close to the source as you were. But they waited in vain, didn't they, and died for their trouble. You selfish, misbegotten and unnatural child! You smelled the smoke. But you were in dreamland taking tea with your friends.[33]

The Jabberwock is not just a big boss or a servant of the Queen; he is Alice's guilt at failing to save her parents. The journey to Queensland, we come to understand, is a journey through Alice's unconscious, confronting and defeating the monsters—fear, self-loathing, grief—she has repressed. That the Queen is a facet of the dreaming girl is made clear in the final encounter, when the ruler shows her true face—and it is Alice's. "Self-pitying dreamers are not wanted here," she declares cruelly.

They cannot survive here. Your pathetic attempts to reclaim your sanity have failed. Retreat to the sterile safety of your self-delusion, or risk inevitable annihilation. If you destroy me, you destroy yourself! Leave now and some hollow part of you may survive. Stay, and I will break you down; you will lose yourself forever.

The Queen is bluffing; her destruction frees Alice and Wonderland, and in a closing "victory" cinematic the dreamworld links back to the real girl. We revisit the various levels of the game, finding peace restored and dead friends brought back to grinning life—the weeping statue in the Vale of Tears transforms into one showing Alice calmly contemplative—and a final tableau dissolves to a pastiche of a Tenniel illustration. Pulling back, we find that Alice is reading the final chapter of her third Carroll adventure, titled "Happily Ever After". The text, again, is quickly gone, but it reads " 'YEA ALICE! You saved us!' And she had done more than that, she knew . . . she had saved *herself* as well."[34] As the camera moves out further and cranes up we see a happy Alice, her hair looking auburn in the autumn sunlight; she closes the book, scoops up Dinah, and sets out into a new life, as the shot closes with the asylum sign in gold. The light and the fallen leaves tell us it is at least late September: as the doctor's journal entries ended on the twenty-fourth of August, it has taken Alice over a month to battle her way to freedom.

McGee's *Alice* Online

In examining responses to this *Alice* from online gaming magazines and among Internet fan communities, I have restricted my body of evidence to ten reviews and five fan sites—*Down the Rabbit Hole*, *Alice's Asylum*, *The Tangle Box*, *Alice Configs*, and *Alice Desktop Art*. I have grouped similar lines of response together for convenience; in fact, many of these reviews combine different approaches and are not always consistent or clear-cut in their assessment of the game and its relationship to other texts.

"This dark Victorian look and feel to the characters I think is more what Wonderland was supposed to be than, say, what the Disney version was."[35] American McGee himself sets up the game in distinction to the 1951 animated version, implicitly acknowledging that this *Alice* will have shaped most players' perception of the character and her mythos, and provided the dominant popular image of what "Alice" means. In fact, five of the ten reviews of my sample did refer to McGee's *Alice* through this comparison.

For those who have read and enjoyed the books—it is completely evident that the creation of the game did not get any of its information from the Disney version of the story.[36]

American McGee's Alice is a creepy, creepy game that plays on the conventions that we're all used to from the Disney animated movie.[37]

Alice in Wonderland. I've watched the movie a million times, played the game almost twice, and I still haven't managed to read the book. That's the way it goes in the U.S.; I guess I'm just an illiterate commie-stomper. [. . .] Alice sounds like a cynical little Briton, a far cry from her innocence in the Disney version, but quite fitting in this macabre world.[38]

Alice finds herself once again chasing after the White Rabbit—he's no longer the adorable bunny people will remember from the Disney cartoon. His face crinkled menacingly, ears bent back behind his head and an overbite that looks like fangs is just an example of how things in Wonderland have been skewed.[39]

As a child, probably everybody read—or at least saw—some version of Lewis Carroll's classic fairytale *Alice in Wonderland*, and enjoyed the positively surreal events that made up the story [. . .] different versions of the literary tale and other books in the series have been portrayed anywhere from a sugar-coated Disney take, making it very kiddie friendly, to more fantasy inspired versions, but probably none have brought to life such a macabre take on Alice as this adaptation of the story.[40]

This last comment is a little different from the three that precede it. Firstly, Enid Burns of *Sharky Games* assumes that her readers will know *Alice* either from a film or the book, whereas most of the others start from the basis that the Disney film will be the most common point of reference. Secondly, she notes that the "original"—whether book or film is unclear, but the *Alice* people first encountered in childhood—was already "surreal", whereas two of her fellow reviewers construct McGee's version as a "skewed" manipulation of the Disney version. Although the last review above does clearly position McGee's adaptation as "macabre" in contrast to the "sugar-coated . . . kiddie friendly" Disney film, it also—accurately, I would say—identifies elements of strangeness in both Disney and Carroll.

The first review, by "The Badger", is also making a slightly different point than the others; it promises that McGee's game actually ignores the

Disney portrayal and bases its characterization on the original books. However, it sees the game—again, as McGee intended—as a grown-up, "darker" interpretation of Carroll, balancing fidelity with novelty. Alice's blue dress is "somewhat reminiscent of our own recollections of the story with the addition of some arcane symbols"; the enemies are "sometimes specific variations of the original *Alice* stories . . . other enemies . . . are definitely not like anything you've seen before"; "this is after all based on *Alice's* Adventures *in Wonderland*—not a mindless massacre."[41]

> Although Alice did have her enemies and trials in the original Lewis Carroll stories, American McGee takes the world of Wonderland to a whole new level. Portraying many familiar places and characters from the original stories and adding more than a few of its own, the player is introduced to a land where things are anything but a pleasant fairy tale.[42]

This summary—which could almost fit on the back cover of the game, so closely does it echo the official pitch—is echoed in a number of other reviews.

> *American McGee's Alice* takes everything you ever thought about the standard *Alice in Wonderland* story and turns it inside out, upside down, and paints it with a definite evil side.[43]

> Many of the bosses are also twisted incarnations of the characters from the original story that the rather snobby Alice didn't get along with, including the Mad Hatter and Tweedle Dee and Tweedle Dum. [. . .] you want to know what happens next and see more of the fascinating, seemingly alive world of Wonderland in its new, depraved form. [. . .] you get to venture forth through an obscenely twisted Wonderland.[44]

> I love the idea that we're going back to Wonderland, and that Wonderland has become creepy (this is not just a remake).[45]

According to this reading, McGee's *Alice* is a "twisted", "obscene", "depraved", "creepy" reworking of Carroll. The implication is clearly that the "original" was innocent, "standard", "familiar", "pleasant"; it's interesting that some of the terms used to describe McGee's game imply sexual corruption, because there seems no obvious evidence of this in the game itself or further development of the idea in the reviews.

In promising that his game represents Wonderland as it "was supposed to be", McGee is positioning Carroll's *Alice* as a "darker" text than Disney's. Some of the reviews—as we saw with Enid Burns—follow this line of interpretation, reading back through the game to the Carroll books, and finding traces of adult meaning, whether surrealism, uncanny undercurrents, or hallucination, in what other reviewers saw as the "innocent" original. The drug interpretation, in particular, finds a new lease on life here, as the *Alice* books are seemingly re-examined through their association with the game.

> This is a game for adults made by adults, don't let the "kid" theme of *Alice in Wonderland* (an opium induced haze to begin with, but I digress) fool you.[46]

> The graphics . . . represent the Wonderland we have all come to know. The upside down, downside up, or sidedown up, the trippy worlds of Alice really come alive in this game . . . it's nearly an exact replica of the Lewis Carroll book.[47]

> Lewis Carroll's timeless literature was a good place to start. Although each of the novels from which American's team drew inspiration was written for children, their disturbing undercurrents are no secret. [. . .] The opening map launches an unending procession of depravities that are somehow true to the spirit of Lewis Carroll's creations . . . [. . .] Lewis Carroll's children's classic, brought to life on the PC as a Grand Guignol drama of blood and gore . . . [48]

> Falling down a well after a white rabbit, encountering talking cats, caterpillars and other fantastic creatures is the making of a surreal adventure. Of course, the Queen's castle and her army of cards certainly top the cake (or tart as the case may be) when it comes to crossing the line to the truly bizarre. Though many have tried to link the creative power behind *Alice in Wonderland* to hallucinogenic drugs, it is argued whether Lewis Carroll ever used drugs . . . *American McGee's Alice* goes beyond the acid trip of the original tale and warps everything even further . . . [49]

In this reading—which, as noted at the top of this section, sometimes overlaps with contradictory theories in the same reviews—Carroll's original was always and already "dark" in some way, and McGee's version doesn't twist and corrupt it so much as faithfully draw out and amplify these "adult" elements.

"The Badger", who assured readers that McGee's *Alice* was a grown-up version of Carroll's books, bypassing the Disney film, also promised that "the anecdotes and words of wisdom spoken by many of the characters will make you 'curiouser and curiouser' to go back and revisit the books yourself."[50] Most of the reviews in this sample show little direct evidence that the author has gone back to the books; their references to Carroll remain, as we have seen, on a vague level. Far more precise are the analyses of McGee's *Alice* in relation to other software, in terms of technical specifications, genre conventions, and game jargon.

> While the game thoroughly lacks in the AI department, the gameplay, weapons, plot and maps make up for it . . . the maps and eye-candy are incredible, but some characters could have used a little more detail and a few more polygons.[51]

> There is also a parade of bosses . . . such as Tweedle-Dum and Tweedle-Dee, who split into smaller versions of themselves and then detonate when fragged.[52]

> In true *Tomb Raider* fashion, your underlying objective is always to push linearly forward, find the exit, and possibly trip upon a few secrets/ bonuses along the way.[53]

> There was exactly one musical puzzle, a la *Loom*.[54]

> *American McGee's Alice* is very much different from some of the recent action adventures I've reviewed, like *FAKK2* and *Rune* in a sense that it is more of a hardcore 'old school' game . . . both *FAKK2* and *Rune* are trying hard to incorporate the storyline, the characters and the plot twists into the action by including as much adventure (narrative style) elements as possible, therefore linking different action sequences into a cohesive action adventure mix . . . [55]

> It takes a lot of the play style of first-person shooters like *Quake* and a lot of the play style of third person jumper/puzzle games like *Tomb Raider* . . . you'll also face big "boss" monsters at the end of major portions of the game. [. . .] But all the eye candy comes at a sometimes steep price. On our test machine, a competent year old workhorse P3-500 with a *GeForce* 256 based videocard, there were some areas where frame rate crawled to a near standstill at 800 × 600 resolution.[56]

Many of the reviews, again, showed no sign of recognizing the characters from Carroll's original texts, or of being concerned to look up their names. The Phantasmagoria is described simply as "the ghoulish apparition soaring through the air";[57] the Mock Turtle is "some sort of bull-crustacean", or simply an "NPC".[58] Justin Robbins' review is comical in its incorporation of Carroll's 1865 characters into a modern street culture:

> You are joined with Cheshire Cat. Cheshire makes a great companion . . . although Cheshire is an obnoxious little sh#$, he is the best resource for help. Cheshire always stops you and tells you what'up, very annoying.[59]

However, one review and two fan Web sites based around McGee's *Alice* do consciously refer the game mythos back to Carroll's books—including *Phantasmagoria* and the *Snark*—in some detail. Perhaps most interesting of all is the review in *Game Revolution*, by "the Mock Dodgson", which attempts a pastiche of Carroll's style and wittily juxtaposes the slightly prim young Alice of the books with the bloodthirsty events of the game. Early in the review's mini-narrative, Alice meets the Tweedle twins—the illustration used is Tenniel's—and agrees to play a game.

> "Yes. Yes. Yes!" agreed Tweedledum. "No. We have a new game. At least it is new for us, but it may be old for you. You never can tell. We have made a game of *you*."
>
> "A game of *me?*" asked Alice. "Whatever does that mean? I imagine I should be quite good at it."
>
> [. . .]
>
> "Aha!" cried Tweedledum, brandishing a sloshing bucket of red paint. "The Queen of Hearts never even noticed I took it." With that, he reached his hand into the bucket and started throwing paint on everything—the road, the bushes, the rocks. Tweedledee got a big handful right in the face and it dripped down him, leaving a circle of red footprints as he continued to run. Some of the paint splashed on the hem of Alice's dress.
>
> "What are you doing?" she asked, backing away so as not to get any more paint on her dress. She was sure it would be difficult to clean.
>
> "Blood, blood, blood." Tweedledum smiled. "I'm coating everything with blood. It's for the game, you see. Blood makes everything better."[60]

This passage combines a number of clever allusions. Firstly, the author—like Noon, Adair, and Greg Roensch, to various degrees—simulates Carroll's style in the *Alice* books. The language is appropriately formal—"I imagine I should be quite good"—and even in this paragraph we see the characteristic italics that seem vital to the Carrollian voice. The detail draws on *Alice in Wonderland*—the gardeners' red paint did belong to the Queen—and on the game, where Alice's apron is stained with blood.

There is one further, interesting reference. "A Game of You" is the title of a graphic novel within Neil Gaiman's *Sandman* series; that is, the comic book that featured *Alice's Journey Behind the Moon*. This could seem an unremarkable coincidence, except for the fact that *The Sandman* is based heavily around Gothic fashion, with the lead character resembling Robert Smith from The Cure, and his sister, Death, wearing arcane symbols very much like McGee's Alice. Given that other fan sites for McGee's *Alice*, as we shall see, pick up on the game's Gothic overtones and link them to The Cure and Marilyn Manson, I suspect the reference was intentional.

The review wryly presents the game as Carroll's Alice might have viewed it; with some distaste and bafflement at the "buildings that dissolved into vortices . . . enormous clockworks, giant chess pieces, disgusting looking emaciated children with nails in their heads."[61] Tweedledee advises her, "to play properly, you must play pretend . . . instead of being a little girl, you must be a surly teenager. Try to be disturbed and full of angst, if you can manage it." "You mean like my sister Edith?" asks Alice. "She sneaked out one night last week to meet her friends at the graveyard. I didn't tell."[62] Edith was in fact younger than Alice Liddell, and a redhead, so not the most obvious choice for Gothic liaisons, but the author has done some research and is playfully locating the game's Alice in the same narrative world as both the book's Alice and the real Alice. Amid the cross-referencing there are some accurate hits at the game's shortcomings: "Isn't this rather a lot of jumping?" Alice enquires.

Down The Rabbit Hole, an extensive *McGee's Alice* site that offers a guide to strategies and enemies, prefaces each of its comments on the game characters with a quotation from Carroll. Some of these are quite imaginative—the Troll Elder gets a verse from "Father William" and the Army Ant, who of course doesn't feature in Carroll's books, is introduced with Alice's line "I don't *rejoice* in insects at all . . . because I'm rather afraid of them—at least the large kinds." Oddly, though, the Ladybird from the game is accompanied with what seems an Americanised passage from *Looking-Glass*—"there was a Ladybug sitting next to the Goat"—the Phantasmagoria with the Unicorn's line about fabulous monsters, and the Snark with a stanza from "How Doth The Little Crocodile". Admittedly, the Snark of the game is a malicious fish with no resemblance to Carroll's description of "those that have feathers, and bite . . . [or] those that have whiskers, and scratch"[63], or Henry Holiday's illustrations, but the Web site does, appropriately, include lines from the *Snark* next to the picture of a Boojum, so this lapse is surprising.

Christkaiser's elegantly, delicately designed fan site for McGee's *Alice*[64] also refers the visitor to Carroll's books. In this case, although the link takes the form of a well-hidden Tenniel illustration on the front page, Carroll is given an extensive corner: a page resembling a library from the game, with "Pick Me" carved on a bookcase and five volumes—*Alice's Adventures Under Ground, Through the Looking-Glass*, the *Nursery Alice*, the *Snark*, and *Phantasmagoria*—turned cover-first towards the visitor. The full text of each is carefully presented, including a scanned version of the handwritten *Under Ground* manuscript. At least some gamers may be led to Carroll by this ingenious route, although they may be surprised to click on a cover showing the horrific Phantasmagoria of McGee's design, and find Carroll's tum-ta-tum rhyme about a domestic ghost who has more in common with something from Harry Potter.

I mentioned above that while the reviews of McGee's *Alice* identified hallucinogenic drug references in the game and by extension in the original books, there were only vague and undeveloped hints that this "darker", "grown-up" version of *Alice* involved any form of sexual depravity. As was the case with illustrated versions and film adaptations, the discourse around Carroll as some form of paedophile, so openly prevalent in recent journalism and cautiously expressed in many biographies, seems to have had no bearing on McGee's game design or on the reviewers' response. However, although McGee's Alice resists the mold of stereotypical female game characters—small-busted, wearing a Victorian dress, and with a posture and expression of grim determination rather than the cheesecake poses of a Lara Croft—she has been read as attractively sexual by more than one fan site, and transformed into a kind of pin-up.

Christkaiser's site, alongside manga and graffiti-style reworkings of McGee's Alice and her enemies, features some remarkable fan images of the character, including her own gauzy digital paintings. In one, she has been superimposed on a screengrab of McGee's Vale of Tears, with the weeping statue in the mist behind her, and dressed precisely like the Gothic girl Death from Neil Gaiman's comic series, complete with ankh necklace; in another, she is completely nude, smudged with violet droplets and holding up a pair of angel wings in front of the Vale of Tears waterfall. Again, this is a clear instance of McGee's aesthetic crossing over with, and appealing to, Gothic culture. "*American McGee's Alice* was made purposely with this target market in mind," Christkaiser suggested in personal correspondence, "as well as the techno/industrial/geek people."[65]

This latter image could actually be seen as a twenty-first-century equivalent of Carroll's photography, especially his portraits of naked little girls with watercolour backdrops—the female form as angelically innocent and set in a pastoral, painted environment. The key difference, apart from the advance in digital image techniques, is that our contemporary morality

Christkaiser's Gothic Alice.

tolerates adult nudes far more readily than it does toddlers without clothes. Far more explicitly sexual, despite being fully dressed, is Arioch's "Bad Alice", a picture of the game's bloodstained heroine perched on a mushroom, apparently indifferent to the fact that she's showing pink knickers.

This further twisting of the already "grown up" but rather coldly asexual McGee Alice into a saucy pin-up figure continues at *Alice Configs*,[66] a site that ingeniously provides "mods" and "skins"—tweaks to the code and appearance of the game. For the most part, these are designed to reinvent the game's dynamic, appearance, and challenges, providing new appeal for players who have finished the "official" version: there are mods to give Alice a personal cadre of Card Guards, or to make the weapons faster, or to offer Alice an "indiglo armband" that lights her way. The skins make McGee's Alice into a dressing-up doll for the Photoshop generation: we have Alice in teal, Alice in violet, Alice, interestingly, in the blue-dress-and-blonde-hair mode from the Disney cartoon, restoring her to a form of nostalgic innocence.

Most of the outfits, though, are in a Britney Spears or Christina Aguilera style—"Queen of Tarts" is a burgundy corseted number, "Pinky" has netting stretched across the bust, and "Summer" is a strange outfit combining a bra top, puffed shoulders, and long skirt with tights. "I tend to enjoy a sexier female character in action games," Aquatarkus told me in an email. "So I pretty much locked into 'sexy' as my particular skinning

"Bad Alice" by Arioch.

style. And not it's a comfort factor that built from the repetition in painting them. All my skins start out as an experiment in curiosity. How would she look as a blond, or a brunette, different make up, different dress, different accessories, more skin or more clothes."[67] Again, though there isn't the slightest overtone of paedophilia—partly because this is an older girl than the heroine of Carroll's stories—this fan site, like Christkaiser's, gives Alice an erotic overtone absent from McGee's design.

Finally, there are sites that elaborate on and around McGee's Alice, building up prequels and sequels. Ken Wong's *The Tangle Box*[68] is an exquisite arrangement of original illustrations and captions that fill out the asylum background to the game. The layout of text and image inevitably recalls comic book panels; more specifically, the pages resemble the art of Dave McKean, who illustrated both *Arkham Asylum* and the *Sandman* covers. Once again, it is hard to believe this is sheer coincidence.[69]

Ken takes the skeleton of his storyline not from Carroll but from the promotional trailer for McGee's game, in which we hear a counsellor in voice over asking Alice what's wrong. "Something's . . . broken," she explains, and when he asks what, she states flatly "I am." The counsellor's offscreen presence is fleshed out by *The Tangle Box* as "a young Ameri-can . . . he's like Charles, in a way. He seems very interested in me, he asks me a lot of questions about Wonderland and the looking-glass." Plate four shows a skinny, sick-looking Alice glancing after the snaggletoothed

Aquatarkus, "Summer" skin for Alice.

Ken Wong, *The Tangle Box.*

Rabbit of McGee's designs; plate six visits Alice's mind again and finds the Cheshire Cat snarling at the Tweedles. A verse reads

> Pretty pussy hasn't eaten
> Yet hunger makes his senses sharper
> For though his body's badly beaten
> His guidance makes my vengeance faster . . . [70]

The poem has something in common with "How Doth The Little Crocodile", but on the whole, the short narrative and its illustrations owe a greater debt to the game intertexts than they do to Carroll. That the Alice of Ken's story refers to Carroll as "Charles", rather than Mr Dodgson, is clear enough evidence that *The Tangle Box*'s expertise lies in the game's promotional material rather than in Victorian culture. On the credits list, Lewis Carroll comes last, below Marilyn Manson, Tim Burton, and The Cure—whose lyrics infiltrate at least one of the site's verses[71]—indicating, again, the importance of modern Gothicism to this strand of *Alice* fandom. "Themes like isolation, madness, not fitting in with the world around you, distorted reality, and the supernatural connect these works," Ken wrote to me, "and I suppose, lead to association with the gothic culture."

> Alice herself embodies these aspects, giving her a depth of character rare for a computer game. She doesn't rely on sex appeal, and is strong, beautiful and courageous. Yet there is a weak side to her that people can identify with, a fragility, the child inside. Her difficulty with facing the world around her and her shifting state of mind are things Goths can relate to, particularly teenage girls.[72]

Alice's Asylum[73] archives further creative efforts from fans of the McGee Alice; tending more towards fiction and poetry than artwork, the material on this site follows the same pattern of referring to the PC game mythos as primary text. "Back to the tea party," reads one morbid verse,

> To celebrate and toast
> Only to find the Hare and Dormouse
> Have been murdered by their mad host[74]

"Bandersnatch Isle", a typical example of the site's fiction, is set after the events of the game; as the title suggests, it introduces a creature from Carroll's work who never featured directly in the McGee mythos. The key characters and settings in the story are clearly modelled on their appearance in the game—the Vale of Tears, for instance, is described in terms of its landmark statue—and elements from the original *Alice* books are brought in to provide novelty, yet modified to fit the structure and tone of the new, "dark" Wonderland. Alice meets the Tortoise, mentioned in Carroll's "Mock Turtle's Story", but the setting is an underwater "skool"—the spelling taken from McGee's "Fortress of Doors" level—and she has to fight off snarks along the way with her vorpal blade. While the author, C. M. Griffiths, has clearly gone back to Carroll, it is the game that provides the dominant framework to this story, and Carroll's inventions are used as a bank of secondary material, adapted to suit if they show potential for expanding the game's mythos.

It would be tempting for a Carrollian purist to dismiss these creative works, or even despair over them: they show Alice becoming distinct from Carroll and closer to American McGee. For these fans, the traditional authorial relationship has certainly shifted; there is an awareness of Carroll, perhaps a sense of distant debt to him as the original creator, but McGee has provided them with a world and a heroine they can more readily connect to, and he becomes their primary reference. One short story on this site displays an even more short-sighted approach to authorship; it elaborates not on Carroll or even McGee's material, but on the relationship between Alice and the doctor depicted in Ken Wong's *Tangle Box*.[75]

Certainly, while semi-professional fiction and art sites based around a popular text are common, this specific type of fandom is odd in my experience. The focus on a recent reworking of a text, to the extent that the original is barely acknowledged, would be equivalent to a *Star Trek* site that only cared about the recent *Enterprise* series and had almost forgotten the names Gene Roddenberry and William Shatner, or a *Star Wars* fan community that revolved solely around the prequel trilogy, hardly aware that Alec Guinness played Obi-Wan Kenobi long before Ewan McGregor took the role.

We can only guess at what will become of this strand of *Alice* fandom; there are, as I have noted, some links back to Carroll, and some afficionados of the game may conceivably follow them up, treating McGee's game as a gateway to Carroll's broader life and work. These curious pools of creativity may, on the other hand, dry up without any further primary texts to sustain them; teenage fans may have short attention spans, and while the Wes Craven adaptation *Dark Wonderland* is still, apparently, in production, there are no new Alice games forthcoming.[76] Ken Wong is now working as concept designer for American McGee; American McGee is working at Carbon6 on *American McGee's Oz*. Whether the amateur writers on *Alice's Asylum* will abandon Alice and immerse themselves in his reworking of L. Frank Baum remains to be seen. In the next chapter, meanwhile, we are looking at a different breed of Alice fan.

Notes

1. Carroll, *Looking-Glass*, p. 202.
2. Much of the my knowledge of the history and conventions of the TPS comes from academic or quasi-academic secondary sources such as J. C. Herz's *Joystick Nation* (London: Abacus, 1997), Steven Poole's *Trigger Happy* (London: Fourth Estate, 2000), and Geoff King and Tanya Krzywinska, *ScreenPlay* (London: Wallflower, 2002).
3. Cover blurb.
4. American McGee on *The Making of Alice*, available for download at *Down the Rabbit Hole*, http://www.3dap.com/alice.
5. The promotional movie for the game, which is also downloadable from a link at *Down the Rabbit Hole*, makes this transformation explicit. "Alice grew up," it announces, tilting up the teenage girl's body; "So did Wonderland."
6. Greg Roensch, "Casebook," *American McGee's Alice* (Rogue/E.A. Games, 2000), n.p.
7. Gardner, *Annotated Alice*, p. 144.
8. Ibid.
9. Ibid.
10. Carroll, *Looking-Glass*, p. 198.
11. See Sacha A. Howells, "Watching A Game, Playing a Movie," in King and Krzywinska, *ScreenPlay*, p. 115.
12. Again, the promotional movie plays up this motif even more explicitly, showing an "Eat Me" pill and "Drink Me" potion slowly rotating downwards alongside a bloodied knife, a dice, a sharpened jack, and a metal syringe; Alice's hand reaches out for the blade. In this intense, condensed version of the game, Alice is actually falling with the objects.
13. Carroll, *Alice in Wonderland*, p. 14.
14. Wee Liang Tong and Marcus Cheng Chye Tan, "Vision and Virtuality: The Construction of Narrative Space in Film and Computer Games," in King and Krzywinska, *ScreenPlay*, pp. 103–4.
15. Howells, "Watching a Game," p. 113.
16. Ibid.
17. Ibid., p. 116.
18. Ibid., p. 118.
19. Ibid.
20. Tanya Krzywinska, "Hands-on Horror," in King and Krzywinska, *ScreenPlay*, p. 216.
21. Interview with Jim Molinets in *The Making of Alice* movie, ibid.
22. She is pleased to see the Cat on their second meeting at the croquet-game, and introduces it as a friend: see Carroll, *Alice in Wonderland*, p. 90.
23. Jason Rutter and Jo Bryce, "Spectacle of the Deathmatch," in King and Krzywinska, *ScreenPlay*, p. 72.
24. Of course, I may not be voyeuristically desiring Alice, but my emotional response to her does depend on my heterosexual male attitude towards a teenage girl alone in a hostile environment.
25. Geoff King also observes this "mixture of pleasure and irritation" in games' spectacular death scenes, and discusses the "moral quandary of offering pleasurable spectacular display at the point of avowed failure." "Die Hard/Try Harder" in King and Krzywinska, *ScreenPlay*, pp. 60–61, Tanya Krzywinska offers an interesting parallel to my own arguments in her chapter on *Undying*, pp. 212–17.

26. Ben Sawyer, Alex Dunne, and Tor Berg, *Game Developer's Marketplace* (Arizona: Coriolis Group, 1998), p. 112; cited in Wee Liang Tong and Marcus Cheng Chye Tan, "Vision and Virtuality," in King and Krzywinska, *ScreenPlay*.

27. The name is a form of signature from Richard "Levelord" Grey, one of the level designers. See *Alice's Asylum*, http://alice.trinitee.net/game/trickery/eastereggs.shtml.

28. If the controls are untouched during the game, Alice balances the knife or cleans her fingernails with it; further evidence of her playful cool.

29. Playing this level for the purposes of analysis, I used the screenshot option to record what I was experiencing, which felt even more like being a tourist taking pictures.

30. King, "Die Harder/Try Harder," p. 57.

31. Sigler, *Alternative Alice*, p. xvii.

32. The weapons or "toys" available to Alice follow the same pattern: the Vorpal Blade and Croquet Mallet are borrowed from Carroll, but the Demon Dice, Blunderbuss, Ice Wand, and Jackbomb are horror/fantasy inventions.

33. Note that here the Jabberwock refers to Alice's family, not just her parents—however, this seems the only hint that the game's protagonist could, like the real Alice Liddell and the fictional Alice, have siblings.

34. The Carrollian italics almost balance up the unfortunate Americanism at the start of the passage.

35. American McGee, *The Making of Alice*.

36. "The Badger," *GameZone*, http://www.gamezone.com/gzreviews/r14078.htm (12 November 2000).

37. Justin Whirledge, *PCGamerWeb*, http://www.pcgamerwb.com/reviews/pc/alice.html (22 January 2001).

38. Sarju Shah, *Firing Squad*, http://firingsquad.gamers.com/games/alicereview (4 January 2001).

39. Richard Greenhill, *Games Domain*, http://www.gamesdomain.com/gdreview/zones/reviews/pc/dec00/alice.html (December 2000).

40. Enid Burns, *Sharky Games* http://www.sharkygames.com/games/reviews/a/alice/ (29 January 2001).

41. "The Badger."

42. Ibid.

43. *Generation5*, http://www.generation5.org/alice_pc.shtml.

44. Richard Greenhill, *Games Domain*.

45. Justin Whirledge, *PCGamerWeb*.

46. Christian Schock, *Intelligamer*, http://www.intelligamer.com/action/alice/alice.asp.

47. Justin Robbins, *Online Game Review*, http://www.onlinegamereview.com/alice.asp.

48. David Laprad, *The Adrenaline Vault*, http://www.avault.com/reviews/review_temp.asp?game=alice.

49. Enid Burns, *Sharky Games*.

50. "The Badger."

51. Anon, *Generation5*.

52. David Laprad, *Adrenaline Vault*.

53. Richard Greenhill, *Games Domain*.

54. Sarju Shah, *Firing Squad*.

55. Uros Jojic, *Actiontrip*, http://www.actiontrip.com/reviews/americanmcgeesalice.phtml.

56. Christian Schock, *Intelligamer*.

57. David Laprad, *Adrenaline Vault*.

58. Justin Whirledge, *PCGamerWeb*. The acronym stands for Non-Player Character.

59. Justin Robbins, *Online Game Review*.

60. "The Mock Dodgson," *Game Revolution*, http://www.game-revolution.com/games/pc/adventure/alice.htm.

61. Ibid.

62. Ibid.

63. Lewis Carroll, ed. Martin Gardner, *The Annotated Snark* (Middlesex: Penguin, 1979) p. 60.

64. Christkaiser, *Alice Desktop Art*, http://alice.trinitee.net/desktopart/high.htm#.

65. Christkaiser, personal email (6 July 2003).

66. *Alice Configs*, http://aquatarkus.20m.com/alice.html.

67. "Aquatarkus," personal email (28 June 2003).

68. *The Tangle Box*, http://tanglebox.cjb.net.

69. Strangely, Ken told me that while he had Gaiman's character Death in mind when he created the site, and regards McKean as "one of today's greatest artists," he wasn't aware of McKean's work at the time of *The Tangle Box*'s creation. Ken Wong, personal email (1 July 2003).

70. *The Tangle Box*.

71. Alice's Vorpal blade is referred to as spurting "blood flowers"; the title of a Cure album.

72. Ken Wong, email.

73. *Alice's Asylum*, http://alice.trinitee.net/community/fan/writing.shtml.

74. "The Dormouse," ibid.

75. Cheshie T. Cat, "Last Day In the Asylum," http://alice.trinitee.net/community/fan/writing/sstories/lastdayasylum.shtml.

76. "The reason no more *Alice* games are being made is because EA and McGee had a falling out—EA still own the rights to the property, but regard it as a failed project." Ken Wong, personal email (4 July 2003).

8

FANS

It is love.[1]

A lice Liddell was born at 19 Dean's Yard, Westminster, on the fourth of May 1852. One hundred and fifty years later, I followed the Lewis Carroll Society into Westminster Abbey—where Alice was married in 1880—and found a security guard blocking me with a politely threatening "Can I help you, sir?" The group from the Society that day consisted of perhaps twenty respectably middle-class, middle-aged people, dressed as if for a wedding: blazers and ties, pastel dresses and skirts. Spike-haired, in a black military jacket and biker boots, I looked more like a bouncer than the security guard himself. He didn't believe I was with the others, and made me give him the name of the man whose memorial we had come to visit before stepping aside. If my participant observation of the LCS had called for a secret infiltration of the group, I would clearly have been a complete failure: I had no kind of disguise, and obviously didn't look like I fitted in.

In other ways, too, I felt, at least initially, like a pretender and an outsider. Until beginning the research for this book in 2001, as I admitted in the Introduction, my interest in Carroll had been genuine but casual. I thought of the *Alice* books with great fondness, owned the *Selected Letters* and the *Annotated Snark*, but had gained my information about Carroll's life from a general and unfocused absorption of magazine articles, Internet sites, book introductions, statue inscriptions, and gift-shop labels over the past couple of decades. My academic research and publications to date were mainly concerned with popular, even trash culture of the late twentieth century—comics, space opera, video games, online communities. I was at least ten years younger than the other Society members I'd met—in some cases, over fifty years younger. My accent was battered out in Woolwich, South East London, and at Kidbrooke, a not especially refined comprehensive school; it sounded far more working-class than anyone else I heard at meetings.

These factors surely shaped my experience of the LCS over the twenty months between January 2002 and August 2003, the time of this writing, and they will inevitably shape my report here. Although my research into Carroll made me far more a fan than I had been previously, and although this increasing knowledge and investment gave me a greater participatory role in the Society, I nevertheless continued to feel, partly through my own sense of cultural identity and my perception of a distinction between myself and them, that I remained somehow on the outskirts of the group. The term participant-observer, with its hyphen bridging two terms, aptly conveys my feeling of straddling the line, of standing both inside and out, a part of the group but still apart.

This inbetweenness makes my analysis of the LCS different from my previous academic work on fandom. Talking to *Star Wars* fan communities, for instance,[2] I was already an expert and could form instant bonds with strangers based on our common knowledge and enthusiasm. My book on this branch of fandom was on one level a study of my own intense investment in the saga. This study of the LCS will also draw on my personal experience, but this is more a story of becoming a fan, and entering at least some of the way into an existing fan community; a more gradual process, and one that left me, at the time of writing, still feeling less expert, less passionate, and less involved than many of the Carrollians I was meeting with and observing. That said, the Society members I encountered very rarely treated me with anything but great kindness, warmth, and generosity. Any remaining sense of detachment I felt from the group was due to my own sense of my age and class and my role as an analyst—someone who was ultimately going to write about them—coupled with my awareness both of having spent less time in Carrollian studies than most other members and of having a potentially shorter-term investment, a means to the end of publishing a book.

The data in this chapter are based primarily on email interviews and questionnaires that I circulated among a small but key group of LCS members. While the sample is very selective—only five people—this allowed me to deal in lengthier and more involved responses than would have been possible with a larger group. Moreover, my correspondents were all at the very heart of the Society, as committee members or ex-committee members, most of them boasting a long-term investment and active service. This group comprised Mark Richards, the chairman; Alan White, the secretary; Roger Allen, the treasurer; committee member Harriet Tait; and Edward Wakeling, who has held the roles of secretary, chairman, and treasurer at various points since he joined in 1975, and now regards himself as a "behind the scenes adviser". Alan White edits the three regular journals and newsletters, *The Carrollian*—a substantial, quarterly anthology of articles—*Bandersnatch*, a more lightweight collection of news and miscellany, and the pamphlet *Lewis Carroll Review*; Edward Wakeling is editor of *Lewis Carroll's Diaries* and co-author with Roger Taylor of *Lewis Carroll, Photographer*.

In addition to circulating these email questionnaires, I attended several LCS meetings—which are held approximately every two months in the Haldane Room of University College, London—the one field trip mentioned above, and the official Christmas party in December 2002. I took unobtrusive notes during these meetings and in one case tape-recorded a lecture. My further data is taken from issues of *Bandersnatch*, *The Lewis Carroll Review* and *The Carrollian*, and in some cases from extended personal correspondence with Edward Wakeling.

According to Roger Allen, the Lewis Carroll Society began in 1969, "as an extra-mural club of the GLC . . . "

> We still have one member who was a founder member from that early time. It moved on to become a National and later International Organisation and there are now several independent LC Societies throughout the world—in the USA, Canada, Japan, Australia, France and Holland. The object of the LCS is to promote the life, works and world of Lewis Carroll and our personal object is to make the Society as professional and as efficient and as appealing as possible.[3]

Alan White confirms:

> As far as I know, the Society started . . . almost as a staff association in the Greater London Council at County Hall. The idea came from Ellis Hillman, who was a London councillor. He press-ganged Anne Clark Amor (then Anne Clark) into being Secretary (she worked for the Council) even though she had no interest in Lewis Carroll. It grew from there.[4]

In this chapter I approach the Lewis Carroll Society from my own background in researching fan cultures. I want to explore what the LCS, a thirty-four-year-old nationwide organisation dedicated to an author who, despite the rumours, remains firmly placed within respectable literary heritage and "high culture", has in common with fandom around contemporary popular culture. Despite the differences in the cultural status of the chosen author and his work; despite the fact that the LCS still depends on printed journals far more than it does online communication; despite the differences in age and social class between the LCS and most popular media fans of my experience, I will be suggesting that the Society operates in a very similar way to other fan groups, yet with some intriguing differences.

In the first section, I set out what I see as some key aspects of popular media fandom, and map the Society's activities onto this framework. In the second, I examine my LCS correspondents' responses to the reworkings and rereadings of Carroll I have been discussing in this book—from the newspaper stories to the Noon novel—in order to gain a sense of their approach to preserving, defending, and promoting Carroll. Finally, I discuss the differences between the LCS and other fan groups with which I have been directly involved or indirectly acquainted, differences that come down largely to the Society's position of comparative cultural power.

Community

A key appeal of fan groups is the sense of being part of a community, of sharing an enthusiasm with others who will understand. I found this sense of belonging vividly expressed by Becky Mackle, an active member of the *Star Wars Chicks* network for female fans of the Lucasfilm saga:

> It adds validation, as in, I'm not alone, I'm not a freak. I think one of the most important things that happened to me in 1999 was finding the Star Wars Chicks . . . I felt not alone any more. I had people to natter with . . . who didn't think I was being stupid.[5]

The same bond through a common interest can be found, explicitly or implicitly, throughout research on fandom: the *Star Trek* 'zine and fanfiction communities of Camille Bacon-Smith's *Enterprising Women*,[6] Janice Radway's Midwestern group of romantic novel readers,[7] the Doctor Who Appreciation Society interviewed by John Tulloch,[8] the *X-Files*-based David Duchovny Estrogen Brigade discussed by Susan J. Clerc,[9] the alt.tv.X-files group studied by Matt Hills,[10] the *Twin Peaks* online groups of Henry Jenkins's research,[11] the action movie enthusiasts of Martin Barker and Kate Brooks's study on *Judge Dredd*,[12] and the fans of *Alien* movies,[13] Batman comics,[14] and the Star Wars saga in my own work.

My LCS correspondents readily admitted that the social aspect of belonging to a group with shared interests was part of the appeal of membership. Alan White listed as the main gratifications "the friendships I have made through the Society and the pleasure of having something constructive to do with my time now that I am retired."[15] Harriet Tait told me that for her, "the main pleasures of the Society are meeting other people who have an interest in the same subject and discovering new things about either Carroll or his works."[16] Edward Wakeling had been retired for two years when he responded to my questions, and his answers echoed those of his fellow members: while he noted "I enjoy the research I have been able to undertake, the scholarships to various US universities, the opportunities to promote Carroll in schools, and the various books I have been fortunate in publishing," the Society's main attraction, overshadowing scholarly achievement on his own part, remained "the social opportunities it provides, and the chance to meet like-minded people."[17] Roger Allen's reply was extremely similar: he primarily enjoyed "the companionship of like minded souls and the opportunity of enjoying mutual collecting."

Only Mark Richards took a slightly different tone, perhaps tinged with the cynicism that comes from chairing an organization and witnessing most of the work being carried out by a few people. His colleague, Alan White, had remarked that some members were "more selfish than others. Very few realise that, as members, they ought to recognise that they have responsibilities and duties under the constitution—to promote the works of Lewis Carroll. They really should give as well as receive."[18] "The 'pleasures' of the Society," Richards explained,

> . . . have changed a bit over the years, as I've grown older and as the Society has changed. My reasons for being involved now are more because I am trying to ensure its survival as a group and because I do get to meet a few interesting people and go to interesting events occasionally. Whereas earlier, the main benefit of membership was learning about Carroll, his contemporaries and general Victorian matters. I think that is still the case for most people.[19]

The faintly begrudging, critical note in Richards' reply is a useful reminder that this kind of community rarely if ever involves absolute consensus—I shall examine internal dissent within the LCS below, but already we can see that the Society is, like every other fan group I have personally encountered, not without its conflicts, disagreements, and resentments. Having said that, Richards' dissatisfaction is far more subtly and politely expressed than it would be in many online popular culture fan groups.

This tone of refinement and careful articulation is consistent across all my correspondents' replies, and again, I will consider it below in relation to questions of "performing" fandom; put simply, my suspicion that Lewis Carroll fans tend to talk and write like Lewis Carroll.

While the expression in all these responses is poised, unslangy, and at times delicately modest—Wakeling's self-deprecating mention of his own books, for instance—these Carrollians, valuing the company of "like-minded people" and the opportunity to share their interest above all other benefits of the Society, have a great deal in common with Becky Mackle and her Star Wars Chicks, with the Bristol Boys' Club who go to action films "with friends cos you've got, like, more of an atmosphere"[20], or the alt.tv.X-files contributor who jokily admits his fanaticism online, confessing "here among the similarly afflict [sic] I am comfortable with my illness."[21]

The sense of shared interest and common knowledge was appealed to and reinforced during the meetings I attended. On May 30, 2002, Wakeling and Roger Taylor delivered a talk to launch *Lewis Carroll, Photographer*; the lecture was punctuated with asides such as "you will know this better than me," and "many of you here won't need telling." This could be seen as another example of Wakeling's modesty, but it also constructs a sense of the group as insiders, people in the know. Furthermore, asides like this offer Society members—or those present—an image of themselves in terms of attitude and approach; they invite complicity with a specific position with regards to Carroll, and offer a sense of superiority for those who align with it.

This latter strategy was obvious during another of Wakeling's lectures, on April 11, 2003. He quoted from the introduction from a Penguin Popular Classics edition of *Alice in Wonderland*; it contains errors that most readers would fail to recognize, such as the assertion that Carroll was the oldest child in the family and that he was "handicapped" by a stammer. Wakeling read the quoted passage wryly, and earned light chuckles from the audience. What struck me most, reading his text for this lecture, was that he knew he would get those laughs.

> I forbear to continue. The text goes on to state that Queen Victoria was bemused rather than amused to receive one of Carroll's mathematical treatises! I hope you spotted the several mistakes. But you have a wider appreciation and understanding of the author. You know better. The vast majority of people reading that would accept it without question. And the myths are born and perpetuated.[22]

Wakeling is not just congratulating his audience in terms of their information, but in terms of their "appreciation and understanding"—their clearer vision, scepticism towards "myths"—essentially, their agreement with a position of superiority based around the study of primary texts rather than the circulation of received ideas. The Society members in attendance are flattered as an elite, a group that shares a higher degree of knowledge. In fairness, he subsequently accepts that some of the "myths" he aims to dismiss will be disputed, and welcomes debate—"It will be a major task . . . but I don't mind the challenge"[23]—but this opening gambit has already gone some way to get his audience on his side.

My impression from my experience of the LCS was that Wakeling would not face much of a battle convincing his listeners on one of his crucial points—that the statement "[Carroll's] relationship with children was unhealthy" is a falsehood. I will discuss my correspondents' reply to this question, and to newspaper reports on the topic, in more detail below—suffice to say for now that there was a consensus between them. The sense of often-unspoken agreement among the Society about Carroll's supposed paedophila, and a corresponding disapproval of journalism's role in circulating this rumour, was brought home to me at the Christmas party on December 13, 2002. I was sitting with Anne Clark Amor and Celia Salisbury Jones—the first is author of *The Real Alice*, and the second serves on the Society's Editorial Board. They were mature, distinguished ladies, in elaborate coordinated outfits and with almost aristocratic bearing; perching between them, I felt not unlike Alice with the Red and White Queens, minding my manners and being put mildly to the test.

I discussed my reasons for joining the Society, and my book, which I explained would deal with the interpretations of Carroll as being "dubious in his relationships with children"—I remember my own phrase, realising at the time that I was carefully choosing a delicate euphemism—and felt a forcefield shiver down between me and the two ladies. I quickly added something like "which of course, I disapprove of myself," and found the air melting again with a relieved chorus of "of course, of course". I had been initiated, and from then on they treated me with absolute charm; I had passed a test and proved myself one of them.

Arcana

The second of what I am proposing are unmistakeable, though not exhaustive, marks of fandom is the penchant for what to anyone outside the group would seem piddlingly obscure detail and trivia. Here are some examples from popular media fandom. First, *Doctor Who* afficionados at a convention in 1982:

I don't think it was all that good an idea to have such strong links between "Logopolis" and "Castravalva", even down to the same incidental music and so on. I mean, the same trick—block transfer computation; the same foe—the Master. They're too similar, which perhaps softens the change too much. You should maybe exaggerate it, as in "War Games"/"Spearhead".[24]

A *Blade Runner* "frequently asked questions" page from the late 1990s:

Q: How can Tyrell tell Roy that "We made you to the best of our abilities," when he deliberately gave him a four year lifespan?

A: Tyrell probably means they couldn't risk making him any better because they can only control them for so long. This assumes Bryant is correct in saying the 4-year lifespan is intentionally built-in. Tyrell also says "the light that burns twice as bright," suggesting improved performance may be a trade-off with lifespan. Since Tyrell's goal is commerce, he may have turned a biological problem into a bene-fit . . . when Sebastian says "there's some of me in you," he might be referring to the intentional use of the genes responsible for Methu-selah Syndrome.[25]

A *Twin Peaks* newsgroup trying to unlock the case of Laura Palmer's murder:

Why hasn't anyone suspected Donna Hayward of offing her best friend? [. . .] She certainly gained a lot by Laura's death—namely, James. Look at their early meetings—this girl was hot for him. And he was seeing her evil best friend. Twice, Donna has made statements that made me confused: first, she convinced James that when they discovered the broken half of the heart necklace was gone, they should NOT go to the police . . . secondly, when Audrey was trying to convince Donna to help her in her own investigation, Donna demanded to know what Audrey had already found out . . .[26]

An online analysis of the differences between the *Star Wars* original movies and the Special Editions:

To the left, some Asp droids (originally featured in *Shadows of the Empire*) are loading cargo into a transport . . . In the sky, a few ships (Imperial Landing Crafts) land and take off, including Dash Rendar's Outrider (again, from *Shadows of the Empire*) . . . A swoop (yet another *Shadows of the Empire* creation) nearly hits the front of the ronto, which rears up like a horse . . . As the landspeeder crosses the frame, two more rontos can be seen below what could be the crashed ship spoken of in *Tales from the Mos Eisley Cantina.*[27]

What these extracts all have in common is an immersion in the detail of the text and often its surrounding intertexts; a sense of monkish study leading to effortless familiarity that tends to inspire contempt or ridicule in those "outside" the culture, or even sometimes from those inside it who regard this kind of obsession as a step too far. It is an internal hierarchy of this kind, separating those who perceive themselves as reasonable fans from others, whom they see as geekily studious, that prompts one of Henry Jenkins's *Twin Peaks* subjects to exclaim, "with a mixture of fascination and irritation",

> Tell me! Tell me! How many times are you people watching *TP*? Do you take notes on every subject as you are watching? Or, when a question comes up you drag out each of the episodes, grab a yellow pad, some popcorn and start watching? Do you have a photographic memory? . . . Do you enjoy making the rest of us feel stupid? Does anyone share my frustration?[28]

This outburst constructs the fan obsessed with obscure detail as a form of swotty student, sitting with a "yellow pad" and taking notes. In my book on *Star Wars*, I compared the Special Edition sites to "the traditional practice of scholarship, the reclusive study of a dense primary text."[29] In both cases, the fan's poring over what to an outsider would seem trivial intricacies in the text is described—whether admiringly, contemptuously, or with a mixture of the two—in relation to academic study.

Matt Hills warns, correctly I feel, that to praise fan knowledge and expression through parallels with academia is patronizing and misguided, based on an assumption that the "official", academic process of research and argument is an ideal model that the "unofficial" fan culture can aspire to and sometimes attain; the expertise of fans is, following this approach, applauded when it approximates the practices of university professors. Hills cites Thomas McLaughlin's praise of "elite fans" who "can come to theoretical questions in ways similar to those of academic cultural critics", contrasted to the "vernacular cultural theory [that] lacks the systematics of academic theory";[30] Hills points out that this comment operates "within an academic imagined subjectivity"[31] where the standards are imposed from within higher education. This point is well made, and my own references to academic conventions in this section are not meant to imply a superior system to fan practices; I agree with Hills that the two are not always leagues apart.

273

Observing that academia consistently enforces a distinction between its own work and that of fandom—for instance, by drawing imaginary lines between the "extensive" nature of the former practice and the "intensive" approach of the latter—and that fandom in its turn tends to snub academic writing as "long-winded" or "boring", Hills argues that despite the boundary being policed on both sides, there is already an overlap between the two practices.

> . . . what I want to suggest is that the circulation of "litcrit" and media studies terms outside the academy threatens the very opposition of intensive/extensive or fan/academic knowledges. And even if the collapse of this opposition is only relevant for certain, well-educated sections of a fan culture, it remains a significant and under-researched fact that fan-scholars have directly drawn on academic knowledge in order to express their love for a text.[32]

Lewis Carroll fandom offers a valuable intersection into this debate because the texts it produces are so hard to pin down on one side of a fan/academic boundary; as such, it supports Hills' argument that the two fields muddy in the middle, with no clear borderline. The regular output of the Society—*The Carrollian, Bandersnatch*, and the *Lewis Carroll Review*—echoes the fan expressions cited above in its obsession with detail and the pleasure it gains from what would strike an outsider as absurd pedantry, but it also follows academic convention rigorously, especially in *The Carrollian*'s longer articles, which engage with extensive secondary, scholarly texts as well as primary documents, and religiously footnote every quotation.

As an example, consider Fernando Soto's "Medico-Linguistic Reading of Carroll's 'Fitful *Agony*' ", which seeks to prove that *The Hunting of the Snark* is about tuberculosis spread by pigs.

> . . . the reader will notice much that is significant for a better understanding of the *Snark*. For instance, this type of tuberculosis disease (ie. Scrofula and/or choreas) was known as "the pig's disease" in both Latin and Greek. What we have here, then, is the first of several words that directly connect tuberculosis/consumptive diseases to a pig! Moreover, Carroll's pigs and Snarks, as well as tuberculosis patients—in their attempts to breathe—are know for their "bellowing". Thus, we may further connect the pig to scrofula, the Snark to the pig, and finally the Snark to scrofula![33]

And a second example, from Simon Nicholls's "Further Glimpses Through The Looking Glass", an assortment of annotations:

In the punning climate created by Dodgson it is inevitable that the brother labeled "DUM" should speak first. By using the familiar elements of a nursery rhyme, Dodgson evokes in this chapter the atmosphere of a recurring dream, where the dreamer recognizes each emerging feature and half-divines its inevitable consequence, as in Michael Balcon's Priestley-influenced film production *Dead of Night*, 1945—which features a haunted mirror—or the *déjà vu* experience conveyed by Rossetti in *Sudden Light* (published in 1870)—"I have been here before."[34]

The Carrollian is a journal produced by fans. It is unashamedly specialist in its subject matter, and serves as the written equivalent of a Society meeting, as a forum for debate and a platform for circulating individual research. There is no money offered to contributors, and no conventionally academic prestige; articles are presumably written and submitted for the hobbyist pleasure of study and of sharing an interest with the community. Some of them have already been presented as lectures at Society meetings, again without any guest lecture fee or honorarium; without any of the obvious rewards of finance or career advancement that accompany academic lectures, conference papers, or keynote speeches.

However, as already suggested, the contents of *The Carrollian* are in many ways indistinguishable from those of an academic journal. They meet academic conventions of surveying the existing knowledge and producing new insights based on fresh reading or primary evidence; they use the conventions of formal expression, citation, and reference required by an academic journal; they often include work by authors who have published books, such as Karoline Leach, Anne Clark Amor, Edward Wakeling, and Ivor Wynne Jones.

Undeniably "scholarly" but not quite like a standard academic journal— its readership, the topics it is prepared to consider, its group of regular contributors are far too narrow for it to fit comfortably in that category— produced with the passion, intensity, and pedantry familiar from other fan cultures, but without the characteristics of unsystematic energy, blinkered single-mindedness, and raw, untrained expression that fandom is supposed to display, *The Carrollian* straddles two camps. As such, it very usefully unsettles the boundaries between those camps. Based around the scholarly study of a respectable, "high" cultural oeuvre, but driven only by the personal satisfaction and pleasure in the text that inspires "amateur" fandom, it bridges a gap between literary criticism within the academy and the unofficial fan practice of poring over films, books, or magazines at home for no obvious reward, and makes more visible the similarities between the two.

Debate

Through a case study of opposing, though to the outsider very similar fangroups—readers of the "underground-indie" trash cinema magazine *Film Threat* and their rivals, followers of the "archivist" trash cinema magazine *Psychotronic Video*—Matt Hills explores the "narcissism of minor differences" that often emerges between neighbouring fandoms. "Moral dualisms can be constructed at two levels; both in terms of legitimating one's own cultural practices against other imagined subjectivities,"—those fully outside the group—"and also in terms of legitimating one's own cultural practices against imagined others whose very cultural proximity also threatens the project of distinction."[35]

This process of attempting to establish a hierarchy within a community, of defining one's own specific branch of the community against an "other" from the same broad group, also comes to light in other fan research. Subcultural fashion followers in David Muggleton's *Inside Subculture* take pains to distinguish their own "authentic" style from that of people who came to the trend late and only appropriated it superficially from High Street shops: a grunge girl complains, "I got very fed up with all the clothes that I was wearing and buying cheap and wrecking being sold for huge amounts of money to people that had probably never heard of . . . Mudhoney or any of the other, like, grunge bands that were fairly big then, and were just buying stuff from Top Shop . . . "[36] The *Star Wars* fans I studied divided themselves into two opposing camps following the release of *The Phantom Menace* in 1999; critical "bashers" and loyal "gushers" came into conflict on message boards and started up their own subgroups, even launching raids on each other's online communities.[37]

I cautioned then against imposing "an imagined consensus on a community that thrives on debate."[38] In the case of the Lewis Carroll Society, the consensus seems to be imposed from the inside. Generally speaking, I found agreement among my correspondents, particularly on the matter of Carroll's relationship with little girls, and in this my questionnaire responses were supported by documents like *The Carrollian* and my experience of meetings. I gained the strong impression that the struggle against the "imagined subjectivity" outside the Society—the ignorant but vocal body of journalists and non-specialist commentators who are charged with peddling myths and sullying Carroll's name—was pressing enough to unite the community on most fronts. However, there emerged a sense that disputes continued to rumble at a deeper level, and that disharmony was sometimes suppressed, possibly for the sake of retaining a united front at a time when Carroll seemed in particular need of defence.

When I asked whether the Society would invite debate in the form of a speaker who believed Carroll was a paedophile, Roger Allen was the most forthright.

> I personally do not for one moment believe that he was a paedophile in any way and most of my colleagues in the LCS agree with me. We all love children and in Victorian times it was not forbidden to show that, as it is now. We have listened to more than enough uninformed "debate" on this subject and I think that we would not be pleased or likely to invite a speaker to speak specifically on that theme. There is more scholarship and knowledge on Lewis Carroll within our Society, both in the UK and in the USA, than can be found almost anywhere else and we do not have to listen to half baked theories based on modern customs and values.[39]

On the more general question as to whether Society members tended to agree about the nature of Carroll's relationship with Alice Liddell, Richards suggested the possibility of an illusory consensus that concealed unspoken disagreements; not through a cynical attempt to hide any dispute but because individual clashes of opinion had grown familiar over time and were no longer mentioned.

> On the whole I don't think there is a consensus on these matters although sometimes it looks as if there is. A few long-standing members who might actually have different opinions tend not to be seen to disagree and hence give the opinion that there is a consensus. I also think that members are better at pointing out what they don't believe (or showing scepticism) than they are at stating their opinions about that they do believe with any degree of conviction.[40]

Alan White's comment that "there are all sorts of views within the Society. I know that Anne believes that Carroll was in love with Alice Liddell and proposed to her, but not everyone believes this"[41] tends to confirm the idea that long-standing debates are known to long-standing members on a personal level, but may not be obvious to newcomers and no longer arise in the Society's meetings and documents. He went on to stress the importance of the Society's image to outsiders, indirectly suggesting its role in promoting Carroll's good name and defending the author from unfortunate associations.

> We have to make sure that the Society does not get that sort of reputation or we shall lose credibility. At one time, we were suspicious that one

member, a police officer, had been 'planted' to find out about us. His membership lapsed after he attended a few meetings and outings. This is why we appear reluctant to invite a speaker on Carroll's sexuality. It might encourage people to get the wrong idea of the Society and attract the wrong sort of members. I know that some people with paedophilic tendencies have, in the past, tried to join but gave up the idea when they discovered that it was innocent. I have had no experience of this myself, but I know the previous secretary had approaches from men who were particularly interested in Carroll's photographs of nude girls: she passed the information to the police immediately.[42]

Richards confirmed that "there is not an official policy on what we would or wouldn't allow as a topic for a meeting. However, I doubt if we would ever schedule a speaker who wanted to make a case for Carroll being a paedophile . . . ", giving as one of his reasons that "it would do no good for the Society—we would look a bit seedy."[43] Edward Wakeling, who, as noted, welcomed challenges to his argument during his lecture to the Society, also denied that the group held any official policy, but felt that there would still be a line drawn against certain topics from certain angles.

> The good thing about the Society is that it does not promote particular views about the various controversies surrounding Carroll—individual members hold their own views—the Society remains uncommitted. I have clear views about these controversies, and some of these have gone into print. But I am the last person to stifle debate. I hope the Society will continue to offer a forum for discussion across the various opinions that pervade, and that members will have the freedom to give their own personal views. It has in the past. I think the Society might resist a talk from a person promoting paedophilia in the name of Carroll, but otherwise, the floor is open to most opinions.[44]

In fact, the single undercurrent of disagreement that did shudder visibly to the surface during my study of the LCS was prompted by Wakeling's article in *The Carrollian* about Carroll's diaries. As was clear from Chapter 1, the cut pages and prayers were fundamental to Karoline Leach's argument, and there was a sense of cold, pursed-lips politeness at best whenever the two authors referred to each others' work. Leach refuses to even speak Wakeling's name in her one nod to his edited *Diaries*: her sneer seems very Victorian. "When I tried to find out exactly what had been removed and from where I realized that no one—including the person preparing the document for publication—actually knew."[45] Wakeling, in turn, credits Leach with her *Times Literary Supplement* article on the cut pages, rather than with what she claims was her discovery of a new document, and will only say that the piece of paper, "uncovered in the Dodgson Family Archives . . . appears to give a very brief extract . . . "[46]

It is telling that in personal correspondence, Wakeling confided a great deal of information about the background to this difference of opinion, and yet asked me to keep it to myself. Of course, I regret not being able to use the material he offered, but the very fact that he wished to keep the dispute private is revealing in itself—in relation to the appearance of consensus within the Society and also to the distinctly late nineteenth-century air of propriety that I constantly sensed around its members and their communication. At any rate, Leach's response to Wakeling's *Carrollian* article is evidence enough to hint at the icy drawing-room atmosphere between the two authors.

> I should like to offer a few developments, observations and corrections on Edward Wakeling's article . . . As the discoverer of the "cut pages in diary document" from which Mr Wakeling is kind enough to quote, and as an author who has devoted a reasonable amount of time and research to the question of the diary prayers and the missing material, I hope it won't seem too presumptuous of me to do so.

As a final note, Mark Richards offered a further revealing comment about Leach's research and the Society's response to it—or rather, the deliberate construction, by a minority, of a collective "Society response" to it.

> The book received a fairly good reception within the Society generally, except in about three cases. And those people have worked hard to discredit her and have tried to give the opinion that the LCS does not agree with her views at all. They have their reasons—and I suppose this is the sort of thing I was getting at earlier about it appearing that there is a consensus.[47]

Alan White's reply was contradictory in some details, but agreed with the general theme:

> A lot of Carrollians rejected the book out of hand without giving it much thought or even reading it, simply because it broke the mould. I think we should welcome new ideas and fresh thought. I do not believe that Carroll had an affair with Lorina Liddell any more than I believe in his paedophilia. They are both possibilities and I await evidence.[48]

Roger Allen, too, stressed that the book had proved controversial within the group, but suggested that not "about three", not "a lot", but the majority of the group had clashed over the validity of Leach's findings. "Her theories are intriguing and interesting but unproven . . . the jury of the LCS majority is not just 'out' on her theories concerning LC's love life and other matters, but most of us are almost certainly in disagreement."[49]

From only twenty months' involvement with the Society—despite my correspondence with high-ranking, active members—I have not been able to draw any clear conclusions about its internal politics and historical tensions. The sense of good manners that seems to shape its members' behaviour and dialogue, while charming and appropriate to the study of Carroll, also makes it more difficult to trace relationships and dig up old resentments. What can be said is that there are clearly debates, some at a deep level; and that unlike other fan groups of my experience, the Society tends to keep these debates—whether from propriety, from over-familiarity, or for the desire to keep a clean face to the outside world—below its surface.

Pilgrimage

The fan practice of actually visiting geographical sites associated with the author, actor, film series, singer, or saga of interest is often overlooked in academic research. Matt Hills is unusual in devoting a chapter to "cult geographies", defining them as "diegetic and pro-filmic spaces (and "real" spaces associated with cult icons) which cult fans take as the basis for material, touristic practices."[50] Some of these spaces are mundane, every-day, and would seem entirely unremarkable to non-fans: in the case of *X-Files* locations in Vancouver, "a back-street alleyway, a university building, a shopping precinct elevator . . . "[51] This category would also include Bruce Springsteen's house, which as Daniel Cavicchi reports, fans trek to and track down despite its ordinary appearance.

> Just recently I drove by his house in Rumson, New Jersey. Friends of ours live close by, and we went to visit them, and they were like, "What do you want to do?" I said, "The first thing I want to do is drive by his house." And sure enough they knew where it was, of course. So, they drove us by, and I got to see his house in New Jersey. No big deal, you know. Could have been anyone's house. (pause) But it was Bruce's house.[52]

Other sites are "commodified fan-tourist experiences",[53] like Graceland for Elvis followers, or a simulation of the Rover's Return for *Coronation Street* enthusiasts.[54] John Urry describes the segmentation of England into imaginary tourist states based around TV shows, authors, and national myths: "there is '*Last of the Summer Wine* Country'," '*Emmerdale Farm* Country', 'James Herriot Country', 'Robin Hood Country', 'Catherine Cookson Country', 'Bronte Country', and so on. Space is divided up in terms of signs that signify particular themes . . . "[55] According to Bronwen Thomas, the film *The English Patient* "was responsible for a growth in the tourism market for the African deserts";[56] while Jonathan Bignell describes an extensive tourist industry around *Dracula*.

> The Romanian Tourist Board offers visitors tours of "Dracula's castle" and Transylvania, even though Stoker never visited Eastern Europe and gathered his information in the Reading Room of the British Library . . . Whitby in Yorkshire, where Stoker stayed and where in the novel Dracula's ship arrives in Britain, hosts The Dracula Experience involving tours of the locations associated with Stoker's visit there and of the places featured in the text.[57]

As a further example, Jenny Rice and Carol Saunders explore the tourist construction of Stamford as "Middlemarch" following the BBC's 1993 adaptation of the George Eliot novel.

> The growth in tourists in search of Middlemarch is contributing to the production of Stamford as a heritage spectacle where the divisions between the "real" and the "fake" become confused. The visitors are not only audience but in some sense actors too; as they follow the town trail or guided tours they can experience going around "Middlemarch", itself a fake. In some cases the visitors even seem confused as to which is the real town, as those who tried to book in at the "White Hart Hotel" (in reality the Stamford Arts Centre) discovered.[58]

Saunders and Rice wryly quote Umberto Eco: "Everything looks real, and therefore it is real; in any case the fact that it seems real is real, and the thing is real even if, like Alice in Wonderland, it never existed."[59]

Carroll's conservatism with regard to travelling is a boon to any fan wishing to follow in his footsteps; he only left Britain once, on a trip to Russia via Calais, Brussels, Cologne, Berlin, and Danzig in 1867. Apart from this uncharacteristic adventure, the sites associated with Carroll—because, of course, it would be hard to create a tourist industry around the locations in *Wonderland* and *Looking-Glass*—are found within a relatively small area: birth in Daresbury, childhood in Croft, Oxford, where he spent most of his life, and Guildford where he died, with secondary nodes of interest around places he visited such as the Isle of Wight, London, Eastbourne, and Whitby. I toured the primary locations, and my own investigations form the basis of the final chapter.

Pilgrimage is an important part of the Society's activities. In addition to a major outing every summer—to Daresbury in 2002 and Croft in 2003—there were several smaller trips during my period of membership, including the visit to Westminster Abbey I mentioned above and a tour around Oxford with Edward Wakeling in September 2002. My correspondents offered some idea of the pleasures involved. Again, Roger Allen was extremely firm, almost blunt: "It is essential and imperative to visit places with a LC connection and particularly to see collections in libraries and universities the world over." Mark Richards, whose responses were always more hesitant, did not convey quite this sense of duty—which again, could be construed as typically "Victorian"—but also suggested the visits were "quite important".

> . . . occasionally one gets a bit closer to the man and his time by being in places associated with him. It also works the other way . . . we tend to use Carroll as an excuse to go to places we might not otherwise visit and to see it in a different way.[60]

Richards' comment is echoed in an anonymous *Bandersnatch* report of the Westminster trip: "Members of the Society often say that one of the greatest benefits of attending meetings is that they find themselves being taken to places that they might not have gone to otherwise . . . with the added benefits of going as a group and being given access to places not normally seen by the public."[61]

The *Bandersnatch* accounts of Society visits give a further sense of the pleasures in Carrollian pilgrimage. Most obviously, there is the appeal of fellowship and community, which is intensified during a longer period with the group, away from home and involving a greater intimacy—traveling together, sharing meals and hotels. Michael O'Connor's diary of the Daresbury trip mentions the "sadness", on the final day, "at having to part from so many fellow Carrollians", and concludes that the greatest joy of the three-day outing was not the "fascinating talks and memorable visits" but "time to talk to one's friends in the Society."

> Lewis Carroll events are always notable for the hubbub of enjoyable conversation, but there rarely seems to be enough time to speak to

everyone you would like to, nor to do so for as long as you would wish. On this occasion, the programme was not as packed with formal lectures as usual, and there were coach and canal trips, and events like the fete where you could just sit and chat to people you too rarely saw. I shan't single out individuals, but will only say that the one-to-one talks I had with friends old—and new—were what I will remember most about the Daresbury Summer Outing, and what made it most special for me . . . once in a while it is equally good just to sit down with like-minded friends, and to talk (of many things). It was splendid![62]

Secondly, there is a sense of the spiritual. Matt Hills argues that media fans exhibit a "neoreligiosity" in their stories of conversion, in their devotion to the text or icon in question, and in their falling back on concepts of irrational "faith" when explaining why they love their chosen object so much. He concludes that "religious discourses and experiences are re-articulated and reconstructed within the discursive work of fan cultures . . . [fandom] seeks to account for its attachments by drawing self-reflexively and intersubjectively on discourses of 'religiosity' and 'devotion'."[63] Fan culture does not, to Hills, represent a collapsing of religion into secular "cults" or a relocation of spiritual faith into a privatized expression of faith based around new "icons"; he makes a clear distinction between traditional religious practice and the neoreligious discourses of fan communities.

In Lewis Carroll fandom—as was the case with the academic/amateur boundary—this distinction is blurred. My correspondents told stories of "becoming" a Carrollian that echo those of other fan groups, albeit with less unrestrained passion.[64] Wakeling, for instance, explained,

> I saw an exhibition put on by the Lewis Carroll Society at Hatfield House in 1975 and was strongly attracted by the subject. I read a biography of Carroll and the edited diaries that summer and joined the Society in October 1975—and haven't looked back.[65]

Michael O'Connor implied an emotional or spiritual bond with Carroll in his confession that seeing "where it all began, Daresbury Parsonage", was "very affecting."[66] There were also declarations of love for Carroll as an author, though these too were properly qualified: Harriet Tait observed "I suppose love is a difficult emotion. Perhaps substitute it in my case for a sense of devotion."[67]

However, it would be wrong entirely to separate this "neoreligious" enthusiasm for Carroll and his work from traditional religion. Due in part to Carroll's extensive involvement with the Church of England, and the

Christian belief that informs a great deal of his writing, the Society outings I witnessed and read about often incorporated Church of England services, ceremonies, and tours. Allen's account of the Oxford trip, for instance, notes, "we visited the beautiful University Church of St Mary the Virgin in the High Street. It would have been here that Dodgson preached and it was to this church that all the great preachers and speakers of the day attracted capacity crowds."[68]

The Westminster Abbey outing provided a fascinating example of a fan visit that involved both religious and neoreligious practice. Anne Clark Amor's talk at the tomb of Dean Stanley was prompted by his connection with the Liddells—he conducted Alice's wedding ceremony—and thus with Carroll. This interest in supplementary and secondary figures is common in other fandoms; *Star Wars* enthusiasts, for instance, will cluster around minor actors from the saga and invite the woman who played Aunt Beru to convention signings.

The visit began with the entire group taking part in Evensong, a ceremony with a specifically Christian meaning. The *Bandersnatch* report describes the experience as "very special . . . simple, yet humbling" and "moving . . . putting us all in the right frame of mind",[69] implying that the religious service was regarded, at least by the author, as spiritual in a more general sense, as an appropriate means to celebrate Carroll rather than to worship God. Similarly, while the placing of a wreath on Carroll's plaque in Poet's Corner could be regarded as a neoreligious act with parallels across other fan groups—I have witnessed Kafka fans laying notes on his grave in Prague, followers of Wilde sticking post-it notes on his Paris tomb, and U2 enthusiasts writing graffiti outside their Old Windmill studio in Dublin—this ceremony combined elements of fan secularity with Christian rites. Caroline Luke, a descendant of Carroll's brother Skeffington, laid the wreath, a Society member marked the occasion with Carroll's line "like pilgrim's wither'd wreath of flowers" from the *Wonderland* prefatory poem, but Canon Michael Middleton of the Abbey conferred the blessing, thanking God for Carroll, "with his perfect understanding of children, his sense of humour and his skill with language."

Carroll's Christianity would inevitably lead the Society to visit Christian sites, but the incorporation of Christian prayer and hymn into these visits is an aspect of the celebration that could feasibly have been omitted. Its inclusion may be partly due to practical reasons. The Society had to gain permission to lay the wreath, and it makes sense to ask the Canon to participate in the ceremony; furthermore, if any kind of fan ceremony is to be held in Westminster Abbey, it makes sense for it to draw on Christian ritual. It could also be sourced to the sense of "performing" fandom that

I have mentioned above and will develop further in the next section—the idea of paying tribute to a Christian author through the form of Church ceremony he would have enjoyed himself, and of enacting what Carroll would have done were he still alive.

However, for some members there are deeper bonds between the neoreligious, fan celebration of Carroll through visits to the sites of his life and the Christian religion that he practiced. Harriet Tait explained,

> I think a lot of his beliefs coincide with mine, which is probably why I feel quite close to him in some respects. The more I read about him, the more I recognise the same aspects in myself.[70]

For Tait at least, the neoreligious practice of becoming "close" to the object of fandom through study and pilgrimage was interlinked with her own faith, and the realization that this was something else she shared with Carroll.

Performance

The process of "performing fandom" is, again, a comparatively under-researched area. Hills discusses the way online fan groups—the alt.tv-X-files community, in his case study—construct themselves as part of an ongoing fan text through their contributions to Internet discussion threads, and are then "read" by other fans. "Alt.tv.X-files does not only celebrate and validate the fan's knowledge, it also mirrors the fan's attachment back to him or her, validating this affective experience itself."[71] Fans perform their own role as X-Philes to an audience of their peers, having their enthusiasm and commitment confirmed and reflected. They are all playing a part in a drama of their own.

> . . . the online *X-Files* audience cannot merely offer a "window" on the programme's offline, socially atomized fandom; it must, instead, perform its fan audiencehood, knowing that other fans will act as a readership for speculations, observations and commentaries. This self-representation and self-performance of the audience-as-text therefore creates a second-order or implied commodification insofar as the online fan audience consumes a textual construction of itself alongside the originating com-modity-text . . . [72]

My own research into various strands of media fandom offers examples of performance that support Hills' argument, particularly his suggestion that the " 'secondary text' of fans' detective work uncannily parallels the hyperdiegetic narrative space of the primary text."[73] On several occasions I found fans to be taking roles and forming communities that, deliberately or unconsciously, echoed those of the protagonists in the original text. Writers to the letter columns of *Batman* comics in the 1960s, for instance, seemed explicitly to be constructing themselves as investigators, piecing together clues about plot developments or simply the identity of the then-uncredited writers and artists. I commented at the time:

> [I]t is tempting to wonder whether this relationship between reader and editor was in any way an unconscious reflection and enactment of the Batman's own role as "darknight detective", musing over the riddles posed by his trickster enemies. It doesn't seem entirely far-fetched to suppose that part of the readers' pleasure in pitting their skills of observation against the comic text came from an identification with Batman and his co-stars, the "ductile detective" Ralph Dibny, and detective J'onn J'onnz, the Martian Manhunter. In this sense, the title *Detective Comics* referred not just to its featured characters, but to the role of the reader; and it was largely the readers who created this role for themselves.[74]

Secondly, my comparison of *Blade Runner* and *Alien* online fan communities identified a contrasting ethos and approach that seemed modelled on the behaviour of the films' main characters—painstaking examination of the primary text in the first case, and macho locker-room banter in the second.

> In place of the obsessive project of detection and enquiry after truth in which the *Blade Runner* fans mimic Rick Deckard, there is more the sense of a marine barracks or mess hall, full of challenge, boast and putdown. Sigourney Weaver is referred to as "Siggy", *Aliens* is described as "pure crap", and fans who "rip on" (insult and disrespect) *Alien Resurrection* are decried as "lousy hypocrites." Here, assertions are backed not so much through the academic rationality we would see on *Blade Runner* sites or the faith and humanism surrounding *Star Wars*, but by an in-depth knowledge of technical production detail and appeals to the craft of screenwriting, informed by a cut-the-crap approach and a military intolerance of sloppy workmanship.[75]

It would be a mistake to generalize that each primary text produces a single performance style in its fandom. In addition to the "faith and humanism" I discovered in the above research, *Star Wars* has inspired a macho, militaristic fandom based on detailed comparisons between the fictional hardware in the movies and the real-life weaponry of the US Army,[76] and a more light-hearted categorisation of opposing groups—the Bashers and Gushers I referred to earlier—into separatist movements and "Defence Forces" that echo the warring factions of the trilogy.

> Members were given military ranks from Private to Corporal based on their persistence in arguing the merits of *Phantom Menace* and their heroic visits to Basher threads or even enemy boards. [. . .] The *TPM* Defence Force and Bashers' Sanctuary have currently agreed a treaty—knowingly reminiscent of the Trade Federation agreement in *The Phantom Menace*—whereby they promise not to flame on each others' home threads. Of course, these wargame heroics are slightly tongue in cheek—"It's fun, in a grade 4 kinda way"—and all the more enjoyable for the way they allow members to play *Star Wars* type roles of mercenary, double-agent, diplomat or hotshot soldier within the arena of rhetorical debate.[77]

Finally, in a comment on a specific discussion-board post, I suggested that the manner and writing style of one online *Star Wars* fan as he reassured another took on the cadences of an elder Jedi. "It isn't too far-fetched, surely, to imagine that Chyren, with his advice to do what 'gives you peace . . . my friend', is—perhaps even consciously—taking on the role of an older Jedi, counselling his skittish padawan-learner."[78]

These findings can be usefully applied to the Lewis Carroll Society, where the phenomenon of fan performance mimicking the primary text is readily apparent, though, as we would expect, in a different form than any of the above examples. In simple terms, as I suggested previously, Lewis Carroll fans often seem to write like Lewis Carroll. As an example, here is Stanley Chapman in an issue of *The Lewis Carroll Review*:

> Everybody in the Society . . . knows the *Alice* books backwards, side-ways, upside down and even the right way round from beginning to end and back again. Everybody's conversation is already packed and peppered, salted, mustarded and vinegared with condiments from the books, and we all know there isn't a single word, comma (inverted or otherwise), hyphen or parenthesis that isn't kept freshly alive by being quoted 1440 minutes every day . . . [79]

Chapman's whimsy may specifically recall the conversation between Alice and the Duchess about whether mustard is a bird or a mineral, but more generally in its playfully extended condiment metaphor and its mixture of fancy and precision—the pretence at knowing an exact number of minutes—it appropriates Carroll's characteristic style just as Adair and Roiphe did. More subtly, I think we can see this tone in Michael O'Connor's report on Daresbury; the pleasure in long-winded wordiness, the modesty and understatement, the faintly jocular and overplayed formality— referring to friends in the Society by full titles—and especially in the mock-shocked effect of the italics.

> Passing quickly over the humbling fact that the coach went off leaving several notable members (and me!) behind at the fete—and *nobody noticed we weren't on it*—we eventually all congregated in the Church. [. . .] While Mr Oultram's reminiscences would normally have made fascinating listening—I am sure I am not the only one who would have liked to have learnt why he and Dr Selwyn Goodacre were once parked in a lay-by listening to "Down Your Way" on the car radio—the sight of the Church staff beginning to close down the little gift stall in the corner before anyone had bought anything provoked muted mutterings of concern finally brought to an end by the gallant Mr Wakeling resound-ingly asking if we could look round the Church while it was still open.[80]

This sense of keeping Carroll's style alive, of at least partially inhabiting a Carollian persona and of carrying out Society duties—including writing up reports—with the mixture of formality and wry charm that the author might have adopted himself, is vividly evident in some aspects of LCS meetings. At the April eleventh session referred to above, Wakeling's lecture was followed by an interval during which members were served Madeira and home-baked biscuits—the two items that are commonly thought to have made up Carroll's customary lunch, probably because of a line in Collingwood's biography.[81] Wakeling later pointed out to me that this was another myth—"He may have had this on a few occasions, and reported it so in a letter. Then everyone thinks this is what he *always* had for lunch"[82]—but this doesn't change the fact that the Society, or whoever decided on and provided the snack, thought it was simulating Carroll's customs. The aim, even if it might have been based on flawed evidence, was to enact what Carroll would have done and perhaps to connect with him through the symbolically loaded food and drink—and in this case we can identify a clear-cut neoreligiosity in the act of communion.

We can see a similar kind of performance-through-dining at the Christ-mas parties. I joined too late to attend the 2001 "Looking-Glass Ball", but *Bandersnatch* gives a full account of the menu:

> [T]he "Forest with no name" looked remarkably like Broccoli Quiche, lamb kebabs substituted for the Sheep's bulrushes, there were Haigha's

ham sandwiches, Humpty's Leggacy (stuffed eggs) and an Undiscoverable Dish (fish pies). Sarah Jardine-Willoughby's mouth-wateringly splendid Looking-Glass cakes were handed round (and cut afterwards) and the choice of red and white wines had been selected for their suitability for use in boiling the Menai Bridge, should any guest be worried about its susceptibility to rust.[83]

Of course, some of the references—to the Looking-Glass rules for cutting cake as decided by the Unicorn, and the White Knight's plan to boil the Menai Bridge in wine—are sheer playfulness rather than actual reportage, but it is still plain that the Society party deliberately attempts to enact both the customs of the *Alice* books and, more generally, perform within a "Carrollian" mode. The prize for the quiz, for instance, was "awarded to he who scored exactly ten out of twenty-five", while in a competition to design and decorate a Humpty Dumpty "the best was identified and the prize awarded to the second-best"; finally, in a direct quoting from *Wonderland*'s Caucus-Race, the raffle ensured that "all should have prizes."[84]

The Christmas Party of 2002, with the theme of "Royalty", followed the same practices. Sarah Jardine-Willoughby had again provided the food, which she ceremonially introduced to the company following the precedent set in *Looking-Glass* where Alice meets the mutton: here were King Edward Potatoes, there the Queen of Hearts' Tarts. The huge salmon on the table, despite having no obvious royal connotations, was nevertheless in keeping with the theme of fish throughout *Looking-Glass*,[85] and was probably—given the Society's intimate acquaintance with the detail of the *Alice* books— included for that reason. We should also bear in mind that potatoes, salmon and home-made tarts would not have been out of place at a middle-class table of the 1860s.

There was an air of modesty and decorum about the gathering that seemed characteristic of the Society as a whole. The winner of the quiz, applauded for getting twenty correct answers, protested meekly, "I'm sure other people did too"; awarded second prize in the costume competition, a woman dressed as Camilla Parker-Bowles piped up, almost unhappily, "Oh, it can't be me." On the other hand, Alan White introduced a note of camp through his second-hand Julian Clary banter about a big hand on the entrance, members getting the clap they deserved, and the number of queens in the audience—a gag repeated in the *Bandersnatch* write-up of January 2003. This could be seen as a form of music-hall performance, especially coupled with Roger Allen's comically overblown theatricals as he read a William McGonagall poem about Queen Victoria—"excuse me," he intoned, "while I strike a pose."

Mark Richards later confided, though, that he felt Society meetings were in danger of putting off anyone under the age of thirty; and I couldn't help thinking that anyone wandering in would see this group as an odd party of very English eccentrics. Most, as noted above, were over the age of fifty, and many were in a form of regal costume, whether rented or handmade—the entrance price of £10 had included a cardboard crown, so everyone, including myself, was dressed up to some extent. I was reminded very strongly of the Christmas party when I later watched Miller's *Alice*, with its well-meaning, slightly bumbling animal-adults; as such, the mood of the Society gathering was entirely fitting, but I had the sense that if one stepped outside the group, or looked back at it from the outskirts like Alice leaving the Mad Tea Party, it might seem a dusty, dated affair—sweet, but a little sad.

The issue of dressing up may seem to invite comparison with other fan communities whose celebration of the text involves costume and disguise—Camille Bacon-Smith provides multiple examples of Trekkers in Star Fleet uniforms, Matt Hills develops a theory around Elvis impersonators, and I found a number of *Star Wars* fans in elaborate Jedi, Stormtrooper, and bounty hunter outfits. However, there is a distinction between these forms of performance and that practiced by the LCS members. In dressing up as historical kings and queens, the Society partygoers are not trying to embody or impersonate either Carroll or anyone from his fictions: first prize went to King Edward IV, Mark Richards was in goldface as Midas, and Selwyn Goodacre, in suit and tie, claimed he was dressed as Prince Phillip.

What the Society may be enacting, instead, is a typically Victorian form of evening entertainment. Carroll had performed charades, directed marionette theatre, and practiced conjuring in "a brown wig and a long white robe" for his siblings at Croft,[86] and continued to perform theatre and magic lantern shows in his adult life.[87] In common with the party fare of potatoes and salmon, the effect is, at least in part, to create a simulation of what Carroll might have done. It results in a kind of time-warp effect, not total or entirely immersive, but nevertheless a feeling that the Society has, in its costumes and customs, meals and manners, captured a sense of Victoriana, a quaint pocket of the past.

It is impossible for me to judge the extent to which the performance I observed at Society meetings and textually, in Society documents, was a deliberate attempt to simulate Carrollian style. I suspect that members would not see themselves as putting on any such performance, outside the obvious examples of naming food dishes after *Alice* characters and making explicit references to Carroll's writing in *Bandersnatch* reports. In my role as part member, part outsider—not cynically detached, but always aware that my experiences were going to form this chapter—I was left wondering whether the Society simply attracted slightly old-fashioned, learned, pedantic individuals whose good manners sometimes seemed cold and sometimes charming; whether the Society had shaped these latent characteristics, or whether these traits were heightened in the company of other members. Whether, in short, the Society attracted people who were already "Carrollian"—that is, Lewis Carroll-like—in their behaviour, or whether it made them that way.

I can't say, and I am not sure that further research would have answered the question: it would take a great deal of self-reflexivity and honesty for Society members to analyse their own "performance" in this way, and it would require a great deal of trust. I don't know, then, whether Edward Wakeling would always have written, as he did in a note to me, "I go to Croft today for the Society's summer outing, and then after a short respite I go to Oxford for a week", [88] or whether this distinctly antique form is due to his twenty-eight year immersion in the life and work of a nineteenth-century author. What I do know is that my own style of writing changed.

When I corresponded with other members I found myself, over time, using a much more formal and polite address than I would ever have used towards, say, the *Star Wars* fans of my previous research. This was far from entirely conscious and deliberate, but I can analyse my own reasons. It was partly born of an awareness that I should meet what I perceived as their expectations of style and expression—a form of mild peer pressure; a sense from the meetings of what was appropriate—and partly a feeling that Carroll was looking over our shoulders; a sense that to adopt aspects of his tone when writing about him and his work was simply the fitting thing to do. In my second questionnaire to Society members, for instance, I found myself writing "May I use your real, full name?"—not excessively polite, perhaps, but probably the first time I had used the phrase "may I" since English lessons at secondary school. In exchanges with Harriet Tait I responded to her self-effacing remark about not being the backbone of the Society with a lame pun about her perhaps being a lesser bone such as a femur—a quibble worthy of Charles Smithson in John Fowles' *French Lieutenant's Woman*, or of the Gnat in *Looking-Glass*. I cannot speak for my fellow members, but in my case, there was a process of becoming more "Carrollian" and of slipping, not quite deliberately, into a mode of expression as if it was a period costume.

Curatorship

The final category in my not exhaustive, but I hope suggestive list of fan traits concerns the feeling of protectiveness and defensiveness around the chosen text or icon—ultimately, the feeling of ownership. For most fan groups, this ownership is complicated by a niggling awareness that they do not have any real claim to the text outside their expertise and commitment. They have no legal rights to it, they didn't create it, they don't produce and distribute it, they can't stop it being cancelled or changed out of recognition. They may have invested thirty years of their lives in love for a TV show or a film series—they may have run a professional-looking Internet site about it, or sold artwork and stories based on it to fanzines, or bought thousands of dollars' worth of merchandise—but if the studio that owns it wants to recast it, relaunch it, or relegate it to production limbo, the fan is helpless. Moreover, if the studio so chooses, it can order the fans to shut down all their amateur spin-off sites and stories under copyright law. It is this paradox that led John Tulloch to dub committed *Doctor Who* fans "a powerless elite", caught "between the power of the industry that makes the show, and the general public upon whose 'votes' its future depends."[89]

This dynamic can be found throughout studies of fandom. Tulloch's Australian *Doctor Who* enthusiasts "started out in combat with the ABC [network], trying to get the programme back on the air," and subsequently had to "battle to get any crumb off the table . . . "[90] The *Doctor Who Monthly Bulletin* voiced a common frustration and anxiety: "Because of the knowledge we have as fans we are more than aware of the rot that has been silently corroding away at the magical essence of a once quite simple, brilliant concept."[91] Tulloch cites an earlier example by his co-author, Henry Jenkins, to support the case from another fan community: "I think we have made *Star Trek* uniquely our own, so we have all the right in the world (universe) to try to change it for the better when the gang at Paramount starts worshipping the almighty dollar." Jenkins comments that "fans respect the original text and their creators, yet fear that their conceptions of the character and other programme materials may be jeopardized by those who wish to exploit them for easy profits."[92]

The same distrust and disquiet was evident in online *Batman* communities around the time of Joel Schumacher's *Batman and Robin* movie (1997):

> The problem is non-batfans and bad script writing. The glorious history of Batman that most batfans treasure is being replaced by some writer or executive's interpretation of it. The only way this will change is if

the next movie bombs at the box office. Even if that happens (which I doubt) the true Batman fan will probably have to look to the comics and not the movies to enjoy Batman the way it was intended.[93]

Compare these responses with the dismay of a long-term *Star Wars* fan who felt let down by *The Phantom Menace*, the first new episode in sixteen years:

> All of us are long time *Star Wars* fans, and all of us were disillusioned. Perhaps it is our age—having grown up before video games became so popular—but we all would have gladly traded about 5 minutes of pod race for some more intimate conversations between major characters that would have fostered more empathy on our part. And who was George Lucas making the movie for, we wondered? The film seemed to have a scattered quality, disjointed in mood and age appeal—as though Lucas were making two films, one full of sophomoric humor and silliness for the kiddies, and one intense in plot and subterfuge, aimed more at adults.[94]

As my responses from the Committee members will demonstrate, the Lewis Carroll Society also has an intense sense of ownership around the author's reputation and work; a loyalty born of so many years' investment, an authority born of expertise. They also feel a need to protect their idea of what "Carroll" is about, who he was and what he was like—which, of course, varies to some extent, although as we saw there was a general agreement on the paedophile issue—and tend to regard themselves, quite justifiably, as an elite. Remember Roger Allen's bold answer: "There is more scholarship and knowledge on Lewis Carroll within our Society, both in the UK and in the USA, than can be found almost anywhere else and we do not have to listen to half-baked theories based on modern customs and values."

The question is, are they powerless? The Society's emotional attachment to Carroll, and its investment in maintaining his public persona according to a certain standard and definition—Wakeling states that "to promote an accurate view of our author" is one of the Society's raisons d'etre[95]—can be paralleled with "purist" Batman fans who flinch when they see their hero behaving "out of character", but there is a significant difference. Batman fans know that the hierarchy of power operates with Time-Warner at the top, DC Comics as a subsidiary, and online discussion boards at the bottom. They may tell themselves that their complaints have led to a reshooting of the *Batman and Robin* trailer—"our criticism seems to have paid off . . . WB have ordered the 'feel' to be amended . . . "[96]—and take heart from previous fan campaigns that seem to have genuinely forced the producers' hand, such as the 1960s protests that saved *Star Trek* from cancellation[97] or the later letter-writing project from gay fans that led to a *Star Trek: The Next Generation* episode exploring sexual intolerance.[98] Ultimately, though—although we may celebrate the creative talent evident in their communities and recognize in it a kind of power over localized meanings—the fans know that the "official" depiction and direction of Batman is out of their hands.

Studies of fandom usually distinguish, then, between this "official" culture and the "resistant" reworkings of the amateur folk culture: the family-oriented heterosexual romances of the Lucas *Star Wars* trilogy, for instance, and the R-rated gay sex scenes of Obi-Wan/Qui-Gon slash fiction. In the case of Lewis Carroll, though, it is the Society that, in many ways, represents the conservative establishment—tending to disapprove of radical interpretations like McGee's game, as we'll see below—and in some ways it has both a legitimate right of ownership and a significant cultural power. I mentioned that Caroline Luke, Carroll's great-great grandniece, is an active member of the group; at the Christmas party I found myself sitting next to Vanessa St Clair, who looked uncannily like her great-grandmother Alice Liddell. From the Society's inaugural meeting in 1969 until his death in January 2003, Philip Dodgson Jacques, Carroll's great nephew and trustee of the Dodgson Family estate, was also a regular member. Symbolically, and in Jacques' case legally, these direct descendants of the two families whose coming together led to *Alice*'s creation hold a position "inside" the institution of Lewis Carroll.

On a different level, a member like Edward Wakeling—far from the only member who publishes and lectures, but one of the most prolific—has a considerable voice in establishing and correcting discourses around Carroll. In a lengthy response, Wakeling listed some of his duties and achievements:

> I began the major task of editing Lewis Carroll's diaries in 1990, with the permission of the Dodgson Family. I was the main organiser of the Society's 25th Anniversary Exhibition at Church Farmhouse Museum, Hendon, in 1994. This exhibition then toured the country for two years and then it travelled to Japan for all of 1997, visiting four major cities. I was the main organiser of the Lewis Carroll Centenary Programme at Christ Church in 1998. I have taken part in many events associated with Lewis Carroll including television programmes, radio interviews, exhibitions, and national events (i.e., the Westminster Abbey Memorial to Lewis Carroll, the Welsh Garden Festival, the unveiling of the Looking-Glass statue in the Castle Grounds at Guildford, the Guildford Festival in 1998, etc.). I was the first Chairman of the Editorial Board.

I now spend quite a bit of time answering questions sent to the Society's web-site, or directed to me from the American Society. I am a founder member of the Lewis Carroll Society of Japan. All these activities, as far as I am concerned, are what the Society is all about. My role has always been pro-active. I like to get involved and do my bit.[99]

These are not localized expressions about what Carroll should mean and represent; Wakeling has a controlling hand over some very public discourses about the author—his major work with Roger Taylor, *Lewis Carroll, Photographer*, providing another example—and keeps a guiding hand on others. "I will help writers to produce accurate statements if I am consulted (and I often am these days)," he reported, and while he holds journalists in contempt, he sometimes manages to shape their stories too: "I often feel compelled to tell them what to write since they lack the intelligence to write anything sensible themselves. I have even dictated copy to them in the past—and they love that."[100]

In some ways, the Society's powers are limited. If members intensely disliked McGee's interpretation, they would have little chance of forcing EA Games to stop distributing it. If they disapprove of a newspaper article suggesting that Carroll had a sexually intimate relationship with Alice Liddell, they have no option of suing. However, they can, if they get the chance, steer the direction of a forthcoming article, or write an article in reply, with a good chance of publication, or dissect it later in a book, as indeed I have in Chapter 2.[101] The Society also has some influence over the public sites of Carroll that I visited for my final chapter: the location of Daresbury Parsonage was restored with signposts and information boards by the Lewis Carroll Birthplace Trust; one of the Guildford statues was, as he states, given an introduction by Wakeling; and the Gogarth Abbey Hotel in Llandudno, once the Liddell holiday home, is being renovated under Society guidance: Shelton Fernando, the new owner, promised "we will cooperate fully with the Lewis Carroll Society."[102] While its relationship with EA Games and Disney is very similar to that between any fan group and the producers of their favoured text, then, the Lewis Carroll Society has a claim to ownership that would be more widely recognized than that of most fan communities, and more clout to put its interpretations into a public arena.

White Paper

"Journalists, in my book, are fair game," Wakeling explained. "I treat them with contempt and a sense of distance. I would never trust a journalist.

I have been abrupt and rude to journalists in the past." Given his usual courtesy and good manners, this is quite an admission, and clearly shows the extent to which the men and women of the press have tried his patience. His intolerance seems mainly due to his investment in protecting Carroll's reputation and in circulating what he regards as factual evidence, as opposed to the newspapers' perpetuation of the "paedophile" story.

> At the end of the day, they publish whatever they like, and most of it is rubbish. I assume most people realise that newspapers are not for truth and information. They are for entertainment, and most of the content is the result of over-active imaginations. The paedophile myth is well past its sell-by-date, but it sells newspapers and magazines. I will always do my best to put journalists on the right track, but it's an uphill task doomed to failure.[103]

Roger Allen took much the same note of resigned impatience.

> The media cannot seem to comment on anything else except this aspect of his affection for children and playing upon the modern almost phobia on the subject, dwell upon it to the nth degree ad nauseam. The paradox that his Alices are still children's classics and acceptable for all children to read does not ever seem to strike the press.[104]

Actually, as we saw, the press does manage to juggle these paradoxical ideas, throwing up the notion that Carroll was a child molester at the same time as it holds the idea of *Alice*, and by extension Carroll, as a jewel in British literary heritage—and warmly recommends new versions of the supposed paedophile's most famous book to child readers. It is interesting to note that Alan White actually takes comfort in this contradictory attitude, reassuring himself that at least the books haven't been branded as immoral and inappropriate as a consequence of the myths around Carroll. For him, resisting the myth is not so much a matter of principle as pedantic correction of the facts, and it sometimes isn't worth the effort.

> Accepting the paedophile myth you could say is sloppy journalism, a reluctance to go back to primary sources and find the truth, but this happens everywhere and it would realistically be impossible to check everything; some things have to be taken as givens. How often do journalists refer to the deserted ship as the *Marie Celeste*? Does it matter that they get the name wrong? It all turns on where you should draw the line. If I get the opportunity to correct the assumption, I do—I

was interviewed once for the *Today* programme on the radio and did just that—but I would not go out of my way to, say, write to a newspaper or magazine. Life's too short. Perhaps we should take comfort from the fact that people do still regard the books as timeless classics.[105]

Finally, Mark Richards's disapproval of the "paedophile" stories took yet another form—that this discourse around Carroll weakens the concept of what a child sex abuser really is.

> I think it is a shame from two points of view. Firstly it gets in the way of good journalism about Carroll—there are interesting things to be said about the man that can be based on fact—without having to continuously resort to speculation. Secondly, it trivialises paedophilia . . . no matter how much Carroll gets accused of it, he will never be seen as evil. The more we associate it with Carroll, the less we associate it with the real monsters like Hindley and Brady and the more innocuous it becomes.[106]

We see here an example of what appears to be a Society consensus, although on closer examination it involves distinctions; there are shades of agreement that certainly blend into a collective view on journalism's treatment of Carroll, but each member takes a slightly different angle and for a different reason. Certainly, there is little tolerance for or trust in journalism. To generalize, I got the impression that Society members regard this form of writing—perceived as sloppy, quick, second-hand, as opposed to the painstaking primary textual work of their own scholarship—as the main enemy in their project to promote and protect Carroll's work and reputation.

Adapting Alice

The Society committee members may seem purists—they may have been forced into this guard-up position, regularly having to witness and sometimes set right what they regard as distortions about Carroll—but my respondents were fairly open-minded about film and television versions of the *Alice* books. Even Roger Allen, whose responses were extremely stern and stubborn, found something to admire in adaptations—with the qualification that they weren't actually useful, and could often be too "free".

> Yes they can be enjoyed and are by most of us. I personally do not go out of my way to see amateur or even professional productions around

the subject of Alice as they are frequently so "free" that I find it difficult to enjoy them as an *Alice* activity. Nevertheless if they are splendidly artistic and skilful productions in their own right, such as an Alice ballet which I saw a few years ago, then I would consider they are worthy activities. They do not normally however increase the knowledge or understanding of Lewis Carroll.[107]

Wakeling explicitly denied a purist approach, seeing film and television as a necessary means of circulating Carroll's work to contemporary audiences.

> They keep Alice in the minds of people today, especially as we live in a visual world dominated by televisual media. Books alone could not do this. Most television programmes and films adapt the material available to them. I'm not a purist. I have a long standing interest in the visual arts. I have a large collection of Alice and Carroll related films and videos . . . and one of my great friends (David Schaefer) is the world authority on Alice films.[108]

"Some are good, some are bad," Alan White mused, although he concluded,

> There are far more dreadful examples than good. Some take a completely fresh approach that can allow you to recognize qualities and nuances in the original that you had not been aware of before. I think Jonathan Miller's TV version is probably the best I have seen on film: it managed to feel that hot, sultry summer afternoon lethargy.[109]

Richards, also taking a relaxed middle ground, agreed with this specific choice in his lengthy, thoughtful answer.

> I have come to accept that, for whatever reasons, film and TV adaptations of any work are rarely true to the original and, for the most part, it does not disappoint or annoy me. Consequently, I don't watch screen versions of Alice with any particular expectations and rather judge them on their own merit. Often, I get a better experience from watching looser adaptations of the story than from those that try to follow the book accurately. Svankmajer's animation and Jonathan Miller's BBC TV version are particularly good, mainly because they are willing to be free with the adaptation of the story (the plot, dialogue, etc.) for the benefit of capturing the general feel and deeper themes of the book. It does not bother me that a screen adaptation mixes characters from *Looking-Glass*, but it does rather spoil it if they mix the basic themes of the two books or interfere with the general progression of the stories.

White and Richards offer different primary reasons than Wakeling and Allen, then; rather than treating them as enjoyable entertainment only when separated from the study of Alice and Carroll, or approving them as a means of promoting the stories in the twenty-first century, they feel that adaptations can grasp something "deep" in the original text and pull out new insights. What matters to Richards is not so much quibbles over detail, which he has given up noticing, but the adaptation's engagement with fundamental ideas in *Alice*—a sentiment echoed by White, with his praise of Miller's ability to capture the "general feel". Free adaptations are therefore more promising and interesting than attempts to recreate the text with superficial accuracy; a view in direct contrast to Allen's more conservative approach.

Dark Wonderland

This pattern of response was repeated almost exactly when I asked my correspondents about *American McGee's Alice*. I provided a link to the official homepage, and for some of them this was their first acquaintance with the game. Wakeling possessed a copy, "but it's still in its wrappers. I think that sums up my view." Richards explained "I know of this PC game and have seen the characters, but have not actually seen the game"; White, similarly, reported, "I have not bought the PC game (yet) although I have the figures based on it." Harriet Tait was unaware of it until she looked at the Web site, and confessed "I must say that my immediate reaction was one of dislike." Roger Allen's reaction, finally, will come as little surprise: "I have no views and no interest whatsoever."

White and Richards's thoughts on the game, based on intertextual material rather than any actual experience of playing, were open to compromise, as we would expect from their earlier responses. "I am somewhat in two minds," White pondered.

> On the one hand, it is a shame that the story has been so obviously corrupted to pander to a market that I think is regrettable anyway. It is so far away from Carroll's original intentions when he wrote the books that it is an insult to him. On the other hand, I take delight in different interpretations of the books. If I am happy to welcome Helen Oxenbury's safe, happy, perhaps sanitised version of the story, then perhaps I should allow American McGee his liberties. There is no doubt that there are some sinister aspects to the *Alice* books: I have occasionally

met people who disliked the books and found them threatening when they were read to as children.[110]

Richards echoed this last point:

> I get the impression that the idea was to appear to be slightly subversive. I'm nearly always pleased to see this type of thing. The amazing thing about the *Alice* books is that they tap in to certain thoughts and feelings within us (and I guess that can be regarded as one of the hallmarks of great literature). If any creative person can distil those concepts and re-present them in a different medium, then, in a way, it is a good thing. And besides, the original books are quite scary.[111]

Both these responses justify the game's interpretation to some extent by arguing that the original contained sinister or frightening scenes; they are prepared to give McGee's work its due on the basis that, as with the free adaptations, it brings out something "deep" that was present, but not immediately visible, in Carroll's text. Note that this reading actually parallels the game reviews that read "surreal" or "disturbing undercurrents" back into the original *Alice*.

On this issue, Wakeling was far less tolerant than he had been towards film and television adaptations. Like White, he viewed it in terms of Carroll's original intentions, and judged it by its distance from them. "I know from reviews that it is a travesty of the story and is a vehicle for aggression, violence and misrepresentation." The notion that *Alice* might always have been violent and aggressive in parts either didn't occur to him or didn't sway him; what did offer consolation was the argument that Alan White suggested above, with regard to the stories' continued popularity despite the paedophile myth. "It won't make a scrap of difference to the people who continue to buy the book for their children."[112]

It was Tait, despite her knee-jerk dislike of the game's Web site, who took up Wakeling's earlier argument about the benefit of new media and new interpretations in ensuring Carroll's continued appeal. Although she too saw the game as a debasement and betrayal of the original intention, she was unable to condemn it entirely.

> . . . it does help to popularise it with a generation or people who might not otherwise have anything to do with the *Alice* books. It keeps the image alive, although I'm not sure if it is the right image! It would be a big debate as to what extent Carroll's works should be so freely used and expanded upon. This type of usage debases the original works which some feel strongly should not be interfered with in any way and

do not need to depart from their original form as they have survived for nearly 150 years on their own. However, would *Alice* die out if it were to remain static in an era so different from our own?[113]

This is an intriguing argument, and one touched on by Richards above. Some of these respondents seem torn between their loyalty to the original and their notion of what Carroll would have wanted on the one hand, and on the other, the belief in *Alice* as a complex work of art that both supports multiple interpretations and, perhaps, must be reinterpreted or re-presented to suit changing times. The Carrollian faces the potential dilemma that protecting the image of *Alice* precisely as its author intended may preserve it as nothing more than a museum piece, with little appeal to young audiences of the present day—which is not, presumably, what Carroll would have wanted. If, as White argues, we accept Oxenbury's reinterpretation—a long way from Tenniel and Carroll's illustrations in most respects—as a useful and positive re-imagining of *Alice* for today's children, then can we legitimately condemn McGee's work as a debasement and insult? If we praise some reworkings despite their distance from the Victorian aesthetic, can we consistently reject others, especially when they do, arguably, build on elements of violence and morbidity in the original text? Does *Alice* need to adapt to remain vibrant, relevant, and alive in the way that Carroll would surely have wanted, even if it means changing his vision of how she must look and behave?

Alice in Disneyland

As Tait says, this is a "big debate", but one key test of where Carrollians find a balance between protecting the author's original intention for Alice and approving of her continued circulation and relevance—even if this involves reinvention—is in their response to Disney's interpretation. As I suggested in Chapter 6, the 1951 Disney film and its related merchandise, not to mention the rides and themed areas at all four existing Disneylands, have probably done more to shape the popular image of what Alice looks, sounds, and acts like than any other film or illustrated version. The film, of course, combines elements from both *Alice* books, changes the plot, cuts and adds dialogue, and inserts new musical numbers. While its image of Alice is fairly close to Tenniel's illustration, other characters like the Cat, Hatter, and Queen of Hearts are far removed from the woodcuts of 1865. However, Disney's parks and *Alice* videos are arguably keeping Carroll's heroine alive and active in the public imagination.

Harriet Tait reconciles these factors in much the same way she was prepared to make some allowances for McGee's game, although she applies the argument with more enthusiasm.

> I loved the film! I thought it was quite a good representation and I like the singing. I also think it makes it accessible to very young children as the language in the original is quite difficult to understand. Perhaps children in Carroll's days could understand it—it seems that language in children's books is over-simplified nowadays compared to those in mid-Victorian times.[114]

Wakeling also took a generous approach to the Disney interpretation, for much the same reasons—objectively, it deserves praise for its role in keeping Alice visible and popular, and on a personal level, for the pleasures of its story, spectacle, and songs.

> I think the Disney video has done more for Carroll around the world than anything the Society has achieved. The Disney film is a confusing mixture of the two Alice books, but it is, nonetheless, very entertaining. Most children I speak to know the Alice story and characters from the Disney video.[115]

Allen, too had fond childhood memories of the film, despite his impatience with its position as the dominant Alice in contemporary culture:

> I enjoyed the Disney *Alice* film when I first saw it as a child and have enjoyed seeing it very occasionally since. I am fed up however with seeing all the ephemera and memorabilia on the Disney theme that seem to appear all the time. The most irritating thing possible, is for someone to say, when Alice is mentioned, Oh yes I have seen the film! as if the film came first.[116]

This sense of saturation was also criticized by Mark Richards, who complained "Overexposure of any kind can become rather tedious, and it is a pity that Disney's *Alice* has supplanted Carroll's." Even while disapproving of it, he acknowledges the power of the Disney version; his refusal to entirely endorse this interpretation goes back to the notion that Carroll's original involved frightening and sinister aspects, and that as a consequence, any wholly "bland" reworking is in some ways a misrepresentation. As White, Wakeling, and Tait did with the PC game, he judges Disney in terms of what he conceives as Carroll's intentions, but in this case the mistake lies in taking out all the "darkness".

The "wholesome" approach that Disney adopts to its output is a mixed blessing. I'm sure Carroll would have approved of their "sanitisation"—avoiding bad language, etc. but they do rather kill the good germs along with the bad ones, making what they do a bit bland in comparison with the strong feelings and senses that were written into the original books. That, to me, is a shame, because the books offer very strong experiences for the reader and might get missed otherwise.[117]

Alan White's response recalls Richards's earlier theory about some adaptations capturing the "feel and deeper themes" of the text despite their infidelity to the detail. Note the "performance" in his reply—what I would regard as a Carrollian italic stress, and the use of Tweedledee's "contrariwise":

> I have long felt that it is a pity that Disney so often felt obliged to tackle classic stories, old favourites, rather than write his own. So often (and this does not apply just to Disney) the film version differs from the pictures in your head, even if the film-maker has stuck to the original script. I have often been extremely annoyed at what Disney has done—I refuse to watch his versions of *Winnie the Pooh*, for instance. Contrariwise, I think that Disney maintained some of the *spirit* of the *Alice* books, even though he took liberties with the story. The scene with the caterpillar blowing smoke letters to accentuate what he is saying is pure Carrollian wit, the cinematic equivalent of wordplay in the books. Consequently, I have many Disney versions in my collection and visited Disneyland last year (I never would have done so without the *Alice* interest).[118]

It has a significant voice within the spheres of scholarly publishing, heritage sites, and to an extent journalism, but against the cultural might of Walt Disney, the Lewis Carroll Society really is powerless. Some members clearly rail against it, regretting its overshadowing of the originals, and others appreciate its role in keeping Carroll and Alice in children's lives for over fifty years. Even for the purist, Disney's Alice cannot be ignored: and so in the last chapter, despite its main focus on locations associated with Lewis Carroll and Alice Liddell, we begin at Disneyland.

Notes

1. Final line of *Sylvie and Bruno* (1893).
2. See Brooker, *Using the Force* (London: Continuum, 2002).
3. Roger Allen, email interview (April 2003).
4. Alan White, email interview (April 2003).
5. Brooker, *Using the Force*, p. 217.
6. Camille Bacon-Smith, *Enterprising Women* (Philadelphia: University of Pennsylvania Press, 1992).
7. Janice Radway, *Reading the Romance* (Chapel Hill: University of North Carolina Press, 1991).
8. Henry Jenkins and John Tulloch, *Science Fiction Audiences* (Routledge: London, 1995).
9. Susan J. Clerc, "DDEB, GATB, MPPB and Ratboy: The X-Files' Media Fandom, Online and Off," in David Lavery, Angela Hague, Marla Cartwright, eds., *Deny All Knowledge: Reading the X-Files* (London: Faber & Faber, 1996).
10. Matt Hills, *Fan Cultures* (London: Routledge, 2002).
11. Henry Jenkins, "Do You Enjoy Making The Rest Of Us Feel Stupid" alt.tv.twinpeaks, the Trickster Author and Viewer Mastery," in David Lavery, ed., *Full of Secrets: Critical Approaches to Twin Peaks* (Detroit: Wayne State University Press, 1994).
12. Martin Barker and Kate Brooks, *Knowing Audiences: Judge Dredd: Its Friends, Fans and Foes* (Luton: University of Luton Press, 1998).
13. Will Brooker, "Internet Fandom and the Continuing Narratives of *Blade Runner*, *Alien* and *Star Wars*," in Annette Kuhn, ed., *Alien Zone 2* (London: Verso, 1999).
14. Will Brooker, *Batman Unmasked* (London: Continuum, 2000).
15. White, email.
16. Harriet Tait, email interview (April 2003).
17. Edward Wakeling, email interview (March 2003).
18. White, email.
19. Mark Richards, email interview (March 2003).
20. Barker and Brooks, *Knowing Audiences*, p. 31.
21. Hills, *Fan Cultures*, pp. 180–81.
22. Wakeling, "The Real Lewis Carroll."
23. Ibid.
24. Quoted in Jenkins and Tulloch, *Science Fiction Audiences*, p. 135.
25. Quoted in Brooker, "Internet Fandom and the Continuing Narratives of *Blade Runner*, *Alien* and *Star Wars*," in Kuhn, ed., *Alien Zone*, p. 61.
26. Quoted in Jenkins, "Do You Enjoy Making The Rest of Us Feel Stupid?" in Lavery, ed., *Full of Secrets*, p. 58.
27. Quoted in Brooker, *Using the Force*, p. 71.
28. Quoted in Jenkins, "Do You Enjoy Making The Rest of Us Feel Stupid?" in Lavery, ed., *Full of Secrets*, p. 59.
29. Brooker, *Using the Force*, p. 64.
30. Thomas McLaughlin, *Street Smarts and Critical Theory* (Madison, WI: University of Wisconsin Press, 1996), quoted in Hills, *Fan Cultures*, p. 17.
31. Hills, ibid.
32. Ibid. p. 19.
33. Fernando Soto, "The Consumption of the Snark and the Decline of Nonsense: A Medico-Linguistic Reading of Carroll's 'Fitful Agony'," *The Carrollian* 8 (Autumn 2001), p. 25.
34. Simon Nicholls, "Further Glimpses 'Through the Looking-Glass'," *The Carrollian* 10 (Autumn 2002), p. 4.
35. Hills, *Fan Cultures*, pp. 60–61.
36. David Muggleton, *Inside Subculture: The Postmodern Meaning of Style* (Oxford: Berg, 2000), p. 141.

37. Brooker, *Using the Force*, p. 96.
38. Ibid., p. 113.
39. Allen, email.
40. Richards, email.
41. White, email.
42. Ibid.
43. Richards, email.
44. Wakeling, email.
45. Leach, *Dreamchild*, p. 56.
46. Wakeling, *Lewis Carroll's Diaries*, p. 214.
47. Richards, email.
48. White, email.
49. Allen, email.
50. Hills, *Fan Cultures*, p. 144.
51. Ibid., p. 149.
52. Quoted in Daniel Cavicchi, *Tramps Like Us: Music and Meaning Among Springsteen Fans* (Oxford: Oxford University Press, 1998), p. 171.
53. Hills, *Fan Cultures*, p. 151.
54. Ibid., p. 146.
55. John Urry, *The Tourist Gaze* (London: Sage, 2002), p. 130.
56. Bronwen Thomas, " 'Piecing Together A Mirage': Adapting *The English Patient* for the Screen," in Giddings and Sheen, eds., *Classic Novel from Page to Screen*, p. 197.
57. Jonathan Bignell, "A Taste of the Gothic: Film and Television Versions of *Dracula*," in Giddings and Sheen, ibid., p. 127.
58. Jenny Rice and Carol Saunders, "Consuming *Middlemarch*: The Construction and Consumption of Nostalgia in Stamford," in Cartmell, Hunter, Kaye, and Whelehan, eds., *Pulping Fictions*, pp. 90–91.
59. Umberto Eco, *Travels in Hyperreality* (London: Picador, 1987), quoted in Rice and Saunders, "Consuming *Middlemarch*," in ibid.
60. Richards, email.
61. Anon, "Westminster School and Westminster Abbey," *Bandersnatch* 116 (July 2002), p. 2.
62. Michael O'Connor, "To Talk of Many Things," *Bandersnatch* 116 (July 2002), p. 7.
63. Hills, *Fan Cultures*, p. 129.
64. Compare for instance Brooker, *Using the Force*, p. 13, and my own story of becoming a *Star Wars* fan on p. xi.
65. Wakeling, email interview.
66. O'Connor, "To Talk of Many Things."
67. Tait, email.
68. Roger Allen, "Day Trip To Oxford," *Bandersnatch* 117 (October 2002), p. 5.
69. "Westminster School and Westminster Abbey."
70. Tait, email.
71. Hills, *Fan Cultures*, p. 181.
72. Ibid., p. 177.
73. Ibid.
74. Brooker, *Batman Unmasked*, p. 254.
75. Brooker, "Internet Fandom and the Continuing Narratives . . . " in Kuhn, ed., *Alien Zone 2*, p. 64.
76. Brooker, *Using the Force*, p. 25.
77. Ibid., p. 96.
78. Ibid., p. 124.
79. Stanley Chapman, "Quotable Alice," in *Lewis Carroll Review* 23 (July 2002), p. 6.
80. O'Connor, "To Talk of Many Things," p. 6.
81. "At meals he was very abstemious always, while he took nothing in the middle of the day except a glass of wine and a biscuit." Collingwood, *Life and Letters*, p. 300.

82.   Wakeling, personal email (17 April 2003).
83.   "The Looking-Glass Ball," *Bandersnatch* 114 (January 2002), p. 8.
84.   Ibid., The line in Carroll is actually "all must have prizes."
85.   "I think—every poem was about fishes in some way. Do you know why they're so fond of fishes, all about here?" Carroll, *Looking-Glass*, p. 276.
86.   Cohen, *Biography*, p. 12.
87.   Wakeling's lecture "The Real Lewis Carroll" gives two such examples from 1855 and 1866.
88.   Edward Wakeling, personal correspondence (6 July 2003).
89.   Jenkins and Tulloch, *Science Fiction Audiences*, p. 145.
90.   Ibid., p. 161.
91.   Ibid., p. 159.
92.   Henry Jenkins, "*Star Trek* Rerun, Reread, Rewritten: Fanwriting as Textual Poaching," in Constance Penley, Elisabeth Lyon, Lynn Spigel, and Janet Bergstrom, eds., *Close Encounters: Film, Feminism and Science Fiction* (Minneapolis: University of Minnesota Press, 1991), p. 192.
93.   Brooker, *Batman Unmasked*, p. 302.
94.   Brooker, *Using the Force*, p. 86.
95.   Wakeling, email interview.
96.   Brooker, *Batman Unmasked*, p. 304.
97.   Jenkins and Tulloch, *Science Fiction Audiences*, p. 13.
98.   Ibid., p. 252.
99.   Edward Wakeling, email interview (July 2003).
100. Wakeling, email interview (March 2003).
101. I should note that Wakeling read and commented on this chapter, providing a further example of his influence.
102. *Bandersnatch* 117 (October 2002).
103. Wakeling, email interview.
104. Allen, email.
105. White, email.
106. Richards, email.
107. Allen, email.
108. Wakeling, email.
109. White, email.
110. White, email.
111. Richards, email.
112. Wakeling, email.
113. Tait, email.
114. Ibid.
115. Wakeling, email.
116. Allen, email.
117. Richards, email.
118. White, email.

┌─────┐
│ 9 │
└─────┘

PILGRIMAGE

How wonderfully young your brother looks![1]

T his final chapter describes a journey around eight places associated with Lewis Carroll. Some of them—most obviously the Disneyland at Marne-la-Vallée, near Paris, but also the rather more downmarket shopping centre at Warrington, North-West England—are included because of an Alice attraction of some kind, rather than because Carroll spent time there. Llandudno, in North Wales, is still the subject of debate with regard to whether Carroll ever set foot in the town, but it does host the Liddells's holiday home, Penmorfa. Ripon, in North Yorkshire, was Carroll's father's place of work from 1852, and Carroll himself only spent odd weeks there, the connection with the city severing with his father's death in 1868. The remaining locations—Daresbury, Croft, Oxford, and Guildford—take us through Carroll's life; they were, respectively, his homes during birth and early childhood, adolescence, maturity, and finally in death.

The sites discussed here do not offer an exhaustive list of Carrollian locations; aside from the many cities crossed in Carroll's trip to Russia, I have omitted the seaside sites of Whitby, Eastbourne, and the Isle of Wight. The chapter describes a specific journey; my journey, or more accurately series of journeys, during May, June and July 2002, with return visits to many of the places a year later. The sites included represent a personal selection, and the chapter is not a guidebook; there exists at least one excellent book of that kind, Charlie Lovett's *Lewis Carroll's England*, for the "literary tourist" who wants to track Carroll's steps more extensively.[2] My project was not to explore every inch or to uncover secrets closed off to most visitors; quite the opposite. I was concerned with the everyday, and with the traces of Carroll that remained near the surface, in the public eye, at this specific moment; I wanted to see what these places showed of Carroll to the casual visitor, and also what some of the locals knew of Carroll.

Disneyland Paris: May 2002

Disneyland Paris opened, as EuroDisney, in 1992. Both Disneyland in Anaheim, California, and Disney World in Florida had featured at least one *Alice in Wonderland* ride, but like many aspects of Disneyland Paris, the attraction went through some changes in translation to Europe. The original Disneyland Alice—which, as noted in Chapter 6, was introduced early on, in 1958—was a "dark ride", where visitors sit in a carriage and are taken on a guided railway tour through various scenes from the film, complete with animated models of the characters, piped-in songs, and the voice of Kathryn Beaumont as a prim commentator. Renovations of Fantasyland in 1983 jazzed up the ride from a primarily two-dimensional to a three-dimensional attraction, knocking out some rooms and adding others, but the general idea remained the same; it currently operates as a two-level tour, with visitors being chugged around outside for part of the ride and taken back in for a Mad Tea Party finale.[3]

Disney World only has one Alice attraction, which was pioneered in 1955 at the Anaheim park and remains there today as an iconic feature: the Mad Tea Party, a carefully controlled chaos of spinning cups that guests sit in as they career around an arena. The Florida version is identical to the Californian except for its ornate roof—added because of the state's less sunny climate—and a centerpiece of the Dormouse emerging from a giant teapot. This ride was carried over to the Tokyo park, which adds another unique Alice feature in the form of the Queen of Hearts' Banquet Hall, a restaurant that plays up the film's surreal tendencies with forced perspective design, psychedelic coloured windows, and columns that appear to be melting.[4]

Despite lacking the dark ride, Disneyland Paris is a strong contender for the park with the most Alice content. In addition to the Mad Tea Party, which combines elements of the two US versions with its protective roof, Japanese-style lanterns, and Dormouse feature, the Paris park gives over a large corner of Fantasyland to Alice's Curious Labyrinth, a series of hedge mazes punctuated with models of minor and some major characters from the film, many of them basic "animatronic" figures that deliver a line of dialogue and perform a simple movement. At one end of the maze is the Queen of Hearts' castle, a bulging peach, mauve, and turquoise monstrosity that visitors can enter and mount to the upper floors from the inside. In the middle, dominating this section of the park, is a huge motif of the Cheshire Cat's face, tricked out for most of the year in coloured flowers that surround revolving, googly eyes.[5]

The first section of the maze takes the visitor left from the entrance into a tangle of hedge corridors that create a surprisingly accurate simulation of the Tulgey Wood in Disney's *Alice* film. An Accordion Owl sits on a high branch, stretching its concertina neck; Horn Ducks, with bulbous purple bodies and yellow trumpet mouths, parp at the passer-by, and a Hammer Bird bends its head to rap on a sign. The Cat, who, fittingly, appears at various points in the attraction, lounges in a tree here, drawling in French. The intended sensation must be that we are ourselves Alice, reliving this part of her adventure—an illusion aided by the movie music playing from hidden speakers—she is the only character who doesn't appear in the maze, and so by implication we must be taking her place, seeing what she saw. This approach to Alice is, as we shall see, consistent throughout Disneyland Paris—she is remarkably absent from the theme park as a whole, and there is a far greater focus on secondary characters.

Without reading absurd depths into the Curious Labyrinth, the fact that the visitor substitutes for Alice can be linked to the interpretation of *Wonderland* and *Looking-Glass* as parables of the passage to adulthood. Many of the guests are, of course, young children, and as they sprint around this part of the maze their height makes it a lot harder for them to get any sense of the layout; they are far more likely to feel genuinely lost, and some of them do look bewildered. I saw a boy of around five years old almost in tears when he opened a little door in the hedge—a device from earlier in the film, rather than the Tulgey Wood—and found another door behind it. In a way, finding a route through the maze on their own, and dealing with the surprising, illogical twists it faces them with—with the treats of various tableaux along the way, and the ultimate prize of the view from the castle at the end—is a small-scale rite of passage for young visitors.

More obviously, we can note that though no mazes feature in Carroll's books, they crop up repeatedly in adaptations and elaborations from *Alice*. There is a knot garden in *Automated Alice*, and a Llabyrinth in *Alice Through The Needle's Eye*; Nick Willing's Alice makes her way through a maze to reach the Mock Turtle and Gryphon, and American McGee's Alice faces the Majestic Maze. One detail in particular provides a very striking link between Adair's novel and the Curious Labyrinth. In *Needle's Eye*, Alice encounters signposts in the maze directing her "THIS WAY? OR THAT WAY?" with two arrows in opposite directions; at the next fork is a sign directing her "HITHER" and "THITHER".[6] The first stage of Disney's labyrinth opens onto a clearing dotted with signs: "WHICH WAY", "THAT WAY", "UP", "DOWN", "YONDER", and "HITHER". Adair's book predates the Paris park, but not the 1951 film from which these signs are taken; it seems hard to avoid the possibility that he drew inspiration for this detail from Disney's version, the *Alice* that purists may turn up their noses at but can never fully turn their backs on.

The maze décor faithfully replicates Disney stalwart Mary Blair's designs for the film; hedges give way to fiberglass faux-stone walls in pastel shades of dusky pink and powder blue, and the hedgerow, the only feature which looks and feels genuinely organic, sprouts giant curlicued leaves of mauve and violet, custard yellow, and burnt orange. The leaves provide a branding and continuity across the Atlantic to the other Disney Alices—they crop up at both the California and Florida Mad Tea Parties, and are dotted around the dark ride. The maze opens into a series of picturesque clearings along the way, providing rewards for successful navigation much as a game provides cut-scenes, and allows the player to relax: first the Caterpillar's lair, where he puffs smoke, then a scene with Card Gardeners frozen on each other's shoulders. A sign at each location points out that this is an ideal place for "La Belle Photo / Photo Stop", guiding the visitor's engagement with the attraction and emphasizing that this is a resting place before further adventure. Again, children in particular are encouraged to pose with the tableau, taking Alice's role alongside the Caterpillar and Cards.

An entire sunken section—a set of concentric hedge circles—is given over to the Caucus-Race, where a Pelican, Parrot, and Toucan are positioned at various points on the spiral, and the Dodo mounts a blue rock in the centre. This area has the added feature of leaping water; jets that arc in cheeky bursts from one fountain to another. On my visits, the Caucus-Race was full of teenagers shoving as they ran to the centre and pushed the Dodo round on his revolving perch, grabbing at the water or trying to catch it in their mouths. A handful of vaguely Gothic girls sulked about wearing studded leather wristbands and Nirvana t-shirts, looking like they'd be happier playing the PC game.

Beyond the Card Gardener "Belle Photo" stop, the labyrinth divides into Cheshire Cat Walk, a calm little garden of low, faux-stone walls and wrought gates with heart designs, and Queen of Hearts Maze. A model Cat grins as he holds a sign, "May Be Difficult. You Could Lose Your

Head!" and nearby another Cat appears, his notice asking "This Way Or That? Par Ici Ou Par Là?" The sense of progression to the Queen of Hearts' stronghold, with her marked territory around it as a last defence, also has some parallels with the McGee *Alice*. This maze has high hedge-walls, some of them twined with fabric ivy leaves, and it holds surprises that could scare young children: Card Guards pop up from around corners, and the Queen herself rises from behind a barrier, roaring and looming over the visitor with the help of hidden hydraulics. Some guests, perhaps the rebellious teens, have shown signs of resistance: the Queen is noticeably battered, and someone has thrown popcorn into her open mouth.

The Queen's castle, too, will seem familiar to afficionados of McGee's game; in its general air of consistent design, with the Queen's motif recurring through all the décor, and in specifics such as the subtle scarlet heart and crown worked into the entrance floor tiles and the glowing heart-shaped lamps on the staircase wall. There is an eerily organic feeling about the place; not so explicit as McGee's "Queensland" levels, where the walls are made of living tissue, but the bulbous bricks of internal-organ colours and the dark red of the staircase do give a sense that the castle embodies the Queen herself. Of course, any link between the design of the attraction and of McGee's game implies a debt on McGee's part, rather than Disney's; and I don't believe the similarities are all in my imagination: although the game was meant to surprise players used to the Disney *Alice*, to define your product against something means you have to study it and know it well.

The exit to Alice's Curious Labyrinth cleverly guides the visitor again: below the word "Sortie" is a large caption, "Unbirthday Party", with the Hatter and Hare's faces on either side. As we leave this attraction, we are given a heavy hint that our next stop must be the Alice ride across the path; or, rather, and even more cleverly, the snack shop on the way to it. The Mad Tea Party at the Paris park is behind March Hare Refresh-ments, a little thatched-roof cottage that looks rather like the house in Harry Harris's film, and is also very similar to the Hare's cottage in Brinsley LeFanu's illustration of 1907.[7] In fact, this detail is present in Carroll's original, though rarely picked up in pictures: Alice knows she is heading towards the Hare's house because "the roof was thatched with fur."[8] The refreshments were closed during my visit, although as they only sold Kit-Kats and Lion Bars this seemed no great loss; in another interesting case of "resistance", the roof and derelict upper floor had been appropriated by sparrows, who were putting the thatch to their own uses.

The music, which constantly surrounds the Disney visitor, providing a shifting soundtrack to the exploration, has effectively segued from "Caucus-Race" to "March of the Cards" in the Queen of Hearts' Maze, and the speakers are now playing "The Unbirthday Song" on a loop. It is striking that this concept, only one of Humpty Dumpty's many conceits, has become such an important part of the Disney *Alice*: it dominates the Tea Party scene in the film, and now jingles away nonstop in the background as visitors line up for the ride. The experience of sitting in the spinning tea cups themselves has little to do with either the book or the film of *Alice*—far less than the Labyrinth, which actually attempts to simulate part of Alice's journey—and aspects of it, like the cod-Japanese lanterns, have no obvious link to Disney's original, let alone Carroll's.

I began asking myself where Carroll remained in, or under, all of this spectacle: was this "Alice" anything remotely to do with the book he wrote in the early 1860s? In terms of characterization, the ride and maze arguably retain some of what Carroll intended. The Horn Ducks and Hammer Bird would have been alien to him, but the Cat still pops up offering sardonic advice, the Queen is still a threatening menace, and the King, who appears as a tiny figure on a castle turret, is still a silly, mild-mannered monarch. The Hare's cottage, as noted, is "authentic" to Carroll's description—accidentally or not—and the Dormouse, who lifts his head occasionally from a giant teapot, on a cloud of steam, is bleary-eyed and dreamy; adult visitors familiar with the 1960s readings may well see a suggestion of being stoned in his blissed-out, cross-eyed expression. The tea cups are a Disney icon now; while they provide the recurring image of "Alice" rides across Europe and the US, featuring in three parks, the concept is almost entirely divorced from anything in Carroll.

Perhaps most noticeable was the absence of Alice. Carroll's heroine and the centre of both stories—so important that he made her name the first word of *Wonderland*—is far less important to the Disneyland Paris experience than are the Cat, the Queen, and particularly the Hatter and Hare. Perhaps the latter pair provide an appropriate zaniness and wacky fun, whereas the Kathryn Beaumont Alice, with her very proper accent and contempt for Mad Tea Parties as silly nonsense, might be a bit of a wet blanket if she was given a greater presence in the attraction design. To stay true to her character in the film, after all, the Labyrinth would have to include a clearing where visitors sit and weep, with these mournful lyrics piping through the speakers:

> I give myself very good advice . . . but I very seldom follow it . . .
> I went along my merry way and I never stopped to reason
> I should have known there'd be a price to pay . . . some day . . .

However, I made it my business for the remaining three days of my visit to track down Alice herself. At the Main Street Town Hall, I asked a "cast member", whose badge showed he spoke five languages, if I could find out where specific characters would be making guest appearances. Did I mean anyone in particular? Yes, Alice in Wonderland. "Oh, *Aleees*," he repeated with some amusement, turning to a colleague and conferring, as if this was something they were rarely asked. They consulted a rota that looked like an employee cleaning chart. "No, she doesn't seem to be booked for anything this morning. It might change this afternoon or tomorrow." I sensed he was bluffing, letting me down gently, and he offered further consolation. "The princesses are meeting and greeting this morning, with their princes! And Snow White will be accompanied by the *sept nains*."

Alice was not present at the Princesses' Parade that afternoon at 4 P.M., but she got a mention. The song, again on a loop as Snow White, Cinderella, Sleeping Beauty, Jasmine, Belle, and Ariel toured Main Street in giant themed floats, exulted that it was a "Disney kind of day" and invited the listener to "take my hand . . . just like Alice in Wonderland . . . it's magic!" Again, I couldn't help thinking how deeply below all this song-and-dance Carroll and his creation were buried. Did whoever wrote those lyrics spare a thought for the 1865 book when they came up with that line, or were they only looking for a rhyme and a reference to part of the Disney canon?

Alice makes a cameo in the picture books available in Main Street shops, although here her relegated position in the Disneyland mythos is even more apparent. The *Classic Stories* version of *Alice in Wonderland* achieves something quite bizarre, along the lines of what *Rosencrantz and Guildenstern* does to *Hamlet*: it takes a major character and makes her minor. The book tells the story of the Tea Party, with the Hatter and Hare as main protagonists, and has Alice turning up as an interesting event in their lives, then leaving and letting them continue with their fun. Further artifacts like cups and towels emphasise her role in the canon, showing her as a small figure alongside Snow White or Winnie-the-Pooh; a postcard depicting her on the spinning tea cups supports my theory that it is the visitor who effectively takes Alice's place on the ride and in the maze.

"Are any characters from *Alice* around today?" I am in the Town Hall, asking a rosy-cheeked woman. She shakes her head, apologetic. "She won't be walking around, but she will be in the parade." The parade? "Yes, the 4 P.M. parade. The best place to watch it is outside the rail station, just here." She's so keen to find some way of helping me out that I almost feel bad about protesting, but these cast members keep trying to fob me off. "But that's the Princesses' Parade," I point out, "she won't be in that." "She is sometimes . . . we never know who'll be in the parade." This is a blatant lie—there is no way the parade, a precision-choreographed affair, could include random guest stars turning up on the day—but her approach to keeping visitors happy clearly involves raising their hopes and having them disappointed later, rather than breaking the news to me now. Alice is not in the parade, although I watch it all the way through again, in the rain.

Further Alice-spotting found her dotted about—appearing for a second in a 2003 cartoon called *The House of Mouse*, in a promotion for the Princesses' Collection, and on a video box for the 1951 movie, now a "*grand classique—d'apres le merveilleux conte de Lewis Carroll*," with a karaoke version of "*La Chanson Non-anniversaire*." Images of Alice can also be found as part of the "heritage" discourse Disney cultivates—the memorabilia for collectors and the exhibits that celebrate the studio's history. A store selling expensive crystal models and porcelain figures stocked a framed picture of Kathryn Beaumont with Walt and a draft illustration of Alice beneath it; the Art of Animation building at the neighbouring Disney Studios also includes framed art from the 1951 film's pre-production. These drawings and paintings, attributed to David S. Hall, are far less cartoony than the film itself, and provide a bridge between Tenniel's detail and the bright simplicity of the animated cells. They are tucked away, though, in a gallery that children and many adults rush through on their way to the next sensation.

"Are there any characters from *Alice* around today?" "Yes," the man in the Town Hall tells me confidently, "the tiger and the rabbit from *Alice* are over by Winnie-The-Pooh's stage." The tiger and the rabbit turn out to be the Tweedle brothers, gooning around some children in wheelchairs. Alice in Disneyland was conspicuous by her absence.

Warrington and Daresbury, Cheshire: June 2002

Stuart Collingwood famously describes Daresbury Parsonage, the site of Carroll's birth, on January 27, 1832, and childhood to the age of eleven, as a place of "complete seclusion from the world", where "even the passing of a cart was a matter of great interest."[9] It is only a little more lively now, and so I stayed in Warrington, some seven miles away. The hotel owner, like most of the people I talked to during my journey, showed a genuine but faint interest when he heard about my work, and clearly felt some vague desire to help out. He was from the Wirral himself, he explained, so didn't know much about Carroll's origins here, but he thought there was a statue in the centre of town.

The tourist office in central Warrington is hidden in the middle of a huge and tatty indoor market: meat slabbed out on a stall next to multi-pack knickers and bags of birdseed, with stacks of canned pet food next to Gareth Gates posters. As I was given directions to Golden Square, I noticed a single Alice artifact in the window: a garish, sub-Tenniel attempt at the Tea Party scene, in the centre of a china plate. There is clearly an awareness of the Carroll connection to Warrington, although little effort has been made to capitalize on it.

Golden Square, near Hatter's Row, was a whirl of miniature fairground rides, including one with five gaudy tea cups—magenta, emerald, mustard yellow—spinning around a teapot. The cups and pot were studded with coloured bulbs, flashing in sequence, and a solitary little girl in a pink t-shirt gripped the rail inside her cup as she circled alone, her bunches swinging out behind her. There must have been some conscious decision behind hiring a poor-man's version of the Disney attraction for the square that holds the Alice statue; most probably, it suggests the power of the Disneyland iconography, the fact that "Alice" is now only a short associative leap away from "Spinning Cups Ride", that one seems naturally to suggest the other.

The statue itself is a few metres away, outside Clinton Cards, and is modeled on Tenniel's designs; the Hatter and Hare on one side of a table, gazing indulgently at the Dormouse slumped between them, and Alice rigidly upright at the end. The figures are made of a warm, red-grey stone; in the middle of the scattered crockery—all of it filled with rainwater—is a gold plate with an inscription.

The Mad Hatter's Tea Party
This sculpture was unveiled by
TRH THE PRINCE AND PRINCESS OF WALES
On the 30th May 1984
By Edwin Russell

That the couple are long separated, and the princess now dead, adds an additional layer of melancholy to this underwater dedication. None of Warrington's shaven-headed lads or its girls in white tops and capri pants seem likely to stop and peer at this gold plate; young mothers wheel pushchairs past the statue without a glance. However, even during my brief visit it was clear that Alice isn't entirely ignored. As I took photographs, a plump, tired-looking woman with a young son stopped for a moment. "Look," she told him, "there's the Dormouse, with his head on the table." They walked on.

Mad Hatter's Tea Party, Washington.

All Saints, the parish church of Daresbury, bears a royal blue sign in its graveyard—where tombs from 1823 and 2000 sit side by side—declaring it the "Birthplace of Lewis Carroll". It was drizzling when I visited; droplets hanging off the sign, giant puddles on the almost-silent roads, wet hedgerow. Daresbury Nuclear Laboratory, a couple of miles away, towered over fields of Friesians. I went through the village first; past the Ring O'Bells pub, which Charlie Lovett says would have been known to Carroll, and up a gentle hill to Daresbury County Primary School. The sign bears little painted figures, based on Tenniel—Alice with the flamingo, the White Rabbit, a Card Gardener, and the Tweedles—and a weathervane on the roof has Alice and the Rabbit rotating opposite the Hatter. I knocked on the school doors and after a while drew out a janitor; a wary young man with a gelled fringe and Liverpool accent. "Yeah, this was the school he went to," the man lied freely, and gave me the wrong directions towards Daresbury Parsonage.

Back at the church, I found the doors left trustingly unlocked. Miscellaneous merchandise, such as Daresbury tea towels and postcards of Carroll's Oxford, was left out on display with only a donation box to handle transactions. A room at the back, kitted out for Sunday School, has *Wonderland* and *Looking-Glass* posters on the door, and inside a series of shrines for Alice, meshed with Christian imagery. Below a table laid with a white cloth, a cross, and a candle is a little tableau made of a tartan blanket spread with tea things, jam tarts, biscuits, and a copy of *Little Women*; perhaps intended to represent the picnic that Alice's sister might have brought out to the riverbank. In the corner of the room, a large Alice doll walks out in front of a mirror into a patch of fake flowers; she is dressed according to Tenniel's illustrations, but her expression is blankly pretty, the face of a mass-produced plastic figure. A stuffed caterpillar sits on a cushion by the radiator. This is a low-budget, knocked-together equivalent of the Disney tableaux, or the Guildford statues I'll discuss later; homely, improvised from available items rather than specially made or designed.

The church's most celebrated feature is its stained-glass window showing Carroll and some of his characters around a Nativity scene; once more incorporating the author and his work, fittingly, into the Christian iconography of his faith. Installed in 1935 as the result of a campaign in Carroll's centenary year, 1932, it depicts the author kneeling piously in white clerical robes, his palms together in prayer. A menagerie of *Alice* characters pose below, lifted from the Tenniel pictures: the Rabbit, the Dodo and Bill, the Mock-Turtle, the Knave, the Cat, and the Queen. Alice herself stands next to Carroll, her hands clasped sadly. It might take a moment to realize what this picture actually represents; it seems a natural pairing, but it's actually quite uncanny. This is not Alice Liddell, but Alice in Wonderland, the fictional girl from the Tenniel illustrations—in a green dress with no apron, but with her characteristic long blonde hair, stockings and shoes, and wearing her usual prim, moody expression. Carroll's face is taken from a photograph; Alice's from a Tenniel illustration. Real and imaginary, creator and character, have been placed next to each other as if they existed on the same level—as if Carroll was a mythical creature like Alice, which, as I suggested in the Introduction, is to some extent true.

A caption reads "In memory of Charles Lutwidge Dodgson (Lewis Carroll), author of *Alice in Wonderland*". The accompanying poem is from Carroll's "Christmas Greetings" of 1867:

> Lady dear, if Fairies may
> For a moment lay aside
> Cunning tricks and elvish play
> 'Tis at happy Christmas-tide.

Carroll and Alice stained glass, All Saints Church, Daresbury.

Again, Carroll's writing has been cleverly interlocked with the Christian imagery that the church, unsurprisingly, chooses to focus on in its celebration of Daresbury's most famous resident: the "Christmas Greetings" are used for their match with the Nativity scene and the birth of Christ. However, there is an interpretive strategy at work here that is just as deliberate in what it excludes and stresses as were the readings of *Alice* books as Freudian allegory or drug experiments. The anarchic, cruel, brutal, and amoral aspects of *Wonderland* have been pushed to one side here and held away, making the story seem uncomplicatedly innocent. There is even the suggestion that *Wonderland* serves as some kind of Christian parable—the main and minor characters are, after all, shown as witnesses to one of the most important events in the Bible. This is arguably a misrepresentation of the actual text, which parodies and burlesques pious verses like Isaac Watts's "The Sluggard" and "How Doth The Little Busy Bee"; the spirit of *Wonderland* is not always reverent by any means. At any rate, the stained glass certainly lifts Carroll and Alice safely away from the discourses about drugs, sex and paedophilia, "rescuing" the author and his work and presenting them as something exceptionally safe and wholesome, suitable for Sunday School.

The last entry in the guest book is two days before my visit, with an average of two comments per week—visitors from Japan, the United States, South Africa. On the sixth of June 2002, Olivia Marsh, the little girl who held the role of Miss Alice Llandudno, visited as part of her duties. On the eleventh of September 2001, there were two visitors to the church; they signed their names but made no comment.

At the vicarage across the road from All Saints, the Reverend David Felix was prepared for my question—he fetched me a photocopied map of the route to the parsonage site. It lies across the M6, hopelessly remote; without the map, I would have had no hope of finding it, and nobody would discover it by chance, as they might quite easily stumble across Alice's Shop in Oxford, the Rabbit Hole in Llandudno, or the statues of Guildford. I passed down narrow lanes, past empty fields. Two houses squatted in the distance; a post van passed, and ten minutes later, a tractor. The fence to the field itself was locked, and I had to climb a gate: kids who surely knew nothing of Lewis Carroll's birthplace had written on the wood, cryptic threats and promises. "Em is a fat slag." "Speedbird . . . f-train when will you stop." "Sophie Tyson, Gareth Hurley 2000."

The field was wet and empty apart from a few benches and two plaques, one so mud-spattered it was illegible. The other, half in English and half in Japanese, explains "at some time between 1856, when he took up photography, and 1883 when the house burned down, Lewis Carroll

Lewis Carroll's birthplace, Daresbury.

probably returned here to take this photograph of his birthplace." The photograph of the parsonage is also mounted in the church, with a far more specific date of 1860; in the careful, uncommitted notice at the site itself, you can hear the scholarly voice of Edward Wakeling or Morton Cohen. "If he had never written the *Alice* books, Charles Lutwidge Dodgson would have been remembered for his photographic work, particularly his use of the collodion process." The top of the plaque shows Alice flanked by Hatta and Haigha, and below it is a diagram showing the Parsonage layout: the location of the School Room, the Parlour, and the Shippon for 4 Cows. At the bottom right corner is a verse from Carroll's "Faces in the Fire", cited whenever his birthplace is discussed:

> An island farm, 'mid seas of corn,
> Swayed by the wandering breath of morn,
> The happy spot where I was born.

The diagram is a map of something that no longer exists, except in the form of what the vicar aptly called a "footprint": a ghost layout marked in brick on the grass, showing where the walls once stood. Weirdly, they don't correspond with what is shown on the plaque. Standing in the middle of a field in what seems the middle of nowhere, I tried to imagine the young Charles racing around what looked like a very small home for a large family, and could only visualize the cut-out silhouette of him as a child of eight, reproduced in Collingwood and Cohen; a two-dimensional shadow.

There has been very little effort to make this site—surely a landmark in literary Britain—into a more commercial venture. The Japanese translation suggests the significant groups of Carrollians who visit from that nation—a phenomenon brought to my attention by tourist guides and shopkeepers in Oxford and Guildford—but there are no merchandise shops, no refreshment stands, not even any signs on the road. Since 1974 there has been a stone pillar to mark this field out from the many identical fields surrounding it, and in the early 1990s the traces of the parsonage walls, the plaques and the benches were added. However, this is still a bleak spot, intended for the dedicated specialist. Perhaps the challenge of finding it, and the fact that it will probably be discovered standing empty, rather than with a group of tourists already clustered around the plaques, gives it a certain appeal to scholars and enables a more personal experience of connection with Carroll. It may have been the weather, but I was left cold.

Croft-on-Tees and Ripon, North Yorkshire: June 2002

Carroll and his family moved to Croft in 1843, installing themselves in the formidable, three-storied rectory; the father took over the parish church, St Peter's, and set about improving the environment, building a school, and repairing the church roof. Carroll himself celebrated their new home in the family magazine, *The Rectory Umbrella*, with a poem that, like the Daresbury verses, is a gift to biographers.

> Fair stands the ancient Rectory,
> The Rectory of Croft,
> The sun shines bright upon it,
> The breezes whisper soft.
> From all the house and garden
> Its inhabitants come forth,
> And muster in the road without,

The Rectory, Croft.

And pace in twos and threes about,
The children of the North.

The poem reminds us that the Dodgson family was a small army, totaling
eleven children—how many British families today can be grouped into

twos and threes?—and also that Carroll's origins were very far from Oxford. We have no recording of his voice, but the accents of his childhood homes in Daresbury and Croft are nothing like the contemporary intonations of South-East England that we might imagine him using.

St Peter's church—blocky and solid, and sitting in a garden of vivid greens—has a hand-written notice outside announcing the dates for communion and services in traditional, inked calligraphy. A newsletter in the doorway brings recent tragedy into this comfortably old-fashioned setting: "Where was God on September 11th? He was in the bravery of individuals." Across the road is Monkend Terrace, and a gateway leading up a leafy path into a private garden. This is, as a carved wooden sign on the pillar points out, "The Old Rectory", and without arranging permission from the owners, this is as far as you are meant to go. The garden is beautifully kept; the path leads to a courtyard of pink gravel and then to the house itself. Bushes and creepers spill around the front walls. The young Carroll illustrated his poem with a picture of a factory-sized establishment dotted with tens of windows; in fact, it only has fourteen on the façade, but it's still a formidable building. The back garden once housed Carroll's first model railway, and provided a lawn for the family croquet. I heard the approach of a gardener on a motorized lawnmower, and retreated; the rest of the grounds remained remote, only glimpsed, like the beautiful garden that Alice struggled to reach.

The bridge over the River Tees bears a plaque celebrating sixty years of Victoria's reign, in 1897—a year before Carroll's death, but he was long gone from Croft and would never have seen it. Teenagers were sitting in the shallows under the bridge arches, splashing, flirting, and swearing at each other. The sun was baking the stones and the water sparkled; apart from their echoing shouts, Croft was lazily quiet, stunned by heat. Only a few glimpses of the present day—a caravan site on the other side of the bridge, a working men's club—disturb the illusion of pastoral heritage, the sense of a pocket of the past. On the opposite bank to the church and rectory is a pub called the Comet, which shares its name with one of Carroll's many family magazines, running for six issues in 1848.[10]

Inside the pub a bookshelf held an odd second-hand collection: *A Town Like Alice*, *Kings and Queens of England*. By the bar was an A4 notice advertising a Mad Hatter's Tea Party with Bouncy Castle, Hair Wrapping, Tombola, and Prize for the Maddest Hat. There was little to link this poster explicitly with Carroll—the picture at the top showed a rabbit pulling a man from a topper—but like the Warrington tea cups, it must have clicked with someone, at some point, that the concept had a local

Bridge over the River Tees, Croft.

resonance. If tourism missed a trick at Daresbury, it entirely dropped the ball at Croft—there is barely any sign that this was Carroll's family home for twenty-five years. Lovett's guide reveals that St Peter's installed a plaque in 1972 and that two nearby streets are named "Lewis Close" and "Carroll Place"; hardly a grand memorial for such a major figure, although it could be considered that the lack of attention to Croft as a heritage site has left it relatively untouched. Much is the same as it was in the 1840s, and some of it the same as it was in the 1500s. Back at the Chequers Inn in Dalton-on-Tees, I told Barry Dowson, the landlord, about my visit. "That sounds like Croft," he offered drily. "Good at doing nothing at all."

Carroll's father became a Canon of Ripon Cathedral in 1852; he subsequently spent thirteen weeks a year in the city, traveling up with the rest of his family in the first days of January. Carroll himself was already living in Oxford by this point, and so his visits to Ripon were shorter—a couple of weeks in January, some Easter holidays—but according to Lovett, it was here that he "had his first photographs taken . . . met some of his earliest child-friends [and] began a register of his correspondence."[11] Ironically, given the brevity of his residence here, Ripon makes far more of its Carroll connection than does Croft. I strolled around the cathedral interior with a white-haired guide in royal blue robes; the Dymo lettering on his badge told me he was Dr R. Geldart. "I think we have a very good Lewis Carroll link . . . don't you?" he enthused. "After all, he was romping around here for many years, he must have seen the rabbit . . . what did you think of that?"

"The rabbit" is one of Ripon's greatest claims to Carrollian fame, according to the cathedral guides; tucked away on the underside of a wooden chair, it is a carved misericord from the late fifteenth century that supposedly depicts that animal running down a hole. In fact, the creature disappearing down the tunnel is showing nothing but its rear end, and its companion looks more like a hippo with long ears than anything from *Alice*, although there is unmistakably a kind of Gryphon chasing them. The fact is, of course, that there are a lot of animals and mythical creatures in the *Alice* books, and they can be found in a great number of rural fields or churches. Cohen makes much out of the fact that Daresbury was the home of "the White Rabbit, the animals in the Caucus-Race, the Caterpillar, the garden of flowers, and much more", claiming that they "owe their origin" to Carroll's birthplace.[12] However, it was surely not necessary for the adult Carroll in Oxford to dredge his memories of the parsonage in order to dream up a Mouse or a Pigeon for his story.

If we look with an eye to finding Carrollian characters, they can be imagined from very vague sources. There is a "carved cat which appears to be smiling" in St Peter's church,[13] but the animal could just as readily be sourced to the carved wooden lions that sat on the Liddells' "Lexicon Staircase", or, as Gardner suggests, to a traditional cat-shaped cheese, or the waning of the moon.[14] Dr Geldart had to point out the Ripon Cathedral "Cheshire Cat", which sits with what the guide booklet describes as the "Queen of Hearts" up on the south trancept; it looked like a face, not an especially cheerful face and not much like a cat face. I showed him the booklet's illustration of another misericord, a pig with bagpipes. "What's that meant to be, then?" he asked. Something from the *Hunting of the Snark*, I told him; the pig blowing a trumpet from one of the illustrations. "Oh well," he concluded, "I don't know if I believe that one. Some of these are a bit of a stretch, aren't they?"

Llandudno, North Wales: June 2002

Henry and Lorina Liddell took their honeymoon in North Wales in 1846, and in 1859 they returned to the area for a holiday, visiting the nascent resort of Llandudno for the first time. During Easter 1861 they brought the entire family and entourage—five children, Miss Prickett, a footman, a lady's maid, a nurse, and nursery-maid—to stay in Llandudno's Tudno Villa hotel. "It was during this visit," writes historian Michael Senior, "that the Dean conceived the idea of building himself a house in the area, and began to seek a site."[15] Choosing an "off-the-peg" design from an architect's window in town, Dean Liddell picked a location on the west shore for his family's holiday home, which was to be called Penmorfa. In August 1862 it was complete, and we know that Alice, her mother and sisters were staying there during Christmas of that year.

Whether Carroll ever visited them—whether he visited once, or many times, whether his visits could conceivably have inspired *Wonderland* and whether he could have written the book there—takes up the entirety of Senior's short but densely argued work, helpfully titled *Did Lewis Carroll Visit Llandudno?* He shows that biographers and journalists have, as is the case with many incidents in Carroll's life, disagreed for decades on the subject, yet often based their views on received wisdom that nobody thought to check, on mistakes that were repeated until they became gospel, and on reports of primary evidence rather than on the evidence itself.

The theory that Carroll not only stayed in the town, but that his walks with Alice on the shores of Llandudno—rather than the boat trips down the Isis—were the source of *Alice's Adventures in Wonderland* seems to have passed from local rumour to public assertion in 1933, when a county court registrar named James J. Marks conveniently recalled a conversation from 1907 with the artist Sir William Richmond. Sir William had supposedly chatted with Marks about his painting "The Three Graces", which depicts the Liddell sisters in front of Llandudno's Great Orme cliffs. He vividly remembered Lewis Carroll staying at Penmorfa while the girls sat for the painting; indeed, he saw the author writing *Alice in Wonderland* and in the evenings he would read to them from the work in progress.

From this evidence—hearsay based on a twenty-five-year-old memory of an old man's eager fancy—Llandudno built itself a literary heritage. In May 1933, the *Llandudno Advertiser* published "Incontrovertible Evidence . . . *Alice* was Written in Llandudno". In September 1933, David Lloyd George unveiled a statue of the White Rabbit outside Penmorfa, announcing

> [W]e are met to commemorate the rambles on these beautiful sands of a famous author with a child, rambles which inspired him to write one of the immoral books . . . it was a holiday at Llandudno that did this. Lewis Carroll had the Llandudno air to stimulate his thoughts and the mountains to elevate him and he had a little child to lead him.[16]

Senior tracks the circulation and evolution of myths and facts, careless errors and wishful thinking, through the biographies of Florence Becker Lennon, Alexander Taylor, Derek Hudson, Anne Clark, Michael Bakewell, Morton Cohen, and Karoline Leach. The scholars tend to come down against the idea that Carroll ever stayed there, despite the town's stubborn, and understandable, adherence to the theory: particularly dogmatic is Michael Bakewell, who writes, "the one person who did not visit was Charles Lutwidge Dodgson. This is rather a tragedy for a town which has always prided itself on its association with Lewis Carroll."[17]

Senior's study comes to a surprising eleventh-hour conclusion that Carroll did in fact come to Llandudno. His decision lies in a letter from Alice Hargreaves to her son Caryl, written in 1933. She tells him, "Dodgson can't have been at Llandudno much before 1862—because we were not there." With this meager first-hand evidence as his most reliable clue, Senior reasons "the answer . . . clearly implies that he *did* come. At the very least it cannot be construed as saying that he didn't."[18] Alice's letter was, he assumes, connected with correspondence from Llandudno; the organizers wanting to verify whether Carroll really had been at Penmorfa before they etched it into white marble below the Rabbit statue.

> She did not, it is now clear, advise her son to tell them that Dodgson had never been there. She was diligent in answering the questions he put to her and "never" forms no part, or implication, of her reply. I therefore conclude, on the basis of Alice's final evidence, and of all of what we now know lies behind it, that Lewis Carroll did visit Llandudno. It is disappointing not to know more about this—but we never will. I do not think that "one day" more will be revealed. I think that is the end of the matter . . . [19]

If we accept Senior's argument, then the notion that Lewis Carroll was in Llandudno at some point rests only on the fact that Alice Hargreaves did not explicitly deny it. This may not be enough for some readers. Hargreaves was eighty at the time, and we have already seen that her recollections of a then-distant childhood with Carroll are not especially useful: her *New York Times* report of 1932 seems to be intended simply to confirm and enhance the "golden afternoon" story, giving people what they want, rather than rocking the boat. Being "Alice" again was giving her new attention and respect in the last years of her life. She was, perhaps, more likely to dodge a straight answer and let Llandudno build its statue outside the home she fondly remembered, rather than flatly deny that he had ever visited, and put an end to all their celebrations. Be that as it may, Llandudno continues to believe the story it has cherished since at least 1933: remarkably, I found it promoting a connection with Alice and Carroll far more visibly than Croft or Daresbury did, and offering more Alice tourist attractions than anywhere outside Oxford.

Llandudno's heritage as a Victorian resort is immediately visible in the architecture of the seafront hotels—the town holds a sense of history very near the surface, unforced and apparently barely changed since the Liddells's visits, although the 1960s and 1970s clearly added some ugly extensions and what would then have been snazzily modern signage. Ironically, the more recent developments—boxy bar annexes, neon fittings—now seem far more dated than the spindly Victorian stylings, the fussy ornamental railings, the fragile-looking facades. This, of course, is a specifically Welsh Victorian design, and the hotel names—"The Sound of the Sea", "The Crest of the Wave", "The Hydro" and "The Grand"—are bilingual, with translations underneath.

The tourist information office has a range of *Alice* books, from the populist and kid-oriented to the adult and almost academic: a Ladybird version, a Disney spin-off, Gardner's *Annotated Alice*, and Stephanie Lovett Stoffel's *Lewis Carroll in Wonderland*. Oddly, this little outpost of Carrolliana also has a range of products from the British Library in London; designed around the *Under Ground* illustrations rather than the more familiar Tenniel pictures, they include address books, notebooks, and "Drink Me" cups. The use of Carroll's original drawings may be intended to stress the Library's role in holding archival documents, including the *Under Ground* manuscript, but I wondered how Carroll would feel, knowing that his technically amateurish sketches were still being circulated so widely; he would surely be surprised, but knowing that his artistic skills never lived up to his ambitions, wouldn't he perhaps be ashamed?

The town's main Alice attraction—I had been sent promotional leaflets for it with my Society material, so it's more than just a local feature—is the Rabbit Hole, on Trinity Square. "An authentic Wonderland rabbit hole has been created in Llandudno by Muriel and Murray Ratcliffe," chatters the leaflet, "and since it was opened in 1987, many thousands of enthralled visitors, provided with an individual stereo recording . . . have re-lived the story, walking through a warren of beautiful life-scenes. It's an ideal indoor venue. IT NEVER RAINS IN WONDERLAND!" I didn't realize until I was staying in Llandudno, during two days of summer downpour, how apposite these last lines were. Aside from this wry recommendation of the Rabbit Hole as a shelter from the weather, it's interesting that the attraction's selling spiel sounds rather Victorian itself. The attempts to make a Walkman seem exciting by calling it an "individual stereo recording", and to dress up homemade dioramas as "beautiful life-scenes", are a little reminiscent of the notices at the 1861 Juvenile Fete for "Cosmoramic Views", "Crystal-ophonic and Musical Rocks", and a "Myriad of Living Wonders."[20]

A teenage girl, probably working at the Rabbit Hole during college holidays, hands me my individual stereo recording. It explains, with no mention of the Llandudno origin theory, that *Wonderland* was written for Alice Liddell—which it pronounces wrongly, with the stress on the second syllable—and tells me "enter the Rabbit Hole when you hear the bell ring." Each life-scene, accompanied by a brief dramatic reading from the book, corresponds roughly to a chapter of *Wonderland*, and also has a curious fit with the McGee game; first the Hall of Doors, then the Pool of Tears. A blonde doll of Alice, looking rather like a shop window dummy from the Little Misses section of a chain store, poses among swathes of cloth, dried plants, strings of fairy bulbs, and handmade models of the secondary characters.

The Duchess is on the slim side, but otherwise the designs have clearly been modeled on Tenniel's pictures; a Hatter with the 10/6 label slowly raising and lowering his slice of bread, a moody blue Caterpillar. Like many film adaptations, the Rabbit Hole's narrative dips into *Looking-Glass* at one point, perhaps because it doesn't want to omit the Tweedles: on the soundtrack, they have country bumpkin, Yorkshire accents. The Cheshire Cat is a huge stuffed head mounted on a fake tree; the Gardeners tableau has some unfortunate discrepancies of scale, with miniature porcelain models of cards next to larger ones. This is clearly not a dark ride on the Disney level, but a creation on a modest budget, improvised from available materials; again, it's a little reminiscent of the Victorian trend for spectacles that didn't quite live up to their billing, like the "Fejee Mermaid" made from a sewn-together fish and monkey.[21]

The adjoining shop stocks porcelain figures, tea sets, and, for £38 apiece, Alice dresses. On the walls are montages of photographs showing children wearing these frocks: all of them female, which doesn't entirely go without saying, and most of them blondes of junior school age, although the display also features a baby, a Chinese girl, and a fourteen-year-old. Priority goes to the Llandudno Alices, the winners of an annual competition that I learned about when I met the then-incumbent in Westminster Abbey during May 2002; Laura Whitworth had been appointed by an adult panel based not just on her appearance but her ability to answer back intelligently in the manner of the original, and her costume had been provided by Muriel at the Rabbit Hole. As we saw, her successor, Olivia Marsh, had taken over the duties and visited Daresbury in June.

This army of near-identical Alices indicates, above all, that Carroll's most famous books still have a genuine appeal to young readers. Visitors to the Rabbit Hole clearly want to pose with the dioramas and dress up as the main character; immune to all the less savoury, or more sophisticated, discourses around Carroll, the *Alice* books are still promoted here as enduring classics, and they apparently touch a note with children who must have been born in the early 1990s, almost a century after the author's death. *Alice*, in this Llandudno stronghold at least, has escaped the taint of the paedophile rumours, but equally, is far more than just a museum piece, a nostalgic Victorian artifact. The diorama models may be creaky in their animation, but something about *Alice* is clearly still vibrant and alive for the young visitors who have their pictures taken in front of them. The pleasures of meeting funny characters, of watching adults in costume being rude or silly, of rapid size switches and location shifts, seem to be as attractive to ten-year-olds of 2002 as they were to the Liddell girls on the golden afternoon.

The All Seasons Hotel is not the only establishment in town with an Alice theme—the St Tudno Hotel, formerly the Tudno Villa, boasts a Lorina Room and a Rhoda Junior Suite, with the Alice Suite topping the rank at £140 per person per night—but it is the only one advertised as featuring a Looking-Glass Lounge. Searching for this promising-sounding attraction took me up to Happy Valley, an 1860s development with a reconstructed Victorian camera obscura and a 1960s cablecar system. From 1955 until 1966, when rain and wind had damaged the models beyond repair, the Valley was home to the *Alice in Wonderland* Illuminated Garden, "a series of tableaux with some of the larger models illuminated from within and others floodlit".[22] A relaunched *Wonderland* Trail, with nine wooden sculptures, was promised for 2002, but the overcast sky and drizzle had reduced Happy Valley to gloom by mid-afternoon, and I had no heart to search for it.[23]

"This is all down to the previous owner," explained Ms Carpenter, the tall, tanned woman on reception at the All Seasons. Her mum and dad had bought the hotel from a Mrs Yates two years ago, and the Alice theming—The Mad Hatter Restaurant, as well as the Looking-Glass Lounge—was there when they moved in. She showed me both rooms. The Mad Hatter Restaurant had an *Alice* duvet cover, with sub-Tenniel illustrations badly printed and gaudily coloured, mounted on one wall. The Looking-Glass Lounge displayed an identical duvet cover, with the distinction that the walls were hung with half a dozen mirrors. They didn't seem to deserve the grand signs outside each room announcing the *Alice* connection, and my disillusionment must have shown. "We can't get rid

The Gogarth Abbey Hotel/Penmorfa, Llandudna.

of it because it's advertised on the Web site," my guide explained. Why couldn't they get rid of the Web site? "She had three of them and we can't find out who's hosting it." As I dutifully took photos of the duvets, Miss Carpenter confessed her scepticism about the previous owner. "She wasn't really into all this . . . she just called the rooms that, but she wasn't really into it." What, was she just doing it as a tourist moneyspinner? "Something like that . . . I don't think she even read the books."

The Gogarth Abbey Hotel[24] stands isolated on the lonely seafront with the Great Orme cliffs rising palely behind it; it looks beached, a Gothic monster. The Liddells' holiday home is identifiable at the centre, with its tower and spiked roof, but the building around it has expanded, as if diseased and spawning extensions or absorbing the surrounding houses. In fact, both are true: according to Ivor Wynne Jones, when Penmorfa lost its name at the end of the nineteenth century and became a hotel, it sucked in two neighbouring houses to the south—adding a "linking structure"—and in the 1930s it spread further north with a new dining room. In November 2002 the link to the adjoining houses was severely damaged by fire, but Penmorfa itself, the heart of the complex, remained

331

intact: the new manager, Shelton Fernando, is, as I mentioned in the previous chapter, keen to cooperate with the Society to enhance the Alice connection. His plans include a Pool of Tears indoor swimming pool and a five-foot statue of Alice herself in the car park.[25]

I visited before the fire and the subsequent redevelopment, and the only statue was the White Rabbit unveiled by Lloyd George in 1933, sited perhaps a hundred metres away from the hotel by a shallow rectangular pool. Persistent vandalism led to the decision during the 1990s to protect it in a spherical cage; the incongruous combination of white marble and curved metal bars make the Rabbit look ludicrous, like a creature in a science fiction teleporter. Yet it also seems sad, especially in the rain, with the roar of waves merging with the swoosh of passing traffic on the wet road; it has become a captured animal, imprisoned for its own protection, but not well-enough protected. Despite the cage, someone has managed to burn its ears—they are disfigured, scorched orange. The inscription beneath is, depending on your point of view, anything from an absurd lie to an exaggeration, or plain wish fulfillment: as if etching it in marble would make it true.

> On this very shore
> During happy rambles with
> Little Alice Liddell
> LEWIS CARROLL
> Was inspired to write that
> Literary treasure
> ALICE IN WONDERLAND
> Which has charmed children
> For generations.

Through a combination of the grim weather, the menacing architecture, the foreboding natural environment, the defacement of the statue, and the ill-conceived attempts to prevent further damage, this place does suggest a sinister aspect to the Alice mythos. You can imagine her up in a little room of Penmorfa, in gales, looking out on the bleak beach as the wind makes the walls sway and creak; imagine what sadism led someone to reach into the Rabbit's cage and burn his ears, to actively try and ruin this old nostalgic icon. I found myself thinking again about McGee's PC game, of a return to Wonderland to find innocence corrupted and old friends tortured. The sign by the Rabbit cage promises this is the home of the REAL ALICE: YR ALICE GO IAWN.

White Rabbit Statue, Llandudna.

Salter's Boat Yard, Oxford.

Oxford: July 2002

On the fourth of July 2002, exactly one hundred and forty years after
Carroll told the story of *Wonderland* in the boat up to Godstow, I stayed
at the Head of the River pub on Folly Bridge, opposite Salter's Boat Yard.
The pub is decorated with boat race paraphernalia and nineteenth-century
signage and etchings—Birds' Blancmange, Robin Cigarettes The Popular
Brand; from my third floor room I could look out directly across the river
to the place where Carroll hired his vessel and set off with Duckworth
and the three girls. The boathouse is the same three-storey building Carroll
would have known, now slightly decrepit and apparently half-deserted;
some of it is taken up by flats, and Hart Publishing has its offices up one
flight of stairs, but some of the windows were always dark and the interiors
beyond looked derelict. A sign for Salter Bros advertises them as Passenger
Launches, Boat Builders and Party Hire, *www.salterbros.fsnet.co.uk:* it's odd
to see the name Carroll knew underlined with an internet address. Behind
the boathouse, taller and wider than the older building, is the cream brick
and emerald glass of the Hertford College Graduate Centre, built in 2000.

To me, of course, the significance of the date was obvious, and *Alice* overshadowed everything I saw: the swans punting along the Isis put me in mind of the "Swan Pie and Greens" chapter in *Through the Needle's Eye*, the "Opium Den" restaurant recalled Carroll's laudanum dream at the end of *Still She Haunts Me*. I was only half-expecting to overhear anyone else mentioning the 140th anniversary, on the site of the story's telling, and so was only mildly disappointed when the conversations around me focused on the difficulties in getting tickets for Wimbledon, the advantages of seeming gay to attract women, and whether Madonna had auditioned for the original *Fame*. I took a £10 tour on a Salter Bros boat; he was only going one way, the wrong way, downstream. The water was the deep, turtle-soup green I had seen in *Dreamchild*. A man dressed as Ali G, in a yellow boiler suit, zoomed past in a speedboat; his jacket boasted "Muff Daddy".

I was expecting some recognition of the anniversary in Alice's Shop, the fifteenth century establishment that Tenniel immortalized as the Sheep Shop. It sells a range of miscellaneous *Alice* merchandise that for the most part rises above pointless tat and in some cases is fittingly based on props from the books themselves: wooden key rings, jumbo magnets, chess sets, tiles of the Daresbury stained glass, Victorian masks, note cards, kaleidoscopes, boxes of tea, porcelain figures, card games, thimbles. The shop is small and the atmosphere is quiet, polite. The Japanese woman behind the counter was pleasant but hesitant and vague. Did she know it was one hundred and forty years since the boat trip? She smiled blankly. I asked if there were any events on. "Well, the museum has an Alice exhibition . . . they're showing Alice Liddell's things from the auction a year or so ago." She gave me the shop's business card, which was half in Japanese and featured the illustrations from the 2001 Royal Shakespeare Company production of *Alice*. "That version was good for people who like Carroll," the shopkeeper mused. The reviews said it was dull, I suggested. "Well . . . it's not for children of today, so much."

Two doors up, past Reservoir Books, is the Alice Tea Shop, a gallery and old-fashioned café; or at least, it was. On my return visit exactly a year later, I found that the Tea Shop had been relegated to a little, three-table affair, with its original location converted into Alice's Shop Too. Sadly, this move seems to have been dictated entirely by commercial prospects. What was a charming and old-fashioned place, hung with original artwork and patronised by elderly women sitting down for a cake and cuppa, is now crammed with spin-offs not just from *Alice* but *Winnie-the-Pooh*, *Harry Potter*, and *Peter Rabbit*, alongside tourist gear from Oxford University. The shop owners have built up their own line of merchandise

Alice's Shop, Oxford.

such as t-shirts and bags; I heard the manager describing his clientele as mainly over-twenties and largely style-conscious Japanese, people who would admire the fact that the bags had been featured in *Vogue*. Of course, business people can hardly be blamed for wanting to make money, but the sacrifice of the full-sized tea shop and the compromising of any Alice identity through the inclusion of barely-related products from other children's books seems regrettable.

At the Museum of Oxford reception desk, a middle-aged woman warned me that the Alice things they bought at auction only form a small part of the display. You also have to go a long way to find them; down corridors, up stairs and back centuries, through the origins of the city and hundreds of years of its history. Finally a sign asked, "Are you looking for Alice?" and I found the little room devoted to her memorabilia. That is, to Alice Liddell and Alice in Wonderland's artifacts, because the two are linked throughout the exhibition. Enlarged Tenniel illustrations, with slightly questionable information beneath—that Mary Hilton Badcock was the model, for instance—stand alongside items that belonged to Alice when she was Mrs Hargreaves. A case holds her letters as head of the

Helpers of Wonderland charity—the paper bears the legend "The Real Alice"—and as patron of the Lewis Carroll Memorial Fund.

Behind glass is her brown taffeta and velvet dress, from around 1875, showing her to be approximately five foot five and very slight in build; alongside it are her parasol and Chantilly lace fan. Nearby we find her possessions from decades later: a Red Cross service medal from World War I, a silver key from 1927. Some of them recall props from *Wonderland*, of course—like the cards and thimble in the Alice Shop—but these items span over fifty years of the woman's life. The connection exists only in the mind of the Carroll fan, although the links are heavily suggested by whoever curated this exhibition and interspersed Alice Hargreaves's auctioned items with miscellany like an 1860 top hat marked 10/6. Other objects, such as the 1892 *Looking-Glass* toffee tin and Lyons Hatter tin, or the *Wonderland* stamp case, are a reminder that Carroll wasn't averse to commercial spin-offs. There are only a few of his own possessions here— like his pocket-watch that sits next to hers—and they are hidden among Alice's belongings. The little room was silent on my visit; I was there alone for half an hour.

I made a detour to the Oxford Experience—an audiovisual tour through the city's past whose nod to Carroll involves an Alice model hurtling through the air after the Rabbit, against a backdrop of huge pages from *Wonderland*—and joined the tour of Christ Church, Carroll's home from 1851 until his death. I found myself trailing after some fifty Japanese students in grey skirts and caps, guided by custodians in black bowler hats. In the courtyard of Tom Quad, visitors are forbidden to wander off the path towards the Lower Common Room—just below what used to be Carroll's quarters—or around the central pond. "Are you a member of this University, sir?" came the sharp rebuke from a bowler hat as I tried to retrace what must have been a daily stroll for Carroll. Fortunately, the official route took me past the Deanery door, and the arch that featured in Tenniel's illustration of Queen Alice knocking at the banquet hall.

Christ Church has its own dining hall, with waiters in ties and a portrait of Henry Liddell above the door; Carroll ate here regularly. It looks grand, but the menu was modest: baked potatoes and filling, lamb casserole, vegetable bolognaise. The posters on the walls outside ignored the Carroll connection and instead promoted its links with Hogwarts School in the *Harry Potter* films. Again, there was no entry for the layperson, and we trooped via the shop—where shelves of *Potter* books outnumbered the *Alice* editions and Carroll diaries—into the cathedral, where a young man was giving out guides in Japanese. Here I found my way to the pre-Raphaelite stained-glass windows of Edward Burnes-Jones: one showing

Edith Liddell as St Catherine, Christ Church, Oxford.

the life of Saint Frideswide, with a corner detail of pilgrims to the Binsey treacle well, and another based around St Catherine. The saint's face is that of Edith Liddell, "Tertia", and the Eaglet—Alice's little redhead sister, who became engaged to Aubrey Harcourt in 1876 but died of peritonitis less than two weeks later.

> *Sacra memoriae Edithae*
> *Henrici et Lorinae Liddell filiae.*
> *Vix quinque dies desponsa.*
> *Morbo correpta subitaneo*
> *Animam Deo reddidit.*

"Scarcely five days betrothed", reads the inscription, when she "gave up her soul to God." The window pins us to another point of Alice's life, between the boat trip from Salter's Yard and the fussy, officious charity patronage that occupied Mrs Hargreaves in the twentieth century; you can't help but wonder how hard the death must have hit Edith's sisters, and how the twenty-four-year-old Alice coped. In some ways, Oxford illuminates Alice more than it does Carroll; within ten minutes you can intersect with locations and objects that invoke visions of her as a stubborn, vivacious girl, a reserved, refined young woman, a strict and perhaps sad elderly lady. Artifacts from most of her eighty-two years are preserved here in one form or another—the boathouse at Salter's Yard, the summer dress from the year before Edith's death, the silver key dating from the year before her husband Regi died. Carroll's rooms and much of his stamping ground at Christ Church is out of bounds; it was Alice Liddell whom I felt I had touched here, and who in return had touched me.

Guildford, Surrey: July 2002

"Caravan sites?" replied the trim, middle-aged woman in the tourist office. "I'm afraid we don't have any information on—"

"No, Carroll sites," I repeated. "Lewis Carroll sites."

Lewis Carroll installed his unmarried sisters and younger brothers in Guildford during autumn 1868. His father had died in June, and the family home in Croft had to be vacated for the new rector, so Carroll took the responsibility of house hunting during that summer. The Chestnuts, a sturdy three-storey place near the castle and High Street, was one of two options he offered, but the scouting group of his sister Fanny and Aunt Lucy liked the house so much they didn't bother to look at the other. It remained occupied by members of the Dodgson family until 1919; Carroll himself passed away there on January 14, 1898. "Unfortunately it's lived in by students now," said the tourist information woman, raising her eyebrows in mild disapproval. "It's a big house," I said. Was it converted into flats now? She didn't know. Were there no plans to convert it into a museum? Another lift of the eyebrows as she allowed herself a little *hmf* of amused contempt, implying years of frustration with local government. "Well, there were plans," she said pointedly, stressing the past tense. "There is still the museum, they're very keen, very helpful."

I asked her for a pamphlet or brochure about Carroll's Guildford. She said they didn't have any, because the only people who asked seemed to be Japanese. She dug out one leaflet, priced 15p. I couldn't remember the last time I'd paid 15 pence for anything. "There's a shop about him in Oxford," she added helpfully, perhaps feeling some kind of common ground, "and one in Wales I think." Yes, Llandudno. "Llandudno, is it?" Yes, I was doing a sort of tour. "Well," she laughed self-consciously, "it all ended here, at the Mount."

Guildford's High Street was busy with midday shoppers: The window glass of Boots and Starbucks flashed next to the Tudor frontage of the Angel Inn, and the faint scent of flowers drifted from hanging baskets, from plant stalls and the nearby castle gardens. I headed down to the museum, past St Mary's where Carroll prayed and preached. As in the Museum of Oxford, the Carroll corner is secreted away, far from being the centre or the highlight of the displays. There are two cabinets in a small, quiet back room at the top of the stairs; during my visit the place was silent, and nobody else came in, or near. The first cabinet holds miscellany from Croft and The Chestnuts—candleholders, dress-up paper dolls made by Dodgson girls, a Life of Christ jigsaw puzzle, and a hand-painted canvas bearing only the word "Jesus"—signs of a modest, pious lifestyle. A huge blow-up of the Tenniel Queen of Hearts stands next to the second cabinet, which displays an odd cow-on-wheels toy and a miniature croquet game.

Two information boards describe Carroll as a "shy and conventional mathematics lecturer" whose life "was to change dramatically on 4th July 1862 [when] he took Alice Liddell, daughter of the Dean of Christ Church, for a boat trip"; he was "never happier than when he was in the company of children." There is no place for Leach's revisionism or Wakeling's myth busting here: the curators offer a pen portrait that will reassure visitors with a casual interest in the author. The image of a stuttering, childlike dreamer is left intact, and reinforced through the authority of a museum setting and a context of authentic artifacts. This is the safe, "heritage" version, unsullied by mentions of obsessions with Alice or nude photography, but also oversimplified in its focus on a single life-changing moment with Alice as sole muse, and its omission of Carroll's confident, socialite side.

In the museum shop, where I bought a 50-page booklet and a postcard of The Chestnuts in 1868, a stout woman of retirement age piped up that she lived next to Carroll's family home, in Castle Gate. She used to be a town councillor, she said, so I tried her with the question about converting it into a museum of some kind. "Ooh, there were plans more than once . . . the council just couldn't afford it, or they could afford it, but they wouldn't find the money." Was it occupied by students now, then? "No, no . . . it's empty, or at least it's got builders in. They're doing terrible things to the front garden, and the plaque isn't there anymore." She was right: the boxy, red-brick house, grand as the rectory at Croft, was missing the plaque that had been there since May 1933. The ten visible windows were dark, with workmen in white t-shirts sometimes appearing inside, slipping from one room to the next.

The Chestnuts, Guildford.

Caught up in back streets, I had to ask a passerby how to get to the Looking-Glass statue in the castle gardens. He was a well-mannered fellow in his seventies, near-bald and with stained teeth; his directions were ludicrously complex and took two minutes to deliver, involving pubs and churches he knew off by heart and seemed to expect me to memorize. Moreover, they were wrong. I ended up going past The Chestnuts again, and made enquiries of a plump man trailing a little brunette girl. "Are you a Lewis Carroll fan?" he puffed. "I forget where it is myself, even though I live next to it . . . go through that tunnel. Good luck." Needless to say, these picaresque little encounters and wrong turns were making me feel, not for the first time, like Alice looking for the beautiful garden.

Within ten minutes I found the castle grounds; they were peaceful and quiet, cushioned in warmth. The keep rose from the centre, a landmark to prevent me from getting too lost. Elderly people sat alone or in couples on benches in front of the bowling green, with its pattern of chessboard tiles; the empty benches bore plaques in memory of loved ones who had spent their lunch hours here. A drunk in a vest staggered past, breaking the idyll a little, and settled down on his back for a sleep with a can held

341

"Alice Stepping through the Looking-Glass", Guildford.

to his chest. I tried to follow the last instructions I'd been given: through a tunnel, up a winding path and a flight of steps, past a bandstand and theatre flats labeled "King Lear set". I spotted the statue across a wall of hedges but couldn't work out how to reach it, and doubled back; down the steps, past the benches, past schoolgirls on mobile phones and teens in groups looking like they hated the place and wanted nothing more than escape.

Finally I found it, in a sunken, hidden garden: "Alice Stepping Through The Looking-Glass", by Jeanne Argent and unveiled in 1989. It captures the Tenniel Alice at the moment where she pushes her hand through the bright silvery mist, but because the gauze has frozen back to glass, she looks trapped, anguished, almost tortured.

Two boys and a girl were lounging around the garden, the lads playing with a Count Dooku plastic lightsaber from the latest *Star Wars* film. They watched me warily as I took notes and photos, then as I left, went up to poke the statue with the bright red plastic blade. I heard one of them complain, as I walked away, "she hasn't got any breasts . . . "

Alice in Wonderland **statue, Guildford.**

The *Looking-Glass* Alice has a twin down by the river, on Millmead; a twin and an older sister, in fact. Guildford's second Alice statue is a bronze of her sitting up and glancing intently off after a rabbit, which is, to use a word Carroll might disapprove of, haring down a track towards its burrow. The figure of a young woman lies next to her, on her stomach, with one hand supporting her head and her bare legs crossed; she is reading a book. This, of course, is Alice and her sister before it all began, on the riverbank, and the contrast between this and the other statue is striking: although they both depict a scene from the opening of the book, just before or at the moment of entry into the other world, the *Wonderland* statue places the two girls in a social scene, on a grassy stretch where office women on a lunch break eat their Boots Meal Deal sandwiches and Shapers crisps. Unlike the *Looking-Glass* piece, isolated in its secret garden, this Alice is very much part of everyday life in Guildford, echoing the lazy lounging of the real people around her. Perhaps accidentally, the two statues pick up on the interpretation of *Looking-Glass* as a "darker", colder, and more sinister book than the supposedly more carefree and sunny *Wonderland*.

As with the Daresbury window, there is an odd blurring of fantasy and reality going on here. This Alice is quite clearly Alice Liddell, with a dark bob, rather than the blonde with shoulder-length hair that Tenniel drew. Furthermore, the book her sister is reading can be peered at over her shoulder: it's *Alice in Wonderland*. So the adventure is about to begin, and yet it's already been written and published—and the older sister is absorbed in a book that, as we know, does have pictures and conversations.

Finally, where it ended. Lewis Carroll died at The Chestnuts, Guildford, thirteen days before his sixty-sixth birthday. His oak coffin was taken on a hand bier from the house along Quarry Street to St Mary's Church, then, following the service, down the High Street and across the river where Alice now sits, to the foot of the Mount. I began to climb the hill to his graveyard. "A steep, stony, country road," wrote his friend Gertrude Thomson, "with hedges close on either side . . . "[26] She was right; it is very steep. I passed a retired couple digging their garden. "Hallo!" I called, naively. "Is this the way to the cemetery?" The man pushed back a straw hat. "Yes, you can't miss it," he chuckled. "It's the centre of town." He laughed, and kept laughing, absurdly, as I kept walking.

The cemetery was almost silent; no people, just a soft bird trill and the wind rustling through willow. I found the grave easily and sat beside it. "Thy will be done," reads the inscription on the horizontal of the white cross. At the base: "Rev. Charles Lutwidge Dodgson (Lewis Carroll) Fell Asleep Jan 14 1898." Asleep, to dream.

It was just me and him now; I had trailed him from birth to death, from that field in Daresbury to this one in Guildford. I felt quite profoundly sad, and deeply connected, with my hand resting on his ground. Matthew Sweet, in *Inventing the Victorians*, frequently finds himself imagining his subjects walking before him. "I can see them," he enthuses, visualizing Joseph Merrick on the Whitechapel Road, and Oscar Wilde in Soho; he talks of "places where the Victorian past will rush to meet you."[27] I couldn't help but bring Carroll back to life before me, as I sat at his grave; I saw him unfold in front of me, tall and slim, bewildered but polite, brushing his dark jacket and trousers down, smiling mildly, blinking. I imagined him looking down on me in my Carroll-hunting gear—my black outfit, rucksack, water bottle, digital and 35mm cameras, mobile and maps, notebook and Palm Pilot—and wondered what he could say to me, what I should say to him.

Before he could see what we make of him in the twenty-first century, I felt I would have to warn him, and apologise. I opened this book with a quotation from Elvis Costello's *Beyond Belief*.

Lewis Carroll's grave, Guildford.

Through a two-way looking glass
You see your Alice
You know she has no sins, for all your jealousy
In a sense she still smiles very sweetly

What we now see is our Alice, and our Carroll. In many ways, the readings that currently circulate say much more about us as a culture than they do about the author, his child-friend Alice Liddell, or his dreamchild Alice in Wonderland. We can see now that the psychoanalytic interpretations of the *Alice* books in the 1930s were a product of a specific moment and movement, and the same is now obvious of the 1960s psychedelic readings. The discourses that I traced in 1990s journalism and in some biographies, that Carroll was emotionally arrested, a repressed paedophile, an obsessive, a stammering social reject, a starched control freak, or a photographic voyeur—and yet that his legacy is an innocent, timeless, very English work of charming fantasy, suitable for reissue to another generation of young readers—have more to do with our own attitudes to childhood and celebrity than they do to the culture Carroll lived through.

As Sweet points out, we like to see the Victorians as hypocrites, keeping themselves buttoned up and curtaining off their piano legs while enjoying a clandestine underworld of sexual perversion. Not only can these myths about Victorian repression be exploded, but we perpetuate too many hypocrisies ourselves to feel complacently superior about the mores of the nineteenth century. Sweet observes that while a host of actors and journalists were celebrating the unveiling of London's Oscar Wilde statue in November 1998, applauding his libertine daring, another section of the press was, on the same day, sneering at him as a borderline paedophile.[28] When the *News of the World* launched its anti-paedophile campaign, trailing pieties about the deaths of little angels, a sixteen-year-old glamour model was flashing her breasts just a few pages away.[29]

We want to retain *Alice* as something to give the kiddies, whether in the cute Oxenbury version, in the starry special effects of Nick Willing's family film, or on the Disney rides in four parks and three nations; but at the same time, we like to dig for dirty secrets and potential smears in Carroll's life, finding something pleasurably creepy in a man who never married yet took photographs of little girls. We want him both ways—the quaint English dreamer-scholar, and the weirdo-paedo who provides shivers of scandal—just as we also want to keep hold of the suspicion that *Alice* might be an opium fantasy, or a cryptic love letter, or in any case something "dark" and odd that the kids don't notice. We want them both in both ways. We're the hypocrites.

So there would be an apology for Carroll; but there would also be reassurance. I could open my rucksack and show him that I was carrying two dog-eared versions of *Alice* everywhere with me, and two biographies of his life; show him that people still cared enough to visit his grave over one hundred years after his death, over one hundred and fifty after Alice Liddell's birth. I could show him the statue at Millmead, where his child-muse is cast in the role of his dreamchild and sits perpetually in the middle of daily life, a friendly landmark of the lunch hour. I could show him the Rabbit Hole at Llandudno, where little girls still enjoy dressing up in blue dresses and white aprons and having their photos taken with the Caterpillar or the Tweedles. I could show him the new Penguin editions of *Alice* in every High Street bookshop, and—steering him away from the biographies for the moment—take him to the children's section to see the picture books by Oxenbury, Zwerger, and McGraw. "That children love the book is a very precious thought to me," he wrote of *Alice in Wonderland* in 1885.[30] Despite all the rumours and readings, children still love the book, and that, I think, would be enough to comfort Carroll. For all the changes we have put her through—perhaps in part because of them—his Alice is still alive.

Notes

1. The first words of the doctor to the Dodgson sisters as he descended from examining Carroll's body, just after his passing. See Collingwood, *Life and Letters*, p. 364.
2. Charlie Lovett, *Lewis Carroll's England: An Illustrated Guide for the Literary Tourist* (London: White Stone Publishing, 1998).
3. Oddly, it also features "Alice's Village" in the Storybook Land boat ride: a church and cottage that are never seen in the film. See Marc Spignese, "Alice in Disneyland," http://laughingplace.com/News-ID503060.asp.
4. See Marc Borelli, "Alice in Tokyo Disneyland," http://laughingplace.com/News-ID503130.asp.
5. Unfortunately, Disney is so rigorously protective of its copyright that I have no hope of including my own photographs in this section.
6. Adair, *Needle's Eye*, pp. 105–6.
7. See Edens, ed., *Alice in Wonderland*, p. 69.
8. Carroll, *Alice in Wonderland*, p. 69.
9. Collingwood, *Life and Letters*, p. 11.
10. See Thomas, *Portrait*, p. 61.
11. Lovett, *Lewis Carroll's England*, p. 16.
12. Cohen, *Biography*, p. 5.
13. Lovett, *Lewis Carroll's England*, p. 10.
14. Gardner, *Annotated Alice*, p. 63.
15. Michael Senior, *Did Lewis Carroll Visit Llandudno?* (Llanwrust: Gwasg Carreg Gwalch, 2000), p. 65.
16. Ibid., pp. 11–14.
17. Bakewell, *Biography*, p. 105.
18. Senior, *Did Lewis Carroll Visit*, p. 79.
19. Ibid., p. 80.
20. Matthew Sweet, *Inventing the Victorians* (London: Faber & Faber, 2001), pp. 1–2.
21. Ibid., p. 137.
22. "New Wonderland Trail for Penmorfa," *Bandersnatch* 115 (April 2002), p. 11.
23. I visited again in the heatwave of August 2003, and in blistering sun found the wooden sculptures of the King and Queen's thrones, the curled Cat, and the Tea Party. Sadly, many of these had already been crudely vandalised.
24. On my return visit I discovered it had been renamed Penmorfa, with signs announcing "The Home of Alice . . . Alice's Tea Room, Mad Hatter's Bar Open to Non-Residents".
25. See Ivor Wynne Jones, "Penmorfa Revisited," *Bandersnatch* 119 (May 2003), p. 20; Ivor Wynne Jones, "The Apotheosis of Penmorfa," *Bandersnatch* 117 (October 2002), p. 6.
26. Quoted in Cohen, *Biography, Lewis Carroll*, p. 526.
27. Sweet, *Inventing the Victorians*, p. 232, p. 222.
28. Ibid., p. 226.
29. Ibid., p. 171.
30. Lewis Carroll to Mary E. Manners (5 December 1885), quoted in Cohen, *Letters*, p. 158.

Appendix A

Disney 1951	Miller 1966	Harris 1985	Svankmajer 1989	Willing 1999
Titles: sketches and song "Alice in Wonderland".	Alice's face through leaves, title card: voice-over recites verse from Wordsworth.	Titles with images and names of cast.		Alice sings "Cherry Ripe" with huge metronome.
Alice on riverbank in Oxford while sister reads "William the Conqueror" passage. "I'm sorry, but how can one possibly pay attention to a book with no pictures in it?"	Maid brushes Alice's hair at home. Alice walks with older sister across garden, through forest to meadow. Alice looks at sister's book, lies back in grass.	Alice in mother's dining room, wishing she could join adult tea party. She goes outside to join sister on riverbank. "What good is a book without any pictures?"	Alice on riverbank with sister. She throws stones into the river.	Alice with nurse and mother. She is preparing to sing formal song at adult garden party. She talks to Dinah.
Alice with Dinah sings "In a World of My Own."		Alice talks to Dinah about wanting to grow up.	Voice-over and titles.	Titles as camera moves across Alice's room, under floorboards.
			Alice's room: she is throwing pebbles into a teacup.	Alice walks through garden party, retreats under apple tree.

(continued)

Disney 1951	Miller 1966	Harris 1985	Svankmajer 1989	Willing 1999
White Rabbit appears: "I'm Late" song.	White Rabbit appears in meadow.	White Rabbit appears on bridge.	Stuffed White Rabbit comes to life, escapes case.	Apple falls, freezes. White Rabbit appears.
Alice follows Rabbit into hole, falls.	Alice follows Rabbit down path, under bridge.	Alice chases Rabbit through forest, into tunnel, falls.	Alice chases Rabbit out of room across field, into drawer in desk.	Alice chases Rabbit into hedge, into hole in tree, falls.
			Alice walks through drawer into tunnel.	
			She walks down passage, spies on Rabbit eating sawdust. Falls into metal bucket, through the bottom.	
Long fall down rabbit-hole.	Crawls under bridge.	Fall through tunnel.	Long fall down hole.	Long fall down rabbit hole.
Lands, races down corridors to door with talking handle. "Curiouser and curiouser."	Finds herself in a white room. Walks down hallway, down stairs, runs down corridor, into library. Finds three doors. Sees beautiful garden through little door.	Lands, chases Rabbit. Down tunnel, through series of doors to vaulted hall with more doors. Sees garden through tiny door. Sees beautiful garden through little door. Looking for way home.	Finds door with small door at base.	Lands, finds herself in a corridor. Enters a circular room full of doors. Sees beautiful garden through little door.
"Drink Me" bottle on glass table. Alice shrinks. Key is on table out of reach.	Finds "Drink Me" bottle, is suddenly tiny.	"Drink Me" bottle appears. Alice shrinks. Key is on table out of reach.	Finds bottle of ink in drawer. Alice drinks, shrinks. Key is on table out of reach.	"Drink Me" bottle appears. Alice shrinks. Key is on table out of reach.

Disney 1951	Miller 1966	Harris 1985	Svankmajer 1989	Willing 1999
"Eat Me" cakes appear. Alice grows.	Finds "Eat Me" cake. "Curiouser and curiouser." Recites "How Doth The Little Crocodile".	"Eat Me" cake appears. "Curiouser and curiouser." Alice grows.	Cake appears. Alice grows. Unlocks small door. Rabbit hits her with oars.	"Eat Me" cakes appear. "Curiouser and curiouser." Alice grows. Rabbit enters, drops fan and gloves.
Begins weeping.	Adults as animals swimming in slow motion. Dissolve into Alice's face.	Begins weeping.	Begins weeping.	Begins weeping.
			Tears fill the room. Mouse arrives, tries to light fire on Alice's head.	
Drinks from bottle again, shrinks, lands in bottle in water.		Rabbit enters, drops fan and gloves. Alice waves fan, shrinks.	Rabbit arrives in boat. She finds cakes, eats them, shrinks.	Alice waves fan, shrinks.
Sea of tears, Alice floating in bottle. Dodo arrives across water.		Falls through skirting-board into river of tears. Meets Mouse, discusses cats and dogs.	Floating on desk in sea of tears. Birds attack her.	Tunnel of tears. Meets Mouse. He leads her into library, sings "I Am An English Lecturer".
	Alice with adult-animals. Mouse reads "William the Conqueror" passage.			Alice with adult-animals. Mouse reads "William the Conqueror" passage.
Caucus race led by Dodo on beach.	Caucus race. Alice gives prizes.	Animals gather on shore. Mouse sings "I Hate Dogs and Cats".		Caucus race. Alice gives prizes.

(continued)

Disney 1951	Miller 1966	Harris 1985	Svankmajer 1989	Willing 1999
Alice chases Rabbit into forest.		Alice in forest meets Rabbit, discusses gloves and fan.	Alice floats down river, meets Rabbit.	White Rabbit enters.
Tweedledum and Tweedledee. They recite "The Walrus and the Carpenter". They begin "Father William"; Alice leaves.				
She arrives at Rabbit's house. He mistakes her for maid, "Mary Ann".	Rabbit calls for "Mary Ann".	"Mary Ann, go home and fetch me a pair of gloves . . . "	"Mary Ann" misrecognition. He sends her for scissors.	"Run home and fetch me a pair of gloves . . . "
In house Alice eats a cake, grows. Accidentally kicks Rabbit out of house.	Alice in White Rabbit's house. "Drink Me" bottle: she grows.	In Rabbit's house. "Drink Me" bottle: she grows.	In Rabbit's house, finds bottle of ink: she grows. Rabbit tries to get in at door, then window. She pushes him away.	In Rabbit's house. Finds bottle: she grows. Her arm shocks him, he falls into cucumber-frame.
Dodo and Bill help Rabbit try to evict Alice. Alice sneezes Bill from chimney.		Rabbit calls Pat, then Bill. Bill scales roof, Alice kicks him out of chimney.	Rabbit calls a group of skull-animals. Bill scales roof, Alice kicks him out of chimney.	Rabbit calls Pat, then Bill. Bill scales roof, Alice kicks him out of chimney.
Alice picks a carrot, eats it, shrinks.	Rocks fly through window, become cakes. She eats them and shrinks.	They throw rocks that become cakes. She eats them and shrinks.	They throw rocks that become cakes. She eats them and shrinks.	They throw rocks that become cakes. She eats them and shrinks.
Alice chases Rabbit. Meets Bread and butter fly, Rocking-horse fly.	Escapes house and flees.	Runs out of house, they chase her.	Runs out of house, they chase her.	Leaves house, meets Puppy.

Disney 1951	Miller 1966	Harris 1985	Svankmajer 1989	Willing 1999
Garden of Live Flowers: they sing "Golden Afternoon".			Animals hunt Alice, catch her, push her into a pot. She grows, encased in a doll shell. They imprison her in a storeroom.	
Flowers shun Alice as a weed.			Alice finds key and escapes.	
Alice meets Caterpillar. "Who are you?"	Alice meets Caterpillar in greenhouse. "Who are you? . . . Keep your temper."	Alice meets Caterpillar. "Who are you? . . . Keep your temper."	Alice meets Caterpillar in room of holes with sock-snakes. "Who are you? . . . Keep your temper."	Alice meets Caterpillar. "Who are you?"
She recites "How Doth the Little Crocodile". He corrects her. "Keep your temper."	She recites "Father William".	He asks her to recite "Father William". They perform it together as song and dance.	Rabbit emerges, leaves. Alice tests mushroom.	He asks her to recite "Father William". Gives her advice on remembering and not being afraid.
Caterpillar becomes Butterfly, flies away.		He vanishes in an explosion.		Caterpillar becomes Butterfly, explodes in a cloud of butterflies.
Alice licks mushroom, grows, meets Pigeon: "Serpent!"	Outside Duchess's house, meets Frog-Footman.	Outside Duchess's house, dialogue between Frog- and Fishfootmen.	Outside Duchess's house, meets Frog-Footman.	Eats mushroom, grows to normal height. Outside Duchess's house, meets Frog-Footman.
Licks mushroom, shrinks to normal size.	Duchess and cook. "Speak Roughly To Your Little Boy".	Duchess and cook sing "There's Something to Say for Hatred".	Finds Rabbit feeding baby. He throws it at her.	Duchess and cook. "Speak Roughly To Your Little Boy".

(continued)

Disney 1951	Miller 1966	Harris 1985	Svankmajer 1989	Willing 1999
Forest with bewildering signs. Alice hears "Jabberwocky". Cheshire Cat appears.	Alice leaves house with baby that becomes pig. Cat speaks to her as voice-over.	Alice leaves house with baby that becomes pig. Cat appears, sings "There's No Way Home".	Baby becomes pig.	Alice leaves house with baby that becomes pig. Cheshire Cat appears.
				She encounters singing tree.
Mad Tea Party. They sing "Unbirthday Song." Dormouse sings "Twinkle, Twinkle Little Bat". Rabbit arrives, Hatter and Hare throw him out. Alice leaves in a huff. Declares she is going home.	Mad Tea Party. Hatter sings "Twinkle, Twinkle Little Bat". Dormouse tells story of three sisters. Alice leaves in a huff.	Mad Tea Party. Hatter sings "Twinkle, Twinkle" and "Laugh". Dormouse tells story. Alice leaves in a huff.	Mad Tea Party. Rabbit emerges from hat. Alice follows him.	Mad Tea Party. Hatter sings "Auntie's Wooden Leg" and "Twinkle, Twinkle". Alice leaves in a huff.
Alice in Tulgey Wood, encounters strange wildlife. Becomes lost, sings "Good Advice" to herself.		Alice in forest meets Fawn and sings "Why Do People Act as if They're Crazy?"		
Cheshire Cat appears, shows her door to secret garden.		Alice finds door in tree, enters secret garden, dances alone.		Alice re-enters room with glass table, finds door with looking-glass portal into secret garden.
Maze outside Queen of Hearts' castle. Card painters sing "Painting the Roses Red".	"Why are you painting those roses?"	"Why are you painting those roses?"		"Why are you painting the roses red?"
Arrival of Queen and court. "Do you play croquet?" Croquet game. Alice fails.	Arrival of Queen and court. Garden party on the grass. Croquet game.	Arrival of Queen and court. Queen sings "Off With Their Heads!" Croquet game.	Arrival of Queen and court. Rabbit executes cards, Hatter, and Hare. Croquet game.	Arrival of Queen and court. "Do you play croquet?" Croquet game.

Disney 1951	Miller 1966	Harris 1985	Svankmajer 1989	Willing 1999
Cat appears. Queen is annoyed by Alice, calls for a trial.	Cat appears. Debate about execution.	Cat appears. Debate about execution.		Cat appears. Debate about execution.
	Alice walks with Duchess. Encounter with Queen.	Alice walks with Duchess. Encounter with Queen.		Alice walks with Duchess. Encounter with Queen.
		Alice walks through wood, talks to baby goat and monkey.		Alice walks through maze.
	Alice meets Mock Turtle and Gryphon. They sing "The Lobster Quadrille."	Alice meets Mock Turtle and Gryphon. Turtle sings "Nonsense".		Alice meets Mock Turtle and Gryphon. They sing "The Lobster Quadrille" and "Turtle Soup".
				Alice walks through maze, past "Cherry Ripe" songbook.
				Meets Red Knight, White Knight.
				Garden of Live Flowers.
				Tweedledum and Tweedledee. They recite "The Walrus and the Carpenter"; they fight. Arrival of crow.
Courtroom. Alice on trial.	Courtroom.	Courtroom. Knave on trial.	Courtroom. Alice on trial for eating tarts.	Courtroom. Knave on trial.
First witness is March Hare.	First witness is Hatter.	First witness is Hatter.		Witnesses: Hatter, Hare, and Dormouse.

(continued)

Disney 1951	Miller 1966	Harris 1985	Svankmajer 1989	Willing 1999
Second witness is Dormouse.	Second witness is cook.	Second witness is cook.		Hatter sings "Twinkle, Twinkle, Little Gnat".
Third witness is Hatter. Sings "Un-birthday Song".	King, Queen, and court sing a miscellany of tunes.			Knave defends himself.
Alice eats mushroom, grows. "You're nothing but a pack of cards."	Alice grows.	Alice grows.		Alice eats mushroom, grows.
Rule 42. "Off with her head."		Rule 42. "You're nothing but a pack of cards."	"Off with her head."	Rule 42. "Are you confident . . . then you don't need us anymore."
Alice flees, chased by court and cards. Past caucus race, tea party, to door with talking handle.		Alice flees, chased by court and cards.	Alice's head changes, replaced by Wonderland characters.	
Sees herself under a tree sleeping. Wakes herself up.		Cards fall, become leaves.		Card house collapses. Apple appears and rotates.
Alice wakes and recites "How Doth the Little Crocodile". Sister tolerant. Takes her home for tea.	Alice wakes in meadow with sister. Voice-over recites Wordsworth verse.	Alice wakes on the grass. Runs back towards house. Title quotation from Carroll.	Alice wakes in her bedroom. Waits for White Rabbit to return so she can cut off his head.	Alice wakes under tree. Runs with Puppy back to the house. Performs "The Lobster Quadrille" to adult applause.

Appendix B

Disney 1951	Miller 1966	Harris 1985	Millar 1985	Svankmajer 1989	Willing 1999
All sing "Unbirthday Song" as Alice approaches.	Alice approaches.	Alice approaches.	Older Alice Hargreaves finds Tea Party in her dining room.	Alice enters room.	Hatter: Have you got any food down there, Dormy?" Alice approaches.
Alice applauds.		Alice: May I introduce myself . . .	Discovers her telephone has vanished.		Alice: I'm lost.
		Hatter: If you want an introduction, get yourself an orchestra.	Looks back, finds dining room is a garden, telephone at end of table.		
		Alice: But I wanted to give you my name.			
		Hatter: Have you finished with it?			
Hat and Hare: No room!	Hat and Hare: No room!	Hat and Hare: No room!	Hat and Hare: No room!	Hat and Hare [voiced by Alice]: No room!	Hat and Hare: No room!

(continued)

Disney 1951	Miller 1966	Harris 1985	Millar 1985	Svankmajer 1989	Willing 1999
			Alice becomes young Alice Liddell.		
Alice: There's plenty of room.		Alice: There's plenty of room.	Alice: There's plenty of room.		Alice: There's plenty of room.
Hare: It's very rude to sit down without being invited.	Hare: Have some wine.	Hatter: Would you like some wine?	Hare: Have some wine.	Hatter changes hats, twice.	Hare: Why didn't you report this sooner, Hatty? Why are you here?
Alice: I did enjoy your singing.	Alice: There isn't any.	Alice: I don't think I should drink wine—I'm too young.	Alice: I don't see any.		Alice: I'm looking for the pretty garden.
		Hare: There isn't any . . . wasn't very nice of you to sit down without being invited.	Hare: There isn't any . . . wasn't very nice of you to sit down without being invited.		
			Alice: I didn't know it was your table . . . it's laid for many more than three.		
Hare: We never get company, Hatter. You must have a cup of tea.			Hatter and Hare: Oooh!	Hare butters a watch.	Hare: Waiter, there's a hair in my soup.
Hare: She doesn't know what a un-birthday is. [he explains]					Hatter: Is it blonde? We're missing a waitress.

Disney 1951	Miller 1966	Harris 1985	Millar 1985	Svankmajer 1989	Willing 1999
Alice: Then today is my un-birthday too.	Hatter: Your um, your er, hair wants cutting.	Hatter: You know, your hair wants cutting.			Hatter: Get your hair cut.
She joins in the song. They give her a cake that becomes a rocket.	Alice: You should learn not to make personal remarks.	Alice: You should learn not to make personal remarks.			Alice: You should learn not to make personal remarks.
Dormouse floats to earth singing "Twinkle, Twinkle".					Hatter: Personal remarks are rude? Egad! . . . Make a note of that, Marchy.
Hatter: Something seems to be troubling you. Wont you tell us all about it.					
Alice tells her story so far.					
Dormouse panics at mention of Dinah.					
Hatter: Time for a clean cup, move down, move down.					
They shift down table.					

(continued)

Disney 1951	Miller 1966	Harris 1985	Millar 1985	Svankmajer 1989	Willing 1999
Hare pours half-cup of tea.					
Hatter: Why is a raven like a writing-desk?	Hatter: Why is a raven like a writing-desk?	Hatter: Why is a raven like a writing-desk?	Hatter: Why is a raven like a writing-desk?	Hatter: Why is a raven like a writing-desk?	Hatter: Why is a raven like a writing-desk? [to Hare] I'm not talking to you.
Alice: I beg your pardon.				Hatter fixes Hare's eye.	Hare: Aren't I good enough?
Hare: Careful, she's stark raven mad.	Alice: I think I can guess.	Alice: I give up . . .	Alice: Lovely, riddles. I believe I can guess that.	Hatter winds up Hare with key.	Alice: You know, I'm pretty sure I can guess . . .
White Rabbit enters, running late.		Hatter: I haven't the vaguest idea . . . I was hoping for an intelligent answer. Alice: How did you become a March Hare? . . . Hare: I started as a January Hare . . . Alice: I didn't mean that.		Hare butters watch.	Alice's biscuit becomes tortoise.
	Hare: Do you mean you think you can find the answer? Then you should say what you mean.	Hatter: Then you should say what you mean.	Hare: Do you mean you think you can find the answer? Then you should say what you mean.	Hatter drinks; tea runs down his insides.	Hatter: You mean you think you know the answer? Then you should say what you mean.

Disney 1951	Miller 1966	Harris 1985	Millar 1985	Svankmajer 1989	Willing 1999
	Alice: I do . . . at least . . . that's the same thing.	Alice: I do . . . at least . . . that's the same thing.	Alice: I do . . . at least . . . that's the same thing.	Hatter: I want a clean cup.	Alice: I do . . . at least . . . that's the same thing.
	Hatter: It's not the same thing at all. You might as well say that "I see what I eat . . ."	Hatter: It's not the same thing at all. You might as well say that "I see what I eat . . ."	Hatter: It's not the same thing a bit, you fool. You might as well say that "I see what I eat . . ."	They move around one place.	Hatter: It's not the same thing at all. You might as well say that "I see what I eat . . ."
	Hare: " . . . I like what I get . . ."		Hare: . . . I like what I get . . .	Hare: Have some wine.	Hare: . . . I like what I get . . .
	Dormouse: " . . . I breathe when I sleep."			Alice: I don't see any.	Hare crushes pie that sprouts crab legs.
				Hare: There isn't any.	
	Long pause.	Hatter: Fresh cups, move down!		Hatter: Your hair wants cutting.	Hatter: Clean cups!
		Alice: Who's the stuffed animal? . . . you look like a plain mouse.		Hatter removes hat, takes out White Rabbit.	
		Dormouse: and you look like a plain little girl. You have another think coming . . . do you want to take it right now?		Hatter: I want a clean cup.	

(continued)

Disney 1951	Miller 1966	Harris 1985	Millar 1985	Svankmajer 1989	Willing 1999
				They move around one place.	
	Hatter: What day of the month is it?	Alice: What time is it?	Hatter: What day of the month is it?	Hatter: What day is it today?	Dance around table.
			Alice is now older Alice Hargreaves		
	Alice: The fourth.	Hatter: 7.27 . . . young lady, are you contradicting me? I am known as a stickler for accuracy. They call me in and I stickle.	Alice: I . . . what . . .		Alice: Mr Dormouse is asleep again.
			Hatter: You stupid half-wit ugly old hag. You should be dead, dead, dead.		
			Alice: It's . . . it's . . . oh dear . . . I think it's the 4th		
Hatter: No wonder you're late . . . clock is two days slow.	Hatter: Two days wrong . . . [entire conversation about watch]	Alice: Are you sure your watch is running . . .	Hatter: The 4th—2 days wrong, wrong, wrong! I told you butter wouldn't suit the works.	Hatter: Two days wrong again. I told you butter would not suit the works.	Hatter: That tells you a lot about your conversation. Sparkle!

Disney 1951	Miller 1966	Harris 1985	Millar 1985	Svankmajer 1989	Willing 1999
		Hatter: Of course it isn't running, its sitting here . . . it's absolutely correct, twice a day.	Hare: It was the best butter.	Hare: It was the best butter.	
Hatter butters and salts the watch. Watch goes crazy, leaping across table. Hatter slams it with mallet.	Hatter: . . . same as my watch. [sings] Oh, when Adam and Eve were first deprived . . .		Hatter: There must be some crumbs in it.	Hare takes another watch from teapot, butters it.	Dormouse wakes, sleeps again.
			Carroll in boat with young Liddell girls and mother.	Hatter: I want a clean cup.	
			Carrol: Shouted the Mad Hatter, shaking the watch very, very angrily.	Repeat move, buttering watch, winding hare, Hare pins watch to Hatter's chest	
			Duckworth: I say old chap, I really think we ought to eat something, you know.		
			Carroll: "What a funny watch," said Alice. Why.		

(continued)

Disney 1951	Miller 1966	Harris 1985	Millar 1985	Svankmajer 1989	Willing 1999
			Alice: It tells the day of the month but not what o' clock it is		
	Hatter: Have you guessed the riddle yet?		Hatter: Have you guessed the riddle yet?	Hatter: Well, why is a raven like a writing-desk?	Hatter: Have you guessed the riddle?
				Montage, growing more rapid: Pours tea. New watch. Butter. Cup. Hare's eye. Turn key. Clock on chest. Move. Tea. Clock. Pour. Butter. Cup. Eye. Turn. Chest. Move. Cup. Watch. Drink. Butter. Cup. Eye. Turn. Chest.	Hatter pours tea for Alice with extended arm.
	Alice: I give it up.		Old Alice: no, I give up. What's the answer.	Hatter now has seven watches on chest.	Alice: I give up.
	Hatter: I haven't the slightest idea.		Hatter: I haven't the faintest idea.	Dormouse snakes from pot across table, licking up dregs from cups.	Hatter: I haven't the slightest idea.
			Alice: Well, I think you should do something more with the time than waste it asking riddles that . . . have . . . no answers.	Hatter: Your hair wants cutting.	Alice: I think you should all do something better with the time . . .

Disney 1951	Miller 1966	Harris 1985	Millar 1985	Svankmajer 1989	Willing 1999
	Hatter performs a lazy dance.		Shot of the river. Carroll and girls in boat.	Hare: Pour yourself a glass of wine.	
			Carroll: You mean, you've never even spoken to time?		
			Lorina: Ah, but she knows how to beat time.		
	[Entire conversation about Time] Hatter: . . . he can't stand beating.		Carroll: He won't stand beating, you know. He's a very sensitive fellow. In the story, that is.		Hatter: If you knew Time the way I do . . . Time took offence to our performance . . .
			Mrs Liddell: Yes, Mr Dodgson. In the story.		Alice peers into bottomless cup.
			Duckworth: Some of us think it's time we had some tea ourselves.		Alice: Could he stop time for me? I have to sing a song.
			Carroll: I'm so sorry!		Hatter: Wonderful, we're all performers here.
			Young Alice: I was so enjoying the Mad Hatter and March Hare. I wish they were real.		Alice: But I don't want to.

(continued)

Disney 1951	Miller 1966	Harris 1985	Millar 1985	Svankmajer 1989	Willing 1999
			River.		Hatter: Stage fright. I remember my first performance . . .
			Hotel room, phone is ringing.		Hatter sings "Auntie's Wooden Leg" with elaborate dance routine, Hare on organ.
		Hare: Every tea party should have a little music.	Older Alice: Mrs Hargreaves speaking. Yes, this is she, Mrs Alice Hargreaves.		Hatter falls from table, re-emerges. Hatter: We're desperate men!
	Hatter sings "Twinkle, Twinkle, Little Bat".	Alice sings "Twinkle, Twinkle, Little Star". Hatter corrects her to "Bat".			Hatter sings "Twinkle, Twinkle, Little Bat".
	Dormouse sings "Twinkle, Twinkle".	Dormouse sings "Twinkle, Twinkle, Little Skunk"; Hare sings "Little Ants".			Hatter improvises "Twinkle, Twinkle, Little Bee".
	Hatter: It's always six o'clock now . . . it's always teatime.	Hatter sings "Laugh".			Hatter falls through table trapdoor.

Disney 1951	Miller 1966	Harris 1985	Millar 1985	Svankmajer 1989	Willing 1999
	Hare: Suppose we change the subject . . . I vote the young lady tells us a story.	Hare: How would you like to tell us a story . . . then the dormouse shall.			Hatter reappears in seat. Hatter: I want a clean cup. Everyone move!
Rabbit: And it was an unbirthday present too.	Dormouse tells story of three little sisters.	Dormouse tells story of three little sisters.			They race around table.
		Dormouse: Treacle . . . molasses to you!			
	Hare: Take some more tea.	Hatter: I want a fresh cup.			
	Alice: I can't take more . . .	Dance around table.			
	Alice: Why were they at the bottom of a well? [entire conversation about treacle]				
	Long pause. Sitar music.				
	Dormouse: Everything that begins with an M . . .				

(continued)

Disney 1951	Miller 1966	Harris 1985	Millar 1985	Svankmajer 1989	Willing 1999
Hatter and Hare: In that case, a very happy un-birthday to you . . .		Alice: Where did they draw treacle from?			Alice: I don't think I like this tea party as much as I thought I would.
They toss him out of the gar-den.		Hatter: If you can draw wat-er . . . eh, stupid?			Hatter: Just because we know you so-cially, Alice, doesn't meant were going to introduce you to our friends.
Alice chases Rabbit out.	Alice [voice-over]: This is the stupidest tea party I was ever at.	Alice stands up and walks off in a huff.		Alice backs to-wards door.	Alice stands up and walks off in a huff.
Alice: Of all the silly non-sense. This is the stupidest tea party I've ever been to in all my life.				Hatter and Hare: No room!	Dormouse: Officer, these men are crimi-nals!

Bibliography

Fiction

Adair, G. *Alice Through the Needle's Eye*. London: Pan Books, 1985.

Anonymous. *Go Ask Alice*. 1971. London: Arrow, 1997.

Barker, P. *The Ghost Road*. London: Penguin, 1995.

Carroll, L. *Alice's Adventures in Wonderland* and *Through the Looking-Glass*. 1865 and 1871. London: Penguin, 2001.

————. *Alice's Adventures in Wonderland*. Illustrated by D. McGraw. New York: HarperCollins, 2001.

————. *Alice in Wonderland and Through the Looking-Glass*. Illustrated by A. Mitchell. London: Oberon Books, 2001.

————. *Alice's Adventures in Wonderland*. Illustrated by M. Peake. London: Bloomsbury, 2001.

————. *Through the Looking-Glass and What Alice Found There*. Illustrated by M. Peake. London: Bloomsbury, 2001.

————. *Alice's Adventures in Wonderland*. Edited by C. Cooper Edens. San Francisco: Chronicle Books, 2000.

————. *Alice's Adventures in Wonderland*. Illustrated by A. Rackham. Singapore: SeaStar Books, 2000.

————. *Alice in Wonderland*. Illustrated by L. Zwerger. New York: North-South Books, 1999.

————. *Alice's Adventures in Wonderland*. Illustrated by H. Oxenbury. London: Walker Books, 1999.

————. *Alice's Adventures Under Ground*. 1886. London: Pavillion, 1998.

————. *Sylvie and Bruno*. 1889. New York: Dover Publications, 1988.

————. *The Annotated Snark*. Edited by M. Gardner. Harmondsworth: Penguin, 1979.

————. *The Annotated Alice: The Definitive Edition*. Edited by M. Gardner. London: Penguin Books, 2001.

Gaiman, N., K. Jones III et al. "Season of Mists." *The Sandman* #22. New York: DC Comics, January 1991.

Gibbons, D., S. Rude et al. *World's Finest*. New York: DC Comics, 1993.

Gibson, W., and B. Sterling. *The Difference Engine*. London: Gollancz, 1990.

Homes, A. M. *The End of Alice*. New York: Scribner, 1996.

Joyce, J. *Finnegans Wake*. New York: Viking, 1959.

Moore, A., and M. Gebbie. *Lost Girls*. Northampton: Kitchen Sink Press, 1995.

Morrison, G., and A. McKean. *Arkham Asylum*. New York: DC Comics, 1989.

Morrison, G., and S. Yeowell. "Zenith." *2000AD* #595. London: Fleetway, October 1988.

————. "Zenith." *2000AD* #602. London: Fleetway, November 1998.

Noon, J. *The Automated Alice*. London: Transworld, 1996.

Roiphe, K. *Still She Haunts Me*, London: Hodder, 2001.

Biographies

Bakewell, M. *Lewis Carroll: A Biography*. London: Mandarin, 1996.

Bjork C., and I-K. Erikssonn. *The Story of Alice in Her Oxford Wonderland*. London: R&S Books, 1994.

Cohen, M. N. *Lewis Carroll: A Biography*. London: Macmillan, 1995.

Collingwood, S. *The Life and Letters of Lewis Carroll*. London: T. Fisher Unwin, 1899.

Hudson, D. *Lewis Carroll*. London: Constable, 1954.

Leach, K. *In the Shadow of the Dreamchild: A New Understanding of Lewis Carroll*. London: Peter Owen, 1999.

Lennon, F. B. *Lewis Carroll*. London: William Clowes & Son, 1947.

Stoffel, S. Lovett. *Lewis Carroll in Wonderland: The Life and Times of Alice and Her Creator*. New York: Abrams, 1997.

Taylor, A. L. *The White Knight*, Edinburgh: Oliver & Boyd Ltd, 1952.

Thomas, D. *Lewis Carroll: A Portrait with Background*, London: John Murray, 1996.

Lewis Carroll

Burke, K. "The Thinking of the Body." In R. Phillips, ed., *Aspects of Alice: Lewis Carroll's Dreamchild as Seen Through the Critics' Looking-Glasses.* New York: Vintage Books, 1971.

Cohen, M. N. *The Selected Letters of Lewis Carroll*. London: Macmillan, 1982.

Cohen, M. N., ed. *Lewis Carroll: Interviews and Recollections*. London: Macmillan, 1989.

Fensch, T. "Lewis Carroll—The First Acidhead." 1968. In R. Phillips, ed., *Aspects of Alice: Lewis Carroll's Dreamchild as Seen Through the Critics' Looking-Glasses.* New York: Vintage Books, 1971.

Gernsheim, H. *Lewis Carroll: Photographer*. New York: Dover, 1969.

Goldschmidt, A. M. E. (1971) "*Alice in Wonderland* Psycho-Analysed." Pages 280–81 in R. Phillips, ed., *Aspects of Alice: Lewis Carroll's Dreamchild as Seen Through the Critics' Looking-Glasses.* New York: Vintage Books, 1971.

Hancher, M. *The Tenniel Illustrations to the Alice Books*. Ohio: Ohio University Press, 1985.

Haughton, H. "Introduction." In *Alice's Adventures in Wonderland and Through the Looking-Glass*. London: Penguin, 1998.

Jones, J. E., and J. F. Gladstone. *The Alice Companion: A Guide to Lewis Carroll's Alice Books*. London: Macmillan, 1998.

Lovett, C. *Lewis Carroll's England: An Illustrated Guide for the Literary Tourist*. London: White Stone Publishing, 1998.

Ovenden, G., and J. Davis. *The Illustrators of Alice in Wonderland*. London: Academy Editions, 1972.

Schilder, P. "Psychoanalytic Remarks on Alice in Wonderland and Lewis Carroll." In R. Phillips, ed., *Aspects of Alice: Lewis Carroll's Dreamchild as Seen Through the Critics' Looking-Glasses*. New York: Vintage Books, 1971.

Self, W. "Introduction." In L. Carroll, *Alice's Adventures in Wonderland*, illustrated by M. Peake. London: Bloomsbury, 2001.

Senior, M. *Did Lewis Carroll Visit Llandudno?* Wales: Gwasg Carreg Gwalch, 2000.

Sigler, C., ed., *Alternative Alices: Visions of Lewis Carroll's* Alice *Books*. Lexington, KY: University Press of Kentucky, 1997.

Smith, Z. "Introduction." In L. Carroll, *Through the Looking-Glass and What Alice Found There*, illustrated by M. Peake. London: Bloomsbury, 2001.

Stoffel, S. L. *The Art of Alice in Wonderland*. New York: Wonderland Press, 1998.

Taylor, R., and E. Wakeling. *Lewis Carroll, Photographer*. Princeton: Princeton University Press, 2002.

Wakeling E., ed. *Lewis Carroll's Diaries*. Vol. 4. Bedfordshire: Lewis Carroll Society, 1979.

Woolf, V. "Lewis Carroll." In R. Phillips, ed., *Aspects of Alice: Lewis Carroll's Dreamchild as Seen Through the Critics' Looking-Glasses*. New York: Vintage Books, 1971.

The Victorians

Kincaid, J. R. *Child-Loving: The Erotic Child and Victorian Literature*. London: Routledge, 1992.

Pike, E. R. *Human Documents of the Victorian Golden Age*. London: George Allen & Unwin, 1967.

Sweet, M. *Inventing the Victorians*. London: Faber & Faber, 2001.

Film

Aycock, W., and M. Shoenecke, eds. *Film and Literature: A Comparative Approach to Adaptation*. Texas: Texas Tech University Press, 1988.

Cartmell D., and I. Whelehan, eds. *Adaptations*. London: Routledge, 1999.

Cartmell, D., I. Whelehan, H. Kaye, and I. Q. Hunter, eds. *Classics in Film and Fiction*, London: Pluto, 2000.

———. *Pulping Fictions*. London: Pluto, 1996.

Giddings, R., K. Selby, and C. Wensley, eds. *Screening the Novel*. Hampshire: Macmillan, 1990.

Giddings, R., and E. Sheen, eds. *The Classic Novel from Page to Screen*. Manchester: Manchester University Press, 2000.

Hames, P., ed. *Dark Alchemy: The Films of Jan Svankmajer*. Wiltshire: Flicks Books, 1995.

Klein, M., and G. Parker, eds. *The English Novel and the Movies*. New York: Frederick Ungar, 1981.

Miller, J. *Subsequent Performances*. London: Faber & Faber, 1986.

Ross, D. "Home by Teatime: Fear of Imagination in Disney's *Alice in Wonderland*." In Cartmell et al., *Classics in Film and Fiction*. London: Pluto, 2000.

Sinyard, N. *Filming Literature*. London: Croom Helm, 1986.

Disney

Bryman, A. *Disney and His Worlds*. London: Routledge, 1995.

Koenig, D. *Mouse Under Glass*. New York: Bonaventure Press, 1997.

Manning, K. A. *Designing Disney's Theme Parks*. New York: Flammarion, 1997.

Fandom

Bacon-Smith, C. *Enterprising Women*. Philadelphia: University of Pennsylvania Press, 1992.

Barker, M., and K. Brooks. *Knowing Audiences: Judge Dredd: Its Friends, Fans and Foes*. Luton: University of Luton Press, 1998.

Brooker, W. *Using the Force: Creativity, Community and Star Wars Fandom*. London: Continuum, 2002.

———. *Batman Unmasked*. London: Continuum, 2000.

———. "Internet Fandom and the Continuing Narratives of *Blade Runner*, *Alien* and *Star Wars*." In Annette Kuhn, ed., *Alien Zone 2*. London: Verso, 1999.

Cavicchi, D. *Tramps Like Us: Music and Meaning Among Springsteen Fans*. Oxford: Oxford University Press, 1998.

Clerc, S. J. "DDEB, GATB, MPPB and Ratboy: The X-Files' Media Fandom, Online and Off." In D. Lavery, A. Hague, M. Cartwright, eds., *Deny All Knowledge: Reading the X-Files*. London: Faber & Faber, 1996.

Hills, M. *Fan Cultures*. London: Routledge, 2002.

Jenkins, H. "Do You Enjoy Making The Rest Of Us Feel Stupid? alt.tv.twinpeaks, the Trickster Author and Viewer Mastery." In D. Lavery, ed., *Full of Secrets: Critical Approaches to Twin Peaks*. Detroit: Wayne State University Press, 1994.

Jenkins, H. "*Star Trek* Rerun, Reread, Rewritten: Fanwriting as Textual Poaching." In C. Penley, E. Lyon, L. Spigel, and J. Bergstrom, eds., *Close Encounters: Film, Feminism and Science Fiction*. Minneapolis: University of Minnesota Press, 1991.

Jenkins, H., and J. Tulloch. *Science Fiction Audiences*. London: Routledge, 1995.

Lavery, D., A. Hague, M. Cartwright, eds., *Deny All Knowledge: Reading the X-Files*, London: Faber & Faber, 1996.

Muggleton, D. *Inside Subculture: The Postmodern Meaning of Style*. Oxford: Berg, 2000.

Radway, J. *Reading the Romance*. Chapel Hill: University of North Carolina Press, 1991.

Cultural Theory

Barthes, R. "Structural Analysis of Narratives." Translated by S. Heath. In *Image-Music-Text*. London: Fontana, 1977.

Brooker, P., ed. *Modernism/Postmodernism*. London: Longman, 1992.

McLaughlin, T. *Street Smarts and Critical Theory*. Madison, WI: University of Wisconsin Press, 1996.

Plant, S. *Zeroes and Ones: Digital Women and the New Technoculture*. New York: Doubleday, 1997.

Urry, J. *The Tourist Gaze*. London: Sage, 2002.

Video Games

Herz, J. C. *Joystick Nation*. London: Abacus, 1997.

King, G., and T. Krzywinska. *ScreenPlay*. London: Wallflower, 2002.

Poole, S. *Trigger Happy*. London: Fourth Estate, 2000.

Sawyer, B., A. Dunne, T. and Berg. *Game Developer's Marketplace*. Scottsdale, AZ: Coriolis Group, 1998.

Articles on Carroll

Allen, R. "Day Trip To Oxford." *Bandersnatch* 117 (October 2002), p. 5.

Allan, R. "Alice in Disneyland." *Sight & Sound* (Spring 1985), p. 138.

Anonymous. "The Looking-Glass Ball." *Bandersnatch* 114 (January 2002), p. 8.

————. "New Wonderland Trail for Penmorfa." *Bandersnatch* 115 (April 2002), p. 11.

————. "Westminster School and Westminster Abbey." *Bandersnatch* 116 (July 2002), p. 2.

————. Off the Shelf. *Guardian,* May 9, 2001, p. 9.

————. *Guardian Education,* May 16, 2000, p. 67.

————. Book Review. *Financial Times,* November 20, 1999, p. 4.

————. Children's Books. *The Sunday Herald,* November 21, 199, p. 31.

————. "The 50 Best Books: Once Upon A Time." *Independent,* November 27, 1999, p. 4.

————. Review of *Alice in Wonderland*. *The Reader,* November 18, 1865.

"AP". "TV's *Alice* fantasy sure to delight kids." *Toronto Star,* December 9, 1985.

Barrett, D. "The Ring of Evil." *Western Daily Press,* Bristol, February 14, 2001, p. 4.

Bassett, K. "Alice Loses the Plot." *Independent,* November 18, 2001.

Billington, M. Review of *Alice in Wonderland*. *Guardian,* November 15, 2001.

Carey, J. "Different Strokes." *Times Educational Supplement,* October 29, 1999, p. 9.

Cleave, M. "Adrian's Adventure with Alice." *Evening Standard*, London, October 23, 2001, p. 30.

Chapman, S. "Quotable Alice." *Lewis Carroll Review* 23 (July 2002), p. 6.

Cohen, M. N. "Who Censored Lewis Carroll?" *The Times,* January 23, 1982.

Connolly, C. "Dangerous Liasons." *Observer,* October 23, 1994, p. 2.

Daley, S. "An Alice Made for the Part." *Chicago Tribune,* December 8, 1985.

Eccleshare, J. "New Faces in Wonderland." *Guardian,* May 27, 2000.

Eck, M. "A Lukewarm Victorian Fantasy." *Times Union,* January 13, 2002.

Edmonds, R. "A Stylish Fantasy Weekend." *Birmingham Post,* December 22, 2001, p. 37.

Fitzgerald, I. "Death of Lewis Carroll." *History Today* 48, no. 1 (January 1998), p. 36.

Gibbons, F. "Looking Through A Glass Darkly." *Guardian,* November 28, 2001.

Gordon, G. "Christmas Light Reading." *The Scotsman,* November 23, 2000, p. 30.

Hall, D. "Christmas Books." *Sunday Telegraph,* November 28, 1999.

Harding, J. "*The End of Alice* Is a Cruel and Perverted Novel." *Daily Mail,* October 27, 1997, p. 8.

Hargreaves, A. "The Lewis Carroll That Alice Recalls." *New York Times,* May 1, 1932.

Harrison, D. "A Thoroughly Modern Alice." *Sunday Telegraph,* August 29, 1999, p. 6.

Haughton, H. "The White Knight's Cult of Little Girls." *Times Literary Supplement,* August 8, 1997, pp. 23–24.

Heptonstall, G. "The Real Lewis Carroll." *Contemporary Review* 275, no. 1603 (August 1999), pp. 104–6.

Januszczak, W. "Victorians and Nudity Are a Dubious Mix." *Sunday Times,* November 4, 2001.

Jenkyns, R. "And Quiet Flows the Don." *New Republic* 215, no.5 (January 29, 1996), pp. 39–42.

Jewel, S. "Britain's Urban Spaceman." *Sunday Star-Times,* Auckland, May 4, 1997.

Johns, I. "Little Wonder." *The Times,* November 15, 2001.

Johnson, S. "Alice Is Cool and Cuddly." *The Times,* October 21, 1999.

Kellaway, K. "The Looking Class." *Observer,* November 18, 2001.

Kenny, M. "What Makes a Paedophile?" *The Express,* December 6, 2000.

Langley, W. "The Real Sin of Alice's Creator." *Mail on Sunday,* March 7, 1999, p. 12.

Leach, K., letter to *The Carrollian* 9 (Spring 2002), p. 55.

———. "Ina in Wonderland." *Times Literary Supplement,* May 3, 1996.

Lockerbie, C. "How Doth The Little Crocodile . . . " *The Scotsman,* October 16, 1999, p. 10.

Maguire, S. "The Perfect Draw." *Scotland on Sunday,* June 18, 2000, p. 13.

Maske, S. "Is Alice a more moral story than Harry Potter?" *Metro,* November 13, 2001, p. 13.

Mason, M. S. "*Alice in Wonderland*: A Dreamy Cast and Fabulous Effects." *Christian Science Monitor* 91, no. 63 (February 26, 1999), p. 18.

McCartney, G., (1992) "Charles Dodgson through the Looking-Glass", *American Spectator*

McCrum, R. Review of *The Alice Companion. Observer,* April 12, 1998, p. 15.

———. "Alice Under the Magnifying Glass." *Observer,* June 3, 2001.

———."Annotated Wonderland." *Observer,* November 19, 2000.

McVeigh, K. "2 Million Pounds for a Piece of Wonderland." *The Scotsman,* March 23, 2001, p. 8.

Nicholls, S. "Further Glimpses 'Through the Looking-Glass.' " *The Carrollian* 10 (Autumn 2002), p. 4.

Nicolette Jones, N. "From Circus Clown to Publisher." *The Times,* August 9, 2000.

Noon, J. "All Kinds of Alice." *The Guardian,* January 7, 1998.

O'Connor, M. "To Talk of Many Things." *Bandersnatch* 116 (July 2002), p. 7.

O'Connor, J. J. "Carroll's *Alice* on CBS." *New York Times,* December 9, 1985.

Parham, M. "What We Choose It to Mean. *New Statesman and Society,* November 1, 1991, p. 36.

Robinson, D. "Letter Shows Alice Author Enigma." *The Scotsman,* November 21, 2001, p. 3.

Self, W. "Dirty Old Man." *New Statesman,* December 25, 2000), p. 88.

Shapiro, A. "Books: First Novels." *The Guardian,* November 4, 2001.

Sorensen, M. "Taking the Wonder out of Wonderland." *Courier Mail,* Queensland, December 29, 2001.

Soto, F. "The Consumption of the Snark and the Decline of Nonsense: A Medico-Linguistic Reading of Carroll's 'Fitful *Agony.*' " *The Carrollian* 8 (Autumn 2001), p. 25.

Spurling, H. "A Subversive World of His Own." *Sunday Telegraph,* January 23, 2000.

Sweet, M. "Malice in Wonderland." *The Independent on Sunday,* March 24, 2002, p. 7.

Wakeling, E. "What Happened to Lewis Carroll's Diaries." *The Carrollian* 8 (Autumn 2001).

Watts, J. "Japan Tackles Child Porn." *The Guardian,* April 27, 1999.

Williams, E. "The Joke's on Them." *Times Educational Supplement Primary Magazine,* January 26, 2001, p. 49.

Williams, M. "Down the Rabbit Hole." *Observer,* October 21, 2001.

Woods, M. "Oxford in the 'Seventies." *Fortnightly Review* 150 (1941).

Woolaston, G. "In the Shadow of the Dreamchild." *The Herald,* April 8, 1999, p. 18.

Wynne Jones, I. "Penmorfa Revisited." *Bandersnatch* 119 (May 2003), p. 20.

———. "The Apotheosis of Penmorfa." *Bandersnatch* 117 (October 2002).

Filmography

Geronimi, Cetal, director. Disney, W., producer. *Alice in Wonderland* (1951).

Harris, H., director. *Alice in Wonderland* (1985).

Millar, G., director. *Dreamchild* (1985).

Miller, J., director. *Alice in Wonderland* (1966).

Svankmajer, J., director. *Alice* (1989).

Willing, N., director. *Alice in Wonderland* (1999).

Web Sites

Actiontrip, http://www.actiontrip.com/reviews/americanmcgeesalice.phtml

Alice's Asylum, http://alice.trinitee.net/

Alice Configs, http://aquatarkus.20m.com/alice.html

Alice's Wonderland, http://www.geocities.com/WestHollywood/Stonewall/6626/

Alice in Disneyland, http://laughingplace.com/News-ID503060.asp

Alice in the Shadows, http://balibeyond.com/alice/index4.html

Alice in Wonderland Film and TV Productions, http://www.alice-in-wonderland.fsnet.co.uk/

Christkaiser, *Alice Desktop Art*, http://alice.trinitee.net/desktopart/high.htm

Down the Rabbit Hole, http://www.3dap.com/alice

Firing Squad, http://firingsquad.gamers.com/games/alicereview (4 January 2001)

Games Domain, http://www.gamesdomain.com/gdreview/zones/reviews/pc/dec00/alice.html

Game Revolution, http://www.game-revolution.com/games/pc/adventure/alice.htm

Generation5, http://www.generation5.org/alice_pc.shtml

GameZone, http://www.gamezone.com/gzreviews/r14078.htm (12 November 2000)

Intelligamer, http://www.intelligamer.com/action/alice/alice.asp

Kino-Eye, http://www.kinoeye.org/02/01/hames01.html

Lady Moonwise, http://www.geocities.com/ladymoonwise/alice.html

Lucy's Little Wonderland, http://www.geocities.com/WestHollywood/Village/7974/MainPage.html

Online Game Review, http://www.onlinegamereview.com/alice.asp

PCGamerWeb, http://www.pcgamerwb.com/reviews/pc/alice.html

Sharky Games, http://www.sharkygames.com/games/reviews/a/alice/

The Adrenaline Vault, http://www.avault.com/reviews/review_temp.asp?game=alice

The Tangle Box, http://tanglebox.cjb.net

WiredPatrol, http://www.wiredpatrol.org/news/archive/ukpaedophiles.html

Archival Sources

Carroll, L. Diary entry. 4 July 1862. Original in British Library, London.

———. Diary entry. 21 April 1863. Original in British Library, London.

Catalogue introduction. Dodgson Family Collection. Surrey History Centre, Woking

DFC.F/2/4/39–45. Derek Hudson to F. Menella Dodgson. 26 February 1953. Surrey History Centre, Woking.

DFC.F/17/1. "Cut Pages in Diary." 3 February 1932. Surrey History Centre, Woking.

DFC F/35/14. Cartoon by Illingworth. 4 October 1963. Surrey History Centre, Woking.

Index

Alice's Adventures Under Ground, 7, 9, 14, 209
'All in the Golden Afternoon', 7, 14
Adair, Gilbert, 158, 162–7, 175
Alcie's Webpage, 51
Alice in Wonderland, 82, 93, 98, 100, 110, 143, 168
Alice Through The Needles Eye, 167–9, 309
Alice, in comic books, 152, 153, 154, 155, 157
Alice: alternatives, 77, 78, 79, 80, 151, 152
Alice: illustrations of, 112–26
Alice: in novels, 160–5
Alice: psychedelic readings of, 80, 124, 211
Alice: surrealist readings of, 77, 79, 207, 216
Allen, Roger, 267, 269, 277, 280, 282, 293, 296, 299
American McGee's Alice, 229–39, 295, 299, 300, 301, 329
  fan response to, 249, 250
  intertextuality, 254–6
  reconfiguring *Alice*, 257–9
  scene descriptions, 240–3
Amor, Ann Clark, 270, 275, 284
Automated Alice, 172–81, 309

Bakewell, Michael, 5, 11, 17, 18, 19, 28, 30–5, 39, 85–7, 130, 327

Batman, 154–9, 286–8
Beaumont, Kathryn, 206, 312
Bjork, Christina, 5, 9–11, 17, 19, 82
Brann, Susie, 238, 9

Card Gardners, 310, 311, 316
Caterpillar, 68, 72, 203, 204, 205, 208, 210, 216, 218, 247, 310
Cheshire cat, 82, 97, 206, 231, 238, 242, 310, 312, 317, 325
Cohen, Morton, 5, 12, 13, 17, 21, 22, 33, 34, 35, 36, 83, 84, 85, 320, 327
Collingwood, Stuart, 1, 2, 3, 4, 8, 28, 66, 314, 321
Croft-on-Tees, 282, 307, 320, 322, 323, 324

Daresbury, 282, 283, 288, 307, 314, 316, 317, 318, 319, 323, 344
Daresbury: site of parsonage, 319, 320
Davis, John, 105–111
Disney's *Alice*, 205, 206, 207, 208, 217
Disneyland Paris, 205, 307, 308, 313, 314
  Alice's Curious Labyrinth, 309–11
  teacup ride, 312
Dodgson and Alice: marriage proposal, 19, 20, 21, 22, 23, 66, 96

Dodgson and Alice: relationship, 3, 6, 7, 9, 16, 19, 33, 58, 61, 90, 91, 155, 176–7

Dodgson and Tenniel collaboration, 106, 113, 137

Dodgson Family Collection, 23, 25, 78

Dodgson, Charles, in novels, 181–194

Dodgson, Charles, and Christianity, 283, 284, 285, 318, 319

Dodgson, Charles, origins of *Alice*, 7, 8, 9, 11, 12–14

Dodgson, Charles, and Mrs Liddell, 83, 186

Dodgson, Charles, and photography, 35–44, 95, 186, 191

Dodgson, Charles, as paedophile, 20, 21, 22, 37, 51, 52, 54, 55, 56, 57, 59, 60–5, 90, 116, 159, 160, 271, 279, 297

Dodgson, Charles, diaries, 5, 6, 7, 8, 16, 22, 26, 27, 28, 30–2, 43

Dodgson, Charles, diaries, censorship of, 17, 18, 19, 23, 25, 185–7

Dodgson, Charles, grave, 344, 345

Dodgson, Charles, sexual identity, 29–31, 32, 36

Dodgson, F. Menella, 4, 5

Dodgson, Wilfred, 22

Dreamchild, 219

Duckworth, Robinson, 7, 8, 9, 10, 11, 83

Eriksson, Inga-Karin, 5, 9–11

Fan fiction, 260, 261

Film adaptations, 201–2

Fitzgerald, Ian, 64–7

Gaiman, Neil, 151, 175

Gardner, Martin, 55, 67, 69, 79, 80, 94, 95, 96, 97

Gibbons, Fiachra, 60, 61

Gladstone, J. Francis, 14, 19, 20, 70, 82, 93, 96

Green, Roger Lancelyn, 5, 27, 29

Gryphon, 91, 204, 212, 218

Guilford, 282, 307, 321, 339, 340, 341, 343, 344

Hargreaves, Alice, See Alice Liddell

Harris, Harry, 200, 212–214

Hatch, Beatrice, 36, 39

Hatch, Evelyn, 36, 39

Haughton, Hugh, 90–3, 96, 97, 99

Henderson, Annie, 36, 40

Henderson, Frances, 36, 40

Homes, A.M., 159, 160

Hudson, Derek, 3–5

Humpty Dumpty, 248, 289, 312

Illustrations; similarities, 128, 129–32, 137, 143, 144

Isle of Wight, 282, 307

Januszczak, Waldemar, 55, 57

Jones, Jo Elwyn, 14, 19, 20, 70, 82, 93, 96

Krzywinska, Tanya, 237–8, 243

Leach, Karoline, 1, 2, 4, 5, 6, 16, 17, 18, 23–25, 28, 33, 34, 35, 37, 83, 275, 278, 279, 327

Lennon, Florence Becker, 1, 2

Lewis Carroll Society, 265, 266, 268, 270, 282, 289, 291
  and debate, 267, 277, 278
  and *Disney*, 301–3
  immersion in the texts, 272–4, 287
  and journalists, 296–7
  origins of 267

Liddell family, 6, 19

Liddell, Alice, 2, 3, 17, 20, 232, 327, 345

Liddell, Alice; as *Alice*, 83, 84, 86, 99

Liddell, Alice; as muse, 6, 16, 21, 62, 171
Liddell, Alice; memories of the boat trip, 8–10
Liddell, Edith, 7, 17, 20, 338, 339
Liddell, Lorina, 7, 16, 17, 20, 24
Llandudno, 307, 325, 326, 330, 331, 333
  Gogarth abbey, 332
Lost Girls, 157
Lucy's Little Wonderland, 50

Mad Hatter, 50, 68, 70, 97, 111, 205, 206, 210–2, 311
Manson, Marilyn, 175, 258
Marsh, Olivia, 323, 329
McCrum, Robert, 67, 69, 70
McGee, American, 85, 229
McGraw, DeLoss, 111, 120, 124, 125, 126, 127, 129, 139, 346
Miller, Jonathan, 200, 209, 210, 211, 223
Mitchell, Adrian, 68
Mock Turtle, 212, 218, 247, 317
Moore, Alan, 156, 157, 158
Morrison, Grant, 154–6

Nabakov, Vladimir, 80, 90
Narrative structure, films, 220–7
Noon, Jeff, 172, 173–4, 175–81

O'Connor, Michael, 282, 283, 288
Ovenden, Graham, 105, 111
Oxenbury, Helen, 111, 112, 114, 116, 118, 120, 126, 127, 134, 346
Oxford, 282, 283, 284, 307, 321, 323, 334–7

Paedophilia, the internet, 53, 54
Peake, Mervyn, 89, 99, 100, 105, 108, 109, 111, 120, 134, 137

Queen of Hearts, 68, 69, 137–42, 203, 247, 311, 317, 325

Rackham, Arthur, 107, 111, 120, 123, 130, 135, 137
Richards, Mark, 269, 277, 278, 279, 282, 290, 298, 299, 300
Ripon, 321, 324, 325
Roiphe, Kate, 158, 182–194
Royal Shakespeare Company's Alice, 68–71

Salisbury Jones, Celia, 270
Self, Will, 55, 56, 57, 61, 70, 98
Sigler, Carolyn, 151, 245
Smith, Robert, 175, 258
Smith, Zadie, 99
St Clair, Vanessa, 294
Star Wars, 268, 270
Starr, Ringo, 212
Steadman, Ralph, 109, 110, 111, 145
Stoffel, Stepahnie Lovett, 5, 13, 14, 17, 19, 38, 78, 127, 328
Svankmajer, Jan, 200, 215, 16, 226, 227
Sweet, Matthew, 54
Sylvia and Bruno, 50, 83, 107, 162

Tait, Harriet, 267, 269, 285, 299, 300, 301, 302
Taylor, Alexander, 2, 3, 4, 5
Tenniel, John, 9, 92, 100, 101, 105, 106, 111, 112, 137, 170, 231
The Cure, 175, 258
The Sandman, 151, 156, 175, 257
The Tangle Box, 257–9
Thomas, Donald, 5, 13 14, 19, 23, 40, 42, 78, 88
Through the Looking Glass, 82, 93, 99, 100, 168, 178
Tweedledee, 233, 254, 314, 316
Tweedledum, 233, 254, 314, 316

Wakeling, Edward, 5, 7, 13, 17, 18, 20, 26, 27, 28, 159, 278, 279
Wakeling, Edward, 267, 269, 275, 278, 282, 293, 296, 300, 320

Warrington, 307, 314, 315, 316
Whitby, 282
White rabbit, 204, 205, 206, 213,
    216, 236, 39, 46, 47, 316, 325,
    332
White, Alan, 267, 269, 277, 279,
    298, 299, 303
Whitworth, Laura, 329
Wilder, Gene, 218

Willing, Nick, 200, 215, 217, 224,
    225, 346
Wonderland, 85–7, 91, 117–19,
    122, 123, 126, 145, 210, 242,
    243

Zwerger, Lisbeth, 111, 116, 120,
    131, 144, 346